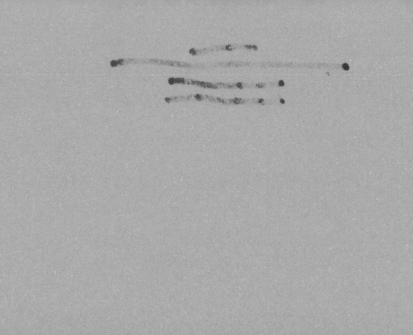

THE WHOLE HORSE WELLNESS GUIDE

Natural and Conventional Care for a Healthy Horse

DIANE MORGAN

Dr. Doug Knueven, D.V.M.
Consulting Veterinary Editor

The Whole Horse Wellness Guide
Natural and Conventional Care for a Healthy Horse
Diane Morgan

Project Team
Editor: Mary E. Grangeia
Copy Editor: Stephanie Fornino
Indexer: Lucie Haskins
Designer: Stephanie Krautheim
Cover Design: Mary Ann Kahn
Consulting Veterinary Editor: Dr. Doug Kneuven

T.F.H. Publications
President/CEO: Glen S. Axelrod
Executive Vice President: Mark E. Johnson
Publisher: Christopher T. Reggio
Production Manager: Kathy Bontz

T.F.H. Publications, Inc.
One TFH Plaza
Third and Union Avenues
Neptune City, NJ 07753

Printed and bound in China

08 09 10 11 12   1 3 5 7 9 8 6 4 2

Library of Congress Cataloging-in-Publication Data
Morgan, Diane, 1947-
  The whole horse wellness guide: natural and conventional care for a healthy horse / Diane Morgan.
    p. cm.
  ISBN 978-0-7938-3201-9 (alk. paper)
  1. Horses. 2. Horses--Health. I. Title.
  SF285.3.M65 2008
  636.1'0893--dc22
                    2007049305

This book has been published with the intent to provide accurate and authoritative information in regard to the subject matter within. While every reasonable precaution has been taken in preparation of this book, the author and publisher expressly disclaim responsibility for any errors, omissions, or adverse effects arising from the use or application of the information contained herein. The techniques and suggestions are used at the reader's discretion and are not to be considered a substitute for veterinary care. If you suspect a medical problem consult your veterinarian.

The Leader In Responsible Animal Care For Over 50 Years!®
www.tfh.com

Table of *CONTENTS*

Introduction   4

Part I
Healing Practices   8

Chapter 1 Mainstream Medical and Surgical Treatment   10

Chapter 2 Nutritional Wellness and Therapeutic Healing   30

Chapter 3 Bodywork   50

Chapter 4 Acupuncture, Acupressure, and Shiatsu   68

Chapter 5 Energetic Medicine   80

Chapter 6 Homeopathy   98

Chapter 7 Western Herbal Medicine   114

Chapter 8 Chinese Herbal Medicine   134

Chapter 9 Ayurvedic Medicine   148

Chapter 10 Aromatherapy and Essential Oils   172

Chapter 11 Flower Essences   190

Part II
Common Equine Diseases and Treatment Options   198

Glossary   262
Resources   268
Index   274

*O*ur earth is charged with power. It has the power to give life and the power to take it away, the power to kill and the power to cure. Its healing treasures surround us everywhere—herbs, chemicals, magnetism, light, fragrances, sounds, vibrations, and crystals. And the almost sacred power of touch.

Introduction

Only a fool, it would seem, would ignore so much of the earth's bounty, and we have been fools for too long. We who live upon this planet are only gradually becoming aware of the healing gifts it has to offer. We are not limited to concocting remedies in a laboratory or confined to gathering herbs by moonlight. Just as there is more than one way to get sick, there's more than one way to get well. Just as there are different kinds of illnesses, there are different ways of healing. One—or more likely more than one—is right for your horse.

The Whole Horse Wellness Guide

The modern horse owner has at her fingertips cures borne from the ancient wisdom of China and India, the marvels of contemporary science, pre-Celtic herbal lore, and more. Work done in nutritional therapy such as orthomolecular medicine and glandular therapy, physical therapies such as chiropractic care and acupuncture, energetic medicine such as low-energy photon medicine and magnetic field therapy, as well as aromatherapy, offer treatments not just for the disease but for the patient. And as we learn more and more about the subtle interconnections between body and spirit, we discover how the right medicine can heal psychic as well as physical ills. We also have come to understand how much easier it is to prevent a problem now than it is to fix it later.

This book explores some of the many treatment options you have for keeping your horse well and for treating an illness or injury. In an ideal world, the treatment method you choose for your horse or yourself would be perfectly safe and completely effective. But this is the real world. There is no such thing as a 100 percent safe and entirely effective treatment, although in some specific cases, you might find a safe treatment that happens to work very well. Others do work very well but may have dangerous side effects. Still others are safer but less effective. Some may even be ineffective *and* dangerous, a bad combination. You will find that you have many choices, and you will learn how to decide which ones are right for your horse.

As we begin our investigation of the many healing practices that are available, we need to look at some of the general terms that are commonly used when talking about different therapies. It is easy to become confused if we don't start out on common ground. Note the sometimes subtle differences in the meanings of these familiar words.

Charged with power, our earth offers us healing treasures that surround us everywhere—herbs, chemicals, magnetism, light, fragrances, sounds, vibrations, and crystals. Just as there are different kinds of illnesses, there are different ways of healing and one—or more likely more than one—is right for your horse.

- *Western*, *mainstream*, and *conventional* are terms that apply to the kind of medicine we in the Western world have become accustomed to. This type of therapy involves interventions such as surgery and pharmaceutical drugs to combat disease.
- *Holistic medicine* refers to a philosophical approach to healing. A holistic practitioner is one who views the patient as a whole—body, mind, and spirit. While Western medicine is focused on relieving symptoms, holistic medicine is more geared toward treating the underlying condition that is responsible for the symptoms. Western medicine treats the disease, and holistic medicine treats the patient.
- *Alternative medicine* refers to any healing technique that is not taught in Western medical schools. Holistic therapies are alternative, but not all alternative treatments are holistic. For example, therapeutic laser treatments (often used to aid the healing of injuries, as will be discussed in Chapter 5) are alternative because this method is not discussed in Western medical schools, but they are not holistic because they are applied symptomatically and not to the patient as a whole.
- *Complementary medicine* applies to alternative therapies that can be used hand-in-hand with Western medicine. This term implies the primacy of Western treatments with alternative methods used to augment its effects.
- *Complementary and alternative veterinary medicine* (CAVM) is defined by the American Veterinary Medical Association as "a heterogeneous group of preventive, diagnostic, and therapeutic philosophies and practices. The theoretical bases and techniques of CAVM may diverge from veterinary medicine routinely taught in North American veterinary medical schools or may differ from current scientific knowledge, or both."
- *Homeopathic medicine* is often confused with holistic medicine, although the two terms are not equivalent. Homeopathy is a specific modality within holistic medicine and will be discussed in detail in Chapter 6. The homeopathic practitioner is guided by the treatment principle "like cures like," which means that a remedy that can cause a certain condition if taken by a healthy individual can be used to treat a patient suffering from a similar condition. Homeopathy is holistic and alternative but not complementary as it does not mix well with Western medicine.
- *Integrative medicine* addresses health care by embracing the best of what Western medicine and alternative medicine have to offer. Surgery and drugs are used if necessary, but if there is a more natural treatment that may help, it is utilized. Often, the two forms of treatment are combined as needed. Integrative medicine implies that Western and alternative therapies are on equal footing.

With this background information in mind, let's begin our look at the many therapeutic options that exist for our horses today.

Part 1

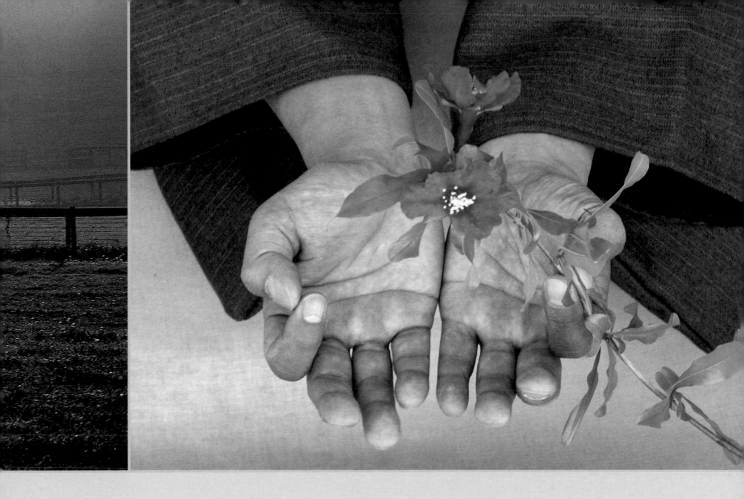

Healing Practices

Chapter 1 **Mainstream**

Western medicine is the kind of therapy most of us know best and trust most. It is both the most powerful and most dangerous way we have to treat illness, which is why its use is largely restricted to licensed professionals. Contemporary Western medicine relies a good deal on strong drugs and advanced technologies to achieve its ends. Critics say it is overspecialized and focuses more on the disease than on the patient. All this is probably true.

Medical and Surgical Treatment

But let me say this. If you must treat a serious disease using only *one* modality, this is the one to choose. The greatest gifts to animal and human health ever developed have come from what cynics and doubters call "conventional" veterinary care. This is such a mistake. Western medicine is not conventional. It's revolutionary.

Mainstream Western medicine has developed three great advances to modern health care: vaccines, antibiotics, and anesthesia. Imagine what your own life would be like without them. Before the advent of antibiotics, people regularly died from wounds and infections. Before vaccinations, millions of animals and humans died from scores of decimating diseases. As for anesthesia, modern surgery would be impossible without it. And while some people object to surgery, there are surely cases where it is needed. When it is, massage, herbs, and acupuncture would not be enough to get your horse through it.

None of these are panaceas, of course. Antibiotics are overused or underused, and they are always playing catch-up with tricky bacteria that seem to mutate at will. And not all pathogens respond to them. Anesthesia can carry the risk of allergic reaction, and it is essentially exposing the body to controlled levels of toxic chemicals, although the benefits of surgery far outweigh the rare instances of these risks. Vaccines can be overdone or underdone and can produce severe adverse reactions in some individuals. Also, we haven't yet developed a vaccine for all diseases—but stay tuned.

Mainstream Western medicine is your best choice when dealing with the following: cancer, emergency trauma, fractures, acute infections, and worms.

VACCINATIONS

ADVANTAGES
- VACCINATIONS ARE PROBABLY THE SINGLE MOST EFFECTIVE WAY TO PREVENT YOUR HORSE FROM BECOMING A VICTIM OF CERTAIN VIRAL AND BACTERIAL DISEASES, INCLUDING THE ALWAYS LETHAL RABIES.
- VACCINES ARE COMPARATIVELY EASY TO ADMINISTER, REASONABLY INEXPENSIVE, AND FAIRLY SAFE.

DISADVANTAGES
- THERE IS SOME DEBATE ABOUT THE EFFICACY OF CERTAIN VACCINES.
- THERE ARE CONCERNS ABOUT THE EFFECT THAT REPEATED VACCINATIONS MAY HAVE ON AN ANIMAL'S IMMUNE SYSTEM.
- SOME VACCINES CAN CAUSE LOCALIZED OR EVEN SYSTEMIC SIDE EFFECTS.

Vaccination is a routine part of health care for most human beings, horses, cats, and dogs in the United States. We vaccinate against encephalitis, influenza, measles, polio, distemper, rabies, and a host of other diseases. We are always seeking new vaccinations against AIDS for humans, equine infectious anemia for horses, and anthrax for other animals. While we tend to think of vaccinations as a modern invention, they are really rather ancient as medical discoveries go.

The first vaccinations were performed in China, with the first recorded inoculation occurring in 1017. At that time, it is believed that a hermit physician inoculated a little girl using smallpox scabs, which he kept in a box next to his body. This kept the scabs nice and warm, which diminished their potency yet made them fairly safe and able to stimulate the body into producing antibodies without causing disease. It is interesting to think that this most "Western" of modalities actually got its start in the East.

Vaccines work, but they don't work perfectly. However, we can say with a good degree of confidence that a vaccine usually prevents the disease for which it was designed, or at the very least, reduces the severity and duration of its signs. Furthermore, most of the diseases we vaccinate against have no specific cure, and treatment is often expensive and unsuccessful.

The American Association of Equine Practitioners (AAEP)

The American Association of Equine Practitioners (AAEP), headquartered in Lexington, Kentucky, was founded in 1954 by a group of 11 charter members. The AAEP now boasts a membership of more than 8,000 veterinarians and veterinary students from 57 countries dedicated to equine health and welfare. You can visit its website at www.aaep.org to get horse health information from experts on a variety of topics, as well as receive access to numerous resources.

Contemporary Western medicine relies a good deal on strong drugs and advanced technologies to achieve its ends.

How They Work

Understanding how vaccinations work requires a thorough understanding of the body's most important defensive weapon: the immune system, which is the mechanism that keeps you or your horse from getting sick (most of the time, anyway).

Because the world is a dangerous place filled with vicious viruses, brutal bacteria, foul fungi, and ferocious foreign proteins, the body must always be ready to fight back. The first thing the immune system has to do is determine which substances are naturally part of the body and which aren't. If a substance is determined to be foreign, the immune system begins to marshal its forces. But if the pathogen is a brand-new visitor, it may take the immune system a little time to recognize and react to it, and the host (i.e., your horse) may get sick before the invader is destroyed. In all probability, the immune system will eventually destroy the foreign agent, although some invaders (like rabies) are so terrible that it is very unlikely that the unfortified immune system will be able to cope with them at all.

When the invader has been killed off, the immune system cleverly tucks away in its cellular memory banks all the particulars of the encounter. If the enemy shows up again, the immune system will be ready to mobilize instantly and destroy the evil agent *before* it can cause sickness.

Lymphocytes

Because the immune system is so important, the body uses two cellular systems to provide immune defenses: humoral immune response and cell-mediated immunity. Both systems involve lymphocytes, which are special white blood cells.

Humoral Immunity: B Lymphocytes

Humoral immune response (HIR), or antibody-mediated immunity, is the part of the body's immune system mediated by secreted antibodies, which are produced by special types of white blood cells called B lymphocytes. These secreted antibodies bind to the surfaces of invading viruses or bacteria and flag them for destruction. This is called "humoral immunity" because it involves substances found in the humours, or body fluids.

B lymphocytes are born and mature in bone marrow, after which they "leave home" so to speak. Some circulate in the blood, but most do their best work in the spleen and lymph nodes, which are located like sentries around the body. When a foreign agent reaches the lymph nodes, it is encircled by these special white blood cells, which then

Vaccinate Early

Vaccines take several weeks to produce a significant immune response in the body. If a horse is already sick or infected with a disease, a vaccination will not do any good at all. The immune system of sick horses will not respond well, and the same is true of horses under stress. The idea behind vaccines is to prepare the immune system *in advance* so that the body doesn't have to get sick in order to recognize future invaders.

engulf and degrade it into smaller particles that the B lymphocytes can recognize as antigens (molecules that stimulate an immune response). At this point, the B lymphocytes have a tough job: They have to figure out how to produce the right antibody to bind to that particular antigen. Once the antibody is identified, the lymphocytes begin to develop into plasma cells, which multiply and circulate in the bloodstream seeking out and killing all invaders containing the targeted antigen. Even after every last one of the invaders is destroyed, many of the B lymphocytes remain on duty, floating around the bloodstream forever (or at least for a really long time) on the lookout for more invaders of the same type. The B lymphocytes are appropriately called memory cells.

All this sounds great, right? But there's still a problem. It takes time for the B lymphocytes to recognize the invaders and figure out what antibody to make. Sometimes it takes *too* long, and an individual can sicken and die before the antibodies have had time to gear up, especially when the horse has not encountered this foreign body before. Vaccines are designed to solve this problem by providing B lymphocytes with antigens in a harmless form that stimulate the production of antibodies and memory cells. When the real killer comes down the pike (or down the bloodstream), the immune system is primed and ready.

Cell-Mediated Immunity: T Lymphocytes

The body is too smart to depend on just one set of defenders. The other part of the immune system, called cell-mediated immunity (CMI), is an immune response that does not involve antibodies. Instead, it is run by T lymphocytes, which are also born in the bone marrow but mature in the thymus gland (hence the "T"). These guys employ T-cell receptors, other special proteins that target antigens and bind to them. In this way, they help to ferret out viruses that have become too "smart" for the B lymphocytes in the body's fluids and have managed to insert themselves inside the cells themselves. Once inside a cell, a virus can subvert its normal function and make more viruses. T cells secrete molecules that destroy the infected cell before it can release a fresh crop of viruses able to infect other healthy cells.

T cells come in three varieties: (1) helper cells, which coordinate the immune response by assisting B lymphocytes to secrete antibodies; (2) cytotoxic (or "killer") cells, which remove infected cells from the body; and (3) suppressor cells, which put the brakes on the B lymphocyte immune response when it becomes hyperactive or "overheats." If the suppressor cells aren't working right, the lymphocytes could develop an autoimmune response, attacking everything in sight—healthy as well as unhealthy cells. Thus, an autoimmune disease may develop when the body has an immune-

Vaccinations are probably the single most effective way to prevent your horse from becoming a victim of certain viral and bacterial diseases.

mediated reaction to its own antigens. (Many autoimmune diseases have a genetic base, but viruses, hormones, bacteria, chemicals, stress, drugs, and other toxins also can trigger them. Unfortunately, vaccines can predispose animals to certain autoimmune diseases too.)

Interferon

In addition to humoral and cellular immunity, a virus-infected cell can fight back by releasing interferon, a natural glycoprotein (a protein containing molecules of sugar) that coaxes the production of other proteins that also fight viruses. Interferons assist the immune response by inhibiting viral replication within other cells of the body.

It is very important for all parts of the immune system to work in harmony; if something goes haywire, the result can be immune system suppression or similar conditions.

All these defenses make up the body's natural immunity.

TYPES OF VACCINES

Vaccines work by jump-starting the immune system so that it goes to work immediately. This way the body doesn't have to get sick to recognize future invaders. The ideal vaccine induces both humoral (B lymphocyte) and cell-mediated (T lymphocyte) responses to protect against invaders. Like natural disease fighters in the body, they come in several forms.

To date, vaccines have come in two "flavors": killed and modified live virus (MLV) forms. Killed (noninfectious or inactivated) vaccines have traditionally been the vaccinations of choice for horse people, followed by a widespread move toward MLV vaccines (also known as attenuated vaccines). Currently, there is a swing back to the preference for killed viruses. As you will see, it's a problematic decision—and there are advantages and disadvantages to both.

Killed Vaccines and Adjuvants

As their name indicates, killed vaccines work by using chemically killed or inactivated organisms. These dead pathogens can't reproduce and therefore cannot cause disease. In other words, killed vaccines are very safe—there is no chance that they can cause the disease they are intended to fight, although the immune response they evoke is usually weaker than that evoked by the other kind of vaccine, the modified live virus (MLV) type. This is why rabies vaccines are always killed virus vaccines. While they may not *perfectly* protect against rabies, there is also no chance that your horse will get the disease from the inoculation.

There is a downside to killed vaccines, though. Because they are weaker, killed vaccines must be administered in larger amounts or more frequently than MLV vaccines. For this reason, substances called adjuvants are added, which increase the effect of the vacine by enhancing the tissue's reaction to the vaccine antigen. Adjuvants can include minerals like aluminum hydroxide, water/oil emulsions, detergents, and plant glycosides.

Because of the many debates about vaccination protocols, research is now being conducted to find new adjuvants for use with killed vaccines to make them stronger and longer lasting. Drug manufacturers are allowed to use some very potent adjuvants in horse vaccines that are not allowed to be used in vaccines produced for use in people. These powerful adjuvants stimulate a strong response but also increase the chances of serious side effects. The more effective the adjuvant, the more likely it is to cause a local reaction (sometimes significant) in horses. However, even if a horse does have such a reaction to one vaccination, that doesn't necessarily mean he will have the same reaction after subsequent vaccinations.

There are some distinct advantages to using killed vaccines. They don't shed viruses into the environment. They are also more stable in storage than

Other Immunity Defenders

It should be mentioned that the body has even more weapons than the immune system to keep it healthy. It also uses enzymes contained in saliva and tears, stomach acids, and "good" bacteria in the gastrointestinal tract.

Extra Protection

If a vaccine is designed to protect against only one disease, it is called univalent or monovalent, depending on whether you're a fan of the Romans ("uni") or the Greeks ("mono"). Likewise, a vaccine designed to attack a number of organisms is called multivalent (Roman) or polyvalent (Greek).

MLVs, and they are much less likely to cause long-term immunity problems. However, killed vaccines tend to cause more irritation or allergic reactions than do MLVs. While killed vaccines may not provide the same level or duration of protection as MLV vaccines, all killed vaccines now on the market have passed safety and efficacy tests required by the United States Department of Agriculture (USDA), which is in charge of these things.

Modified Live Vaccines (MLVs)

MLV vaccines incorporate organisms that are too weak to cause sickness. However, these pathogens are still alive and so can replicate in the body to provoke an immune response. Because MLV vaccines most closely resemble the viruses they are designed to fight, they induce fast, long-lasting protection, usually requiring fewer boosters than a killed vaccine for the same disease. There is also less chance of allergic reactions because they do not require adjuvants (immune stimulators). MLVs are also less expensive than killed vaccines.

MLV vaccines do pose their own set of problems. There is a slight chance the animal may actually contract the disease it is being vaccinated against. This is called retained or residual virulence. Animals with weakened immune systems are most at risk. The challenge is to develop an MLV vaccine that is the least virulent form possible while at the same time achieving maximal protection.

In the early days, some MLV vaccine viruses underwent mutations, causing reversion to the wild type when inoculated back into the original host. In other words, the vaccination caused the patient to get the disease it was designed to protect him against. This occurred with both early MLV rabies vaccines, and in human medicine, with the polio vaccine. Today this unfortunate outcome is unlikely thanks to recombinant DNA technology, which allows us to isolate specific genes and control cell mutation. Still, although the possibility of such a wild-type mutation developing is extraordinarily slim, no one wants to take any chance at all with inoculations such as rabies vaccines.

Another concern is that modified live viruses can be shed into the environment, causing false positive tests and possible long-term problems. For example, other animals in the area with weakened immune systems may get sick. While healthy horses in a safe environment can handle the minimal risk of developing a disease from an MLV vaccine, the same cannot be said for animals that have an immunological deficit. This also can occur in animals that have a genetic predisposition that leads to adverse responses to new viruses. Horses who have recently undergone surgery or experienced other illnesses, as well as stressed horses moved to a new environment, are at greater risk of having an adverse response to a vaccine.

Vaccines do not generally prevent infection. The offending pathogen must first get inside the body before it is attacked by the vaccine-stimulated active immune system.

Recombinant Gene Vaccines

New types of vaccines are the product of recombinant gene technology. They include subunit, gene-deleted, and vectored vaccines. The genetic material has been artificially modified in these vaccines.

Subunit vaccines comprise just the part of the microorganism that will induce an immune response. They are similar in many ways to killed vaccines and have a low probability of causing an adverse reaction. Like killed vaccines, however, they cannot replicate and thus don't provide as strong an immunity as do modified live vaccines. They are also more expensive to produce.

The gene-deleted vaccine works by blocking specific viral organisms from

Horses who have recently undergone surgery or experienced other illnesses, as well as stressed horses moved to a new environment, are at greater risk of having an adverse response to a vaccine.

invading cells. It involves isolating and removing viral genes that code for "nonrequired" proteins. This process is intended to decrease the virulence of the virus making it safe for administration in a vaccine. However, the degree of protection it offers could be limited since immune response is restricted only to those antigens present on the surface of the virus.

Another recombinant gene vaccine is the vectored vaccine, in which genetic engineering is used. The first such vaccine on the market was Recombitek, made for canine distemper. To make this vaccine, researchers use the canarypox virus. (Canarypox is harmless to dogs no matter what it does to canaries.) The virus is genetically altered to produce only the portions of the canine distemper virus that allow both humoral and cell-mediated immune response immunity to develop. So genes that code for distemper antigen are inserted into the DNA of the canarypox virus. This harmless but living organism is injected into the body as the vaccine. The virus replicates so it stimulates the immune system without adjuvants yet it cannot revert to a disease-causing organism. The theory is that this kind of vaccine will cause fewer reactions. However, some studies have suggested that current recombinant vaccines may damage T lymphocytes, among other things.

Vaccine Safety and Effectiveness

Few medical treatments are completely safe and effective. Vaccines are generally considered to be effective and safe, but they can cause adverse reactions in some horses, which in a very few cases can be severe. It is always possible for a horse to have a bad reaction to a vaccination.

So when is a vaccine worth the risk? This is a touchy call. Some viruses, such as rabies, African horse sickness,

and West Nile virus, can be deadly, but many other diseases we commonly vaccinate against cause only temporary or minor illness. It's a classic case of whether the disease is worse than the prevention. Some horses do seem to be allergic to vaccines. (If the reaction gets worse with every injection, it likely is a true allergic reaction.) The most severe allergic reaction is anaphylaxis, which occurs when the immune system responds too strongly to the antigen that's administered. In a worst-case scenario, a horse can die. However, this kind of reaction is extremely rare.

If side effects or adverse reactions occur, they tend to be less serious. Sometimes these reactions have nothing directly to do with the vaccine. For example, if your horse shows signs of respiratory distress following a vaccination or it appears that a vaccine may not have worked, it may be that the animal was harboring an infection before the vaccination anyway, and that the stress of the vaccine exacerbated an underlying disease. More commonly, there may be a local reaction at the site of the injection. This can range from a sore muscle to an abscess. In most cases, the abscess occurs because bacteria were introduced under the skin during the vaccination procedure, but there's also something called a "sterile abscess," in which there are no bacteria present—it's just an odd response to the vaccine. To keep post-vaccination swellings down, rubbing the injection site area vigorously often helps.

Controversies about vaccines boil down to four major topics: efficacy, safety, frequency, and the efficacy of combination vaccinations. The decision about how often to vaccinate and for what diseases comes down to a risk/benefit analysis, one that will be different for each horse owner. No one protocol will suit everyone. Before you and your veterinarian can choose the right protocol, you'll need to consider such factors as your horse's age and general health, disease concerns in your area, stabling conditions, and activities you engage in with him. In some cases, of course, you may not have much of a choice. For example, if you are boarding a horse, the barn's management may require certain vaccinations.

When They Don't Work…

It is well known that vaccinations sometimes appear to fail, by which we mean that the vaccinated animal contracts the illness for which it was vaccinated. (Indeed, few things are 100 percent effective.) The quality of the vaccine used is often blamed for the failure, but in point of fact, many vaccinations fail simply because the vaccine was not stored or administered properly. Vaccines are rather fragile entities, especially the modified live variety.

While vaccines produced by FDA-licensed manufacturers are potent when they leave the factory, several things can occur to inactivate them. If exposed to heat or cold (especially the former) or if improperly stored, their efficacy is diminished. This is particularly likely to happen with vaccines purchased from feed stores or through the mail. (If the vaccines arrive too warm at the vet's office, your vet will send them back, but you can't count on a store clerk to be so conscientious.)

Storing vaccines for too long also will reduce potency. After vaccines are made, they are "lyophilized," a fancy word for freeze-dried. This is done by rapidly freezing and dehydrating the vaccine under high vacuum to create a more stable product. However, when the vaccine is actually administered, the lyophilized product is mixed with its accompanying diluent. Once this is done, the vaccine has to be given right away; storing it will make it much less potent.

Another blow to a vaccine's efficiency can occur if the diluent of one company is used with a different company's vaccine, as sometimes happens. In fact, different vaccines should not even be administered with the same needle or syringe. (Luckily everyone uses disposable syringes and needles these days.) Letting two different brands of vaccine interact, even just a little bit, may inactivate the components and inhibit an immune response.

Duration of Immunity

It turns out that the duration of immunity from vaccines is quite variable. Some vaccines are short lived; others seem to last for many years. Many vets recommend yearly or even more frequent semi-annual vaccinations. This is a topic that is still under investigation.

The most common reason for animals to come down with an infectious disease after being vaccinated against it is that the vaccine was simply given too late.

The route of administration is also critical. The manufacturer of each vaccine provides directions for correct administration. Most MLV vaccines are approved for subcutaneous injection (under the skin—the easiest way), but a few require other routes such as intramuscular (into the muscle) or intranasal (into the nose). A killed vaccine administered by a route other than indicated may trigger a severe adverse reaction from the adjuvants. Such mistakes can cause vaccine failure.

The most common reason for animals to come down with an infectious disease after being vaccinated against it is that the vaccine was simply given too late. Vaccinations do not work on animals that are already infected. Unfortunately, it takes longer for the body to produce a sufficient antibody level after vaccination than the incubation period of most infectious diseases. If a horse is exposed to an infectious agent shortly before or after the vaccination, it's too late to protect him—and too easy to blame the vaccine for the occurrence of the disease. This happens because some irresponsible horse owners don't bother to get their horses vaccinated until they hear something is "going around." By then, odds are the disease has already "gotten around" to the horse in question. Infection is especially likely if the animal has never been vaccinated. Horses who have been vaccinated but need a "booster" are still able to mount a rapid response to an onslaught of the disease, and antibody formation may beat the incubation period.

Yet another problem with vaccines is connected to the notorious shape-shifting abilities of many viruses. It is very expensive for vaccine companies to keep up with fast-mutating viruses. Manufacturers are more likely to accept less effective but significantly less expensive antigen concentrations, and comparative studies between vaccines are quite rare. Veterinarians tend to be as brand loyal as the rest of us, and that can be unfortunate if the favored company is not producing the best vaccine. Even two batches of a vaccine from the same company are not automatically equal.

For the best outcome:
- Keep all horses on the same vaccination schedule if possible.
- Learn what diseases are endemic in your area.
- If you wish to economize by giving vaccinations yourself, learn how to do it correctly.
- Be sure to get the vaccines from a reliable source. If the vaccines have not been properly stored in a dark, refrigerated area, they are useless or dangerous.
- Network with other horse owners to find a veterinarian you can trust to keep your horses on a safe and effective health maintenance schedule.

OWNER RESPONSIBILITY

Despite the occasional ineffective vaccination or adverse reaction, horses are still safer being vaccinated than not, just as humans are. But beyond the medical necessity, there is also an issue of responsibility because those who avoid vaccinating their horses are putting others at risk and possibly allowing their animals to carry disease. When all or nearly all the animals in a given area have been vaccinated, they have what is called herd immunity. Unvaccinated horses are unlikely to get the disease because they have no one to get it from. So it is indeed true that your unvaccinated horse will probably not get sick—until other people start doing the same and as a result introduce more and more susceptible horses into the population. This is an ethical consideration that should play a part in your own decision as to whether or not to vaccinate.

It is possible for modified live vaccines to shed into the environment. A vaccinated horse can still shed disease organisms, infecting other horses, especially those with weakened immune systems. If the other horses are not vaccinated, they can get sick. However, some types of vaccines, notably aerosols, make this shedding less likely. On the other hand, animals vaccinated with killed vaccines do not shed viruses at all.

Every vet has her own vaccine protocol, which partly depends on the part of the country in which you live and how much contact your horse has with other horses. Broodmares, performance horses, and boarded horses typically require a different protocol than solitary horses who remain at home all year.

While some countries require periodic testing of live vaccines, the United States (so far) does not. Nor are drug manufacturing companies required to demonstrate duration of immunity. While dog and cat owners have regularly switched to less frequent vaccinations, the American Association of Equine Practitioners (AAEP) still recommends annual vaccines for most diseases. You can visit this link on its website for more information: www.aaep.org/pdfs/AAEP_vacc_guide.pdf

Anti-Vaccine Myth

One anti-vaccine myth, which is revived every few years, is that vaccines really had nothing to do with the disappearance of deadly diseases like human smallpox and canine distemper. The myth claims that these diseases were on the decline anyway when vaccines were introduced and would soon have faded away of their own accord. Scientific evidence supports the opposite view. While some kinds of epidemics do rise and fall, such as influenza, smallpox remained a steady killer of millions of people throughout the world for centuries. It stopped posing a threat when worldwide vaccines became available. This is not a coincidence.

THE CONVENTIONAL VS. HOLISTIC DEBATE

For a long time, vaccines were regarded as exceptionally safe tools with rare and minor side effects. And as a matter of fact, vaccines are generally safe when used responsibly. (This is true of all vaccines, not just ones for horses.) As a result, concerns voiced by the holistic veterinary community went largely unheeded by the establishment for years. But in 1983, Dr. W. Jean Dodds, a well-known veterinarian with expertise in hematology and immunology, suggested that certain autoimmune diseases that had begun cropping up in animals were possibly due to overvaccination. The basic idea was

that repeated exposure to vaccines may trigger autoimmune diseases. As more reports and papers were published, concerns arose. In the end, while a powerful tool in fighting disease, vaccination was found to be not entirely benign. Like all medical procedures, vaccines have some side effects, most minor, with a rare few serious or deadly.

Some problems causing adverse effects stem not from the vaccine itself but with its adjuvants or the mixture in which the vaccine is suspended. This suspension material may include other antigens, protein from egg yolks or tissue culture, antibiotics as preservatives, and carriers that enhance an immune response. Fortunately, vaccine production techniques have improved immeasurably over the years, so we are seeing fewer problems in this regard, at least in the short term. Other conditions that can increase the risk of adverse side effects may include genetic defects, a weak immune system, steroids, poor diet, health at the time of vaccination, exposure to the disease immediately before or following a vaccine, stress, improper handling of the vaccine, or simply a bad vaccine.

Many holistic veterinarians continue to have concerns about vaccines. There are a number of conditions, such as eczema, arthritis, epilepsy, allergies, autoimmune diseases, pancreatic insufficiency, and even warts that these vets feel are linked to overvaccinating animals. Homeopaths, in particular, are anti-vaccination and have coined the word "vaccinosis," which refers to any condition brought on by vaccines. The theory is that vaccines can disturb an animal's energy system and predispose him to disease. Evidence, admittedly anecdotal in nature, is that some diseases (at least in the homeopathic practitioner's experience) emerge within three months after vaccination, either following a first shot or a booster.

In fact, most homeopathic practitioners think vaccines should not be given at all. They believe that poor

When all or nearly all the animals in a given area have been vaccinated, they have what is called herd immunity.

Actually getting and recovering from a disease will produce a higher antibody level and presumably more protection than vaccination. But that's not usually worth the risk.

nutrition and vaccines are responsible for most chronic diseases. Most holistic veterinarians are not so much against vaccines as they are against overvaccinating. This includes giving boosters too frequently, giving vaccines that have not proven to be effective, vaccinating for relatively minor diseases, and vaccinating for diseases that the individual is not likely to contract. Many also object to the preservatives, mutated microorganisms, foreign animal proteins, and other compounds that are injected along with the vaccine. In general, holistic vets think it is best for the horse's health to keep unneeded chemicals and debris out of his system.

However, the possibility of immune system problems poses a concern for many proponents as well as opponents of vaccines. Unfortunately, the immune system can go awry in a variety of ways. It can be overactive (causing allergies and other problems), it can be immune deficient (resulting in diseases in which protective responses may fail), or there can be an autoimmune disease (in which the body attacks its own cells).

Opponents suggest that vaccines cultured on animal tissue can contain extraneous proteins that may cause autoimmune diseases. And indeed there are studies that link animal vaccines to autoimmune diseases.

We do know that immune-suppressant viruses in the retrovirus and parvovirus categories have been implicated in bone marrow failure, immune-mediated blood disease, lymphoma, leukemia, dysregulation of humoral and cell-mediated immunity, liver and kidney failure, and endocrine disorders such as thyroiditis, Addison's disease, and diabetes. Some claim that vaccines can cause thyroid disorders, which in turn can lead to autoimmune disease. The jury is still out.

Many holistic veterinarians have concerns about vaccines. They believe it is best for the horse's health to keep unneeded chemicals and debris out of his system.

THE FREQUENCY PROTOCOL DEBATE

Did you get your measles vaccine this year? Polio shot? Diphtheria? No? Of course not. There is an obvious paradox here. The average person lives into his or her 70s or 80s with only a childhood series of vaccinations, but many people unthinkingly trot their pets to the vet to get them vaccinated every year whether they need it or not. If a human vaccine can be expected to last ten years or more, is it unreasonable to expect an equine vaccine to last five or more years?

No one seriously proposes that horses have a radically different immune system from our own or that equine vaccines operate on wildly different principles from human ones. Today the frequency protocol of vaccinations is set not by practicing veterinarians or independent researchers but by the manufacturers of each drug. It is in the financial interests of manufacturers to recommend that their product be used as frequently as is consistent with safety. Although it would be unethical for a veterinarian to recommend a series of shots simply because it is profitable, the fact is that according to the Compendium of Veterinary Products (which reviews approved pharmaceuticals, pesticides, and other products and their dispensation), all vaccines

other than rabies have been required to have label recommendations for an annual vaccination. Thus, vets who do not follow the recommendations of the manufacturer could conceivably be liable for damages if they routinely ignore them and animals in their practice get sick.

Until recently, everyone was sure that vaccines were by and large extremely safe. However, as might be expected, the longer we vaccinate, the more problems we see arise. It may be that less frequent vaccinations are desirable both because they are not needed and because frequent vaccination can indeed be harmful.

> ## Veterinary Immunologists
> Interestingly enough, very few veterinarians have specialized training in immunology (as they might in neurology or ophthalmology). In fact, there are currently only about 45 active board-certified veterinary immunologists in the whole country. Any veterinarian can address immunological issues, of course, but she cannot technically be called a "specialist" in the field.

Adult booster shots are another issue. Modified live vaccines probably confer sufficient immunity on an adult animal without a booster. According to the Council on Biologic and Therapeutic Agents (COBTA), which has researched this issue extensively, adult vaccines provide no additional immunity or protection to a previously vaccinated animal. Some veterinarians insist on a booster shot for adults anyway, but it is probably not necessary. The reason for the frequency protocol is that researchers initially assumed immunity would fade in some animals, so to ensure that all animals in the population were protected, all needed to be vaccinated.

Opponents to yearly vaccination claim that frequent vaccination causes adverse reactions and may even compromise the long-term health of the animal. In the past it was believed that even if annual vaccinations were unnecessary, they at least did no harm. That attitude is changing, along with the increased incidence of anaphylaxis and other adverse reactions. In some cases and with some vaccines, horses properly immunized as foals do not need further vaccinations because early vaccination stimulates the memory cells that enable them to call up immunity. But ultimately, this is a decision that should be made with the advice of your vet. And let's not forget that good hygiene and preventing contact with infected animals goes a long way in preventing all kinds of transmissible diseases overall.

What About Polyvalent Vaccines?

For some time, the trend has been to combine multiple vaccines into one dose, a so-called polyvalent vaccine. The reason is simple: It's cheaper, it's easier, and it's more convenient. Experience shows that horse owners are most apt to comply with a simple and less frequent vaccination schedule.

But there are dangers with the polyvalent approach. It is very hard to accommodate the immunology of the animal, the various properties of the pathogens, the changing epidemiologic situation in an area, or the age and living environment of the horse by using one "magic bullet." Also, the more components we shove into one vaccine, the more likely it is they will interfere with each other so that an optimal response cannot be mounted. A kind of "competition" develops between the antigens, and the horse may not be able to respond normally to each separate component—and might even become immunocompromised. One reason for this immunosuppression is simply antigen overload, a state in which the animal has received so many antigens that the immune system can no longer respond. And there's also the adjuvant problem: Only one or two adjuvants can be used in a single injection, but different adjuvants are best with different antigens. So a polyvalent vaccine often shortchanges the horse.

Proponents of polyvalent vaccines argue that the immunosuppression resulting from vaccines, while sometimes significant, is temporary, lasting only between seven and ten days. For most horses, this is not a problem, but it can become so if (1) the horse has a nutritional deficiency; (2) the horse has a hereditary immune disorder; or (3) a susceptible horse is exposed to a serious illness within that seven- to ten-day window. We should say that if the horse does become ill during that period, the vaccine did not *cause* the sickness; it simply reduced the horse's immune system temporarily so that the horse was not able to fight it off. Monovalent vaccines are less likely to produce immunosuppression because the system is not being overwhelmed.

Basic Vaccination Guidelines

When trying to decide what the best vaccination protocol is for your horse, consider the following:

- *Health and Physical Condition*: Horses with compromised immune systems (overactive immune systems, autoimmune disorders, or immune-deficient disorders) are at increased risk of adverse reactions to vaccines. This may include certain elderly horses. Horses with fevers should not be vaccinated because a fever inhibits the body's response to vaccine agents.
- *Location*: Your geographic area will help to determine whether or not your horse needs to be vaccinated with a particular vaccine. Check with your vet to see what is needed in your area.
- *Exposure and Activities*: If your horse is out and about on trail rides, horse shows, or is boarded with strange horses, he has increased exposure. This is not necessarily a bad thing. Such animals often get a so-called "street booster" by having their immune systems challenged. Stay-at-home horses may be at more risk of coming down with the disease after exposure simply because they have had no way to give their immune system a workout.

In consultation with your veterinarian, continue boosters on a regular schedule. Add supplemental vaccines only if your horse is at risk.

Horses who have had an allergic reaction to vaccines should have titer tests to determine their level of immunity. An antibody titer is a laboratory test that measures the presence and amount of antibodies in blood.

If possible, give vaccines in monovalent form. They are more likely to be more effective than polyvalent ones and to cause fewer reactions.

> ### USDA Approval Guidelines
>
> To be approved and licensed by the United States Department of Agriculture (USDA), a vaccination must demonstrate that it produces a certain increase in the number of antibodies (referred to as a "rise in antibody titer following administration"). There is a problem with this criterion, however, because we don't always know that more antibodies will stave off the disease. We hope so, but we're not always 100 percent sure.

ANTIBIOTICS

ADVANTAGES
- HIGHLY EFFECTIVE AGAINST MANY BACTERIAL DISEASES.
- RELATIVELY NONTOXIC.

DISADVANTAGES
- INEFFECTIVE AGAINST VIRAL DISEASES.
- CAN SOMETIMES CAUSE ALLERGIC REACTIONS.
- IMPROPER USE CAN LEAD TO RESISTANT BACTERIA AND MORE DANGEROUS FORMS OF DISEASE.

Antibiotics are a staple of mainstream veterinary practice today. Some of them work by killing bacteria directly; others only stop them from multiplying. Antibiotics have no power over viruses, however.

While they are truly miracle drugs, antibiotics are not without adverse effects. For one thing, they may disrupt the normal population of "friendly microbes" dwelling in the intestinal tract. These helpful little guys not only

help to digest food but are also the first line of defense against infections. Antibiotics also can decrease the number of circulating white blood cells, leaving the body more vulnerable to infection. Antibiotics can be hard on the liver and kidneys, which are responsible for ridding the body of toxins. While a normal liver can usually process toxins without trouble, a compromised one may not be able to do so.

In addition, harmful bacteria are very good at developing immunity to antibiotics. Part of this is due to the use of low-dose antibiotics or to changing antibiotics before giving the first prescription a chance to work. Many people also neglect to use antibiotics properly. Some use them for even the slightest infection, which is better left for the body to fight on its own. Others fail to take the antibiotic for the prescribed length of time, the result of which is often to kill off the weaker pathogens while the stronger and more resistant ones go free to reproduce. This is one reason why there are more and resistant "bugs" out there.

Highly effective against many bacterial diseases, antibiotics are a staple of mainstream veterinary practice today.

The use of antibiotics also may increase the growth of fungi (which are generally unaffected by antibiotics). This occurs because the fungi and bacteria may be fighting for a place at the table, so to speak, and thus are keeping each other in check. When one of the "combatants" is killed off, however, the other can run wild. As a result, killing off the bacteria leads to increased fungal problems.

In any case, antibiotics should not be used lightly, nor should you second-guess your vet about which antibiotic should be used. Different bacteria respond to different antibiotics, and unless you know the particular pathogen involved, you can make the situation worse.

Antibiotics can be administered in three ways: by injection, topically right onto the skin, or orally. Only two or three oral antibiotics work with horses, however. Use antibiotics with caution and always under the guidance of a licensed veterinarian.

OTHER DRUGS COMMONLY USED IN EQUINE PRACTICE

Anti-Inflammatory Drugs

Anti-inflammatory drugs work by removing inflammation and thus pain. The more commonly used anti-inflammatory drugs in horses are the nonsteroidal anti-inflammatory drugs (NSAIDs) phenylbutazone (bute), flunixin, and vedaprofen. Common side effects of NSAIDs include gastrointestinal ulcers.

Steroids (corticosteroids) are another class of anti-inflammatory drugs, which are modified versions of the natural cortisol found in the body. They are often used for skin problems, allergies, and inflammations. While they work extremely well, they can cause serious side effects and must be used carefully. They can cause abortion in pregnant mares and reduce a horse's natural immune mechanisms. They have also been linked to laminitis, especially in ponies. Steroids come in injectable, pill, and topical forms.

Dimethyl Sulfoxide (DMSO)

Since the 1960s, DMSO has been one of the most popular of all supplements, but it can't really be called "dietary" because it is a chemical solvent usually applied to the skin. However, it would actually be safe enough to drink or even use (diluted) intravenously if you really wanted to. It's mainly used as an anti-inflammatory, working in much the same way that corticosteroids do, and it can be used with other drugs. It also may provide needed sulfur, so in this way it could be considered a nutritional supplement.

DMSO and MSM

Dimethyl sulfoxide (DMSO) is not permitted for some performance events because its anti-inflammatory capabilities may be considered performance-enhancing. Methylsulfonylmethane (MSM) is an edible, less powerful derivative of dimethyl sulfoxide (DMSO) that retains many of the latter's beneficial effects. MSM is also a source of sulfur.

This substance is so easily absorbed through the skin that it is often used as a "carrier" for other substances such as antibiotics. It quickly enters the circulatory system, gets into the lungs, and is breathed out. (It tastes like garlic and can smell up the entire stable!) It can be found in the bones and skin within an hour after application. DMSO is available in liquid and gel form. Rubber gloves must always be worn during application.

Veterinarians and horse owners use DMSO for a wide range of problems—everything from joint disease to swellings, colic, and skin disease. However, its effects have not been thoroughly studied, and the verdict is still out despite its extraordinarily wide usage.

Hyaluronic Acid (Sodium Hyaluronate)

This substance (derived, believe it not, from rooster combs) is used as treatment for joint inflammation and is usually injected into the joint. Your horse also makes hyaluronic acid naturally; it acts as a lubricant within the joint.

This is a very safe, nontoxic substance, and it seems to work quite well. Some horses experience a temporary joint flare after treatment, so all horses should be rested before returning to work.

BRONCHODILATORS

Bronchodilators open restricted bronchioles in the lungs and increase airflow in horses with pulmonary disease such as asthma or allergies, which are common conditions in stabled horses. These drugs can be used alone or safely combined with anti-inflammatory drugs for treatment of more severely affected horses. Bronchodilator drugs can be given orally, by injection, or by inhalation. Oral administration is most convenient, but inhalation therapy is most effective; proper administration of bronchodilators by inhalation requires the use of a special mask.

Common bronchodilators include clenbuterol, pirbuterol, albuterol, ephedrine, atropine ipratropium bromide, and aminophylline (a derivative of theophylline). Some last for 12 or more hours; others must be given hourly. Side effects are usually minimal but may include sweating and excitation.

SEDATIVES

Sedatives can be literal lifesavers for horses. These excitable animals often need to be sedated for diagnostic tests, minor surgical procedures (such as castration), and dental care. They also calm fractious animals.

The two types most commonly used are acepromazine (ace) and xylazine hydrochloride. Ace is a very safe sedative, but it is not the drug of choice for animals with heart, respiratory, or neurological problems. With training, an owner can learn to administer this drug. Rompun is both a tranquilizer and a muscle relaxer. It should be administered only by a vet.

Anti-inflammatory drugs work by removing inflammation and thus pain.

Banned Drugs

The United States Equestrian Federation (USEF) (formerly the American Horse Show Association) has banned the use of many substances in performance animals. This doesn't mean that you can't use some of these substances therapeutically, but their use is regulated or restricted. Some of these forbidden substances are:

- acepromazine
- albuterol
- aminophylline
- amphetamines
- atropine
- azaperone
- benzocaine
- caffeine
- chlorpheniramine
- chlorprothixene
- clenbuterol
- cocaine
- detomidine
- dextromethorphan
- diazepam
- diphenhydramine
- DMSO (sometimes)

- dyphylline
- ephedrine
- etorphine
- haloperidol
- homatropine
- hydromorphone
- hydroxyzine
- isoxsuprine
- levallorphan
- levorphanol
- lidocaine
- mazindol
- mepivacaine
- methylphenidate
- morphine
- nikethamide
- oxymorphone

- phenobarbital
- phenylephrine
- piperacetazine
- prethcamide
- procaine
- promazine
- propionylpromazine
- propoxyphene
- pyrilamine
- reserpine
- strychnine
- tetracaine
- tripelennamine
- tropicamide
- xylazine

This is not a complete list. If you are unsure about whether a particular substance is permitted, restricted, or forbidden, contact the USEF at 800-MED-AHSA.

ANESTHESIA

ADVANTAGES
- PERMITS SURGICAL PROCEDURES TO BE PERFORMED.

DISADVANTAGES
- CAN BE DANGEROUS.
- CAN BE EXPENSIVE.

Another significant contribution Western medicine has made to health care is anesthesia. While horses do not undergo anesthesia as frequently as cats and dogs, it is necessary for major surgical procedures. Conditions that would have inevitably led to death in earlier days, such as some kinds of colic and broken legs, may respond to

STEM CELL THERAPY

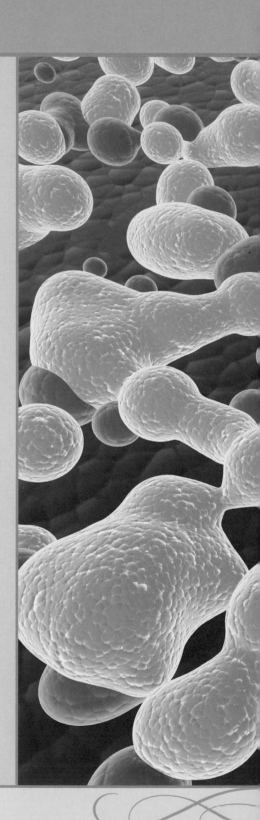

Recent research suggests that stem cell therapy is effective in treating certain diseases in animals. Stem cells are unlike other cells in that they have the ability to change their function and become different types of cells. For instance, stem cells can become specialized cartilage, bone, tendon, fat, muscle, or nerve cells.

Many of the long-term consequences of injury or disease occur because the body's structures cannot repair themselves adequately. For example, equine tendon injuries heal slowly because they produce scar tissue which, while strong enough to allow some activity, is very different mechanically from a normal tendon. This is why horses who have sustained a tendon injury often re-injure the tendon in the future and may not be the good athletes they were before. Using stem cells, the quality of healing can be improved by providing cells that have the ability to recreate normal tendon tissue rather than simply just scar tissue, resulting in more complete healing.

HOW IT WORKS

One experimental kind of treatment for horses using stem cell therapy involves the veterinarian taking a small sample of the horse's own fat in a minimally invasive procedure and re-implanting it two days later at the site of trauma. The procedure is used to help heal tendons, ligaments, joints, and fractures. Strains or tears of the suspensory ligament and bowed tendons are said to improve, usually within 45 days, as detected by ultrasound. Even arthritic horses may benefit, according to its proponents, typically within two weeks. The treatment is also thought to work well with bone cysts and osteochondritis. However, practitioners caution that stem cell therapy is not intended to get performance horses back to work faster—it just heals them better.

While stem cell therapy is certainly "Western medicine," this procedure is not considered standard therapy. It is controversial at the present time and is intended to be used in conjunction with standard remedies.

surgical treatment, which would otherwise not have been made possible without the use of anesthetics.

Anesthesiology is now routinely used in field procedures such as castration. With the use of newer anesthetics such as sevoflurane, it is safer than ever before but requires the supervision of a veterinarian trained in its use in horses both during and after the procedure. Horses are large animals, and they recover from anesthesia less easily than a dog or cat. Their responses to it can be unpredictable as well.

Anesthesia can be inhalant or intravenous, depending on the procedure and the preference of the veterinarian. Intravenous anesthesiology is usually the drug of choice for procedures lasting less than an hour, while inhalants are generally used in procedures lasting an hour or more.

Anesthesia is best done under the guidance of a vet who is a member of the American College of Veterinary Anesthesiologists (ACVA).

MAINSTREAM RELIABILITY

Mainstream veterinary medicine continues to be the health care staple for most horse owners. It's extremely effective and generally safe. It covers the entire range of horse health issues, from broken legs to a case of the sniffles. It is responsible for saving thousands of equine lives every year. However, professional veterinary care is not only expensive but increasingly difficult to find. (It's not easy to locate someone who's willing to get up in the middle of the night and drive out to your place when your horse has colic.) Many equine vets seem to be heading toward the more lucrative field of small animal care. As a result of high costs, low veterinary availability, and a desire to take a more active role in their horses' health care, many owners are looking for complementary or alternative forms of health care. In the pages that follow, we'll take a look at some of these options.

Chapter 2 **Nutritional**

Wellness and Therapeutic Healing

*M*aybe the ancient Hindus got it right. In the Taittiriya Upanishad (Book 2), it is written "From food, verily, are produced all creatures—whatsoever dwells on earth. By food alone, furthermore, do they live, and to food, in the end do they return; for food alone is the eldest of all beings, and therefore it is called the panacea for all." In modern terms, that translates to the more familiar saying "You are what you eat." It should come as no surprise, then, that proper nutrition is as vital to the health and longevity of horses as it is to our own health and longevity.

THE RIGHT DIET

Build a healthy horse from the inside out! The right diet can keep your horse healthy, and the wrong diet can kill him. A therapeutic diet is one designed to address a specific disease condition or nutrient imbalance. But as they say, prevention is always the best medicine. So by offering your equine companion a balanced diet that mimics what he eats in the wild, one that is naturally suited to his system, you will ensure his general good health. Furthermore, you cannot offer any therapeutic protocols unless you first understand the basics of equine digestion and nutrition.

The Equine Digestive System

Horses have a different digestive system than ours. They have a very small stomach relative to their body size, so if you overload your horse with a large meal you will cause him digestive distress. Long periods without food are also problematic because, unlike humans, horses continually produce digestive acids, which can irritate the lining of an empty stomach. This is why horses are natural grazers and must eat small, frequent meals throughout the day.

The first step in proper nutrition is trying to recreate a horse's natural grazing state by allowing him plenty of time in grassy pastures, and when stabled, providing him with a constant supply of good-quality hay. Combined, these can offer the average horse in moderate work all the calories and nutrients that he needs. To maintain good weight, some horses may also need additional calories provided in the form of grains. Different foods have different nutritive values, so it is necessary to understand and assess this relative to your particular horse to keep him at his best weight and energy level.

Basic Principles of Equine Nutrition

Grass is the natural food of horses in the wild. In theory, it is the complete feed, offering all the essential nutrients

and fiber in the right proportions. When domestic horses are fed mostly hay (dried grasses), they have a much lower incidence of colic. Those fed a mostly grain diet may suffer fluid shifts, acid-base shifts, and changes in microbial flora. Along with quality, quantity is also important. Horses are healthier when they are fed frequently so that their digestive tracts are kept full. After all, they evolved mostly to graze all day. (Wild horses eat 16 to 17 hours a day!) Those who get insufficient fiber lack the important digestive bacteria that live on it. And an unhealthy intestinal bacterial population leads to all kinds of other trouble. Again, the number-one rule in any equine feeding program is to feed small, frequent meals throughout the day for proper digestion.

Knowing the principles of equine nutrition and being constantly aware of your horse's individual needs will go a long way toward keeping him in optimum condition.

Hay

Roughage (hay, grass, and other high-fiber feed) is not only the healthiest and most natural form of nutrition for horses, but it also provides most of their daily dietary requirements. As Shakespeare wrote in *A Midsummer Night's Dream*, "Good hay, sweet hay, hath no fellow." As usual, the Bard knew what he was talking about. However, because hay can vary a great deal in quality, you want to be sure that you select the right kind—one that is not only appropriate and palatable for your horse but that is also safe.

Evaluating Hay Quality

Don't judge a book by its cover. Before purchasing hay, ask to have a bale opened so that you can examine the inside. The outer layer may have been subject to stresses that do not affect the true quality of the hay. Also, a bale that looks good on the outside may not be entirely good on the inside. It may contain dirt, debris, weeds, or plants that may be toxic to horses. It also should be free of mold, moisture, dust, and discoloration (which indicates sun bleaching). It will need to be inspected for insect infestation as well. Seeing the inside will ensure the overall quality of the bale.

Good hay is soft to the touch and leafy, with fine stems. In most cases, the greener it is, the better it is. Early-bloom hay, which has been harvested before the seed heads have formed, is best. Buy hay within a year of harvest. The older it is, the less nutrition it provides. Most hay is best when cut right before mid-bloom, or early maturity stage. After that, it may lose nutritional value, especially protein. In late-cut hay, only 50 percent of the protein might be digestible. On the other hand, first-cut hay tends to be high in weed content, especially if the fields have not been carefully tended.

Nutritive Value

Ideally, horses would live on grass rather than hay, but few enjoy a domestic environment in which grass is available all year round. Roughage is necessary to digestion, but it is also high in calcium and low in phosphorus. Most grains are the opposite, being high in phosphorus and low in calcium. Feeding both helps to deliver a balanced diet to the horse. Hay is also a great source of vitamins A, D, E, and K, although the amounts of these nutrients decline over time when stored. If hay is sun-cured, it tends to lose a lot of vitamin D, although sun-curing also can

Equine Digestion

Although the equine digestive system is complex, it can be broken down into fairly simple stages.

After the horse swallows his food, the stomach begins to digest protein, mostly through the action of pepsin and hydrochloric acid. The acid environment of the stomach also ionizes minerals so that they are more easily absorbed by the body. The small intestine (which contains mostly fluid and is more than 70 feet [21.3 m] long) hydrolyzes fats, carbohydrates, and the rest of the proteins so that they can be absorbed. The cecum, or hindgut (which people don't have), breaks down and ferments long-stem fiber and produces vitamins and fatty acids. The cecum can hold about 10 gallons (37.6 l) of food and water. After food leaves the small intestine, it passes along to the colon, which finishes the digestive process and removes most of the remaining water from the food (which it then redistributes to the rest of the system). The large intestine has no digestive juices, only fermentation bacteria and mucus to help the fibrous food move along. (Horses who spend more time foraging grass and eating hay develop longer colons than grain-fed horses.) The remaining waste products enter the rectum and are eliminated. The whole process takes about 72 hours, on average.

Hay provides many of a horse's essential dietary requirements.

reduce the amount of some of the other vitamins as well. The amount also depends on how moist the hay is: The more water per ton (about 907 kg), the lower the vitamin content. Hay that is too moist is also at greater risk of spoiling or being contaminated by mold. On the other hand, hay can't be completely dry at harvest or it will not process correctly because it is moved though baling equipment. This is especially true of alfalfa and clover hays, which can "shatter" under such conditions.

GRAINS

Technically, grains are the dry, one-seeded fruit of cereal plants like corn or oats. Each individual grain consists of the seed head of the plant, which contains the nutrient for the plant embryo. Certain grains (like barley and oats) have, in addition, a husk that provides more fiber, while others, like corn, do not. Almost all grains are suitable for equine consumption, but each grain has its special attributes.

You can feed your horse one type of grain, or you can select a specific mix. (Many pre-mixes are available.) Horses, who are conservative by nature, tend to stick with the grain they are used to and are loath to test a new variety. This is surely an evolutionary adaptation. If grain is switched suddenly, a horse does not have enough proper intestinal bacteria to process it properly; this can lead to a lactate buildup, which lowers the pH value in the intestine. Your job is easier with balanced, commercial pre-mixed feeds, which are custom designed for various life stages and exercise levels.

Grains are the most convenient way to add calories and proteins to your horse's diet. They are also critical to pregnant and lactating mares, growing colts, and performance horses. Four to eight times heavier than an equal

amount of baled hay, they have about 50 percent more calories than moderately good hay. Many grains are low in protein, but if the protein is of high quality, horses can make do with a relatively small amount. However, when grains and manufactured feeds contain substantial amounts of proteins, the amino acid availability can be damaged by heat and improper drying techniques. The length of storage also can reduce the amount of available proteins. This is why many companies fortify their feeds with the essential amino acids lysine and methionine.

Feeding Grains Properly

Grain is not really a natural food for horses, and many will not even eat it unless it is sweetened by molasses. (Molasses isn't a natural food for horses either, but they do have a sweet tooth.) An idle horse may not need grain at all, but it is essential for most riding, growing, and breeding horses.

Excess energy in the form of grain is more dangerous than excess energy from grass forage. This may be because grain energy comes from starch, not from the volatile fatty acids that grasses produce. Starch stimulates insulin production, which may in turn result in bone problems like osteochondrosis. One rule of thumb to follow is never to feed your horse more than 5 pounds (2.3 kg) of grain at any one meal. Most healthy horses need much less.

The digestibility and palatability of many feeds can be improved if the feed is rolled, ground, or crushed. This is because crushing "pre-chews" the feed, making it more available for the microbes and enzymes to work on. That doesn't mean that crushed or rolled grain is always the correct choice, however. The very process that makes it easier to chew and digest also leaves the grain more vulnerable to oxidation and decomposition. This is especially true of grain that must be stored for a long period. Unless you have an aged horse with poor teeth or a foal who is just learning to chew, certain whole grains, especially oats, are sometimes the wisest (and least expensive) choice.

Types of Grain

Whole grains are more natural, but they are difficult to assess nutritionally because the variability is so high that owners have to rely on an average. Differences in grain quality are largely due to the source of the grain and storage conditions, both of which may be unknown to the owner. You need less high-quality grain to keep a horse in condition than lower-quality material, but sometimes the only way to know is by experimentally feeding your horse to see the results.

Horses seem to like oats the best of any grain, followed by corn, wheat, barley, rye, and crushed soybeans, pretty much in that order. In fact, they like oats so much that

Dollar Value

If you are buying hay en masse, it is wise to have it analyzed by a forage laboratory to determine its nutrient content. There is no point in spending a lot of money for nothing. More importantly, you want to be sure that your horse is getting the best possible nutrition. One simple rule is to purchase local hay whenever possible. It will be fresher and less expensive than hay hauled in from afar.

Complete Feeds

Pellets can consist entirely of grain, but many kinds include hay or might even be all hay. Check the label. Some pelleted feeds combine hay and grain to make a "complete" food. Complete it may be—natural it is not. Some horses fed pellets develop colic.

Complete feeds, which include both forage and grain, are valuable under certain conditions and for certain types of horses, notably hard keepers or horses with certain health problems. However, it is such an unnatural way to feed a horse that many on this diet eventually develop stable vices, like cribbing, out of sheer boredom. Horses who are fed hay keep busy simply through the endless process of chewing the stuff. Those fed pellets finish their meal in seconds and have little to do but stand around, wondering when the next meal is arriving and getting into trouble as a result. The happiest horse is an outdoor horse foraging for his own food.

it is one of the few grains to which you don't need to add a sweetener to tempt their taste buds. Oats are a sensible choice for horses because they are the safest of all grains and the least likely to cause digestive upset. They are also highly digestible. Nowadays, however, horses are more likely to be fed the cheaper but distinctly second favorite, corn. Corn also has the highest available energy (calories) content of any grain—about twice as much as oats, which makes it a "natural" choice for performance horses. However, it has a lot of starch and little fiber, which can be a dangerous combination. It is also less digestible than oats.

Grain Pellets

A popular choice for many owners is pelletized grain, which provides easy storage and clean, pest-free food. Many horses also love it. Horses receiving pelletized grains do need to drink plenty of water to stay hydrated. It is best if the grains used in pellets are coarsely rather than finely ground. Finely ground grains are dustier, less palatable, and possibly more likely to cause gastrointestinal problems.

Pelleted foods are almost dust-free, a great advantage for horses with respiratory problems. They are easy to measure for horses who need a very specific measured quantity of food. They are much easier to eat than regular grains or hay, so they may be the food of choice for older horses or horses with dental problems. Pellets also produce less waste (and less manure). Whether this is a good or bad thing is a matter of debate. The passing of waste is a natural part of the digestive system, after all.

Also, because they contain much less molasses, pellets don't freeze in the winter as sweet feed sometimes does. Another advantage is that because they combine their ingredients in an indivisible whole, picky eaters cannot select only their favorite grains and thus not get complete nutrition. They are especially good for performance horses who may need fats in their food. Horses don't naturally take to fat, so disguising the stuff in pellets is a good way to get it down painlessly.

Keep in mind that pellets are much more expensive than hay or grain. When buying pellets, deal with a source you trust. Another factor to consider is that it's a lot easier to sneak bad ingredients into pellets than into grain or hay. Horses also eat them faster than either traditional feeds or extruded feeds.

WATER

All horses need a constant supply of clean water. In fact, about 70 percent of your horse *is* water. Water carries nutrients, flushes waste, aids certain chemical reactions, lubricates joints, helps to regulate body temperature, and is a major component of saliva, blood, mucus, milk, and sweat. (It is well to recall that horses and humans are among the only animals who sweat. Pigs, for instance, do not sweat, despite the phrase "sweating like a pig.")

While the amount they drink varies according to the temperature and the amount of exercise they are getting, most horses take in two or three times as much water as food. Generally, they need to take in about 8 gallons (37 l) a day. Factors influencing just how much they need include temperature and humidity, feed type and amount, exercise level, and lactation. Too little water can cause your horse to get colic, among other things. To make sure that your horse is getting high-quality water, test it frequently and use filters if necessary.

POISONOUS PASTURE

In keeping with "you are what you eat," Paracelsus, famous Swiss alchemical genius and physician of the Middle Ages, said, "It better benefits a man to know one herb in the meadow, but to know it thoroughly, than to see the whole meadow without knowing what grows on it." This is especially true if said herb is a poisonous one.

Spring and summer bring about the growth of many plants, herbs, and weeds that may be poisonous to horses. It's important to do regular inspections of fields and pastures in which your horse may graze, paying particular attention to hedges where many species tend to grow.

For most plant poisonings, there is unfortunately no treatment a lay person can give. Human beings, dogs, and cats have the ability to vomit if they are poisoned, and most treatment involves making the victim throw up. Horses, however, cannot vomit, and the first obvious signs of poisoning may occur hours or even days after ingestion. If you suspect poisoning, call your veterinarian; don't make things worse by dosing your horse with tranquilizers or pain medication. Get him to a quiet place, blanket him if necessary, and wait for the vet to arrive.

Prevention is the best cure. Remove all poisonous plants from your pasture—or else just keep your horse out of the pasture. While the list is long, don't get too frightened. Many of these plants are not tasty to horses (although some are irresistible). In addition, not every one of these grows everywhere! The following plants can be toxic (in varying degrees), although some have medicinal use when applied judiciously:

- alsike clover (*Trifolium hybridum*)
- arrowgrass (*Triglochin maritima*)
- autumn crocus (*Colchicum autumnale*)
- avocado (*Persea americana*)
- black locust (*Robinia pseudoacacia*)
- black walnut (*Juglans nigra*)
- bindweed or morning glory (*Convolvulus arvensis*)
- boxwood (*Buxus sempervirens*)
- bracken fern (*Pteridium aquilinum*)
- burning bush (*Euonymus atropurpureus*)
- buckwheat (*Fagopyrum esculentum*)
- buttercup (*Ranunculus acris* and others)
- castor bean (*Ricinus communis*)
- chinaberry (*Melia azedarach*)
- common nightshade (*Solanum americanum*)
- crimson clover (*Trifolium incarnatum*)
- death camas (*Zigadenus spp.*)
- dogbane (*Apocynum cannabinum*)
- Easter lily (*Zephyranthes atamasco*)
- European hemlock (*Conium maculatum*)
- Eve's necklace or Texas sophora (*Sophora affinis*)
- false hellebore or Indian poke (*Veratrum viride*)
- fitweed (*Corydalis spp.*)
- golden chain or bean tree (*Laburnum anagyroides*)
- groundsel (*Senecio spp.*)

Extruded Feeds

Extruding (a process invented in 1957) is a special method of cooking feed. The resulting product is more digestible than ordinary grain mixes, and it also stores very well. Horses chew these foods more slowly than pellets, which makes them an excellent choice for horses who tend to bolt their food or for those who are susceptible to bloat or colic. On the downside, extruded grains are about half the weight of pelleted foods but may cost as much per bag—so you are paying more for less.

DEADLY PROTEIN

Probably the single biggest dietary factor that makes horses sick is simply feeding them too much protein. Horses are designed to live on grass, which is not particularly rich in protein. Horses are quite thrifty and can make do with a comparatively small amount. A full-grown mature working horse can do very well on a diet of 9 to12 percent crude protein, lactating mares may need 14 percent, and weanlings may need as much as 16 percent.

Excess protein in horses also results in more urea in sweat and plasma, increased blood ammonia concentrations, and increased post-exercise orotic acid excretions. While these are not pathological conditions in and of themselves, they are abnormal and should probably be avoided.

More significantly, excess protein leads to:

- increased water intake
- higher heart and respiratory rates
- higher rates of sweating and dehydration
- lower muscle glycogen concentrations, leading to early fatigue and loss of stamina in endurance horses
- increased urinary nitrogen excretions, which affects respiratory health
- increased urinary calcium and phosphorus loss

Excess protein has even been shown to slow racing times in thoroughbreds. Another study showed that horses fed 25 percent extra protein (that's a lot) suffered slower growth rates and developmental bone disease. Nature simply did not design horses to eat protein like tigers do.

When misguided owners start overloading their horses on protein-rich hays like alfalfa, they are just asking for trouble. Alfalfa can be as much as 20 percent protein—way more than almost any horse needs, and even worse, this protein cannot always be fully used by the horse. If the horse can't eliminate all the excess, he is at risk for problems such as colic, and in young horses, developmental bone disease. Alfalfa is also high in calcium and low in phosphorus. This can be disastrous for horses, interfering with proper muscle development and producing knuckling over and epiphysitis, osselets, bone spavin, and navicular disease. It also can throw the parathyroid gland out of whack, leading to even more trouble. Alfalfa is comparatively low in fiber, which is really critical for horses, and it has also been linked to kidney stones. Some of the imbalance in alfalfa can be countered by judicious use of grain, but this must be done carefully. All foods need to be given in the right proportions to provide balanced nutrition, good digestion, and optimal health. For more information on the proper diet for your horse, please read my book *Feeding Your Horse for Life*. (See Resources.)

- horse chestnut (*Aesculus hippocastanum*)
- horsetail (*Equisetum arvense*)
- hound's tongue (*Cynoglossum officinale*)
- hydrangea (*Hydrangea spp.*)
- kochia (*Kochia scoparia*)
- Indian paintbrush (*Castilleja spp.*)
- jimmyweed (*Haplopappus heterophyllus*)
- jimsonweed (*Datura spp.*)
- Labrador tea (*Ledum columbianum* and *Ledum glandulosum*)
- locoweed (*Astragalus* and *Oxytropis spp.*)
- lupine (*Lupinus spp.*)
- mesquite (*Prosopis glandulosa*)
- milkweed (*Asclepias spp.*)
- mistletoe (*Phoradendron villosum*)
- mock azalea (*Menziesia ferruginea*)
- monkshood (*Aconitum napellus*)
- oak (*Quercus spp.*)
- oleander (*Nerium oleander*)
- peach (*Prunus persica*)
- pieris japonica (*Pieris floribunda*)
- ragwort (*Senecio jacobaea*)
- rape (*Brassica napus*)
- rattlebox or rattlepod (*Crotalaria spp.*)
- red clover (*Trifolium pratense*)
- red maple (*Acer rubrum*)
- rosary pea (*Abrus precatorius*)
- sacahuista or beargrass (*Nolina texana*)
- saltbush (*Atriplex patula*)
- sagebrush (*Artemisia spp.*)
- senna or coffeeweed (*Cassia spp.*)
- silver nightshade (*Solanum elaeagnifolium*)
- snakeroot (*Eupatorium rugosum*)
- sneezeweed (*Helenium spp.*)
- Saint-John's-wort (*Hypericum perforatum*)
- sudangrass (*Sorghum sudanense*)
- sweet clover (*Melilotus spp.*)
- sweet pea (*Lathyrus spp.*)
- tall fescue (*Festuca spp.*)
- tarweed (*Amsinckia intermedia*)
- water hemlock (*Cicuta maculata*)
- wild cherry wilted leaves (*Prunus spp.*)
- wild jasmine or day-blooming jessamine (*Cestrum diurnum*)
- yellow jessamine (*Gelsemium sempervirens*)
- yellow star thistle (*Centaurea solstitialis*)
- yew (*Taxus* family)

Selenium Accumulator Plants

Selenium is one of the few elements that a number of plants absorb in amounts sufficient enough to make them toxic to horses. Some plants, including cereal grains, absorb so much selenium that eating them can poison your horse. Wild-growing selenium soakers include:

- beard tongue (*Penstemon spp.*)
- broom (*Gutierrezia sarothrae*)
- golden weed (*Haplopappus engelmannii*)
- gumweed (*Grindelia spp.*)
- Indian paintbrush (*Castilleja spp.*)
- prince's plume (*Stanleya pinnata*)
- saltbush (*Atriplex spp.*)
- two-grooved milk vetch (*Astragalus bisulcatus*)
- white prairie aster (*Aster falcatus*)
- woody aster (*Xylorhiza glabriuscula*)

Selenium poisoning is incurable (resulting in blind staggers and other conditions), so strong preventive measures should be taken. Most accumulator plants are broad leaved and can be killed with the proper herbicide. Grass does not accumulate selenium, so if the level in your soil is high (it can be checked), keep it well covered with grass. However, choose carefully; for example, alfalfa is one of the hays that may accumulate selenium.

VITAMINS

Vitamins are organic compounds essential for your horse's growth and maintenance. While needed only in small amounts, they are critical for the proper functioning of his body. They help enzymatic reactions in the body, scavenge free radicals, release energy from food, help to metabolize amino acids and proteins, maintain cell membrane activity, support bone development, maintain calcium balance, help blood clot, support normal eye function, and aid nerve impulse transduction. They come in two basic varieties: fat soluble (vitamins A, D, E, and K) and water-soluble (vitamins C and B). Fat-soluble vitamins are stored in the body and need dietary fat to be used, while water-soluble vitamins need only water. Water-soluble vitamins are not stored in the body and need to be given every day.

There are a huge number of supplements and additives that you can add to your horse's diet, but it is important to know how much supplementation is really necessary. Good nutrition generally offers all the nutrients a horse needs. Supplements should only be used to correct deficiencies in a diet or when needed by horses with special requirements

Nutraceuticals

Many nutritional therapies rely on nutraceuticals, substances that act partly as nutrients and partly as medications. Most of them are made from substances that occur naturally in the body.

(like performance horses, mares, seniors, and invalids).

The following are necessary vitamins in any good equine diet.

Vitamin A

Vitamin A maintains the normal structure of cell walls, and it is necessary for bone growth and good vision. Horses store vitamin A in the liver, just as we do. Green forage (consumed in spring) has a high concentration of beta-carotene, a precursor of vitamin A, making it a good source for this vitamin. It is also present in alfalfa in greater amounts than in grass hays.

A deficiency in vitamin A can produce night blindness, poor growth, impaired reproduction, respiratory infections, and a rough coat. Too much can lead to unthriftiness (failure of a young animal to grow or gain weight at a normal rate in spite of an adequate diet) and depression. Broodmares in the last trimester may need a vitamin A supplement, especially in the fall or winter.

Vitamin B Complex

The B vitamins perform a wide variety of functions, and because they are water soluble, they are not stored in the body and need to be replaced regularly. B vitamins are great for the immune system, and they help to manage stress, allergies, and infections. They are often considered together because particular B vitamins require other B vitamins for synthesis or activation, and they are usually supplemented together.

While healthy horses make their own B vitamins, animals with chronic diseases often can benefit from supplementation. Deficiencies of vitamin B_1 (thiamine) are occasionally reported—some kinds of plants interfere with its function in the body.

One B vitamin, biotin, is particularly helpful for horses with poor hoof condition. In fact, biotin is just about the only feed supplement that has actually been proven to improve hoof quality. However, results will not become apparent for several months, as the hoof grows downward from the coronary band, where the biotin is incorporated. Unfortunately, some horses may not be helped by it.

Vitamin C

Water-soluble vitamin C is an important antioxidant that supports cells in times of physical or environmental stress. It recharges other antioxidants within the body to keep them active.

While horses can make their own vitamin C (unlike humans) in their livers, aged horses (20 years plus) are shown to have lower vitamin C levels. In addition, certain conditions, such as increased stress (from surgery or other events) may produce a need for a little extra in the vitamin C department. Powdered, oral supplementation (4.5 to 20 grams) may be administered. Vitamin C also may be helpful in the treatment of tying-up syndrome or Cushing's disease due to pituitary adenoma (benign tumors). It also protects lung function.

Apples, by the way, are excellent sources of vitamin C, and horses generally love them.

Vitamin D

The main function of vitamin D is to regulate the absorption, transport, and deposition of calcium, and to a lesser extent, phosphorus.

If your horse spends any amount of time outdoors, he absorbs enough vitamin D, the so-called sunshine vitamin. Horses also receive it from good-quality food, especially in sun-cured hay. However, eating the wild jasmine plant (*Cestrum diurnum*), which is high in vitamin D, can cause damaging toxicity and possibly death. Too much vitamin C causes calcium deposition in soft tissues, which in turn can damage muscles, blood vessels, kidneys, and even the heart.

Vitamin E

This antioxidant vitamin is important for reproduction, muscle development, and red blood cell function.

Vitamin E deficiency has been shown to be present in equine motor neuron disease. A supplement (6,000 IU per day) may help with equine degenerative myeloencephalopathy, a diffuse degenerative disease of the spinal cord and brain

Thiamine, or vitamin B_1, is sometimes used as a "natural sedative." However, its effect is too spotty to be reliable.

Antioxidants

Several vitamins, such as C and E, are also antioxidants that destroy damaging free radicals. A free radical is a reactive compound that contains an unpaired electron. Desperately searching for a pairing electron, the free radical will snatch one wherever it can—often from a nearby fatty acid. The fatty acid then becomes a free radical itself and raids the fatty acid next door to it and so on down the line. There is something truly vampire-like about all this, and the eventual result is cell membrane rupture and the death of the cell. That's why antioxidants are good! Yet, it is possible to get too much of a good thing. Because the immune system uses free radicals to fight disease, high doses of antioxidants can reduce the effectiveness of the immune system. This is a case where more is not necessarily better.

stem. It can be combined with selenium to fight against tying-up syndrome. Performance horses also may benefit from vitamin E supplements.

Vitamin K

This vitamin is an important blood-clotting agent. Alfalfa hay is loaded with it. It is also produced by the microbes in the cecum and colon and absorbed there.

Dicumarol, a compound produced by a fungus on both dry and green sweet clover, can cause a deficiency of Vitamin K. However, not many horses subsist on sweet clover any more, so this isn't usually an issue.

MINERAL SUPPLEMENTATION

Minerals are inorganic substances (as opposed to vitamins, which are organic in nature). They cannot by made in a laboratory or in your horse's body. We must rely on Mother Nature's good will to hand them out to us. Minerals participate in nearly every bodily function; they build teeth and bone, work with enzymes, help muscle contraction, and aid nerve impulses.

Very few horses need mineral supplementation of any sort because most get what they need from their diets, if the soil is adequate. (If it's not in the soil, it can't get into the plant.) The following are necessary minerals in any good equine diet.

Calcium (Ca) and Phosphorus (P)

These minerals should be treated together because they must be in correct balance. Both are critical for healthy bones and teeth. The ratio of calcium to phosphorus should be between 1.5:1 and 2:1. An overbalance of phosphorus can cause osteodystrophy, in which bones become very weak and the tendons may detach from the bones. Too little phosphorus causes rickets, overgrowth, and fragile bones and can lead to fractures and lameness. A calcium deficiency also can cause rickets, as well as osteomalacia (brittle bones).

Calcium is the main inorganic component of bone. It is also an essential mineral needed for muscle contraction, blood clotting, temperature regulation, and heart function. Most horses get plenty of calcium through their natural diet, especially if they are eating alfalfa hay, which is loaded with the stuff. However, in some cases of heavy work and consequent sweating, or in lactating mares (especially draft breeds), significant amounts of calcium can be lost. A calcium deficiency also can occur in a high grain/low legume diet. In such cases, calcium-containing solutions can be given. These solutions should *not* be given as "prevention," however, because they can actually make the problem worse. In many cases, so-called calcium deficiency has more to do with the availability of phosphorus rather than with calcium. And high levels of iron in the water can impede the absorption of phosphorus. You see, everything is connected, and things are never as simple as they seem. Supplementing calcium in excess is probably the most

common cause of mineral imbalances in horses. It usually occurs when the amount is not properly coordinated with phosphorus.

Cobalt (Co)

This trace mineral is required for vitamin B_{12} synthesis and the formation of red blood cells. In most parts of the world, cobalt deficiency is rare in horses. However, some people maintain that cobalt supplementation increases microbial fiber digestion.

Copper (Cu)

Copper is an important mineral that helps to build bone, connective tissue, and blood cells. It is necessary for proper iron utilization and hoof integrity. Most adult horses get plenty of copper in the diet, but some researchers have found that young growing horses may benefit from a copper supplement to help to prevent osteochondrosis, a disease that affects bone growth. Pregnant mares supplemented with copper have foals with a lower incidence of developmental orthopedic diseases. Horses with a deficiency of copper typically have dull or discolored coats. Copper deficiency is widespread in some parts of the United States.

Iodine (I)

Iodine is a component of thyroid hormones, which regulate metabolism and growth.

Foals born to iodine-deficient dams may be stillborn or born weak and unable to nurse. Horses with a low thyroid panel may benefit from an iodine supplement. However, feeding excess iodine can interfere with thyroid function. Kelp and other marine products may contain excessively high levels of iodine. This is important to remember because these products are frequently sold as supplements. For accuracy, any supplement should be fed by weight, not volume.

Iron (Fe)

Iron is a vital component of blood hemoglobin and essential for oxygen transport. The highest percentage of iron is found in the red blood cells. It is absorbed mainly from the small intestine and stored in the liver, spleen, and bone marrow.

True iron-deficient anemia is rare in horses; most often anemia comes from an excess or deficiency of copper or vitamin B_{12}. It is not thought necessary to supplement the diet of most horses with iron.

Magnesium (Mg)

This mineral is needed for muscle and nervous tissue function. In fact, the average horse walks around with about 1/2 pound (227 g) of magnesium in his body.

A deficiency can result in nervousness, fatigue, and muscle tremors. Magnesium is usually plentiful in the diet (it is found in green plants, especially alfalfa), but it has been found that a magnesium supplement may be helpful to horses with tense muscles or tight backs.

Manganese (Mn)

Manganese is important because it is needed for cartilage development and for the proper utilization of other trace minerals. It is a component of many enzymes and is stored mostly in the liver.

Manganese is low in grains and alfalfa, two products commonly fed to performance horses. Thus, these horses may be need supplements. In addition, as with all minerals, soil pH affects the absorption of manganese in forage plants.

Potassium (K)

Potassium is an important electrolyte needed to maintain the cell's acid-base balance and internal cellular fluid pressure. In hot weather and/or during exercise, the potassium requirement can increase significantly. Otherwise, potassium deficiency is rare in horses because forage is an excellent source for this mineral.

Chelated Minerals

Some manufacturers claim that chelated minerals are more effective as supplements than ordinary minerals. Chelated minerals are usually bound to amino acids, which apparently makes them more easily absorbed by the body. There is no evidence to support the claim that chelated minerals are any better than any other kind, and they cost more. Very few healthy horses need mineral supplementation of any sort.

Selenium (Se)

This trace mineral works like an antioxidant and works closely with vitamin E. Supplementation is usually provided in a mineral mixture, complete feed, or trace-mineralized salt. Commercial oral formulations of this vitamin/mineral combination are also available for horses with a tendency to tie up. Selenium deficiency also results in weak foals, impaired movement, and difficulty in nursing. Interestingly, nonruminants like horses are much more likely to be victims of selenium poisoning than ruminants like cows. Absorption in nonruminants is 77 percent in contrast to 29 percent for ruminants. On the other hand, if the soil lacks selenium, horses are susceptible to white muscle disease. Too much selenium in the soil can cause lameness and swelling around the coronary band.

Sodium Chloride (NaCl)

Sodium chloride is the major blood electrolyte needed for the regulation of body fluids. A tendency to chew on salty objects may indicate a deficiency. Many commercial feeds are low on sodium and chloride, so horses should have access to iodized or trace-mineralized salt.

Sulfur (S)

Sulfur is a component of three amino acids (methionine, cystine, and cysteine). It is important in maintaining cell permeability. It is essential for the synthesis of biotin, thiamin, insulin, and chondroitin sulfate (a building block of synovial fluid and cartilage). In the body, sulfur is largely taken up in the joints, skin, and hooves. It helps to produce insulin and also kills bacteria and fungi.

Sulfur is found in many raw fruits and vegetables. Hay may not provide enough sulfur, but grain supplements almost always compensate for this. Water also may contain significant amounts of sulfur.

Zinc (Zn)

Zinc is important for healthy skin, bones, hooves, and connective tissue, and it is a component of more than 200 enzymes. It is critical in reproductive function. Brittle, crumbly hooves and a poor coat can be signs of zinc deficiency. Zinc is found in most trace-mineralized salt products. It also can be found in oats.

OTHER SUPPLEMENTS

Glucosamine and Chondroitin

Glucosamine and chondroitin sulfate are substances found naturally in the body. Glucosamine is a form of amino sugar that is believed to play a role in cartilage formation and repair. Chondroitin sulfate is part of a large protein molecule (proteoglycan) that gives cartilage elasticity.

Both glucosamine and chondroitin sulfate are sold as dietary or nutritional supplements. They are extracted from animal tissue: glucosamine from crab, lobster or shrimp shells; and chondroitin sulfate from animal cartilage, such as tracheas or shark cartilage.

Coenzyme Q10 (Ubiquinone)

This substance helps to break down fat and helps it become usable energy. By acting as an oxygen free-radical scavenger, it stabilizes mitochondrial cell membranes. It is naturally produced in the body, but aging animals make less of it, even though their need for it increases. It has been shown to be helpful in animals with heart disease, but the dose required for horses (about ten times the human dose) has made it prohibitively expensive. It has been used in cases of laminitis.

Colloidal Silver

This mineral supplement is developed from electromagnetically charged silver suspended in deionized water. It was first widely used in the 1940s. Given orally, colloidal silver is used to fight certain bacteria, fungi, and viruses. It is sometimes used in a spray form to "sterilize" the stable area.

As a supplement, colloidal silver is not shown by any controlled studies to be effective against disease, and if used, should be administered only under the guidance of a veterinarian and for the shortest possible time. Some maintain that because bacteria have grown to be so resistant to antibiotics, colloidal silver fulfills a useful function. It is often prescribed along with the herb thuja. This supplement should never be injected or used on horses with liver problems.

Digestive Enzymes

Digestive enzymes such as lipase, amylase, protease, and disaccharidase are produced within the body to help to break down nutrients.

Sick and elderly horses may have fewer digestive enzymes, and some owners buy powdered commercial preparations in the belief they will help their horses with digestion. They are simply added to the food, with older animals receiving more of the supplemental enzymes. Clinical studies to show their effectiveness are lacking.

Dimethylglycine (DMG)

DMG, a dietary supplement, is a natural substance already present in many foods. It is supposed to enhance oxygen usage at the cellular level. This is especially important for broodmares. It is also said to lengthen peak performance periods, shorten recovery time after hard exercise, and reduce lactic acid buildup and cramping. Some also believe that DMG improves a horse's immune response by over 400 percent to protect against pathogens, and it helps older horses with limited respiratory function. Despite the hype, these effects are not proved. This is a very safe supplement, however, which can be purchased commercially.

Flaxseed Oil

The flax plant is an annual herb believed to have originated in Egypt. Flaxseed oil is a plant-based source of omega-3 fatty acids as well as omega-6 fatty acids. Flaxseed is also a rich source of lignans (phytoestrogens), which support the immune system.

Horses in need of fatty acids typically have dull, dry skin and poor hooves. Omega-3 fatty acids are helpful in stimulating natural steroid production, regulating nerve transmission, mediating immune response, and constructing strong cell membranes. There is some evidence that this supplement can have a calming effect on horses. It is especially recommended for pregnant mares because pregnancy is one of the conditions most associated with omega-3 fatty acid deficiency.

Methylsulfonylmethane (MSM)

MSM, an organic source of sulfur, is an edible, stable, odorless derivative of DMSO (see Chapter 1) and has many of its same anti-inflammatory properties, although not to the same degree. It has been used to treat chronic muscle soreness, epiphysitis, scar formation, ulcers, acute laminitis, recurring digestive tract disorders, and arthritis.

MSM occurs in many raw fruits and vegetables; its primary source in horse supplements is kelp. These supplements evaporate quickly, so they must be administered fresh and not allowed to sit out.

Perna Mussel (*Perna canaliculus*)

This New Zealand mussel has been shown to be effective in treating degenerative joint disorders. It is also an anti-inflammatory. This is a great supplement for an older horse, but some show a pronounced distaste for it.

Probiotics (Bacterial Supplements)

Probiotics are a live or freeze-dried microbial feed supplement. They include *Lactobacillus bulgaris* and *Lactobacillus acidophilus*, which supply nutrients and aid digestion. Probiotics are supposed to be particularly useful in times of stress, such as during weaning and shipping and when exposed to disease organisms. They also may be helpful to horses switching to a new feed. Some people believe that they improve the performance of race horses, possibly by increasing aerobic capacity. However, there are some questions about the real usefulness of these supplements. One is how these bacteria manage to survive in a container for weeks and weeks without nutrients. Are you inadvertently feeding your horse dead bacteria? Even if they are alive, it's uncertain how they live through the trip through a horse's stomach, where the stomach acid kills off most of the bacteria.

Shark Cartilage

This chondroitin-containing substance is touted as a miracle cure for arthritis. Its benefits have not been thoroughly studied, and because sharks are rapidly becoming endangered the world over, I believe the use of this material is unethical, especially because its widespread use would result in even more killing of sharks.

THE BASICS OF NUTRITIONAL THERAPY

ADVANTAGES
- NATURAL.
- NONINVASIVE.
- CAN USUALLY BE PRACTICED BY A HORSE'S OWNER, ALTHOUGH THE PROCESS SHOULD BEGIN UNDER THE ADVICE OF A TRAINED EQUINE NUTRITIONIST.

DISADVANTAGES
- IMPROPER NUTRITION CAN CAUSE PERMANENT DAMAGE.
- THE PROCESS CAN TAKE A LONG TIME, AND CHANGES MAY BE INCREMENTAL.

In its strictest sense, nutritional therapy practiced by alternative practitioners is based on the idea that nutritional imbalances play a role in many diseases. Proponents believe that when the body is particularly low in one or more nutrients, it manifests in some form of disease or symptoms. Their theory is that by correcting these deficiencies with appropriate changes in the diet and adding a custom vitamin or mineral supplement, the symptoms will disappear due to the improved health of the horse.

Practitioners who use equine nutritional therapy say it also strengthens the immune system, enhances energy levels, and improves performance in any stage of a horse's life. Knowing how to feed a horse based on his life stage, they feel, is the first step toward balancing his nutrition.

Nutritional therapy is different than conventional medicine in that it considers and treats the horse as a whole, taking into consideration the interrelationships of the various organs and systems of the body. More importantly, the body's self-healing ability is recognized at all times.

Equine nutritional therapy uses your horse's diet and body chemistry along with custom-designed vitamin and mineral supplements to encourage the body's own natural healing processes. Analysis is done to see if your horse has any nutritional deficiencies, toxic levels of heavy metals, stress response and recovery issues, inflammatory tendencies, or endocrine and enzyme dysfunctions. Quite often the nutrition program may be complemented by additional alternative therapies that balance body structures, such as chiropractic, acupuncture, electromedicine, cranial rhythm, infrasound, biosonic repatterning, and photon therapy.

While it is obvious to everyone that some illnesses have such a foundation in inadequate nutrition, not everyone

will agree that a nutritional imbalance or deficiency is always to blame. It is certainly true that a sound, balanced diet is critical for optimum health. Indeed, a small dietary change can make a dramatic difference for good or ill. The National Research Council (NRC) provides general guidelines (within a wide range) of the proper nutritional levels. Of necessity, of course, these guidelines are meant for the average individual. Every horse's needs are different, even within a class (such as with a performance horse, lactating mare, and so on).

Therapeutic Protocols

There are many approaches to nutritional therapy. Many such protocols consist of:

- detoxifying the body from heavy metal contaminants
- correcting vitamin and mineral deficiencies
- restoring healthy digestion
- reducing internal stress

Heavy metal contaminants include mercury, cadmium, arsenic, nickel, and lead. Aluminum is sometimes considered a "heavy metal" in this therapy also, although it is actually very light. Aluminum is particularly concentrated by cereal grains and alfalfa, which make up a significant portion of a horse's diet. In addition, aluminum containers are used to feed and water horses, as well as to store food. Water contaminated by acid rain also may be considered a source of metal contamination. Diseases blamed on heavy metal contamination include allergies, ataxia, colic, depression, diarrhea, excitability, gastroenteritis, hair loss, inability to recover from stress, lameness, laminitis, mood swings, shedding problems, ulcers, weight loss, and "unexplained illnesses." In other words, almost everything. (There is a widespread theory in some circles that we are all being poisoned by heavy metals; this is probably not true.)

Many nutritional therapies rely on a mineral hair analysis and a feed ration analysis for diagnostics and treatment. In the former, a small sample of the horse's hair is taken. The hair is dissolved and burned at a high temperature. Each mineral present gives off a characteristic spectrum of light. Proponents claim to be able to tell a lot from this, including your horse's metabolic rate, stress level, immune system status, energy levels, and carbohydrate tolerance, as well as adrenal and thyroid glandular activity and proclivities to more than 30 illnesses, long before they actually appear. Further, a hair analysis is supposed to tell you if your horse is prone to anxiety, mood swings, aggression, or spookiness. This is certainly a safe, noninvasive diagnostic tool, and it is certainly true that hair analysis is a good way to check for toxic metals, but its efficacy in determining anything else has not been proved.

The other diagnostic tool, ration analysis, evaluates your horse's current diet by comparing it against the National Research Council's equine nutrient requirements to see how it compares with the needs of your horse. Requirements for maintenance horses, breeding stallions, lactating mares, performance horses, growing foals, and aged horses over the age of fifteen are taken into consideration. Nutrients analyzed include crude protein, lysine, calcium (Ca), phosphorus (P), magnesium (Mg), potassium (K), sodium (Na), iron (Fe), zinc (Zn), copper (Cu), iodine (I),

selenium (Se), manganese (Mn), vitamin A, vitamin D, and vitamin E, along with digestible energy.

When the needs of the horse have been thoroughly analyzed, the animal may be placed on a vitamin or mineral supplement, digestive aids, glandular therapy (see section "Glandular Therapy"), anti-inflammatory drugs, or joint supplements. Diseases such as Cushing's syndrome and laminitis have been treated with nutritional therapy.

Nutritional therapy is believed to allow deeper healing to occur as toxins and other body stressors are eliminated and supplements are added to support the restorative process. Eventually, the supplement program can be reduced as the improvements become permanent.

Other natural therapies that balance the horse's body can also be integrated with this protocol. Progress will often be enhanced when the nutrition program is coupled with therapies that balance body structures (chiropractic) and energy flows (acupuncture, acupressure, electromedicine, etc.).

An important caution: As with any alterative therapy, always consult with your vet before beginning treatment.

ORTHOMOLECULAR MEDICINE

Orthomolecular medicine is defined as the use of optimum amounts of naturally occurring substances, especially nutrients, to treat disease and maintain health. Orthomolecular practitioners believe that the currently recommended dietary levels of vitamins and other nutrients are based on the minimum amounts to avoid deficiency diseases. Therefore, animals require much higher levels to achieve and maintain health. Vitamin or mineral supplements are key elements of this therapy. The usual vitamins included are A, C, and E. Practitioners believe that mega doses of vitamin A may help to fight infections, while vitamin E can fight liver disease. Vitamin C and E together have antioxidant and anti-inflammatory properties. Increasingly, fatty acid supplementation is also used.

While it is an axiom that a proper diet provides all necessary nutrients, orthomolecular medicine suggests

that the variability in food quality, often a result of soil depletion, may necessitate higher doses of some nutrients, especially certain vitamins. Before supplementing any vitamin, however, discuss safe dosage levels with a vet who is well acquainted with the basic principles of orthomolecular medicine. Orthomolecular therapy may involve single substances or combinations thereof.

The key to proper supplementation is balance. If you supplement too much of one vitamin, for instance, it can throw off the absorption or metabolism of others. For example, supplements containing vitamin C or E should not be added to feeds containing iron or copper supplements. (Iron and copper can destroy vitamins C and E.) Supplemented mineral oils also can absorb the fat-soluble vitamins A, D, and E and make them unavailable for the horse. Don't supplement, especially with a mineral, without getting a go-ahead from your vet first.

It is safe to combine orthomolecular medicine with other types of veterinary care.

GLANDULAR THERAPY

Glandular therapy uses supplements made from glandular tissue. It is sometimes used as replacement therapy for horses whose organs are not functioning well. Thus, a horse with thyroid trouble might be given thyroid glandular material. Before the 1940s and the development of modern synthetic hormones, glandular extracts were widely used. Glandular products include purified extracts from glands such as the thymus, thyroid, and adrenal glands, as well as other organs like the heart, liver, kidneys, and spleen. They are typically used when the horse's own endocrine system is underproducing or undersecreting a specific hormone or when an organ is diseased or weakened. The extract is believed to supply necessary raw material so that the diseased or weakened organs can begin to regenerate.

Because this is an animal product and not a plant product, some horses may not accept glandular tissue extracts. (In addition, the extracts can be expensive.) However, the material often can be injected, and supporters of glandular tissue therapy say that the gentle action of glandular therapy has many advantages over standard pharmaceuticals, which while quick and inexpensive, also bring about many side effects. Many of these materials are also sources of active lipids and steroids, and some may have advantages over pure hormones.

Most scientists object to glandular principle on theory; they believe that all ingested substances are quickly broken down into their constituent molecules. Glandular therapy supporters, on the other hand, maintain that large "macromolecules" such as larger hormones, enzymes, and peptides can indeed be absorbed nearly intact across the gut wall (which is why oral vaccines work). Supporters of glandular therapy believe that they have the scientific evidence to show that large tissue-specific molecules can be absorbed and exert significant benefit upon the organism.

THE HAND THAT FEEDS

In sum, your horse is what he eats. The good thing about all of this is that *you* control, to a large extent, what goes into his tummy. After all, your horse is not likely to walk into the kitchen and make himself a peanut butter sandwich. Your job as a responsible owner is to make sure that your equine companion gets plenty of the good stuff and none of the bad stuff. It's that simple—and it's also that challenging.

Chapter 3

From the beginning of time, both people and horses have known the healing power of touch. It is physically relaxing, but it also can be emotionally stabilizing and psychologically empowering. A good rubdown has been thought to be beneficial to horses for at least 1,000 years. The basic principle is nothing new, but as with every other modality, we are discovering different approaches and techniques all the time.

Bodywork and touch therapy can be used to recondition the body, but it also can treat a variety of common equine conditions. Many chronic muscle and spine problems

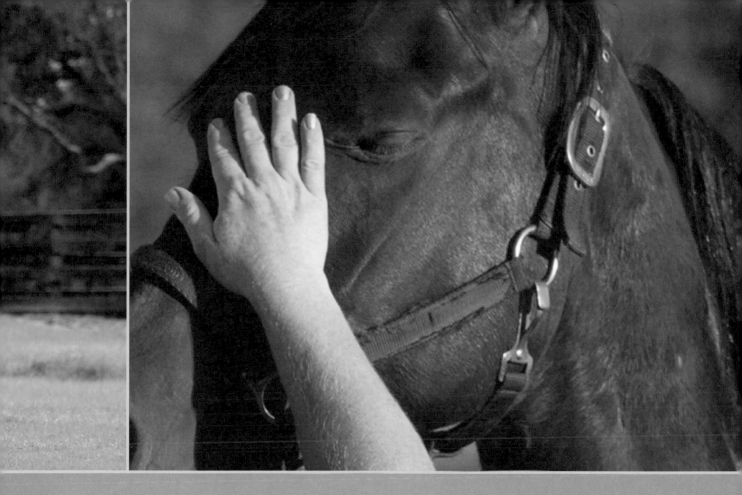

Bodywork

are caused by poor saddle fit, shoeing problems, incorrect bitting, and unbalanced riders. And of course, strenuous physical work like jumping, barrel racing, and dressage also can wreak havoc on joints and muscles. Careful owners watch their horses for signs of physical pain, but some signals are still often mistaken for behavior problems. Determining the actual source of your horse's problem is essential to his well-being, and these bodywork modalities can help to sort out a number of concerns.

Bodywork is a wonderful adjunct and complement to mainstream veterinary care. Indeed, it is often used to keep a horse feeling fit and limber, but it also can be used as a healing technique. While various sorts of physical and energy therapies may differ in operating principles, all depend on a thorough knowledge of equine anatomy. Although you can learn massage and many other forms of bodywork and touch therapy yourself, you'll get the best results from studying your horse's body and working under the guidance of a mentor until you become proficient.

Bodywork offers many important benefits other than physical ones. For example, massage therapy has psychological advantages—it has something to offer both you and your horse. Unlike other forms of alternative health treatments, which may consist of sticking needles into your horse or feeding him herbs and tonics, massage creates a strong emotional bond with him. Also, most bodywork is done without the need for any anesthetic, which is definitely a plus! It is very important to use only qualified individuals for these sorts of therapies—especially when manipulations of the spine are involved.

To find a good therapist, check with your vet or horse mentor. You also can contact the International Association of Animal Massage Therapists (IAAMT) or visit their website at www.iaamt.com for more information. Many good therapists have an Equine Sports Massage Certification. A good equine massage practitioner will not, by the way, diagnose your horse's condition but will work with your vet for the benefit of the animal.

MASSAGE THERAPY

ADVANTAGES
- NONINVASIVE.
- EFFECTIVE FOR MANY MUSCULAR STRESSES.
- HAS A CALMING EFFECT.
- STRENGTHENS THE EQUINE–HUMAN BOND.

DISADVANTAGES
- TIME CONSUMING.
- PHYSICALLY RIGOROUS ON THE PRACTITIONER.
- CAN BE COUNTERPRODUCTIVE IF INCORRECTLY APPLIED.

Massage is one of the most ancient of all therapies, the origins of which were first documented in China around 2700 B.C.E. The word "massage" is related to both the Arabic verb *mass*, meaning "to touch" and the Greek *massein*, meaning "to knead."

Massage affects the whole body because joint mobility and health are essential to proper body functioning. However, its benefits go beyond improving muscle tone and limbering up joints. You can use it to improve your horse's performance and general well-being, as well as to treat specific problems. Equine massage is a recognized professional sports therapy designed particularly for horses. It offers the following benefits:
- lowers risk of injury
- increases circulation
- strengthens muscle tone
- relaxes spasms
- increases range of motion
- speeds healing
- reduces swelling and inflammation
- releases lactic acid buildup

- triggers the release of endorphins, turning an irritable or nervous animal into something more closely approximating a teddy bear
- deepens the bond between horse and owner

Truly, there is magic in your fingers. The glory of massage and massage-related therapies is that they are not only effective, but proper techniques are safe enough for horse owners to learn easily for themselves. However, the official position for the practice of equine massage developed by the American Association of Equine Practitioners (AAEP) is that it should only be performed by a graduate of an accredited massage school who has specialized training in equine anatomy, physiology, and veterinary ethics. Some states have laws that restrict those who may and may not engage in the practice. None of these laws restrict what the horse owner herself can do, of course, although it's advisable not to attempt a deep muscle massage on your own. However, if you are planning to hire a massage therapist for your horse, be sure to check her credentials thoroughly, and get references.

THE BENEFITS OF MASSAGE

Musculoskeletal problems are probably the most common cause of poor performance, and good massage therapy can make all the difference. It can loosen tight muscles, increasing range of motion and circulation, which in turn improves your horse's power, endurance, coordination, and reflexes. A separate advantage of massage therapy is that it is very inexpensive—no fancy machines or dangerous drugs are needed. And just as important, it employs techniques you can easily learn from an accredited practitioner. The more you physically demand from your horse, the more valuable massage will be in attaining your goals.

Skeletal muscle composes 60 percent of a horse's total body weight. That's a lot of massage!

Massage can loosen tight muscles, increasing range of motion and circulation, which in turn improves your horse's power, endurance, coordination, and reflexes.

However, therapeutic massage is not the same as a rubdown; it is a specialized technique designed to treat a specific ailment. A good massage follows a particular sequence of muscle manipulations and includes stimulating certain pressure points.

An average session takes about an hour, so wait until you have that much time to give to your horse. Rushing a massage or leaving it partially undone may be worse than not doing it at all. If you are working a horse for a particular problem (usually related to a muscle spasm), you will find that one or two sessions will do the trick. If more than three are required, it's a good indication that something deeper is troubling your animal. In some cases, the "something deeper" is a systemic illness that is being expressed in the muscle. At other times, the problem could stem from something as straightforward as a bad hoof trim, poorly fitting saddle, or bad riding.

Getting Started

Before you begin a massage, brush your horse thoroughly. This will make the experience more pleasant for both of you. It's no fun rubbing a dirty horse—especially because the action will serve to rub any grime deeper into his coat or skin. Brush away all dirt, mud, hair, and dried sweat first.

Equine massage generally begins with gentle even stroking to get the horse accustomed to the feel of it. You don't want to start out digging around for muscle spasms. It proceeds with a light touch in the same direction as the hair growth and moves longitudinally along the muscle. As the massage continues, the stroking can become deeper. (If you are doing it correctly, the horse becomes relaxed, almost soporific, as you go along.) At this point, your strokes change direction and you begin moving your hands in the direction of the venous flow—toward the heart—because you are improving circulation in the blood and lymph nodes. Massage parts of the horse in the same order every

time. Pick the largest muscles first: over the back, shoulders, and hindquarters.

To work into the muscles more, use the heel of your hand or a loose fist and press and release it on the body in a circular, rhythmic motion. Begin with light pressure and gradually work more deeply into the muscle. A horse's hide is a lot thicker than human skin, so it will take more pressure to have the same therapeutic effect. On thicker muscles you can press harder, but on thinner muscles covering bone near the face, head, and shoulder areas, be gentler.

Always be aware of your horse's expression or twitches on the skin that may indicate that you are working in a tender or sensitive area. Head jerking, snorting, etc., and obviously nipping and kicking also indicate discomfort. If there is a specific problem, approach that area last. Massaging the whole body often has a more therapeutic effect than aiming just at one troublesome muscle group. Remember that everything is connected!

You will need to set up a regular routine and stick to it. As your horse learns what to expect, he will relax into the massage and it will be more effective. Always move slowly so as not to startle the animal, and work to create a sense of peace. Some quiet music playing in the background also will help to create a positive environment. Talk quietly to reassure and calm your horse.

Massage should be done with your whole attention. Letting your mind wander off to play in the field of quantum mechanics or pondering the next segment of your favorite television show will detract from the benefits of this therapy. Concentrate on your horse's body and mood, and feel what is beneath your fingers. You are dealing with a very large life force here. More than one horse has been known to give his owner a gentle nip to remind her to pay attention! If your horse steps away from you, try beginning the massage in a different place.

Never attempt massage if your horse is acutely ill, especially with a fever, general infection, or shock. Massage lowers blood pressure, just what you don't want in a case of shock.

The 4 T's

Massage is not only a therapy; it's a diagnostic tool as well. Many massage therapists talk about the "4 T's" they use to determine a horse's state of health: temperature, tenderness, texture, and tension. (Remember that a massage therapist is not a veterinarian and should not be used in place of one where diagnostics are concerned.)

A good therapist can feel a change in a horse's body temperature. While not as accurate as a thermometer, this can give a quick warning that something might be wrong. Tenderness refers to the animal's degree of sensitivity and can indicate a painful spot. Texture refers to the feel of the horse's coat and skin—its softness, pliability, and quality. Tension refers to the tightness of the muscles. This tightness can interfere with good circulation and can be a sign of pain or stress.

By making massage part of your regular routine, you can stay on top of your horse's physical condition.

Massage Techniques

Many massage systems were originally designed for people, but they work equally well with horses. There are currently well over 200 massage techniques, many of which were first designed for human beings and then adapted to horses. Here are just a few of them.

Canadian Deep Muscle Massage

This form of therapy was first written about in the late 1800s in New York City, not in Canada, as one might suspect by its name. (The originator of the technique was a woman named Therese Pfrimmer. She claimed to have had her own paralysis reversed by this technique.) Don't be too frightened of the word "deep," either. Deep doesn't mean hard. When done correctly, even deep muscles can be reached with a minimum of pressure.

Unlike many other techniques, this is not a whole-body relaxation massage. Rather, it is a cross-fiber massage that addresses particular muscles and muscle groups. Meant to address very specific problems, its primary goal is fast relief from pain or stress.

The technique begins gently and progresses deeply as the outer muscle fibers relax, allowing the second and third layers of muscle to be worked on. The theory is that it is necessary to massage all three layers of muscle to free the muscle fibers completely. In order to restore maximum muscle strength and flexibility, each muscle fiber must work independently.

Here's the biology behind the theory. A tight, painful muscle has lost its lubrication and becomes painful. Without lubrication, the muscle fibers stick together, compressing the muscle. When muscles are dry they become stiff, inflexible, and compressed. Canadian Deep Muscle massage effectively restores fluid to the muscle fibers. During the massage process, stagnated toxins are said to be carried away and the muscle is able to absorb more oxygen, reducing the pain. The fibers are once again lubricated, resulting in more flexibility and strength.

This therapy is used to:
- alleviate soreness and pain
- relax muscle spasms and adhesions
- increase range of motion
- enhance muscle health and function
- improve circulation
- help to prevent injury
- improves the rate of recovery should an injury occur
- calm the horse

Obviously, if you wish to attempt this modality on your horse, you need to employ someone who is trained in this technique.

Equine Muscle Release Therapy (EMRT)

According to its practitioners, EMRT is a dynamic technique used to relieve spastic muscles and similar problems. It works by signaling the brain to initiate healing via specialized nerve cells found in the fascia, a thin, semi-elastic connective tissue that covers every muscle rather like plastic wrap. Because the fascia is body-wide and can entrap nerves affecting the central nervous system (CNS), trauma in one part of the body can affect another part. It's like an information highway carrying signals from the body to the brain. Any dysfunction of the CNS and/or blockages in other parts of the body can also affect the involuntary nervous system. The purpose of this holistic bodywork technique is to rebalance the nervous system, thereby reducing stress and accelerating injury recovery rates by helping the tissue to regain its pliability.

EMRT is noninvasive and nonmanipulative; it does not distort or twist the muscles as do some other forms of treatment. The therapy consists of administering a series of gentle, rolling moves over the muscle in a particular sequence to release spasms. In the process, energy flows are stimulated and balanced, encouraging the body to reset and heal itself, producing rapid and lasting relief from pain and discomfort. EMRT also can be employed to treat organic and glandular conditions and can be applied in conjunction with other healing modalities such as herbal medicine.

This therapy is used to:
- treat strains of the muscle or tendon
- address skeletal problems
- improve circulation and speed healing
- help kidney infection
- help dry or cracked hoofs

Thumpers

You can buy a mechanical massage unit, colloquially known as a "thumper." These devices have oscillating, vibrating heads that make the job of massaging a large animal a lot easier on the owner. The problem with them is obvious, however. You won't be able to feel the horse's muscle tense or relax in response to the pressure, and there is a possibility of muscle damage as a result. Most of these units are designed for human beings rather than horses, anyway, and they may not stand up to barn use.

- remove toxins associated with tying-up syndrome
- treat growth disorder
- relieve stress and restore emotional balance
- help to prevent any of the above

Originally derived from the Bowen Technique, practitioners are accredited by the Bowen Therapy Academy of Australia (BTAA) through the Equus College of Learning and Research and recognized by both the Holistic Animal Therapy Association of Australia (HATAA) and the British Holistic Veterinary Medicine Association (BHVMA). Practitioners can give follow-up advice for the full rehabilitation of your horse. I should also note that this technique was used by the Australian Endurance team, which got the gold medal at the World Cup in France in 2000.

Equine Sports Massage (ESM)

ESM was developed by Jack Meager, massage therapist for the U.S. Olympic Equestrian Team. It uses techniques derived from Swedish massage but concentrates on muscles strained from specific sports activities. Small muscle injuries can take up to 90 days to become apparent, usually through a change in attitude, decreased performance, or lameness. The sports massage is designed to prevent that from happening.

ESM is the therapeutic hands-on application of massage techniques for the purpose of increasing circulation, relaxing muscle spasms, relieving tension, enhancing muscle tone, and increasing range of motion in high-performance horses. With a thorough understanding of anatomy and the interaction of bones, joints, and muscles, the therapist looks at the horse as a whole and attempts to consider all possible causes and effects of any tension while interpreting his reactions and expressions.

As your horse learns what to expect, he will relax into most bodywork therapies, and they will be more effective. Talk quietly to reassure and calm your horse before and during any treatment.

ESM helps to:
- relax the muscular system
- remove undesired spasms and adhesions from the muscles
- increase muscle flexibility and range of motion
- speed recovery from muscular injuries
- prevent injuries
- prevent disease before it occurs
- reduce stress and promote relaxation

Lymph Drainage Massage

Lymph Drainage Massage was developed in the 1930s by Hans Vodder, a Danish doctor, who observed a connection between swollen lymph glands and colds, infections, and other ailments. It is a "first-line" defense against disease. Because the lymph system is designed to remove bacteria and toxins from the body, Vodder hypothesized that massaging the lymph system would help it function better.

In this form of massage, the strokes are always with the muscle fiber rather than the cross-fiber, because the lymph system runs in the direction of muscle

Not all horses are suitable candidates for massage. Those who are not include horses with tying-up syndrome, infections, influenza, or lymphangitis. Any horse who has an undiagnosed problem should see a vet first.

fiber. Massage with light drainage (effleurage movements) will assist lymphatic circulation. It can help to speed up recovery. Basically, the purpose of this type of "recuperation routine" is to prevent lactic acid buildup after strenuous activity.

This massage technique uses extremely light strokes, and is very effective for swollen legs. It has been beneficial in treating the following conditions:

- post-traumatic (injury-related) edema
- postoperative edema
- degenerative tendon conditions
- tendonitis
- tumescence
- chronic inflammatory reactions to infection
- excessive swelling due to stagnation

SWEDISH MASSAGE

This is "traditional" massage that combines Far Eastern, Middle Eastern, and European folk massage techniques. It makes use of long strokes, kneading, and friction on the outer layers of muscle tissue to stretch and relax the muscles, tendons, and ligaments. Equine Swedish massage can help to:

- promote muscle relaxation and restore movement
- increase range of motion
- enhance gait quality and performance
- release stress, tension, or fear
- increase stamina
- improve lymph flow
- release spasms and cellular memory
- stimulate circulation
- reduce swelling from injury
- dissolve scar tissue adhesions
- flush metabolic wastes from the tissues
- enhance the oxygenation of blood
- promote healing
- improve behavior and disposition
- improve quality of life

Trigger Point Therapy

Trigger points are places where the body accumulates waste products around a nerve receptor. They feel like small nodules and can cause referred pain or discomfort in other areas of the body. Releasing trigger points is said to flush toxins from the body and relieve pain. Most trigger points are in the same locations as acupoints, but the theory behind the technique differs from that of acupressure because it does not make use of the idea of meridians, the invisible channels of energy coursing through the body.

Trigger Point Therapy works to:

- reduce pain by relieving muscular hypertonicity

Never massage a horse around an infected area or a suspicious lump. Manipulation of the area could spread the infection to other parts of the body. Massage is counterproductive on any wound or tumor.

- take pressure off nerves and blood vessels
- restore coordination and strength
- reset muscle fiber length for full range of motion and maximum power.
- promote optimum athleticism

BASIC MASSAGE STROKES

No matter what kind of body therapy you may practice, some of the same stroking techniques appear in different modalities. Most strokes begin gently and gradually go deeper into the tissues. You need to gently loosen the muscles bit by bit. In addition, if you start off too powerfully, your horse will respond negatively.

Here are a few of the most fundamental strokes:

Compression: This is the application of sustained pressure on affected muscles to release the muscle fibers, encourage better circulation and oxygen flow, and relieve spasms. It is often used on larger, thicker muscle groups such as the gluteal muscles and triceps. You can use your palm or the back of your hand, taking advantage of your knuckles.

Deep Digital Pressure: This technique uses your whole body to apply the pressure evenly as you press your fingers against suspect soft tissue. You gradually increase the pressure against the tightness until you feel it release. Never use this method over bony protuberances or on the spine.

Rolling plays a very important role in your horse's health. When he rolls, he is stretching all the muscles in his body, which helps him to maintain flexibility and health.

When to Use Massage

Use massage:

- while grooming or after a ride

- during rehabilitation as recommended by your vet

- to help to prevent injuries due to muscle stress

- during intense or competitive training

- as a follow-up to a chiropractic adjustment

- for the ongoing health and wellness of your horse

Do not use massage when:

- there is abnormal heat or swelling

- the horse is weight bearing lame

- an injury is less than seven days old

- the horse is lethargic or off feed

- there is evidence of an elevated pulse, abnormal respiration, or fever

- there are skin lesions from a viral or bacterial infection

- recent hematomas or undiagnosed lumps or bumps are present

- an area is too painful to touch

Cross-Fiber Friction: Helping to break up muscle adhesions, this technique involves placing your fingers at right angles to the muscle fibers and pressing (not too deeply) back and forth over them. It is effective on neck muscles.

Effleurage: Sweeping, steady, flowing strokes that can be applied at various levels, effleurage usually begins with lighter strokes and proceeds to firmer ones. It is particularly effective used on a horse's back. You can use the flat of your hand, but it's important to apply pressure with your whole body, not just your arm.

Jostling: This technique involves cupping your hand over the crest of the horse's neck, thumbs toward yourself, and then gently rolling the crests toward you. This will release tension in the neck. As you continue, you should be able to use more pressure and go deeper.

Percussive Strokes: Percussive strokes, such as pounding with your fist or "hacking" with the side of your hand, are used to stimulate specific soft-tissue areas. This technique works to improve circulation and release muscle tension as it triggers the release of endorphins. Percussive strokes can be used on the shoulders and rump but not directly on the spine. These strokes should not make up an entire routine but can be incorporated into a general therapy session. Hands and wrists must remain as relaxed as possible.

Petrissage: Petrissage consists of massage movements with applied pressure that are deep and that compress the underlying muscles. Kneading, wringing, skin rolling, and pick-up-and-squeeze are the principal movements. They are all performed with the padded palm of the hand, the fingers, and also the thumbs.

Rocking: This massage technique uses gentle or vigorous, rhythmic movements to create sufficient motion to move the body part and then allow it to return to the original position. It relaxes tight muscles.

Shaking: As you might guess, this involves directly shaking the "belly" of the muscle, the large mass of muscle that powers the work of movement. The action is done by grasping either the muscle belly, for direct shaking, or the limb furthest away from the body, for indirect shaking. The tissue also may be rhythmically moved back and forth, from gently to vigorously.

After any massage session, it's a good idea to take your horse for a brisk five-minute walk to prevent stiffness that may develop. It will relieve your stiffness as well.

The goal of many touch therapies is to restore harmony within the body so that the body makes its own adjustments and achieves its own cure.

TOUCH THERAPY

ADVANTAGES
- TOTALLY NONINVASIVE.
- COMPARATIVELY EASY TO LEARN.
- COMPLETELY HARMLESS, NO MATTER HOW MANY MISTAKES YOU MAKE.

DISADVANTAGES
- NO REAL EVIDENCE THAT IT HAS OBJECTIVE BENEFITS, ALTHOUGH IT MAY RELAX THE HORSE.

While touch therapy is cousin to massage and has many similar techniques, it is fundamentally different in principle. It is based not on pressure but on awareness of energy and works under the principle that a horse (or a human being, or a butterfly for that matter) is not so much a physical object but an energy field or energy system that is constantly exchanging energy with other areas of the environment. This energy can be categorized as physical, mental, or spiritual (etheric). During the session, one focuses not so much on the muscle or area of pain but on the horse as a sentient being, an energy center with whom you try to connect. The basic idea is that touch itself is healing and sacred.

Techniques are extremely variable and may be combined with aromatherapy, massage, and acupressure.

BOWEN TECHNIQUE

The Bowen Technique is a healing, hands-on therapy developed in the 1950s by the Australian healer-therapist Tom Bowen. Technically, the technique is not considered massage, chiropractic, or acupressure because no manipulation, adjustment, or force is used. The practitioner uses his thumbs and fingers to gently move muscles and tissues. Part of the therapy involves rest periods between a series of massage movements within each treatment session. These pauses and the gentleness of the treatment are what make Bowen different from other modalities.

This technique is designed to allow the body to absorb the healing process. The moves themselves are a gentle but precise manipulation of soft tissues. The goal is to restore harmony within the body so that the body makes its own adjustments and achieves its own cure. It may offer rapid, long-lasting relief from all kinds of pain and discomfort, and it helps to speed up recovery time. Also, because it is so gentle, it can be used on individuals of any age for a wide range of conditions, including:

- muscular, skeletal, or nerve imbalance
- chronic pain due to injury
- uneven gait or irregular action
- uneven wear of shoes
- muscle atrophy or uneven development
- stiffness on one rein
- sore back
- sluggish lymphatic system or weakened immune system
- uncharacteristic change of temperament or deterioration of performance

EQUINE CRANIOSACRAL THERAPY (ESCT)

Within the craniosacral system the cerebrospinal fluid moves like a gentle tide. The craniosacral system of a horse is made up of several parts: the bones of the head (cranium), the tailbone (sacrum), and the spinal column. This work is generally specialized in these areas, but it is not limited to them, nor is it limited to the physical.

ESCT practitioners believe that healing can be promoted by manipulating the head, spine, and pelvis to release "blocked" spinal fluids. The gentle touch helps the fluid become more rhythmic and balanced, and it optimizes body movement. It also restores balance to the central nervous system and is used to treat various other conditions such as the following:

- facial nerve paralysis
- head shaking
- head injuries
- lameness
- nervous disorders
- colic
- cribbing
- spinal injuries

Initially, the practitioner begins by doing an overall assessment of the horse and then watches the animal walk and move. Working with the owner, she does an overall analysis of the animal's behavior problems and history. She then performs an initial physical exam, looking for inflammation, vertebrae out of alignment, and other signs of stress in the horse. In follow-up sessions, she uses sensitive and exact finger pressure to palpate the cranial wave on different areas of the horse. In doing so, she can tell where there is lack of movement or other related problems. This is similar to an acupuncturist palpating the flow of energy through meridian pathways.

A gentle, hands-on method, most owners can learn and practice craniosacral techniques that will enhance healthy movement and release muscular and skeletal restrictions throughout the horse's body. Especially with performance animals, craniosacral massage can be highly effective in treating musculoskeletal imbalances. Applied on a regular basis, it can be a way of maintaining the overall health and well-being of horses between competitions.

The therapy is focused on:

- promoting optimal cerebrospinal fluid flow
- rebalancing the central nervous system
- stimulating the body's natural healing mechanisms
- optimizing body movement
- reducing stress

Horses who undergo TTEAM demonstrate an increased willingness and ability to perform. As an added benefit, a deeper bond grows between horse and rider because of increased understanding and more effective communication.

TELLINGTON TTOUCH THERAPY

This system of touch therapy combines massage therapy with ground work and riding exercises. It was developed by Linda Tellington-Jones. The entire program is known as The Tellington TTouch Equine Awareness Method (TTEAM), and it has its roots in the Feldenkrais Method of Functional Integration massage.

The basic theory behind the method is that posture dictates behavior, and one goal of the therapy is to help horses become active rather than reactive. It helps reluctant horses gain more propulsion but also settles down anxious ones. Different postures indicate different problems, and Tellington TTouch (TTouch) therapists are skilled at learning and interpreting these postures. TTEAM therapy encourages optimal performance and health and presents solutions to common behavioral and physical problems.

The target organs of the TTouch method are those of the central nervous system. It addresses what practitioners consider to be the five instinctive responses to stress: flight, fight, freeze, faint, and fool around. The massage used in this system is very gentle and absolutely noninvasive.

Tellington bodywork is designed to:
- help relieve the memory of pain
- reduce stiffness
- improve posture
- free movement for a more fluid, natural outline
- calm a disturbed horse and restore self-confidence to a shy one

Horses who undergo TTEAM demonstrate a marked improvement in athletic skills and an increased willingness

and ability to perform. As an added benefit, a deeper bond grows between horse and rider because of increased understanding and more effective communication.

ZERO BALANCING

This technique was developed by Dr. Fritz Smith, an osteopath and acupuncturist, in the 1970s. It was originally designed for people but has also been used with horses. Zero Balancing has its roots in osteopathy, acupuncture, Rolfing, and meditation. Relaxing yet energizing, it integrates fundamental principles of Western medicine with Eastern concepts of energy using a powerful hands-on method of aligning body energy with body structure. The actual practice focuses on joints and bones and consists of a series of gentle finger pressures, stretching, and bending to release tension.

Zero Balancing also offers the possibility of healing by addressing the energy flow of the skeletal system. By correcting imbalances between energy and structure, zero balancing:

- provides relief from pain, anxiety, and stress
- can correct skeletal alignment

A Zero Balancing session generally takes 30 to 40 minutes. Combined with other modalities, it can provide additional ways to adjust energetic and physical structural balance through touch.

CHIROPRACTIC

Hippocrates, the ancient Greek physician, said, "Look well to the spine for the cause of disease." This is an idea that has applied to animals as well as people. In fact, B.J. Palmer, believed to be the founder of chiropractic, ran a veterinary clinic as part of his chiropractic school, in which he claimed to have adjusted the vertebral subluxations (misalignments) of sick animals. In his later writings he commented, "Many doctors of chiropractic think that we should soft-pedal the animal application of chiropractic. They fear the public might call them horse-doctors." Indeed.

Chiropractors concentrate on the interactions between neurological mechanisms and the biomechanics of the spine. This is a field that is undergoing tremendous expansion in veterinary medicine.

Unfortunately, chiropractic is not currently taught in veterinary schools, which makes it difficult to find qualified care. However, one certification course for veterinarians and chiropractors is offered by the American Veterinary Chiropractic Association (AVCA).

Relaxation

During touch therapy, your horse may show varying degrees of relaxation. Common responses are:

- licking and chewing
- yawning
- wobbling lips
- stretching
- stomach gurgling

Complementary Medicine

Veterinary chiropractors do not dispense or inject medication, perform surgery, or replace regular veterinary care. Although chiropractic is often done along with other forms of treatment or therapy, such as acupuncture, it should not be considered a replacement for conventional medicine. As with any physical or behavioral problem your horse may experience, it is always advisable to consult your vet so that she can assess him for any underlying medical conditions that could be causing similar symptoms.

ADVANTAGES
- NO MEDICATIONS ARE REQUIRED.
- IMPROVES PERFORMANCE.
- ENHANCES HEALTH.
- ANIMALS USUALLY REALLY ENJOY IT.

DISADVANTAGES
- THERAPY MUST BE PERFORMED BY A SKILLED PROFESSIONAL, PREFERABLY ONE WITH A CERTIFICATION IN VETERINARY CHIROPRACTIC.
- THIS THERAPY CAN BE HARMFUL IF INCORRECTLY APPLIED.

The word "chiropractic" comes from the Greek words *cheiros,* meaning "hand," and *praktike,* meaning "practice." Veterinary chiropractic deals with the relationship of the vertebrae in the spine and the spine's relationship to the rest of the body. The theory is that the bones and joints are ordered in a specific way, and the nerves surrounding each joint and vertebral articulation communicate to the central nervous system and the brain. All organs also receive input from the nerves that exit between the vertebrae. Physical trauma, problems during birth, mental stress, or poor nutrition can cause a misalignment, or "subluxation," between the vertebrae. The good thing about equine chiropractic is that because horses are so strong and their ligaments are so strongly attached, most adjustments need be only very slight.

Even a small subluxation has a negative effect on the nervous system, muscles, and joints (a sort of "butterfly effect" in miniature). If untreated, it can cause degenerative pathologies to other joints. Distant organs can be affected. Adjusting these misalignments alters the nervous system input and affects blood flow to the whole body, as well as hormone and neurotransmitter levels directly affecting the organs, glands, skin, and joints.

Horses who begin to turn in reduced performance or display behavior changes like cinch sensitivity or bucking may be candidates for an adjustment.

The American Veterinary Chiropractic Association (AVCA)

The American Veterinary Chiropractic Association (AVCA) was formed in 1989 by a group of veterinarians and chiropractors interested in furthering the profession of animal chiropractic.

The AVCA has a three-fold mission: to function as a professional membership group, to promote animal chiropractic to professionals and the public, and to act as the certifying agency for doctors who have undergone animal chiropractic training. One of its goals is to provide the public with unhampered access to ethical doctors trained in this field. Some members of the association are veterinarians and some are chiropractors. They receive complementary training for certification. Veterinarians receive training in chiropractic theory and technique, while Doctors of Chiropractic learn common animal diseases, comparative anatomy, and animal handling techniques.

You can visit the AVCA on the web at www.animalchiropractic.org.

THE CHIROPRACTIC EXAM

An initial chiropractic exam includes evaluating the patient's history, athleticism, general state of health, past injuries and problems, and prior X-rays and tests. It includes a neurological exam, stance and gait analysis, and motion and static palpation. When a full assessment has been done, the treatment can comprise the adjustment of vertebral joints, extremity joints, and cranial sutures.

In each subsequent equine therapy session, the chiropractor attempts to correct the horse's particular problem by first making adjustments to the spine, although other areas, including the knees, shoulders, hocks, ribs, or even tail docks are sometimes adjusted. By definition, an adjustment is defined as a short lever, high-velocity, low-amplitude controlled thrust by hand or instrument directed in a specific direction on a specific joint to correct vertebral subluxations. It sounds scary but just means that the practitioner applies pressure to the bone and "unlocks" it from its improper position. The bone will then be free to align itself correctly. (The concept of "subluxation" is not accepted in mainstream veterinary or medical care, however.)

Most horses show no signs of pain or distress during chiropractic examination or treatment, although they may be leery of the first approach to the painful area. Many actually seem to become more relaxed. With animal chiropractic care, the practitioner uses the gentlest possible technique to alleviate pain before making the needed adjustment. This process will reset the nervous system, letting the horse regain normal interaction with gravity and other natural forces.

An average treatment takes an hour or so. Chiropractic adjustments usually take a series of two to five treatments, varying anywhere from one week to one month apart; chronic problems may require more treatments than do acute injuries.

CHIROPRACTIC BENEFITS

Chiropractic care is not intended to replace traditional veterinary medical or surgical care. However, it is intended to detect and treat problems that interfere with gait and thus the performance of the horse. Horses who begin to turn in reduced performance, have problems executing desired movements, exhibit short stride or gait imbalance, or display behavior changes like cinch sensitivity or bucking may be candidates for an adjustment. In addition, conditions like arthritis, muscle spasm, and related injuries may respond. A specialty of chiropractic care is back injuries, which influence so much of a horse's behavior. It seems to be most successful in dealing with movement and gait problems, although it claims success in other areas, including allergies. Chiropractic can also be used to treat internal disorders such as gastrointestinal disease, bladder dysfunction, and reproductive problems. Some practitioners maintain that there is a connection between bone alignment and the immune system, especially in relation to viral infections.

Follow-Up Treatments

Follow-up examinations are usually performed four to six months after the initial visit. Sometimes horse owners say they can tell that their horses need a readjustment. For example, by feeling along the side of the neck or the lumbar region of the back, they may notice bumps or swellings that seem to indicate something is out of alignment. However, because "the knee bone is connected to the thighbone," so to speak, it's likely that the chiropractor will work on a larger section of the horse's skeleton. Most will not charge extra for working on a larger section of the horse.

Many horses show immediate improvement after an adjustment; others seem tired for a day or so but then return to normal. Several sessions may sometimes be necessary. Some horse owners use chiropractic as a maintenance technique for performance horses and bring them in for prophylactic treatments every month or two.

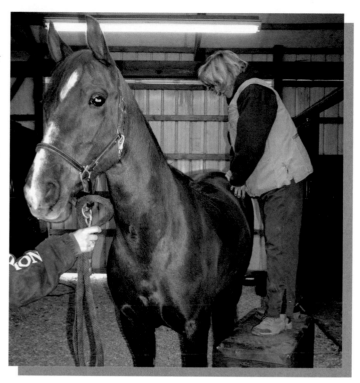

When to Seek Chiropractic Care

Many owners seek veterinary chiropractic care for their horses to help with the following:

- lameness or gait problems
- back, leg, or neck pain
- navicular disease or laminitis
- neurological problems
- geriatric or arthritic conditions
- recovery from illness or injury
- chronic health problems
- postsurgical care
- allergies
- head shyness or reluctance to take a lead or move in a certain direction
- behavioral changes
- improvement of athletic performance

While this technique is a "touch" therapy, it can be very dangerous if not done by a qualified professional. A very precise touch is needed. Chiropractic is considered a complementary therapy to be used in conjunction with other therapies. It is not meant to replace conventional veterinary medicine. To find a certified equine chiropractic practitioner near you, visit www.avcadoctors.com.

All massage and touch therapies are most effective when used in conjunction with other forms of veterinary care. When applied properly they can often extend the life, usefulness, and happiness of your equine best friend.

Chapter 4 **Acupuncture,**

Acupressure, and Shiatsu

$\mathcal{A}$cupuncture and its kin, acupressure and shiatsu, belong in a category all their own, although they are sometimes lumped in with physical medicine (along with massage therapy and chiropractic). These modalities also can be related to what is sometimes referred to as "energetic medicine," which includes magnetic field therapy and photon therapy. The truth is that most energy-related modalities can be categorized in a number of different ways, but they all rely on using powerful invisible channels, called meridians, through which energy pulses can be stimulated at certain points to effect treatment and healing.

ACUPUNCTURE

ADVANTAGES
- NONINVASIVE.
- APPEARS TO BE EFFECTIVE IN THE TREATMENT OF MANY COMMON CONDITIONS.
- MOST HORSES ENJOY THE RELAXING ENDORPHINS RELEASED INTO THE SYSTEM BY NEEDLING.
- NOT USUALLY ASSOCIATED WITH SERIOUS SIDE EFFECTS.
- CAN BE USED TO TREAT CONDITIONS FOR WHICH WESTERN MEDICINE HAS LITTLE TO OFFER.

DISADVANTAGES
- BECAUSE IT MAY BE EFFECTIVE IN CONTROLLING PAIN, IT CAN SOMETIMES MASK MORE SERIOUS CONDITIONS.
- IT IS POSSIBLE FOR NEEDLES TO DAMAGE SOME TISSUES.
- IT IS NOT A PANACEA.

Today, the ancient art of acupuncture has been found to be as beneficial to horses as it has been to humans. In fact, it was used on horses before it was used on humans, at least if Chinese chronicles are to be believed.

Developed in China nearly 6,000 years ago, acupuncture is a healing technique that stimulates the body's ability to sustain and balance itself so that the patient can live in harmony with her surroundings. The earliest written account of acupuncture is found in the *Nei Jing*, the Yellow Emperor's Book of Internal Medicine. Based on the Taoist philosophy of balancing energy meridians within the body, it is designed to restore health and well-being. Practically speaking, fine needles are painlessly inserted into the skin at key points corresponding to specific organs to relieve pain and cure disease and dysfunction.

Acupuncture has been found to be as beneficial to horses as it has been to humans.

THE THEORY

In theory, acupuncture is all about Qi (pronounced CHEE and sometimes spelled "chi"), the life force. If the term "life force" is a little too vague for your taste, you can call it "electrical energy" because it amounts to the same thing. Acupuncturists believe that if the electrical energy in the body is blocked, disease can occur. Acupuncture helps to remove the blockage and allows the blood and its nutrients to move unhindered.

No one is really sure how acupuncture works exactly, but it has been shown to have an effect on the body's endorphin receptors. Endorphins are the body's own painkillers, an opioid-like chemical similar to morphine. They also participate in other body functions. The latest research shows that treating an acupuncture point has an immediate effect directly on the brain. In understanding how acupuncture regulates the body through

Don't Try This at Home!

Don't attempt acupuncture yourself. It should be performed only by a qualified practitioner. You can go to www.ivas.org to find a qualified veterinary acupuncturist in your area.

An acupuncturist will work with you and your horse to find the root of his problems rather than just treating the symptoms. Aside from possible health issues, other important considerations include saddle fit, training, and riding techniques. Sometimes a horse needs adjustment of misaligned joints for the treatment to be complete. Through this therapy, general health can be improved and chronic pain often can be resolved so that healing can take place.

Always bear in mind that acupuncture is not a substitute for veterinary care. It is always important to get a proper diagnosis from your vet to rule out possible medical sources of any physical or behavioral problems your horse may be having.

these mechanisms, you have to envision the body as a web of electrical circuits. The energy that goes through these circuits is the Qi, which is what the practitioner works to rebalance.

How It Works

The word "acupuncture" means "needle piercing." (The earliest needles were stone!) The piercing is designed to stimulate particular acupuncture points (acupoints) known as Shu Xue. (The ancient Chinese discovered 173 acupoints in horses.) Shu means "passing through," and Xue refers to an outlet. The acupoints are located at concentrated nerve bundles and blood vessels, and the regions where they are located have increased electrical conductivity. When a needle is placed in an acupuncture point, a signal travels along that peripheral nerve to reach the spinal cord to block pain, release endorphins (chemicals that help to regulate the body), and increase blood flow.

Each acupoint "communicates" with a specific organ through eight invisible channels called meridians (*jing luo*), which travel along the surface of the entire body. Each meridian is related to and named after a specific organ or function. There are, in addition, eight special meridians that are considered to be reservoirs supplying Qi and blood to the twelve regular channels, and these have a strong connection to the kidneys.

Meridians are paired into functional duets. The twelve main meridians are named after organ systems:
- lung and large intestine
- stomach and spleen
- heart and small intestine
- bladder and kidney
- pericardium and triple heater
- gall bladder and liver

In addition, the "governing vessel" meridian runs along the dorsal (back) midline, and the "conception" runs along the ventral (belly) midline. (There are also some deep "esoteric" meridians, but that's a topic beyond the scope of this book.)

Diagnosis and Treatment

According to acupuncture theory, disease is a form of imbalance. The Chinese believe that the imbalance is between the yin and yang forces. These are not opposite forces but complementary ones that must exist together in harmony. The yin and yang influence the body, mind, and spirit. Yin is commonly considered to be cool, feminine,

NAET

A treatment sometimes administered along with acupressure or acupuncture is NAET (Nambudripad's Allergy Elimination Technique), which is used for horses suffering from allergies. The creator of the technique, Devi Nambudripad, Ph.D., is a Californian acupuncturist, chiropractor, kinesiologist, and registered nurse.

The basic premise here is that allergies are caused by energy blockages that can be diagnosed with muscle testing and then cured with acupressure or acupuncture. In humans, the allergy is diagnosed by having the patient hold out an arm while holding the suspected allergen in the palm of the other hand. The practitioner then pushes down on the extended arm to gauge its strength. Obviously, this doesn't work with horses, so "surrogate testing," or in some cases an electrodiagnostic device, is used to measure skin resistance to a small electric current emitted by the device. In surrogate testing, the practitioner muscle tests the person (or surrogate) who holds the allergen against the horse. Muscle weakness indicates an allergy. (Nambudripad does suggest that conventional Western diagnostic techniques also can be used.)

To treat the allergy, the allergen is pressed against the body of the horse along several meridians in a particular sequence. This is a harmless treatment, to be sure, but its effectiveness has not been documented.

and moist, while yang is hot, masculine, and dry.

When an organ is diseased, the corresponding acupoints may be abnormally tender or show other alterations. The practitioner inserts very fine needles (usually less than 1/2 inch [1.27 cm]) at specific points along the meridian to either stimulate or diffuse the life force to correct the imbalance.

Despite all this needle sticking, acupuncture is practically painless. In fact, many horses immediately calm down once the treatment is begun. The needles remain in the horse for 5 to 20 minutes depending on the condition being treated. The good effects of acupuncture remain for days or even a month after each treatment. In some cases, it is entirely curative.

While Western acupuncturists may not agree with the Chinese understanding of anatomy and physiology, they believe that acupuncture releases hormones that help the body respond to injury and stress. Science has further shown that acupuncture stimulates the immune system and regulates circulation, blood pressure, the rhythm and stroke volume of the heart, gastric acid secretion, and red and white blood cell production. Equally important, it relieves pain. Acupuncture can be enhanced by electrical stimulation—attaching small electrical clips to the needles. It is often used with other modalities such as acupressure and massage.

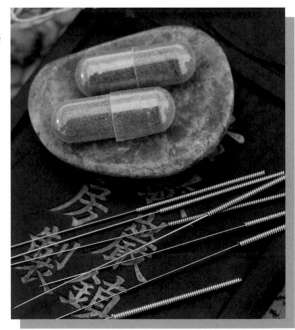

Acupuncture has been successfully used to treat all sorts of equine conditions, including:

- arthritis
- back problems
- behavioral problems
- colic
- conjunctivitis
- chronic obstructive pulmonary disease (COPD)
- diarrhea

- immune system deficiencies
- injuries
- lameness
- laminitis
- navicular disease
- neurological problems
- performance problems
- periodic ophthalmia
- reproductive problems
- ringbone
- ulcers

ACUPRESSURE

ADVANTAGES
- TOTALLY NONINVASIVE.
- NOT ASSOCIATED WITH SIDE EFFECTS.
- CAN BE USED WITH OTHER MODALITIES.
- CAN BE USED BY NONPROFESSIONALS.

DISADVANTAGES
- NOT GENERALLY CONSIDERED AS EFFECTIVE AS TRUE ACUPUNCTURE.
- STRESSFUL TO THE HANDS OF THE CLINICIAN.

Acupressure is similar to acupuncture, but it is performed without needles. Instead, practitioners use the hands or even the knees to work along the meridians. Like acupuncture, it is a traditional part of Chinese medicine, and it is sometimes called "acupuncture without the needles."

How It Works

Like acupuncture, acupressure works by accessing and releasing blocked meridians. It is used for the same conditions as acupuncture. This noninvasive technique relieves pain by stimulating the release of endorphins and promoting circulation. Unlike acupuncture, acupressure is completely safe, so horse owners can try their hand (literally) at it. Like acupuncture, it stimulates the immune system, decreases pain, and helps the horse relax. It is often useful for digestive upsets

Acupressure can resolve injuries more readily by increasing the blood supply and removing toxins.

of all sorts, arthritis, and muscle spasms. To know the correct amount of pressure to apply, try it on yourself first!

DIAGNOSIS AND TREATMENT

In acupressure, the practitioner manipulates acupoints by pressing them. She usually uses her fingers to press a point, but in some cases, the hands, elbows, knees, or feet are also used. These points are very small, so it is important to get just the right spot. Stimulating the wrong spot will cause no harm but will simply have no effect.

From a traditional Chinese medicine perspective, the way the points are stimulated depends on the horse's condition. To simplify, pain is associated with an excess condition and weakness is considered a deficiency problem. The practitioner wants to tone up a deficiency by massaging the points in a clockwise direction for a relatively short time (about 30 seconds). She reduces an excess condition by massaging the point in a counterclockwise direction for a longer time (about two minutes).

Acupressure points are precisely the same as those used in acupuncture. And as in acupuncture, there are scientific studies showing it is effective for certain conditions.

Acupressure is used to:

- build the immune system
- resolve injuries more readily by increasing the blood supply and removing toxins
- balance energy to optimize the body's natural ability to heal
- release endorphins necessary to increase energy or relieve pain
- release natural cortisone to reduce swelling and inflammation
- relieve muscle spasms
- strengthen muscles, tendons, joints, and bones
- replenish the animal's physical and emotional energy
- release emotional blockages
- enhance mental clarity and calm required for focus in training and performance

Practitioners believe that this form of hands-on therapy not only supports your horse's physical health and emotional well-being, but it creates a lasting bond that will have positive effects on your relationship with him and also on training and performance.

Equine Communication Through Touch

A sister therapy to acupressure, shiatsu has been used to treat people for centuries but has only been adapted for use with horses in the last 25 years. One of the pioneers in this field is Pamela Hannay, senior instructor of the Ohashi Institute in New York. She believed that horses would respond particularly well to shiatsu therapy because touch is a natural form of communication for them.

Because every living body is born with an essential life force or energy that travels through the body in channels known as meridians, shiatsu serves to balance this energy flow through the sense of touch. Using pressure, rotation, and stretching of the limbs, the shiatsu practitioner can stimulate and guide energy to reestablish the balance of energy flow in the body, which is needed to maintain good health and performance. Treatment can either be toning or sedating, depending on whether energy is deficient or in excess.

SHIATSU

ADVANTAGES
- NONINVASIVE AND GENERALLY SAFE.
- PROBABLY EFFECTIVE FOR SOME CONDITIONS.

DISADVANTAGES
- MAY BE DANGEROUS WHEN APPLIED TO THE NECK.
- NOT SUITABLE FOR ALL CONDITIONS.

Shiatsu, which is similar to acupressure, is a classic Japanese bodywork therapy that uses both pressure and stretches. It is recognized as a valid medical therapy by the Ministry of Health and Welfare in Japan. The word literally means "finger pressure," but other techniques are used as well, including stroking and flat hand pressure. It was developed for horses by Pamela Hannay in the 1980s. It can be used for both prevention and treatment of disease.

How It Works

Shiatsu increases the flow of blood to injured areas and reduces inflammation and joint swelling. It also increases range of motion. It is generally used to treat soft tissue injuries, strains, sprains, spasms, and aches located in the back, shoulders, neck, and hindquarters.

Shiatsu is particularly beneficial for aches and pains caused by work, injury, or old age.

DIAGNOSIS AND TREATMENT

The practitioner will first do a physical evaluation of the horse's overall condition, as well as interview you about his history, problems, and environment. She will use her fingertips to explore and feel along the body to see if there are any gritty/grainy places or soft spongy spots. She also will take note of subtle changes of temperature (cold areas lack energy and hot areas have too much energy) and make note of subtle variations and skin textures that may change with time and touch. Once she has diagnosed problem areas, she will apply pressure to the appropriate meridians in an effort to release energy blockages.

The word "shiatsu" is derived from the Japanese *shi*, meaning "finger," and *atsu*, which means "pressure."

As with traditional acupuncture, shiatsu relies on paired meridians, although instead of needles, the thumbs and fingers are used. One of each pair is the yin and one is the yang. So-called "ting points" at the end of each meridian help to regulate the flow of energy along the meridian. Pressing on the ting points increases the function of the whole meridian. Each meridian also affects the external body area it travels over.

When doing shiatsu, you use one hand to support and protect yourself from sudden movements and the other hand to work along the meridian. Check for hot or cold spots, which are indicative of too much or too little Qi flowing along the meridian. As in classical acupuncture, it is important to balance the forces.

Shiatsu is particularly beneficial for:

- aches and pains caused by work, injury, or old age
- mishandling
- chronic injuries
- nervous tension
- cribbing
- behavioral problems

ABOUT EQUINE MERIDIANS

The ancient Chinese discovered 173 acupoints in horses. Acupoints are found within meridians, the channels that form a network interconnecting all organs to maintain equilibrium in the body. Toning or sedating of points lying along meridians moves life energy, or Qi, rebalancing it and relieving or preventing blockages and excesses that can cause discomfort, pain, and disease.

Using meridian charts, practitioners identify points that show an excess or deficiency. The traditional five-element meridian chart helps to determine which points require sedation or stimulation to correct any imbalances.

IMPORTANT MERIDIANS

The bladder meridian is one of the most important for back pain and emotional problems such as fear and depression. It can be used prophylactically to keep the back supple and flexible. The bladder meridian runs from the eye to the hind foot on either side of the spine.

The "mate" to the yang bladder meridian is the yin kidney meridian, which runs along the underside of the horse. It starts at the bulb of the hoof of the rear leg, and travels up the inside of the leg, then up the underside of the body, entering the body at the side and top of the sternum near the base of the neck. It helps to generate the core metabolic mechanism of the horse and is responsible for good functioning of the circulatory, respiratory, and digestive systems. Massaging the kidney meridian helps to prevent exhaustion.

The lung meridian begins within the horse's abdomen and rises to the surface of the chest. It then travels along the front surface of the foreleg to just above the hoof. Shiatsu equine practitioners believe that a badly fitting harness or breast plate can interrupt its flow. The lung meridian helps to protect the immune system and fight off respiratory

BLADDER MERIDIAN

KIDNEY MERIDIAN

STOMACH MERIDIAN

LUNG MERIDIAN

SIDE VIEW   FRONT VIEW

or foreleg pain, including knee problems and laminitis.

The stomach meridian is responsible for transporting food. If the energy becomes unbalanced along the stomach meridian, it can lead to problems like colic, a result of too much Qi along this meridian.

CREDENTIALS NECESSARY

Acupuncture, acupressure, and shiatsu are ancient therapies that have stood the test of time. Acupuncture is one of the most scientifically proven of all alternative modalities. Many practitioners and patients alike have found the therapies to be beneficial in the treatment of pain caused by injury or arthritis. They are often combined with other forms of healing therapies such as massage and chiropractic, and they appear to be showing up more in mainstream health care. However, as mentioned earlier, because these therapies can be dangerous if administered incorrectly, make sure that the person performing them (preferably a vet) is qualified and experienced working with horses. And of course, always consult with your vet before trying them.

Different Technique, Same Effect

Curiously, Korean and other forms of acupuncture use different acupoints than does the Chinese system, but they appear equally effective. Some Western experts theorize that the place the needles are inserted is irrelevant and that acupuncture works simply by stimulating the nerves. However, studies show that acupoints do have unique electrical, anatomical, and histological characteristics.

Chapter 5

From high-tech lasers to ancient crystals, energetic medicine (or vibrational healing) has long been a part of the healing arts. Energetic medicine is a general term for many different therapies, all of which subscribe to the theory that every living thing has its own élan, its own life force.

Energetic Medicine

According to energetic theory, health or emotional problems are glitches in the programming of our vital energy fields. Therefore, healing can be accomplished by rebalancing these disturbances to restore natural health. Based on noninvasive modalities, energetic medicine enables the body to heal itself naturally by correcting the information fields of the body.

CRYSTAL HEALING

ADVANTAGES
- IT IS COMPLETELY HARMLESS.
- IT IS RELATIVELY INEXPENSIVE.
- IT CREATES A GREAT BOND BETWEEN OWNER AND HORSE.
- IT MAY HELP WITH CERTAIN CONDITIONS.
- IT CAN HAVE A POWERFUL PSYCHOLOGICAL EFFECT.

DISADVANTAGES
- ITS ACTUAL EFFECTIVENESS IS NOT SCIENTIFICALLY PROVEN.

A crystal is defined as a solid, homogenous substance with a highly regular atomic structure. However, in crystal medicine, substances that are not crystals, such as metals, pearls, or even petrified wood, have been used to the same effect.

For some, crystals go well beyond the area of natural cures into the realm of the supernatural. But most crystal healers deny there is anything supernatural at all about their powers. And crystals certainly have a long history of earthly application. They have been used for healing by all cultures throughout the ages. Healers believe that crystals can structure, store, amplify, focus, transmit, and even transform all sorts of physical and emotional energy.

While crystal and mineral healing is "way out there" for some people, others swear by its benefits. Crystals are said to carry vibrational energy (one of the basic principles also of homeopathy). They may or may not cure disease, but at the least I think that they exert a powerful psychological effect on horse owners. Using them as a protection creates "good vibrations" between horses and owners, the value of which cannot be denied or overlooked. Besides, crystals are beautiful and fun—and the practice, for instance, of attaching malachite or turquoise to a horse's bridle is so traditional in some cultures that one dare not overlook it completely.

Energetic medicine is a general term for many different therapies, all of which subscribe to the theory that every living thing has its own élan, its own life force.

THE MASTER STONE

The first step in gemstone healing is to find a master stone that matches your horse's personality. Different healers use different criteria to find this stone. The criteria may depend on color, structure, or some other aspect. Thus, in some systems, all beryl stones (aquamarine, green beryl, and emerald) have the same healing effect, while in others it's the color that makes the difference. So emerald and tsavorite, both being bright green, would have the effect

of "green stone" upon the horse, even though they belong to different mineral families and even different crystal systems. For these healers, color is often more important than the particular type of stone, although most declare that glass won't work. It must be a true crystal, which has a regular structure and not a random one as does glass. (Glass cannot "channel" energy.) Most healers say that a natural crystal (although not necessarily a faceted one) is best, although in a pinch a synthetic crystal also will work.

CRYSTAL POWER

Let's look first at crystal power by color, which is the most traditional method. (Ancient healers had no good way to distinguish a ruby from a spinel or a sapphire from lapis lazuli.) Using this system, you would look for a stone of pure, deep color. Pale rubies and emeralds are more properly termed pink sapphire and green beryl and lack the depth of hue you need. You are better off using a deeply colored, less expensive stone than a "real" ruby of insufficient color. For most uses, too, the fewer flaws the stone has, the better. Some natural stones such as emeralds are nearly always flawed, however; in this case a synthetic stone might be your best choice.

> ### Synthetic Stones
>
> You can purchase synthetic stones, which are chemically indistinguishable from natural ones. Some crystal workers, however, believe that only the natural stones, formed eons ago, have the desired effect. Others disagree. Because natural rubies and emeralds, which have the preferred rich, deep color, are not easily obtainable, most of us have to be satisfied with synthetic stones.

In olden days, crystals were ground up and taken internally with honey, wine, milk, or other substances (including, in one famous Egyptian formula, cat feces). Most people now simply place the crystal against the relevant part of the body.

Red Stones

Red stones are primarily used to strengthen and give courage. They are also traditionally used for heart and circulatory ailments. Equally important, they are stones of balance. For the best effect, a stone of pure hue and medium saturation is chosen. The most powerful (and expensive) red stone is the ruby. Garnets (rhodolites), spinels, bloodstones, red jasper, and rhodocrosites also can be used. Synthetic rubies are inexpensive and of the same crystal structure as natural stones. There is no reason why they shouldn't work as well. Red is a yang, or masculine, color.

Blue Stones

Blue stones can be used to refine, regulate, and focus energy. They are said to be spiritual in nature and can help to turn a coarse, earthy horse into a lighter, more spiritual animal. They are also supremely good for jumpers. The most powerful blue stone traditionally is the sapphire, although aquamarine, blue lace agate, azurite, turquoise, and lapis lazuli also can be used. A very dark (indigo) blue stone helps to increase intuition and sensitivity. Blue is a yin, or feminine, color.

Green Stones

Green stones are used to calm the animal and restore balance and "rootedness." The most powerful green stone is the emerald. However, malachite has a long and honored place in equine culture as a stone that can prevent falls. Green, of course, is also the color of fertility and is a good stone for broodmares. In addition to the emerald, aventurine, chrysoprase, malachite, green tourmaline, and jade can be used. Green is a yin, or feminine, color.

Orange and Yellow Stones

Yellow to deep orange stones are used to increase energy and vitality. They are excellent for top-level performance horses in any sport. The most powerful orange stone is said to be the carnelian, but the yellow citrine works very well also. Yellow is a yang, or masculine, color and orange is a yin, or female, color.

Violet Stones

Violet stones are used to increase grace and poise. This is probably the best color for dressage horses. The most powerful violet stone is the amethyst, but other violet or purple stones can be used. Violet is a yin, or feminine, color.

White Stones

White stones are used to heal the whole horse and improve general well-being. All horses benefit from this color. The most powerful white stone is the diamond, but quartz is also effective. White balances yin and yang forces.

Black Stones

Black stones, such as jet, obsidian, and onyx, absorb negative energy and help shy, awkward horses become more independent. They are especially good for young animals. Black stone carries neither yin nor yang energy but can absorb both.

SELECTING THE MASTER STONE

In selecting a master stone for therapeutic reasons, consider the following:

The first step in gemstone healing is to find a master stone that matches your horse's personality. Different healers use different criteria to find this stone. The criteria may depend on color, structure, or some other aspect.

- If your horse is self-assured, patient, and athletic but strong minded with a tendency to anger or rebellion, his master gemstone color is red.
- If your horse is highly energetic, alert, outgoing, and impulsive, his master gemstone color is orange.
- If your horse is courageous, active, and strong, with a good character but sometimes rebellious, his master gemstone color is yellow.
- If your horse is well grounded, calm, balanced, willing, and trustworthy but perhaps self-indulgent, gluttonous, or confused, his master gemstone color is green.
- If your horse is intelligent but aloof and proud, his master gemstone color is blue.
- If your horse is intuitive, sure-footed, passionate, and persevering but mistrustful, bitter, or fearful, his master gemstone color is indigo.
- If your horse is loyal, responsive, graceful, and tolerant but overly cautious, depressed, or fearful, his master gemstone color is violet.
- If your horse is self-assured and good with a number of different tasks and riders but cold, his master gemstone color is white.

The Metal Connection

If you wish to increase the power of the crystal by using it on the horse's halter and bridle, consider these settings:

- If your horse is strong, vital, and proud, his master metal is gold.
- If your horse is emotional, responsive, moody, and changeable, his master metal is silver.
- If your horse is affectionate, beautiful, and in harmony with you, his master metal is copper.
- If your horse is enthusiastic, brave, and passionate, his master metal is iron.
- If your horse is focused, stable, and down to earth, his master metal is lead.
- If your horse is kind, willing, and honest, his master metal is tin.

CRYSTAL SHAPE

The shape of the crystal you use is also said to have importance. Spherical crystals represent the totality of the universe; they are often used to help to focus and energize the mind. They are also said to produce stability, strength, invigoration, and peace. These crystals are helpful when training horses, when focus and discipline are important. While any form of crystal can be therapeutic, most practitioners believe that spherical gems or cabochons (gemstones that have been shaped and polished as opposed to faceted) have the best power to heal. Faceted gemstones also can effect very powerful changes, but these changes may be out of balance. They should be used with caution. Crystal clusters bestow healing "group energy" on a collection of horses. They foster cooperation and friendship; they also break up negative energy in the environment.

When several crystals are strung together on a halter and worn, they are believed to produce changes that affect the entire body. Placing a crystal on a specific part of the body concentrates its energy there. If you get a stone in the form of a rondel or flattened sphere, you can tape it to the affected part or attach it to the bridle or halter. Placing the stone on the front center of the headpiece has a general and mild effect on the whole body. A placement on the right side encourages masculine, or yang, energies; a placement on the left side affects feminine, or yin, energies.

> ## Crystal Clearing
>
> According to one theory, you must "clear" a crystal before you use it. The simplest way to accomplish this is to rinse the crystal under pure water, then place it in the sun for a few hours to absorb solar energy. It doesn't hurt to put it under the moon, either. This way you will get both yin and yang energy.

CRYSTALS FOR CHAKRA REBALANCING

For people who practice Indian medicine, crystals can be used to rebalance or clear the chakras, which are points of physical or spiritual energy in the body. According to Tantric tradition, every being has seven chakras, or energy centers, that serve as junctions between the body and consciousness. They are open channels that receive, assimilate, and express our vital life energy. When the flow of energy in any of the chakras becomes blocked or misaligned, they cannot function properly and we may develop physical and mental illnesses.

These are the equine chakras:
- First chakra: The base chakra is located at the place where the tail meets the body.
- Second chakra: The sacral chakra is at the point of the hip.
- Third chakra: The solar plexus chakra runs through the midsection of the back, down through the belly.
- Fourth chakra: The heart chakra runs diagonally from the point of the shoulder to the elbow.
- Fifth chakra: The throat chakra runs from the crest to the gullet.
- Sixth chakra: The third eye chakra is in the center of the forehead.
- Seventh chakra: The crown chakra is between the ears.

Each of the seven chakras is said to be cleared by use of the following crystals, respectively: black tourmaline, carnelian, citrine, green aventurine, rose quartz, blue lace agate, amethyst, and clear quartz. Begin with the first chakra, at the base of the spine, and work forward along the horse.

STONES, MINERALS, AND METALS FOR HEALING

Use of stones, minerals, and metals for healing is another similar therapy system chosen to cure or act as protection against specific health or behavior problems. You can hold them in your hand to help to concentrate healing energy toward your horse and also incorporate them into his halter or blanket.

These can be used in conjunction with crystals to achieve more individual results. It is best if you can match emotional and physical needs. For example, several crystals may be listed as good for muscle problems. However, fearful horses may have a different response than stubborn horses. Choose the remedy that best suits your horse's mental and physical conditions.

How It Works

In theory, the tissue of all living mammals has vibratory properties compatible with those of crystals. Liquid crystal molecules combine to form cell membranes, nerve sheaths, connective tissue, etc. So, when crystals are used for healing, their vibrating resonances interact with the body's tissue to stimulate various healing effects.

A crystal healing session begins with a consultation during which the practitioner gauges your horse's needs based on any problems and concerns you relate. She then places the most appropriate crystals on and around the body to direct healing energy to those areas. All crystals are usually chosen intuitively based on their particular healing potential.

Here are some of the most commonly used crystals and stones, along with their traditional properties:

[*Note:* Not all stones are used for physical, emotional, and spiritual purposes, just as not all medicines have the same effects. The properties listed are those that apply to each specific stone; if a particular property is not listed, that means it does not apply.]

- **Agate**—*Physical*: Helps intestinal troubles; skin disease. *Emotional*: For courage; calming; strength. Improves self-confidence and banishes fear. Green varieties increase fertility. Blue-laced agate calms anger and reduces inflammation.
- **Amazonite**—*Physical:* Improves condition of the throat and bronchi; nervous system.
- **Amber**—*Physical*: Energizer and motivator. Helps heal sore throat (especially swollen glands or strangles); bladder; ears; intestinal troubles; fever. *Emotional:* Changes negative energy into positive energy. Used with turquoise to calm and focus.
- **Amethyst**—*Physical:* Heals blood diseases; eyes problems. *Emotional*: For courage; grief; calming; combats negativity.
- **Ametrine**—*Physical:* Detoxifier.
- **Anhydrite**—*Physical:* Kidneys. *Emotional:* Helpful in retraining horses; used to overcome bad habits.
- **Anyolite (Ruby Zoisite)**—*Physical:* Enhances fertility and increases physical vitality.
- **Antimony**—*Physical:* Promotes vitality and improves circulation. *Spiritual:* For protection.
- **Apatite**—*Physical*: Fights viruses. Yellow variety used for arthritis and other bone problems. *Emotional:* Quiets emotional stress (blue variety); improves communication.
- **Aphthitalite**—*Physical:* Improves balance and harmony between horse and rider. *Emotional:* Increases self-confidence.
- **Apophyllite**—*Physical:* Stimulates the reproductive organs in breeding horses.
- **Aquamarine**—*Physical:* Improves breathing; liver; glands; nervous system; eyes. *Emotional:* For courage; communication.
- **Aventurine**—*Physical:* Improves circulation; antidepressant; general healing (blue variety). Helps heart function; stress; eye conditions (green variety). *Emotional:* Increases mental agility.
- **Azurite**—*Physical:* Helps arthritis (joints); trauma; eyes. *Emotional:* Calms phobic or panicky horses.
- **Barite**—*Physical:* Muscle stimulant, particularly useful for jumpers. (People have said it makes them feel as if they are flying!)

- **Beryl**—*Physical:* Energizer; general healing; helps heart function.
- **Bloodstone**—*Physical:* Stops bleeding. *Emotional:* For courage; victory; fights depression.
- **Calcite**—*Emotional:* For centering; calming (blue variety).
- **Carnelian**—*Physical:* Treats wheezing from allergies; helps arthritis; helps heal wounds; prevents fevers. *Emotional:* For courage; enhances self-esteem; quells anger.
- **Celestite**– *Physical:* Eases breathing.
- **Chalcedony**—*Spiritual:* For safety in travel.
- **Chrysoprase**—*Physical:* Heals burns; relieves neck and shoulder pain.
- **Citrine**—*Physical:* Treats digestion and stomach problems; blood purifier; energizer; skin toner; helps spinal alignment (place on spine); improves circulation. *Emotional:* Quiets panicky, fearful horses. *Spiritual:* For protection.
- **Copper**—*Physical:* Treats kidney parathyroid trouble; mental clarity.
- **Diamond**—*Physical:* For general healing
- **Dolomite**—*Emotional:* For sorrow and grief.
- **Elbaite**—*Emotional:* Helps you improve a difficult relationship with your horse (watermelon tourmaline); heals emotions.
- **Emerald**—*Physical:* Enhances mental abilities.
- **Feldspar**—*Physical:* Helps to heal muscle and skin injuries.
- **Fluorite**—*Physical:* Strengthens teeth and bones; balancing; pneumonia.
- **Garnet**—*Physical:* Strengthener; energizer; releases toxins; helps anemia; helps skin disease. *Emotional:* For relaxation.
- **Gold**—*Physical:* Strengthens the back, spinal column, and thymus gland.
- **Hematite**—*Emotional:* For grounding.
- **Iron**—*Physical:* Heals muscles and improves renal and genital systems. *Spiritual:* Traditionally, a protection against demons.
- **Jade**—*Physical:* Heals kidney disorders; for general healing.
- **Jasper**—*Physical:* General healer, especially for stomach problems (green variety). *Spiritual:* For protection.
- **Jet**—*Physical:* Protects from illness; helps toothaches. *Emotional:* Dispels fear.
- **Kunzite**—*Physical:* Treats bones and spinal cord problems; anemia. *Emotional:* For communication.
- **Lapis Lazuli**—*Physical:* Treats

Using crystals, stones, and metals as a protection creates "good vibrations" between horses and owners, the value of which cannot be overlooked. The practice of attaching them to a horse's bridle is traditional in some cultures.

How Color Affects Us

The body absorbs light that is made up of all the colors of the spectrum. Likewise, all living things, including the cells in the body, "vibrate" at an atomic level at different wavelengths. Much like sounds, each color in the spectrum has a frequency, wavelength, and energy associated with it. The color frequencies that the body absorbs are decoded by the brain and then passed on; they have an effect on the nervous system, the endocrine system, and subsequently on the release of hormones and other organic substances within the body. They trigger an array of responses, some conscious, many others subconscious.

Some researchers believe that color affects all our senses of sight, sound, smell, taste, and feelings. Because of this, color can be used to affect healing. In crystal healing, the powers of crystal vibration affecting the body at a cellular/subconscious level heal and influence the body both emotionally and physically.

heart and skin problems. *Emotional:* For depression; imparts courage.

- **Lead**—*Physical:* Improves skin; spleen; teeth; bones. (*Do not place lead in direct contact with the skin.*)
- **Malachite**—*Physical:* Treats diarrhea; overstressed nervous system; asthma; improves eyesight. *Emotional:* For power.
- **Meta-Ankoleite**—*Physical:* Blood purifier; central nervous system; conditions affecting the head.
- **Moonstone**—*Physical:* Good for hormone imbalances in mares; aligns the vertebrae; digestive aid. *Emotional:* Calms emotions; offers grounding.
- **Obsidian**—*Emotional:* Grounding stone. *Spiritual:* For protection.
- **Onyx**—*Physical:* Helps lung problems (yellow variety). *Emotional:* For emotional balance.
- **Opal**—*Physical:* Improves skin and coat (white); improves eyesight.
- **Quartz (clear)**—*Physical:* Energizer; air purifier; treats diarrhea; relieves pain. *Emotional:* For balancing and clearing.
- **Pearl**—*Physical:* Energizer; improves eyesight; heart; urinary tract.
- **Peridot**—*Physical:* Improves digestive system; heart; lungs. *Spiritual:* For protection.
- **Petrified Wood**—*Physical:* Energizer; improves circulation; helps skin inflammation; helps back, hip; muscle diseases; improves longevity.
- **Rhodonite**—*Physical:* Improves mental clarity; lung problems; ear; trauma; vitamin absorption.
- **Ruby**—*Physical:* Treats weakened muscles and muscle problems resulting from overexertion; anemia; arthritis pain. *Emotional:* Imparts power and cheerfulness; overcomes fear.
- **Sapphire**—*Physical:* Treats nervous disorders; arthritis; blood problems. *Emotional:* For nervousness.
- **Sea Shells**—*Physical:* Treats calcium deficiencies and bone disorders.
- **Serpentine**—*Spiritual:* Protects against venomous creatures. (To be effective, the stone must be in its natural state and never come into contact with iron.)
- **Silver**—*Physical:* Treats problems of the esophagus; stomach; pancreas; intestines; liver. *Emotional:* For maintaining balance.
- **Smithsonite**—*Physical:* Relieves muscular tension. *Emotional:* Reduces anger.
- **Smoky Quartz**—*Physical:* Removes toxins; treats abdominal problems. *Emotional:* Treats depression. *Spiritual:* For protection.
- **Sodalite**—*Physical:* Balances the metabolism. Good for endurance horses. *Emotional:* For courage.
- **Thermonatrite**—*Physical:* Helps sore throats. *Emotional:* For stubbornness and anxiety.
- **Tin**—*Physical:* Improves liver and pituitary gland problems.
- **Topaz**—*Physical:* Strengthens the immune system; for general strength; helps with flu.
- **Tourmaline**—*Physical:* Strengthens the immune system; helps eye problems; heals central nervous system

conditions; helps lower back pain (black variety); improves lymph. Also excellent for horses who have had radiation therapy. *Spiritual:* For protection.
- **Turquoise**—*Physical:* Fights viruses and treats sore throats. *Spiritual:* This is definitely a rider's stone! It is said to keep you from falling off your horse. *Emotional:* For communication and courage.
- **Wulfenite**—*Physical:* Stimulates circulation.

Crystals should not be the only therapy option; use them in conjunction with other modalities to achieve the best results.

LIGHT (PHOTON) THERAPY, OR LOW-LEVEL PHOTOTHERAPY/LASER THERAPY

ADVANTAGES
- AFTER SOME BASIC TRAINING, THE OWNER CAN USE IT HERSELF.
- IT CAN SPEED HEALING.
- IT CAN BE USED TO STIMULATE ACUPUNCTURE POINTS OR IT CAN BE APPLIED DIRECTLY OVER THE INJURY.
- USED AWAY FROM THE EYE, IT IS SAFE.
- NO SIDE EFFECTS.

DISADVANTAGES
- CAN BE DANGEROUS IF THE LASER STRIKES THE EYE.
- MACHINES LARGE ENOUGH TO DO MOST WOUND HEALING MUST BE RENTED.

[*Note:* The effectiveness of this treatment is strongly debated. The British Journal of Rheumatology, in a double blind study, found lasers ineffective for tendonitis. The Journal of Athletic Training, however, in a review of scientific studies, found it effective for subacromial impingement syndrome (shoulder pain). These studies were done on human beings, of course. The same review found that ultrasound therapy was not helpful. As for wound healing, the Agency for Healthcare Research and Quality (AHRQ) found low-level laser treatment ineffective, but most studies available were deemed to be poorly done.]

The term "laser" is an acronym for "light amplification by stimulated emission of radiation." Lasers emit light in a special form. Low-Level Laser Therapy (formerly called "cold laser therapy"), or biostimulation, is the use of low-powered laser light to create therapeutic effects. Therapeutic lasers work by supplying energy to the body in the form of photons of light, and this stimulates the body's ability to repair itself. The "biostimulating" effect of the laser is in its anti-inflammatory, analgesic, and anti-swelling effect on tissues.

The difference between "hot" and "cold" lasers is the amount of peak power they deliver. Hot lasers deliver up to thousands of watts of power. These are the lasers that are used in surgery because they can make a very clean incision with little or no bleeding. So-called "cold" lasers produce an average power of 100 milliwatts or less; this is the type of laser used for therapeutic purposes. It is usually pulsed, meaning that the light is on for only a fraction of a second. Therapeutic laser light is generally either visible (usually red) or invisible (infrared).

HOW IT WORKS

While lasers were once confined to research laboratories and high-tech hospital facilities, they are now available everywhere and to everyone. Some veterinarians and other practitioners use them freely, especially for eye, back, muscle, and tendon problems, as well as to help to heal wounds.

At wound sites, lasers are used to speed up healing. However, many holistic vets use them in conjunction with

acupuncture at the acupuncture sites. The smaller, almost pen-sized lasers can be used at acupoints near the eye, although extreme caution must be used not to direct the laser directly into the eye because it could cause extreme pain. Although people who work with lasers claim they are extremely effective for ocular problems, even a slight jerk of the horse's head could result in catastrophe. Larger units, designed for serious wound healing, have to be rented or leased.

Some studies have suggested that the good effects of laser therapy actually come from the light itself, not from any unique properties of lasers. According to this theory, lasers are just machines that produce this healing type of radiation, nothing more. However, proponents of light therapy assert it can accomplish the following things:

Some veterinarians and other practitioners use laser therapy freely, especially for eye, back, muscle, and tendon problems, as well as to help to heal wounds.

- increase circulation by increasing the formation of new capillaries, which replace damaged blood vessels
- stimulate the production of collagen, an important protein for repairing tissues
- stimulate the release of adenosine triphosphate (ATP), the major carrier of energy to all cells; this allows cells to receive nutrients faster and get rid of waste products more quickly
- increase lymphatic system activity, helping to reduce edema
- increase RNA and DNA synthesis
- reduce the excitability of nervous tissue, thereby relieving pain
- stimulate fibroblastic activity that helps to form collagen fibers
- increase phagocytosis, the process of scavenging and ingesting dead cells
- stimulate tissue granulation
- stimulate acetylcholine release

ELECTRO-ACUSCOPE MYOPULSE THERAPY

ADVANTAGES
- NONINVASIVE.
- NO SIDE EFFECTS.

DISADVANTAGES
- CAN BE EXPENSIVE.
- EFFECTIVENESS NOT PROVED.

Electro-Acuscope Myopulse Therapy uses an electronic medical instrument to treat a wide range of neuromuscular conditions commonly affecting equine athletes. Using electricity, it treats pain by stimulating the nervous system (without puncturing the skin). Don't worry about electrocuting your horse; the amount of electricity produced by the acuscope is measured in microamps (millionths of an amp). This low level can produce the most beneficial effect on the cells. A companion instrument, the myopulse, gently stimulates muscles, tendons, and

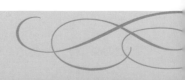

ligaments to reduce spasm and inflammation and to strengthen trauma-damaged tissue.

The goal of the treatment is to reduce pain and increase range of motion. The therapy has been used with barrel racers, polo ponies, cutters, endurance horses, racers, and other performance and event animals.

How It Works

Usually between 5 and 15 treatments are needed, although a more severe injury such as a bowed tendon may take up to 30 or 40 treatments, with an additional 60-day rest period before resuming work. The acuscope has a cumulative effect on the body, and the pain relief following each treatment will last longer. In addition, each successive treatment will require a shorter period of time to be effective.

Proponents recommend this therapy for inflammatory conditions such as:

- arthritis
- bursitis
- capped joints
- carpitis
- deep tissue infections
- hematomas
- laminitis
- ruptures
- strains
- torn muscles or tendons

Other conditions for which it has been used include:

- constriction of the annular ligament
- contracted heel
- fibrous scar tissue
- loose stifle
- muscle atrophy
- osteitis
- scratches
- seedy toe
- skin problems (cuts, infections, and post-injection tissue reactions)
- stocking up
- stringhalt
- thrush
- tying-up syndrome

LEDs

Light emitting diodes (LEDs) are a related form of light therapy. They are similar to lasers but differ in the way that the light energy is delivered. However, their healing effects are the same.

MAGNETIC THERAPY

ADVANTAGES
- FREE FROM SIDE EFFECTS.
- NONINVASIVE.
- EASY TO USE.
- THE USE OF PULSATING ELECTROMAGNETIC FIELDS MAY IMPROVE THE HEALING OF SOME FRACTURES.

DISADVANTAGES
- EFFECTIVENESS NOT PROVED.

GOOD VIBRATIONS

In a way, practitioners of energetic medicine have Albert Einstein, Werner Heisenberg, and quantum physics to thank. Energetic theory relies not on the mechanistic Newtonian concept of absolute space, time, and objects but on a fluid world in which matter and energy flow through each other. In this world, unlike the classic Newtonian world, "objects" are seen as fluctuating states of being. In the world of Newton, the body is a machine. It is a beautiful and complex machine, but it's only a machine.

Energetic medicine has a broader and deeper view. The body is more than a machine—it's an energy field, and its perfect health depends on a proper energy balance. Using religious language, we might call it spiritual. Energetic medicine, in fact, makes no distinction between body and spirit. They don't merely affect each other. They don't merely interpenetrate each other, or even become each other. They are each other at every moment. What seems solid and physical—like a horse's hoof—is really mostly whirling energy. What seems empty, like air, is filled with pulsating particles. There is only one world with infinite faces.

This field of medicine is the most modern, most ancient, most unitary, most diverse modality of healing ever produced. It is a true mirror of the universe. This is philosophy, of course, but energetic medicine has its highly technical side as well, which derives from its philosophy. The basic idea is that the body has an electrical-biochemical connection. This connection is subtle and difficult to perceive; however, that does not invalidate its existence. Bioenergy operates differently than ordinary electricity (to which it is often compared). Bioenergy is "alive" in a way that ordinary electricity is not and seems directed in a way that inorganic electricity can never be. It is the subtle "substance" that guides the life process from birth to death. Bioenergetics is dedicated to the idea that the body can naturally heal itself if given an opportunity to do so.

The energy field that is us extends beyond us to connect us to the environment. This is one reason why a bioenergetic modality doesn't draw boundaries around the patient as if she is contained entirely within her skin. Thoughts, feelings, and even "physical" phenomena like voices carry energy from the body, just as receptive organs like the eye and ear draw it in. Truly, this is a holistic universe.

Bioenergetics is opposed to mainstream medicine—indeed its practitioners hope that one day it will be the mainstream choice. Of course, in one sense it already is. MRI, CT scans, and X-rays, all examples of bioenergetics, have long been part of diagnostic medicine. Healing is the next logical step.

Everything on earth generates electrical impulses, which in turn causes all things to be influenced by magnetic forces and thus magnets. Magnetic therapy is a form of alternative medicine involving magnetic fields. Proponents claim that subjecting certain parts of the body to doses of magnetic fields has a beneficial and healing effect.

HOW IT WORKS

Any horse who is ridden regularly is at risk of developing repetitive stress-related injuries. He can be subject to a vast array of ailments, many of them joint, muscle, ligament, or tendon related because a horse suffers pressure and shocks to his joints during exercise, especially in competition. However, on the flip side, if horses cannot exercise, they are subject to a host of other health problems. Exercise enables their bodies to function properly and helps them maintain their circulatory system. Therefore, it's important to treat musculoskeletal injuries right away to ensure that the horse is inactive for the briefest possible amount of time. Vets and horse owners have been using therapeutic magnetic devices, such as magnetic blankets and wraps, which may take care of common equine ailments for quite a few years.

Magnetic therapy comes in several forms, and there is a difference in theory between magnetic therapy, electromagnetic therapy (sometimes referred to as Pulsating Electromagnetic Field Therapy, or PEFT), and static magnetic therapy. In PEFT, it is theorized that application of the right amount of electrical current, either directly (through the application of electric wires) or indirectly (by indirect induction via a magnetic field) may affect body tissues. Horses do have electricity running through them at all times, as do the rest of us. It can be measured in the beating heart and even in the production of bone.

PEFT has been studied (mostly in humans) in healing fractures as well as in soft tissue injuries. The Task Force for Veterinary Science says that PEFT therapy may have limited value for the treatment of tendon injuries, perhaps in part because there is no apparent electrical activity to affect in these tissues. It is most effective on old rather than fresh traumas. It may possibly help to heal fractures, although probably not as well as it heals tissue injuries.

Another therapy, Static Magnet Therapy, relies on magnetic pads (bars, beads, or strips) that radiate an unchanging magnetic field. Supporters claim that the therapy works by application of Faraday's law and a concomitant effect called Hall's effect. These laws state that a magnetic field will exert a force on a moving ionic current, and that when a magnetic field is placed perpendicular to the direction of the flow of an electric current, it will deflect and separate the charged ions into opposite directions, depending on the magnetic pole encountered and the charge of the ion. (However, this force is not based on the attraction of like and unlike charges.) In the body, the electrical conductor, that "moving ionic current," is nothing other than the blood that flows through the blood vessels (arteries and veins). If the blood vessel is perpendicular to the magnetic line of force, the magnet produces a voltage in the blood by forcing the separation of charged ions. In other words, if the magnet is properly oriented, it can affect the flow of blood. (Thus, the orientation of the magnet is very important in this modality.) Opponents of the therapy argue that Hall's effect is too small to make a difference in healing. (The power of a magnet is measured in units called "gauss," the number of lines of magnetic force passing through one square centimeter. A small magnet has about 10 gauss; an MRI has about 10,000.)

Both magnetic therapies have been used to treat pain, sprains, inflammation, swelling, and infection. Its advantages are legion. It's drug-free, humane, and noninvasive. In the entire field of equine

health literature, no side effects have ever been reported, although in human medicine, they may interfere with pacemakers, defibrillators, insulin pumps, and liver infusion pumps. Its major uses are to improve elasticity of muscles and to promote greater range of motion. It has been used with success for tendonitis, bowed tendons, bucked shins, and muscular sprains.

In horses, magnets have been applied in healing the following:

- tendon injuries (bowed tendons, tendon rupture, tendonitis, digital flexor tendon injury)
- ligament injuries (inflammation of the ligaments, desmitis)
- knee injuries (carpus)
- hind leg (stifle joint) injuries (patella ligament tears, menisci (cartilage) tears, quadriceps muscle damage)
- bony injuries (metacarpus, cannon bone, pastern bone, hock injury [bone spavin])
- back, loin, or croup injuries
- withers, shoulder, and flank injuries

MAGNETIC DEVICES

You can buy magnetic blankets, magnetic leg wraps, magnetic hock wraps, magnetic bell boots, tiny hoof magnets (known as Cor-Mags) placed along acupuncture meridians, and even magnetic massagers. While many horse owners claim to have gotten great results with these, opponents suggest that any kind of bandage, magnetic or not, would work equally well.

The magnetic blanket is probably the most popular magnetic device used for horses. One type uses thin static magnets attached to the underside of the blanket. The other uses electrical pulse magnets. The magnet hock bandage is equally popular, but it has not been shown to be any more effective than a regular hock bandage. Magnetic hock bandages should not be applied to hot or seriously injured hocks.

There are dozens of variants of magnet therapy—in fact, one estimate puts the number of magnetic therapy devices at more than 5,000!

WHEN TO USE MAGNETIC THERAPY

Horses respond to magnetic therapy in much the same way as humans and other animals do. However, because they have massive circulatory systems, horses should only be exposed to magnets while they are resting, stabled, turned out, or during travel. It's not safe to use magnets during exercise because horses are prone to overheating during exercise, and one action of magnets is to stimulate the circulatory system, which in turn increases body temperature. As with all animals, overheating is potentially dangerous to a horse's health.

If your horse has an existing injury or develops a new one, magnets should be applied as soon as possible to reduce inflammation around the injury site and to encourage new cell growth. They should be placed as close to the point of injury as possible. If your horse is not exercising because of the injury, the magnets can be left on until activity is resumed, and then they must be removed. Also, magnets should be placed on the horse only when he is completely cool. As with all therapies and OTC meds, always consult with your vet before beginning any at-home treatment.

Proponents of magnetic therapy believe it has the following benefits:

- Magnets ease post-exercise aches and pains, and if any damage has occurred during exercise, the magnetic field will start reducing inflammation around the injury.
- Using magnets before exercise will warm and loosen the muscles, tendons, and ligaments before a workout, which will help to prevent strains and sprains.

- Magnets are easy to use; they can be applied overnight, when the horse is stabled or turned out. They can be placed under blankets or used alone. The body increases the rate at which it heals during rest, so this is an ideal time to use magnetic therapy to treat chronic or recent injuries.
- Magnets can be used during travel to prepare a horse for competition or exercise. They have a calming and soothing effect, which is beneficial for horses who are nervous travelers.

Many horses who are treated with magnets show signs of reduced discomfort, increased mobility, and increased energy/activity levels.

REIKI

ADVANTAGES
- SAFE.
- NONINTRUSIVE.
- CAN BE DONE BY OWNER.

DISADVANTAGES
- NOT SCIENTIFICALLY PROVEN TO BE EFFECTIVE.

In Japanese, Reiki (pronounced RAY-key) means "universal life energy." The practitioner regards herself as a channel for this energy, which is "drawn" to the area that needs to be healed. The history of this therapy is a little muddled, but some believe that it originated in Tibet and then moved on to China and Japan. In modern times, this gentlest of all natural healing techniques was further developed by Dr. Mikao Usui in Japan, who says that he found a description of the therapy in ancient manuscripts.

Reiki was introduced to the United States in the 1930s by Hawayo Takata. It works by transmitting life energy, *ki* (the Japanese version of Qi), to the horse by placing your hands gently in specific positions either on or above the body. During a session, energy enters through the practitioner's head and exits through the palms of the hands, so it is not necessary always to touch the body. Practitioners believe that it has powerful spiritual benefits as well. Reiki is designed to relieve pain, heal illnesses, and restore vitality.

It is used to:
- remove energy blocks and congestion resulting from emotional trauma, illness, injury, and stress
- improve confidence and general behavioral problems
- stimulate healing

Reiki is like a combination of animal communication and acupuncture—without ever actually touching the horse. The healing hands are held near the chakras of the animals. The major chakras in Reiki are:
- the crown chakra, located on the poll between the ears
- the brow (third eye) chakra, located in the middle of the forehead
- the throat chakra, located just behind the jaw at the top of the neck
- the heart chakra, located just behind the withers
- the solar plexus chakra, located right under the cantle of the saddle
- the sacral chakra, located at the top of the hips
- the root chakra, located at the base of the tail

As you become more sensitive to your horse's aura, you may be able to feel the differences in energy at these points. Reiki is often used not only to heal but to train horses through improving mobility, increasing energy levels, inducing greater calm and focus, and enhancing communication.

ANIMAL COMMUNICATORS

ADVANTAGES
- ABSOLUTELY NONINVASIVE.
- FUN, AND YOU MAY LEARN USEFUL INFORMATION.

DISADVANTAGES
- CAN BE FRAUDULENT.
- NO SCIENTIFIC EVIDENCE IT WORKS.
- MAY REQUIRE A SPECIAL "EMPATH," OR PERSON WITH CERTAIN INTUITIVE SKILLS.

Horses are much more complex beings than we once thought. They have minds and emotions as well as bodies. Many people believe that animals express pain, discomfort, and sorrow in ways that are too subtle for ordinary people to pick up on, partly because we are not gifted with the kind of "horse sense" (if you will pardon the pun) that makes it easy for us to understand their clues. Animal communicators claim to be able to read these subtle signals and respond to them. Some attempt to diagnose a condition; others try to use their skills to treat the ailing animal. Some even say that they are having a "conversation" with the horse. Whether it's a matter of closer and more intense observation or whether this is a spiritual gift is not clear.

HOW IT WORKS

Many animal communicators believe that all animals talk to each other through telepathic communication and that it is possible for specially trained or intuitive people to tap into this channel. This intuitively derived knowledge may arrive in mental images (clairvoyance), mental sound (clairaudience), inner feelings (clairsentience), or even "knowing" (claircognizance).

Certainly animals suffering loneliness, depression, or neglect may benefit from the attentions of animal communicators and may "perk up" during a session. However, the fact is that people who call in animal communicators are not the ones likely to neglect their horses in the first place. Many trained practitioners, however, do specialize in psychological problems such as shyness, aggression, fear, and bad habits like rearing or kicking.

Animal communicators believe that animals are on the same "level" as human beings and are just as evolved, intelligent, and soulful in their own way. Proceeding from this platform makes them compassionate and caring when it comes to their clients. They do not regard a horse as an object whose total function in life is to carry a person around on his back without complaint. They wisely understand that horses, too, are spiritual beings who can be approached in a mental as well as physical way.

It is also obvious that, as in any field, there are charlatans and misguided people who believe that they can perceive things they cannot. Most suspect (to me) are animal communicators who feel they can talk to your horse over the telephone. However, some people swear this "therapy" has produced positive results in which they discovered the secret sources of their horse's symptoms and stresses.

LEARNING TO COMMUNICATE

Proponents of animal communication believe that it can be helpful for many common problems with domestic animals of all kinds and that it can improve and deepen your relationship with them. Here are some common applications:

Cellular Intelligence

Developed by animal behaviorist Linda Tellington-Jones, TTouch is a gentle, hands-on, holistic healing method that can be used to:

- enhance healing and health

- improve behavior

- develop an animal's ability to learn without fear or force

- deepen the bond between humans and animals through increased awareness and communication

The main focus of TTouch is bodywork that consists of circular movements and lifts all over the body. Although it might look somewhat like massage, TTouch is actually designed to work at the cellular level to increase an animal's awareness and enhance his ability to learn and focus.

Based on groundbreaking research by neurologist Sir Charles Sherrington, which showed that severed nerves grow back together because each cell of the body has its own intelligence, Tellington-Jones hypothesized that nonhabitual touch could stimulate cell intelligence and quickly "turn on" and repattern corresponding brain cells. She also hypothesized that the circles of TTouch provided a means for this "cellular intelligence" common to all life to become a method of communication—the cells of one being could make a direct connection with the cells of another. Through this special form of touch, TTouch communicates across species barriers from being to being, helping to stimulate the body's healing mechanisms with the transference of healing energy and information to reeducate the body and reprogram the brain.

TTEAM, the Tellington TTouch Equine Awareness Method, an innovative training technique that evolved out of TTouch, is a holistic way of training and healing by affecting the body, mind, and spirit and by recognizing the individuality and special needs of each horse. It can be used to improve athletic skills and increase the horse's willingness and ability to learn. This method presents solutions to common physical and behavior problems by using special touches, lifts, and movement exercises to release tension, increase body awareness, and identify soreness and discomfort. It also incorporates a variety of obstacles in ground exercises that teach self-control, focus, cooperation, balance, and coordination. A deeper bond grows between horse and rider because of more effective communication.

- to solve behavior problems (fear, aggression, separation anxiety, unwanted behaviors)
- to address quality of life issues (find out what your animal wants and needs; improve relationships), especially during illness and near death
- to enhance training
- to help animals interact better with each other
- in the case of adopted animals, to find out about an animal's past

In cases where a disease is undiagnosed or in very serious cases where little hope is held out, it may be that animal communicators have something of real value to offer our equine companions.

While it is widely believed that only certain people have the skill to communicate with an animal on a deep level, most animal communicators insist that each of us has this ability locked up inside us. They show that by being quiet, alert, and receptive, many an owner (whom they usually refer to as "guardians") can learn to communicate with her horse. Part of the strategy depends on truly respecting and loving the animal as an individual being, not as a possession, and understanding that a horse is truly a "person." A horse is not a human being, of course, but a person in the philosophical sense of having needs and rights. These needs and rights come from the fact that he is a living, sentient creature, just as humans are, one who can feel pain and suffer emotional stress.

Chapter 6

Homeopathy

The word "homeopathy" comes from two Greek words that mean "like disease." A holistic approach to treatment, this system is based on the idea that substances that produce symptoms of illness in healthy people will have a curative effect when given in very dilute quantities to sick people who have the same symptoms. The remedies made from these substances are believed to work by stimulating the body's own healing processes. Homeopathy has been found to be effective in treating animals and is now being used by holistic veterinary practitioners for a variety of equine conditions.

ADVANTAGES
- ALL MEDICATIONS CAN BE PURCHASED WITHOUT A PRESCRIPTION.
- MEDICATIONS ARE ORAL AND CAN BE ADMINISTERED BY THE OWNER.
- MOST REMEDIES ARE INEXPENSIVE.
- DESIGNED TO TREAT MOST CONDITIONS.
- GENERALLY SAFE.

DISADVANTAGES
- DIFFICULT FOR OWNERS TO USE SAFELY ON THEIR OWN BECAUSE APPROPRIATE MEDICATIONS AND DOSAGES ARE BEST DETERMINED BY A HOMEOPATHIC VETERINARIAN.
- EFFECTIVENESS IS DISPUTED.
- NOT APPROPRIATE AS THE ONLY TREATMENT FOR TRAUMA AND EMERGENCY CONDITIONS.
- NOT SUPPOSED TO BE USED IN CONJUNCTION WITH STANDARD MEDICATIONS.

[*Note:* Despite the lack of support from the mainstream medical community, homeopathy has devoted adherents in the United States. It is more widely accepted in Europe and India.]

BASIC PRINCIPLES

A system of medicine developed by Samuel Hahnemann (1755–1843), homeopathy is based on a simple concept that "like cures like." This is called the Law of Similars. Many centuries ago, the Greek physician Hippocrates proposed the same idea. The basic theory behind it is that the cure for a condition that produces, say, a rash might be a tiny portion of a substance (plant, animal, or mineral) that in *large* doses would produce those same signs of illness in an individual. For example, if someone has a painful red swelling, the homeopathic cure might be apis, which is made from honeybees.

This all seems straightforward enough. But there's a twist. Homeopathy operates on a strange, even paradoxical principle—the more the remedy is diluted, the more powerful it is. As a matter of fact, most homeopathic remedies are so dilute that they contain *none* of the original substance. This seems odd, even ridiculous, to skeptics because diluting a substance is conventionally considered to make it weaker.

However, homeopaths maintain that if the dilution is carried out in a particular way, the remedy is strengthened, or "potentiated" or "potentized," not weakened. The particular method used is called "serial dilution" and "succussion" or shaking vigorously. Homeopaths contend that the shaking causes an imprint (or memory) of the diluted substance, despite the fact that no molecules of the original substance may remain. And, the less of the substance, the more energy is in the remedy.

Homeopaths believe that every individual has a unique energy pattern called it's "vital force." The vital force is the mechanism that maintains the health of the organism. From this perspective, the underlying cause of illness is a disturbance of the body's vital force. Because all disease is

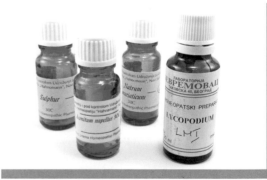

Homeopathy is based on the idea that substances that produce symptoms of illness in healthy people will have a curative effect when given in very dilute quantities to sick people who have the same symptoms.

a reflection of this energetic imbalance, sickness must be addressed energetically to be eradicated. Treatment with these diluted remedies can harmonize and rebalance the body's energy, thereby restoring health. This is what makes homeopathy a vibrational or energetic method of healing more than a medicinal one.

How It Works

Homeopathic medicines begin as a tincture of exact proportions called the "mother tincture." In the next stage of preparing a remedy (and all homeopathic medications are called remedies), 1 drop of the mother tincture is added to 99 drops of water and then succussed one hundred times (by a machine nowadays). This is called a 1C potency. Homeopaths believe that this violent shaking causes a strong energy transfer from the original substance to the water. So if you want a 6C remedy, you take the 1C substance and dilute it 5 more times, a hundredfold each time, succussing it with each dilution.

At 2C, the remedy is only 1 part in 10,000. At a homeopathic potency of 30C, the remedy dilution is an astronomical figure but something less than a drop in the ocean. The remedy is then taken in liquid form or placed onto a sugar pill.

Most contemporary Western scientists dismiss the idea of homeopathy as voodoo and wishful thinking. After all, even if the principle were found to be valid, there's only so much dilution that is possible. You can't get less than a molecule! Yet conventional medicine has yet to embrace the concept that there is more to the individual than the physical body.

Homeopaths believe that this modality works for both acute and chronic conditions. Critics charge that the gradual improvements seen for many chronic conditions treated homeopathically are due more to time than the remedy and that the animal would have recovered anyway. Homeopaths point to examples where acute flare-ups of disease also responded to homeopathic treatment, although many of the examples are drawn from human experience, in which psychosomatic factors may play a role. However, homeopaths and their clients continue to believe that these remedies work and work well. Some practitioners even maintain that of all animals, horses seem the most responsive to homeopathic remedies.

Remedy Potency

Homeopathy uses several scales of potency. In the "X," or decimal potency remedy, the dilution factor is tenfold with each dilution. It begins with one drop of mother tincture in nine drops of water. In the "C," or centesimal potency, the dilution factor is one hundredfold at each dilution. It begins with 1 drop of substance in 99 drops of water. This is the most commonly used scale. In the "M," or millesimal scale, the dilution factor is one thousandfold for each dilution. It begins with 1 drop of mother tincture in 999 drops of water.

Homeopaths believe that it is best to start with the lowest effective potency, especially if the signs you observe are mostly physical rather than mental or emotional. The use of higher potencies (above 30C) is best left to experienced practitioners.

A HOMEOPATHIC ALTERNATIVE TO VACCINES

Some alternative veterinarians, especially homeopaths, advocate using nosodes or potentized oral vaccines rather than conventional vaccinations for animals at high risk from conventional vaccines. A nosode is a homeopathic medicine derived from a product of the disease and thereafter potentiated. Nosodes can be used in two ways: prophylactically (to prevent the disease) and therapeutically (to treat the disease). An oral vaccine, on the other hand, is prepared from the actual organism that causes the disease. In many cases, the terms "nosode" and "oral vaccine" are used interchangeably because both serve the same purpose.

In some cases, the nosode is what is termed "isopathic"—in other words, taken from the very disease it is meant to fight against. In other cases, the nosode is homeopathic, or taken from a similar disease. For example, the isopathic nosode medicine *Distemperinum* was developed from the mucous secretions of a dog affected with distemper. The nosode for canine parvovirus is made from parvo-infected feces, vomitus, or blood, potentized to a very high degree and administered orally. Supposedly, what is captured is not just the virus but the essence of the disease.

Homeopathy Versus Herbal Medicine

It is important to remember that homeopathy is *not* herbal medicine. Many of the remedies used in homeopathy would be deadly if given in an herbal dose. They are safe only because the amount used is so tiny but "potentiated" (or "potentized") by the dilution and shaking of the remedy.

Because some of these substances are toxic when given in inappropriate doses, it is imperative that veterinary homeopathy be practiced only by licensed veterinarians who have been educated in veterinary homeopathy. (Don't try shaking up some watered-down weed juice yourself. You won't get the same effect.)

Most homeopathic nosodes are oral rather than injected and are given at 30C. An autonosode is extracted from the patient on whom it is to be used. There are nosodes for many ailments of horses, including influenza and herpes virus. Advocates say that the nosodes can provide good protection similar to that of a vaccine, and they also can be used afterward to help the horse convalesce.

Nosodes are not commercially available and must be prepared by a homeopathic veterinarian.

How They Work

The use of nosodes as a preventive is a matter of great controversy, even within the homeopathic community, although some practitioners have found it effective if the nosode is given about the same time as the exposure to the disease, preferably during the incubation period. They admit, however, that it does not work well if given more than a few days in advance.

In general, the efficacy of homeopathic prevention has not been proven. The only way to test it would be to experiment on healthy animals, something most homeopathic practitioners refuse to do on ethical grounds. These humane considerations have not hindered conventional clinical researchers from their investigations, however. In a study published in 1996, researchers Larson, Wynn, and Schultz found that nosode-administered dogs were completely unprotected from subsequent challenges from parvovirus. Another study, by W.B. Jones and published in *Alternative Therapy Health Medicine* (1996), had better luck (in fact better than any other researcher) finding that nosodes protected 22 percent of the subject dogs from a subsequent exposure to parvovirus. However, "protect" here simply means that the nosode-administered dogs took longer to get the infection before they died from it. In the same study, vaccinated dogs were protected 100 percent; none were infected (let alone died). And there is no valid independent evidence to show that nosodes are effective in protecting horses at all.

In short, homeopathic nosodes don't seem to be the most effective or convenient way to deal with infectious diseases, although I suppose it is better than nothing if your unvaccinated horse has actually been exposed to a disease, a period during which vaccines are ineffective. Many holistic vets use nosodes *along with* (not instead of) vaccination as a preventive. One advantage is that they are safe for animals too young to be vaccinated conventionally. It is probably safe to say that nosodes should be used alone only in animals who for one reason or another cannot be vaccinated any other way.

Legal Issues

Another problem with nosodes (leaving aside for the moment the question of whether or not they actually work) is that, legally speaking, a nosode is not a vaccination. While some may say that this is the great advantage, the fact is that for purposes of boarding, traveling, and so forth, a nosode is not (yet) an acceptable substitute. In other words, your homeopathic veterinarian cannot sign documentation stating that your horse has received the required vaccine when in fact he has not.

PRESCRIBING HOMEOPATHIC REMEDIES

Generally, homeopathic remedies are prescribed according to key symptoms that the individual is experiencing. Each remedy is catalogued according to the symptoms of specific parts of the body, such as the head, extremities, gastrointestinal system, and so on, or to symptoms related to emotional disorders.

The sourcebook for homeopathic remedy symptoms is called the repertory. The repertory lists the symptoms that all the remedies might cause if given to a healthy individual in large doses, such as trembling, muscle pain, or seizures. The theory is that giving minute but potentiated doses of the same remedy to a sick animal will treat the disease. In some situations, more than one remedy may be applicable, in which case the practitioner will choose the one that most closely matches all the symptoms.

The potency of the dose given depends on factors such as the strength of the horse's vital force (which is much like the immune system), the seriousness of the disease, and whether the disease is chronic or acute. Generally, younger horses with more vital force are given higher potencies than elderly ones. Higher potencies are also given for diseases that cause strong mental symptoms such as fear or depression. In cases where an organ is diseased or there is serious tissue damage, a lower potency is believed to be safer. If the remedy obtains a result, it should not usually be repeated because more does not always equal better, and homeopaths warn that overmedication is a great danger in all remedies. Most practitioners discourage using homeopathic remedies at the same time as Western drugs.

ADMINISTERING HOMEOPATHIC REMEDIES

The simplest way to give a homeopathic medication is to place the dose in a small syringe with water and then squeeze it gently into the horse's mouth. If you have the remedy in a tablet form, you can plant it inside his underlip, where the mucous membranes will absorb it.

The list of typical symptoms for which each remedy is prescribed is accompanied by what homeopaths call a "generality," which contains more information about the symptom such as "worsens with cold" or "worse at night."

COMMONLY USED HOMEOPATHIC REMEDIES IN HORSES

Homeopathic remedies should only be used under the supervision of a veterinary homeopath. Details for dosing depend on many factors and are best determined by a trained professional. It is helpful for those interested in

applying homeopathic remedies to their horse to have a homeopathic remedy kit on hand so they can administer medications as the homeopathic vet prescribes them. Many homeopaths will work over the phone with the client once they have seen the patient. The following are those most commonly used for equine conditions and illnesses:

It is easy to confuse homeopathic remedies with herbal remedies. A homeopathic remedy will clearly say "homeopathic" on the bottle.

Aconitum napellus (**Monkshood, Aconite, or Wolfbane**)

- **Parts used:** The whole plant, including the root, at the time when the plant begins to flower.
- **Applications:** Fever, anxiety, respiratory disease, systemic infection, uveitis, shipping fever, laminitis, shock, surgical recovery, exposure to weather extremes, complications from rainrot, diarrhea following a fright, tying-up syndrome to relieve muscle tension.
- **Indications:** Horses who benefit from aconite are those whose signs grow worse when exposed to the cold and who are worse at night. They often have a strong, bounding pulse and are very thirsty.
- **Note:** The active ingredient is aconite, a toxic alkaloid, but the amount used in the remedy is so minute that there are no harmful effects. It is primarily used at the first sign of any sudden ailment, especially one following a scary episode.

Aesculus hippocastanum (**Horse Chestnut**)

- **Parts used:** The whole fruit, including the capsule.
- **Applications:** Hock swellings such as bog spavin, chest congestion, and coughing, especially when the weather is cold and dry. It is sometimes used for digestive upsets as well. Signals that a horse may need this remedy include yawning, irritability, enlarged blood vessels, and pain in the sacral area.
- **Note:** The effect of this remedy is most noticeable on the bowel.

Antimonium crudum (**Black Antimony Sulfide**)

- **Parts used:** Triturations.
- **Applications:** Vesicular stomatitis.
- **Indications:** Stomach problems following too much food.

Apis mellifica (**Apis Mel or Honeybee Venom**)

- **Parts used:** The entire insect.
- **Applications:** Swelling from insect bites and bee stings, indeed any rapid hot swelling that pits on pressure (when you push on the spot with your finger, it leaves an indentation and doesn't spring back), or any allergic reaction such as hives; bog spavin; thoroughpin; windgalls; swelling under the eyes; acute navicular disease; nephritis: ovarian cysts; irritability; suspiciousness.

Arnica montana (**Leopard's Bane**)

- **Parts used:** The whole fresh plant.
- **Constituents:** Sesquiterpene lactones, which reduce inflammation and decrease pain.
- **Applications:** Bruises; trauma of any type, especially bruising; muscle or tendon inflammation; splints (first signs); corns; rainrot; before/after surgery. (Arnica helps the body reabsorb blood from bruised tissue.)
- **Indications:** Restless horses who seem sore to the

Leopard's Bane

touch or who have inflammations in joints and muscles.

- **Note:** Arnica is best used for injuries that bruise but where the skin remains unbroken. It is also a standard remedy for broodmares recovering from the birth process. (Despite its name, arnica is not really from Montana, which simply means "mountain." Arnica is a daisy-like alpine flower.) Do not apply arnica to open wounds because it can be an irritant.

Daisy

Arsenicum album (**Arsenic**)
- **Parts used:** Triturations from the toxide (active remedies diluted from the arsenic).
- **Applications:** Allergic asthma, chronic obstructive pulmonary disease, poor coat, dry and/or scaly skin, eczema, restlessness, mud fever, sweet itch, wheezing and coughing, dust allergies, appetite loss, diarrhea after eating to excess, stall-weaving.
- **Indications:** Animals needing this remedy are often restless and thirsty. The symptoms tend to be worse at night and in cold, wet conditions.
- **Note:** This remedy is often called "the horse remedy." It is especially useful in the care of thoroughbreds.

Baptisia tinctoria (**Wild Indigo**)
- **Parts used:** The fresh root and bark.
- **Applications:** Equine influenza.
- **Indications:** Horse is lethargic and weak and often stiff as well. Great muscular soreness and a putrid discharge are usually present.

Belladonna (**Deadly Nightshade**)
- **Parts used:** The flowering plant.
- **Applications:** Fever, inflamed joints, acute laminitis, convulsions, muscle twitches, earache, arthritis (where joints are swollen and hot), heatstroke, inflammation of glands, infections (when horse has a fever and full pulse), acute encephalitis.
- **Indications:** Horses who are quarrelsome, disobedient, aggressive, enraged, or fearful. Horses requiring belladonna typically have a leaping, pounding pulse. The animal may seem worse when touched or moved suddenly. Homeopaths believe that belladonna is especially useful for injuries occurring on the right side of the body. Belladonna is indicated for horses who seem to get worse in bright light. They do better with rest, warmth, and darkness.
- **Note:** Belladonna works well with aconite and is frequently used after administering that remedy.

Bellis perennis (**Daisy**)
- **Parts used:** The whole fresh plant.
- **Applications:** Deep bruising, especially around the pelvis. Even old injuries may respond.
- **Indications:** It is indicated for horses who are stiff and unwilling to move. Excellent for aged horses.
- **Note:** Bruises that do not respond to arnica may respond to bellis. Daisies, of course, are part of the natural diet of horses.

Most homeopaths discourage using homeopathic remedies at the same time as mainstream Western drugs.

Berberis vulgaris (**Barberry**)
- **Parts used:** The bark of the root.
- **Applications:** Liver and kidney dysfunction; tying-up syndrome.
- **Indications:** Horse may be twitchy and have pain when walking.

Bryonia alba (**Wild Hops, White Bryony**)
- **Parts used:** The root of the plant, before flowering takes place; also the whole fresh plant.
- **Applications:** Deep-seated, gradual-onset lameness in the muscle or bone, such as navicular disease, arthritis, bone spavin, synovitis, or tendonitis. It may be used for mastitis and to help to normalize the milk production in mares. It also can be used for dry, harsh coughs, such as those from pleurisy. It helps traveling horses who suffer from constipation and may also help those who are irritable and barn-sour.
- **Indications:** Bryonia is indicated for horses who get worse in the evening, upon rising, and after eating.
- **Note:** It has sometimes been called the "grumpy bear" remedy, although its efficacy on bears is not documented.

Marigold

Calcarea carbonica (**Oyster Shell**)
- **Parts used:** Trituration and distillation in water of oyster shell.
- **Applications:** Ringbone, splint, osteochondritis dissecans (developmental disease of the bone), respiratory problems, facial warts.
- **Indications:** Horses requiring this remedy are often stubborn or aggressive. This is a particularly potent remedy for warmbloods.

Calcarea fluorica (**"Calc Fluor," Fluoride of Lime**)
- **Parts used:** Fluoride of lime.
- **Applications:** A variety of aliments due to overstraining the muscles or bones; also pedal ostitis, navicular disease, bad teeth, laminitis, splints, corns, ringbone, sesamoiditis (inflammation of the sesamoid bones).
- **Indications:** Horses requiring this remedy are often worse when the weather changes. They may crave salt.

Calendula officinalis (**Marigold**)
- **Parts used:** Leaves and flowers.
- **Applications:** Wound healing. It promotes rapid healing and granulation of the tissue.
- **Indications:** This remedy is especially indicated with horses who seem to be worse in damp weather.
- **Note:** Do not use in cases of deep puncture wounds because it can irritate them further.

Carbo vegetabilis (**Vegetable Charcoal, "Carbo Veg"**)
- **Parts used:** Trituration of the vegetable charcoal from beech, poplar, or birch.
- **Applications:** Cases of sudden collapse, surgical support. It is a well-known remedy for flatulent colic, constipation, bronchitis with wheezing, poor digestion.
- **Indications:** Horses requiring this remedy are usually worse in damp weather and react badly to changes in temperature. It is especially good for obese horses and horses who do not appear to have fully recovered from illness.

Causticum (**Potassium Hydrate**)
- **Parts used:** A distillation of equal parts slaked lime, EPM (electrolytic pH modifier), potassium bisulfate.

- **Applications:** Paralysis, especial facial paralysis of the right side; wobblers. It is given to clear warts that are resistant to thuja (another homeopathic remedy).
- **Indications:** Horses requiring this remedy are usually worse in dry, cold, windy weather.

China (**Cinchona**)
- **Parts used:** The bulb of this Peruvian plant.
- **Applications:** Dehydration and shock.
- **Indications:** The horse is unusually sensitive to noise and irritable around the ears.

Cicuta virosa (**Water Hemlock**)
- **Parts used:** The fresh root when the plant flowers.
- **Applications:** Adjunct therapy in cases of tetanus, fits, convulsions.
- **Indications:** Horse will have a stiff neck and tight muscles.
- **Note:** Remember, this is a homeopathic remedy. Do *not* give your horse the fresh or dried herb; it can kill him.

Colchicum (**Meadow Saffron**)
- **Parts used:** Spring bulbs.
- **Applications:** Gas-related colic or bloat, especially if the signs are acute and severe and arise from eating excessive amounts of clover.
- **Indications:** Horses who seem worse at night.

Colocynthus (**Bitter or Squirting Cucumber, Bitter Apple**)
- **Parts used:** Pulped fruit.
- **Applications:** Gaseous or tympanitic colic of unknown cause.
- **Indications:** Horses requiring this remedy tend to be worse in the evening.

Cuprum metallicum (**Copper**)
- **Parts used:** Trituration of the metal.
- **Applications:** Muscle cramping or other myositis in performance horses, especially jumpers and racers.
- **Indications:** Horses requiring this remedy are usually worse in the cold.

Curare (**Arrow Poison**)
- **Parts used:** Dilution of the poison in alcohol.
- **Applications:** Post-influenza weakness.
- **Indications:** Horse has slow reflexes, nervous debility, or trembling.
- **Note:** Curare in any normal dose is deadly.

Dulcamara (**Woody Nightshade**)
- **Parts used:** Fresh leaves before flowering.
- **Applications:** Colic.
- **Indications:** Horse seems chilled and wet. Horses with allergies seem to benefit most.

Echinacea (**Purple Cone Flower**)
- **Parts used:** Flower and roots.
- **Applications:** Infected tissue, including postpartum infections. It also can be given in low doses to horses worn down by illness or infection.
- **Indications:** Horse may seem tight in the chest.

Homeopathic remedies should be stored away from direct sunlight and extreme temperatures. They should also be kept away from strong electromagnetic fields such as those generated by a microwave oven.

Purple Cone Flower

Homeopathic remedies are said to work by stimulating the body's own healing processes.

Elaps corallinus (**Coral Snake**)
- **Parts used:** Coral snake venom triturated with sugar of milk.
- **Applications:** Tying-up syndrome.
- **Indications:** Extremities may feel icy cold.

Eupatorium perfoliatum (**Thoroughwart or Boneset**)
- **Parts used:** Whole plant.
- **Applications:** Influenza, windgalls, synovitis.
- **Indications:** Horse may have stiffness and bone pain.

Euphorbium (**Spurge Gum**)
- **Parts used:** Resin.
- **Applications:** Gaseous colic.
- **Indications:** Horse also may have a runny nose or sinusitis.

Euphrasia (**Eyebright**)
- **Parts used:** Whole plant.
- **Applications:** Diseases of the eye, applied both orally and topically. Acute conjunctivitis, corneal abrasions, stubborn uveitis.
- **Indications:** Horses requiring this remedy typically have eyes that water in sunlight. They tend to be worse in the dark or when the wind is southerly.

Ferrum phosphorus (**Phosphate of Iron**)
- **Parts used:** Trituration of the salt.
- **Applications:** To alleviate early inflammatory conditions that fail to respond to aconitum. It is good for bleeders.
- **Indications:** Horses requiring this remedy are usually nervous and sensitive.

Gelsemium sempervirens (**Yellow Jasmine**)
- **Parts used:** Bark of the root.
- **Applications:** Equine influenza and radial paralysis.
- **Indications:** Horses requiring this remedy are usually worse in damp weather.

Graphites (**Plumbago or Black Lead**)
- **Parts used:** Triturations of finely divided black lead.
- **Applications:** Skin conditions that produce a clear, wet, sticky discharge, such as greasy heel; mud fever; brittle hoofs; sweet itch; rainrot; ear infections with discharge.
- **Indications:** Overweight horse with unhealthy looking skin.

Hamamelis (**Witch Hazel**)
- **Parts used:** Root and fresh bark of the plant.
- **Applications:** Remedy for venous bleeding and nosebleeds.
- **Indications:** This remedy is indicated for horses who are worse in humid conditions.
- **Note:** It is similar to Veg Carb but used for less extreme conditions.

Hecla lava (**Volcanic Ash**)
- **Parts used:** Prepared from the trituration of the ash.
- **Applications:** Skeletal and lymphoid systems.
- **Indications:** Navicular disease, ringbone, dental and

St. John's Wort

facial bone problems, including tumors on the bone.
- **Note:** The ash contains alumina, lime, and silica.

Hepar sulphuris calcareum (**Hepar Sulph**)
- **Parts used:** Ash resulting from burning calcium carbonate (oyster shells) and sulfur.
- **Applications:** Chronic abscesses, hoof infections, swollen glands, respiratory diseases that produce pus, fistulas.
- **Indications:** Horses requiring this remedy are typically irritable on approach and seem worse in cold drafts.

Hypericum perforatum (**Saint John's Wort**)
- **Parts used:** Whole fresh plant.
- **Applications:** Radial paralysis and other nerve injuries (including spinal injuries), puncture wounds that can lead to exposure to tetanus toxin. It also may heal proud flesh.
- **Indications:** Horses requiring this remedy are typically worse on movement and in damp air.

Club Moss

Kali bichromicum (**Potassium Bichromate**)
- **Parts used:** This is a potassium salt of chromium.
- **Applications:** Windgall, greasy heel, cellulites, and lymphangitis.
- **Indications:** Horse may have a stuffy nose.

Kali phosphoricum (**Kali Phos**)
- **Parts used:** Phosphate of potassium.
- **Applications:** Stress, anxiety, exhaustion, weakness in the back or legs. It is believed to act on the nervous system and is helpful for horses recovering from surgery or illness.
- **Indications:** May be useful during early tumor formation.

Lathyrus (**Chickpea**)
- **Parts used:** The remedy is prepared from the flower or pods.
- **Applications:** Diseases of the urinary system, extremities, respiratory system, and gastrointestinal system. Grass sickness, roaring, and after a bout of influenza.
- **Indications:** Can be used in cases considered hopeless.

Ledum palustre (**Marsh Tea**)
- **Parts used:** Whole fresh plant.
- **Applications:** Used with hypericum (in alternate dosings) to guard against tetanus, as it is specific for deep puncture wounds. It is also used for painful bruising and joint problems, especially the hock.
- **Indications:** Horses requiring this remedy are often worse when warm.

Lobelia inflata (**Indian Tobacco**)
- **Parts used:** Dried leaves.
- **Applications:** Convalescence after a bout of influenza. Also good for gastric upset.
- **Indications:** Horse may have weak or flabby muscle tone.

Lycopodium (**Club Moss**)
- **Parts used:** Spores or the whole plant.

In general, higher potencies work for longer periods of time than lower potencies.

- **Applications:** Chronic colic or for horses with depraved appetite.
- **Indications:** Horse may have swollen, tighten pasterns.

Magnesia phosphorica (**Magnesium Phosphate**)
- **Parts used:** Solution distilled in water.
- **Applications:** Gaseous colic.
- **Indications:** Horse may have twitchy eyes and legs.

Millefolium (**Yarrow**)
- **Parts used:** Whole fresh plant
- **Applications:** Hemorrhage after an injury.
- **Indications:** Any bleeding.
- **Note:** This remedy also can help in cases of poisoning.

Nux vomica (**Poison Nut**)
- **Parts used:** Trituration of seeds.
- **Applications:** Horses requiring this remedy are usually worse early in the morning and don't wish to be touched. They improve with rest. This remedy is used mostly with male horses.
- **Indications:** Digestive upsets, including grass colic (mild), bowel blockage, and constipation; laminitis; COPD.
- **Note:** Nux vomica is also a good remedy to start with in many diseases, as it is supposed to clear away the bad effects of previous medications.

Phosphorus (**Phosphorus**)
- **Parts used:** Trituration of red phosphorus.
- **Applications:** Alleviates profuse bleeding and can be used after surgery. Also very important for use in rapid-onset pneumonia.
- **Indications:** Weak, rapid pulse; tenderness in the stomach area. Horse may seem frightened.

Plumbum metallicum (**Lead**)
- **Parts used:** Trituration with lactose.
- **Applications:** Grass sickness in its sub-acute stage, radial paralysis.
- **Indications:** Best used in mares. Stool may seem sticky.

Pulsatilla (**Windflower, Pasque Flower**)
- **Parts used:** Whole fresh plant.
- **Applications:** Shyness with gentle mares, mastitis, irregular season, ovarian underactivity, chronic coughing with thick yellow discharge, conjunctivitis.
- **Indications:** Pulsatilla is associated with mares and often used for inflammation of the reproductive system. Generally, the mare has a gentle or sad disposition. Symptoms are usually worse in heat but better in motion and in the open air. The animal may not exhibit much thirst.

Rhus toxicodendron, Rhus Tox (**Poison Ivy or Poison Oak**)
- **Parts used:** Fresh leaves before flowering.
- **Applications**: Tendon/ligament sprains, bone

Homeopathy appears to have no side effects.

Pulsatilla

spavins, conjunctivitis, skin infections, muscle soreness, arthritis that improves with movement. It also can be used to treat Lyme disease.

- **Indications:** Horses requiring this remedy are worse in damp, cold weather.
- **Note:** Rhus Tox is sometimes called the "creaking gate" remedy because it helps with stiffness.

Ruta Graveolens (Rue, "Ruta Grav")

- **Parts used:** Whole, fresh plant.
- **Applications:** Damaged connective tissue, such as cartilage, also for cannon bone injuries.
- **Indications:** Horses requiring this remedy are worse when the weather is cold.

Scutellaria (Skullcap)

- **Parts used:** Fresh plant.
- **Applications:** Nervousness and muscle twitching.
- **Indications:** Works best on highly strung horses.
- **Note:** It does not cause drowsiness.

Sepia (Ink of the Cuttlefish)

- **Parts used:** Dried liquid.
- **Applications:** Female reproductive system and with mares indifferent to their young. But it is also used for skin problems such as abscesses and fungal infections like ringworm.
- **Indications:** Useful for individuals who show lack of interest and those suffering from physical overexertion and fatigue.
- **Note:** Its use is similar to pulsatilla except that the sepia horse tends to be more unpredictable.

Silicea or *Silica* (Flint, Silicon Dioxide)

- **Parts used:** Pure flint.
- **Applications:** Poll-evil, abscesses, cysts, fistulous withers, chronic foot infections, sand crack. It is also used for bone problems and deep wounds, conjunctivitis, and slow-healing infections.
- **Indications:** Horses requiring this remedy are worse with cold.

Sulfur (Sulphur or Pure Flint)

- **Parts used:** Solution in alcohol.
- **Applications:** This is a deep-acting remedy used for chronic dry, red, hot, itchy skin conditions. It is also useful for allergies, insect stings, sweet itch, ear mites, and arthritis. Sulphur is most effective for recurring complaints.
- **Indications:** Horses requiring this remedy are typically constantly hungry and may crib. They are worse in the heat.
- **Note:** Sulfur also aids the power of many other homeopathic remedies.

Thuja occidentalis (Arborvitae)

- **Parts used:** Fresh green twigs.
- **Applications:** Warts around the scrotum and sheath. It is also recommended against negative effects of vaccinations and for skin conditions and spinal cord problems.

Homeopathic remedies are derived mostly from plants and minerals or taken from animal sources, usually in the form of secretions such as snake venom or bee sting.

Special licenses are required for veterinary homeopaths in Arizona, Connecticut, and Nevada.

BIOCHEMIC TISSUE SALT THERAPY

This therapy was developed in the 1870s by Wilhelm Schuessler (1822–1898), a German homeopathic physician. It is related to homeopathy because it is actually based on 12 potentized mineral salts he called tissue salts. (They are also called cell salts.) His theory was that imbalance or a deficiency of any of the tissue salts causes disease, which can be rectified and body equilibrium reestablished by administering the same mineral salts in small quantities. Tissue salts are naturally part of the body, but Schuessler believed that if they are potentiated like homeopathic remedies, they can be used as preventives or to treat existing conditions.

HOW IT WORKS

Preparation involves mixing one part of the mineral salt with nine parts lactose. This mixture is diluted again with nine parts lactose. The process is repeated six times in total. The tissue salts are available as tablets to dissolve in the mouth. The most common prescription is three tablets twice daily for three weeks. For acute problems, you can double or triple the frequency.

Tissue salts are extremely safe and free of side effects, but for best results, practitioners warn not to touch the tablets with your hands as this might contaminate them. This handling precaution applies to all homeopathic remedies.

These 12 main tissue salts are:

Calcium Fluoride (Calc Fluor): Called the "elasticity salt," it is useful for problems in connective tissue, bone, teeth, muscle, and ligaments.

Calcium Phosphate (Calc Phos): This "nutrition salt" is used to help cell development, especially in the bones, muscles, and blood. This is a "general nutrition" salt.

Calcium Sulfate (Calc Sulph): Calc Sulph is a blood purifier; it is also used to treat purulent (pus-like) discharges from wounds.

Iron Phosphate (*Ferrum phosphoricum* or Ferr Phos): Ferr Phos is an anti-inflammation salt used for localized infection with acute pain and heat. It is said to boost the oxygen capacity of the blood and is helpful if given twice a day three days before surgery.

Magnesium Phosphate (Mag Phos): Mag Phos is a neuromuscular coordinator and nerve relaxant used for any condition arising from trouble between the muscles and nerves. It can be used to relieve muscle spasm. It works well with thiamine and valerian for calming a skittish horse.

Natrum Muriaticum (Nat Mur): Nat Mur is used to treat hives. It is considered a "water distributor" and is used to treat sneezing, dry mucous membranes, and muscle soreness due to muscle fatigue. Nat Mur is just another way of saying sodium chloride, or table salt.

Potassium Chloride (Kali Mur): Kali Mur is used to remove congestion and to treat slow-healing injuries and puffy legs.

Potassium Phosphate (Kali Phos): Kali Phos is the "nerve nutrient salt," and it is used for horses who are irritable, depressed, or nervous.

Potassium Sulfate (Kali Sulph): This "skin salt" restores oxygen to the cells and is used for mucous discharges, inflammation, and flaky, dry skin.

Silica: This is the "calcium reorganizer" salt and is used for conditions in which there is an abnormal calcification of the bone. It is known as the "cleanser."

Sodium Sulfate (Nat Sulph): Nat Sulph regulates the density of intercellular fluid and helps the body eliminate toxins.

- **Indications:** Horses requiring this remedy are typically worse in wet, cold weather.
- **Note:** It is used more for chronic than for acute signs.

Veratrum album (**White Hellebore**)
- **Parts used:** Fresh roots.
- **Applications:** Gaseous or flatulent colic.
- **Indications:** Horse may have gushing, watery diarrhea.

Zincum metallicum (**Zinc**)
- **Parts used:** Trituration with lactose.
- **Applications:** Recurrent cases of gaseous colic and anemia.
- **Indications:** The horse will have a fever.

Zingiber (**Ginger**)
- **Parts used:** Dried rhizome.
- **Applications:** Gaseous colic.
- **Indications:** Any symptom of digestive upset.

A NONTOXIC ALTERNATIVE

Many holistic practitioners and horse owners prefer using homeopathy, alone or in combination with other therapies, because it offers a safer, more natural, or gentler alternative to mainstream care. It's true that it is natural: Homeopathic remedies are derived mostly from plants and minerals or taken from animal sources, usually in the form of secretions such as snake venom or bee sting. And because these remedies consist of the tiniest microdoses, proponents maintain that they are completely nontoxic and without side effects when used properly, making them a safe form of health treatment. But again, bear in mind that conventional veterinary care may be mandatory for more serious or life-threatening illnesses. Always consult your vet prior to beginning any new treatment plan.

Chapter 7

Western Herbal Medicine

*H*orses are natural herbalists. After all, they have been grazing on plants for millions of years. Wild horses may possibly even possess deep-seated inner knowledge about which herbs are good for the immune system or which ones might prevent colic. Whether today's horse has the same instincts is more debatable, however. Most of the time, modern horses depend on their owners to care for their health care needs.

ADVANTAGES
- HERBAL MEDICATIONS AND SUPPLEMENTS ARE AVAILABLE WITHOUT A PRESCRIPTION.
- SOME ARE VERY EFFECTIVE; MANY ARE THE SOURCES OF MAINSTREAM VETERINARY MEDICATIONS.
- SOME ARE QUITE PALATABLE TO HORSES.
- THE ACTIVE INGREDIENT IS IN A MORE "NATURAL" STATE AND MAY PRODUCE FEWER SIDE EFFECTS THAN THOSE OF STANDARD MEDICATIONS.

DISADVANTAGES
- HERBS CAN BE TOXIC AS WELL AS HEALING.
- SOME ARE DIFFICULT TO PREPARE AND ADMINISTER.
- THEY ARE NOT USUALLY AVAILABLE IN CAREFULLY CALIBRATED STRENGTHS; THERE IS A WIDE RANGE OF EFFECTIVENESS/TOXICITY BETWEEN BATCHES.
- SOURCES ARE NOT CAREFULLY REGULATED.
- GATHERING WILD HERBS CAN BE DISASTROUS TO THE ENVIRONMENT.

NATURAL HERBS

Herbal medicine can be strong stuff. In fact, these remedies can accurately be called "drugs," a word that originally meant "dried herbs." After all, they are the basis of many modern pharmaceuticals. Herbs are not magical, although you can buy books on magical ones. (Those herbs must have spells put on them, I suspect!) They can be used in the same way ordinary medicines are, and they work basically in the same way. Like regular medicine, they can be toxic, irritating, or ineffective. They also can cure.

Many horse owners prefer to use natural herbs rather than the synthetic drugs derived from them because they feel that herbs work in a gentler and more gradual manner and are less likely to produce dangerous side effects. However, it is well to remember that "natural" does not always equal "safe." Rattlesnake venom is natural. Castor beans, the source of the deadly toxin ricin, are natural. So be aware that herbal medicine can be extremely strong, and proceed with caution. Better yet, don't proceed at all unless you are guided by a competent herbal practitioner, such as a veterinarian who uses herbs. Herbs can contain anthraquinones, coumarin, oxalic acid, alkaloids, salicylates, saponins, sterols, tannins, and volatile oils—all of which can be dangerous in the wrong doses or when used for the wrong ailment.

In most varieties of Western botanical medicine, herbs are classified by their action on body processes and not with reference to specific diseases, so it's vital for the practitioner to fully understand the way the body functions. As you learn the effects of certain herbs, you can administer them more confidently. But herbology is such a complex topic that the average person can expect to learn the uses of no more than half a dozen or so plants.

Caution: Same Plant, Different Dose
Keep in mind that while homeopathy and herbal medicine may be based on the same plant material, these are not interchangeable remedies. Homeopathy uses minute quantities of herbs that are shaken and vastly diluted. It also makes use of ingredients that would be lethal if taken in the same manner as an herb.

EFFICACY

One problem with herbs is their efficacy can be hard to validate scientifically. That's because most scientific analysis requires the breaking down of an herb into its constituent parts. And that, herbalists claim, is the problem because herbs are meant to work "holistically;" the very splitting apart that is needed to analyze them destroys their efficacy. Also, say herbalists, isolating the various components of natural herbs may create a physical dependency and depress the body's ability to extract needed nutrients from whole foods. They believe that whole herbs retain all the necessary ingredients to balance the so-called "active" ingredients and thus transport to the body a more thoroughly balanced substance that will produce better healing. You might compare it to the Mona Lisa—break it down and all you have are innumerable specks of dried paint splattered on a canvas. Only when taken as a whole does the power, beauty, and mystery of the painting emerge. Proponents of contemporary Western medicine might roll their eyes at my analogy, though, because they regularly take apart and reassemble various drug components all the time to examine how they work and to make them work better.

THE NAME'S THE GAME

All plants and animals have two names: their common everyday one, such as catnip, and their scientific one, for catnip, *Nepeta cataria*. All scientific names have at least two parts: The first part is the genus name and the second is the species name. If a subspecies is referred to, that name follows the species name. The whole thing is written in italics, with the first letter of the genus name capitalized and the rest not. For example, we modern humans are *Homo sapiens sapiens*, to differentiate us from ancient European humans, the *Homo sapiens neanderthalis*. Sometimes a

In the wild, horses are natural herbalists.

"manmade" form or cultivar is added to the species name; that is not italicized.

Curiously, it is done this way all over the world, even in countries like Saudi Arabia and China, regardless of the fact that they do not use a Latin alphabet. It is really important to use the scientific name when buying herbs, also. For one thing, an herb might have two everyday names: "catnip" and "cat mint" both refer to *Nepeta cataria*. Or two completely different plants might go by the same common name. The term milk thistle, for instance, usually refers to *Silybum marianum*, which also can be called St. Mary's thistle, but it also may refer to *Sonchus oleraceus*, which can be called sow thistle. So, you see, common names can be even more confusing than the scientific ones.

DRIED OR FRESH

There can be a difference in potency between fresh and dried herbs. In some cases, the fresh herb is more potent, and in some cases it's the dried herb. In a few cases, *only* the fresh herb or *only* the dried herb is really effective. Some herbs need at least partial drying to be effective. It is easy to serve fresh herbs to your horse—simply add some leaves to his feed (but make sure that he eats them). Quite often, a small handful of the chosen herb once or twice a day is sufficient.

Dried herbs are most commonly used because they can be readily purchased. Dried herbs obviously keep longer than fresh ones, and roots keep longer than leafy material. However, a few herbs lose most of their potency within a few days after they are dried, and all herbs lose some of their power over time.

How to Judge Herbal Quality

Whether you use herbs to treat an ailment or to supplement a diet, it's important to be able to judge their quality. Dried herbs, if they are well prepared, should look, smell, and taste very much like their fresh counterparts.

Store your herbs in amber glass if possible, out of sunlight and in a cool area (but not in the refrigerator). Carefully label and date every herb you use. If properly prepared and stored, herbal flowers will last one year, and bark and root products will last two years. For the very best quality, grow your own herbs! That way you will know that you have not poisoned their birthplace with pesticides.

Gathering Wild Herbs

It may be a tempting idea, but the wild harvesting of herbs is a bad idea for several reasons:

- It's easy to get confused and pick the wrong one. Some deadly herbs bear a scary resemblance to harmless and helpful ones. Play it safe and purchase your herbs from a reputable dealer, or raise your own.
- Wild herbs may have been sprayed with pesticides, soaked with exhaust fumes, urinated on by dogs or wildlife, or infested with strange molds.
- The wild gathering of some herbs has led to their decimation and in some cases almost complete extinction. (Goldenseal is a perfect example.) Protect Mother Earth and purchase your herbs from a reputable dealer who grows them.
- Gathering wild herbs is illegal in some places.

Potency Variance

Most herbs are not officially classed as "medicine" and are not under the aegis of the Food and Drug Administration (FDA). Independent testing has shown that two apparently similar bunches of herbs may include widely varying amounts of the active ingredient. Also, herbs work more slowly than standard medicines, so you have to be patient.

USE OF HERBS IN NATURAL CARE

Herbs have several different roles in a holistic equine health care plan:

- prevention
- tonifying
- recovery and aid to healing
- as primary or adjunctive therapy in the treatment of illness

Many commercial companies sell herb mixtures designed to address specific problems. These are convenient but are not suitable when fresh herbs are required or preferred.

ADMINISTRATION OF HERBS

Herbs can be used for various purposes. For example, they can be used as a dietary supplement or as a treatment for an illness, and as such, they are administered in different forms.

THE EASY WAY

You can sometimes add dried herbs (leaves and flowers only) to your horse's feed without having to cook them first, but don't overdo it. Roots need to be ground up before being added. Because many horses object to the taste of medicinal herbs, it's important to gradually increase the amount in your horse's feed over a period of several days.

Herbal medicine can be extremely strong, so don't administer it to your horse unless you are guided by a competent herbal practitioner.

If you are using dried leafy herbs, perhaps the easiest and most effective way to serve them is to soak them overnight in apple cider vinegar. Don't strain them, but add them just as they are to your horse's food. It is believed that vinegar acts as a catalyst to the herbal action. Do not let this mixture sit around, though. You don't want the herbs to ferment! You cannot use this method for roots, bark, or seeds unless they are thoroughly ground up first.

CAPSULES

Some herbs are obtainable in capsules. You can use these with your horse, but because they are mostly designed for smaller animals, you'll need a lot of them. This can be expensive as well.

EXTRACTS

Some herbs are extracted with alcohol or glycerin in tinctures. A tincture is a solution of the herb in alcohol or water and alcohol. An alcohol tincture is the strongest and probably the most versatile way to prepare an herb. Alcohol is a strong solvent, so when you place a fresh or dried herb in a mixture of water and pure grain alcohol, the alcohol extracts the active ingredients from the herb. This product is called a menstruum. The amount of alcohol needed to make a menstruum depends on the herb. After a varying period of time, depending on the herb, the menstruum is strained and pressed. The liquid product contains the strong active ingredients and can be stored for a long time. The big problem is that the tincture is usually about 50 percent (at least) alcohol, and horses aren't crazy about the taste (wisely). There is also some controversy about the use of alcohol in herbs prepared for horses, with some practitioners maintaining that it can cause fermentation in the horse's gut. Others assert that alcohol is absolutely necessary to trigger a catalytic response in the body.

Glycerin-extracted herbs are much more palatable than alcohol-extracted ones. The glycerin is usually obtained from coconut oils. These are not as strong as alcohol extracts and have a shorter shelf life (just a year or so). However, their benefits may outweigh the drawbacks.

Furthermore, horses have a very long digestive tract, which makes using fresh or dried herbs rather than extracts a more attractive option. (Carnivores have a shorter digestive tract, which makes it more difficult for them to get the direct benefit of herbs.)

Herbal Teas (Infusions)

More traditionally, and most simply, herbs are administered through an infusion or decoction. An infusion is just a fancy word for tea made from the leaves or flowers of the herb. These teas are most useful for conditions of the skin and coat, as well as for a general tonic.

To make a tea, just pour boiling water over the fresh or dried herb. Cover tightly, and let it steep for 10 to 15 minutes. (The time is not usually critical, but steeping the herb for a much longer period may inactivate the important agents.) Strain the material, and place it in a container. Then pour the liquid over the feed. Depending on the size of your horse, the kind of herb, and the seriousness of your horse's condition, you may need anywhere from 1 to 4 cups (1 cup=240 ml). It's best to make it fresh every day, although you can store it for a week or two in a cool spot away from sunlight.

The main problem with teas is that they are so diffuse that they have a weak effect. You have to give your horse a lot of tea before you'll bring about any changes. You also can use an herbal infusion to bathe the skin.

Decoctions

You also can make a decoction, which is used to prepare heavier, denser plant material like roots, seeds, or bark. These materials need to be ground into a powder before preparing. The word "decoction" simply refers to the liquid made by boiling the ground herb in water.

Place the material in a pot and simmer (do not boil) for 20 minutes. Let it cool for another 15 minutes. Strain the herb, and serve it the same way as an infusion. Decoctions tend to be stronger than infusions.

For all dosages, follow the advice of the veterinary herbal practitioner. A cup (240 ml) should be the maximum dose, and many herbs should be administered in much smaller doses. If you are combining herbs, the maximum for the combination should still not be more than 1 cup (240 ml) unless your vet directs otherwise. Don't administer more than three doses a day.

External Use for Poultices, Compresses, and Salves

You can use either dried or fresh herbs for a poultice. A poultice is a bandage or wrap, and its main purpose is to reduce inflammation or swelling. Typically, a hot poultice (a "sweat") is used to draw out infection and speed healing, while a cold poultice is used to reduce swelling and inflammation. A hot poultice is also used to increase circulation in the affected area.

When making a poultice, the herbs are spread on a cloth and rolled into a bandage. Chamomile, cleavers, kelp, marshmallow, and slippery elm are all good for this purpose. Preparation begins with mashing the herbs with water or vegetable oil until they form a paste. Then they are folded into a washcloth or other soft material. The warm or cool cloth is placed on the horse and held on the affected area until the cloth is at body temperature. This process may be repeated several times. It's important never to leave a poultice on for more than 12 hours and to be careful to wash the area thoroughly afterward. If you don't want to make your own, commercial poultices are available.

You also can make a compress. However, a compress requires advance preparation, so it won't work in an emergency unless you have the material already prepared. To make a compress, fresh herbs are placed in an airtight container filled with vegetable oil. After three days, you can strain the oil, dip a cloth in it, and apply it to your horse just as you would a poultice.

Salves are another option and offer a different type of application because they are thicker and pastier and placed directly on the skin. To make a salve of the chosen herb, a good oil is used as a base, the ground herb is placed in the oil, then cocoa butter or beeswax is added. You can store this in your refrigerator for several months.

Some people recommend using cold-pressed, organic olive oil to make compresses. Olive oil has good preservative qualities, but be aware that this oil may be too acidic for the skin of sensitive horses.

Use as Internal Medicine

Herbs tend to work more slowly than conventional drugs. While this can be dangerous in an emergency, most conditions for which herbal remedies may be used are not life threatening. Herbalists believe that the slower route of action results in a better cure. In general, herbs are most useful in the treatment of chronic ailments.

Just as with conventional medicines, some herbs treat the disease, while others only alleviate the signs of the disease. Symptomatic treatment can be better than nothing—for instance, there is no cure for a cold, so we treat it symptomatically. However, if the underlying condition itself can be treated, it's obviously better to get at the root cause than to try to camouflage it.

COMMON HERBS AND THEIR USES

The following are herbs commonly used with horses. (It's always a good idea to check with your vet before using them.)

Aloe Vera (*aloe spp.*)
- **Parts used:** Juice of the leaves.
- **Action:** Internally, used as a stimulating purgative. Externally, used as a healing herb and emollient.
- **Indications:** Ulcers (taken internally); wound healing (externally); tendon injuries (externally); to counter the side effects of NSAIDS (internally); mud fever (external); gastric ulcers (internal); immunostimulant (internally); appetite stimulant. Also can be sprayed directly onto ringworm.
- **Preparation:** Place directly in the horse's mouth when using internally, or place in food or drinking water. Water not drunk or food not eaten should be discarded.
- **Note:** This herb has been in therapeutic use for 5,500 years. Aloe should be used cautiously when taken internally. This plant is actually a member of the lily family. Do not give a product meant for external use internally. Aloe vera should not be used as a dewormer, although some people do so.

Angelica (*Angelica sinensis* or *Angelica archangelica*)
- **Parts used:** Root powder, leaves, and stems.
- **Action:** Reduces flatulence and expels gas from the intestines; diaphoretic; stomachic; tonic; expectorant.
- **Indications:** Muscle damage; problems in the female reproductive system. Also serves to increase perspiration and stimulate gastric juices.
- **Preparation:** Externally, it can be used as a poultice for arthritis and chest problems. The essential oil from the root can be used as a general tonic. Syrup made from the stems and leaves can be stored and diluted. Tea made from the dried leaves soothes nerves, coughs, and arthritis.
- **Note:** Angelica is a robust, aromatic, short-lived perennial. It is considered a "warming herb." Some experts advise against its internal use, although it has been used successfully for thousands of years. In any case, horses taking angelica should not be exposed to direct sunlight. The plant bears a close resemblance to

Herbs are classified by their action on body processes and not with reference to specific diseases, so it's vital for the practitioner to fully understand the way the body functions.

deadly water hemlock—don't get them mixed up. Never feed this herb during gestation.

Aniseed (*Illicium verum*)

- **Parts used:** Dried seed or fruit.
- **Action:** Expectorant.
- **Indications:** Coughs that spring from secondary bacterial infection. Also used to treat poor appetite, hives, colic, bloating, wind, or gas.
- **Preparation:** A tea is normally brewed from the fruit after being lightly crushed before brewing. Aniseed can be used with eucalyptus as a chest rub for bronchial and respiratory complaints and also as a rub for external parasites.
- **Note:** Aniseed, a Mediterranean plant, is an annual, aromatic cousin of fennel and has many of the same qualities. This plant also can be prepared as an essential oil.

Arnica (*arnica spp.*)

- **Parts used:** Whole flowering plant, fresh or dried.
- **Action:** Works on the muscles and capillaries; discutient.
- **Indications:** Wound healing, including closed tissue injuries, sprain, and fractures; sore muscles; inflammation from insect bites; swellings from fractures; bruises.
- **Preparation:** This can be given as an infusion or poultice, but you also can buy a commercially made gel, cream, ointment, liniment, salve, or tincture. Arnica should only be used internally by licensed veterinarians; only very dilute tinctures should be used.
- **Note:** Arnica is an aromatic, bitter, fragrant rhizomatous perennial with basal hairy leaves and yellow daisy-like flowers. In fact, it is a member of the sunflower family. It is generally found in mountainous areas of Canada, the northern United States, and Europe. Do not use arnica internally because it can produce serious side effects such as dizziness and tremors. Prolonged use may irritate the skin.

Astragalus (*Astragalus membranaceus*)

- **Parts used:** Mature (at least three years old) roots.
- **Action:** Immunostimulant; antiviral; anti-inflammatory; diuretic.
- **Indications:** Viral infections of the respiratory tract and heart. It improves adrenal gland and digestive function.
- **Preparation:** It can be prepared as a tincture or infusion.
- **Note:** This perennial plant with small yellow flowers, a thick root, and a yellowish, tough skin, is native to northern China and Mongolia. It is a member of the pea family. The herb is used mostly in traditional Chinese medicine but is also used for Western therapies, especially as an immune system booster. Scientists have isolated a number of active ingredients, including bioflavonoids, choline, and a polysaccharide called *Astragalan B*, which seems to control bacterial infections, stimulating the immune system and protecting the body against toxins. This herb should not be taken in the presence of fever or during an illness.

Bladderwrack or Kelp (*Fucus vesiculosus*)

- **Parts used:** Dried mass of root, stem, and leaves.

Bladderwrack Seaweed

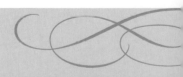

- **Action:** Alterative; nutritional.
- **Indications:** Hypothyroidism (it balances the metabolism in horses receiving insufficient iodine); coat and hoof conditioning; helps to shed the winter coat; aids muscle development in young horses; restores balance to the intestinal system after worming; arthritis.
- **Preparation:** Bladderwrack can be taken internally or used externally as a poultice.
- **Note:** Bladderwrack is found in northern oceans only. It is an excellent source of iodine, which is very important for the thyroid gland. Bay and chestnut horses get a real bloom on them from bladderwrack, but be careful of your source. Seaweeds such as bladderwrack are very beneficial but also prone to picking up heavy metals and other contaminants that may be on a dirty beach.

Avoid the "shotgun" approach when giving herbs. More is not necessarily better. It often can be ineffectual, or worse, downright harmful. In many cases you will find that you only need to use a small (not homeopathic small, but small nonetheless) dose to trigger the desired effect—the horse can do the rest by himself.

Burdock (*Arctium lappa*)

- **Parts used:** Root.
- **Action:** This bitter herb is a general internal cleanser and diuretic. It stimulates the liver.
- **Indications:** Skin conditions that do not respond to topical treatment such as eczema and allergies; blood purifier; laminitis. Helps horses with a poor appetite.
- **Preparation:** Burdock can be purchased as a dried root powder, decoction, tincture, or fluid extract.
- **Note:** Burdock is a biennial herb grown in China, Europe, and the United States. Use of burdock root goes back to the Middle Ages. The roots of burdock closely resemble those of belladonna or deadly nightshade, so buy only from a reputable source. Burdock combines well with dandelion, and it's safe for long-term use. Do not give it to pregnant mares because it may damage the fetus.

Calendula or Pot Marigold (*Calendula officinalis*)

- **Parts used:** Crushed petals or whole flower heads. When harvesting the flowers, remove the flowers and separate the petals.
- **Action:** Antifungal; astringent; antispasmodic; antibacterial; anti-inflammatory. There is evidence recommending calendula for some viral infections.
- **Indications:** Wound healing; burns; dermatitis; digestive tract. It has also been shown to stimulate the development of granulation tissue.
- **Preparation:** You can use the dried herb or you can make an infusion from the fresh petals. Aromatherapists use calendula oil for its skin-healing properties.
- **Note:** Calendula is a bushy, aromatic annual that can be used both internally and externally. It is propagated easily by seed in fall or spring. Do not give to pregnant mares.

Cayenne (*Capsicum spp.*)

- **Parts used:** Dried seed pod.
- **Action:** Dilates blood vessels; helps the skin. Cayenne pepper has a tonic, antiseptic effect, stimulating the circulatory and digestive systems and increasing perspiration. Although it is a "hot" spice, it has many cooling properties.
- **Indications:** Circulation in the legs and joints; digestive problems. It also may help heart disease.
- **Preparation:** Applied topically to the skin, capsaicin, the active ingredient in cayenne, causes a sensation of pain relief and warmth, which can cause extended but reversible insensitivity of the skin (nerve block). This is useful in treating topical pain such as arthritis and spasms. Used externally for sprains, itching, arthritis, unbroken chilblains, neuralgia, and pleurisy. It can be administered internally in large capsules.

- **Note:** Scientists believe that capsaicin assists digestion by stimulating the flow of both saliva and stomach secretions. Do not use near the eyes or on injured skin.

Celery Seed (*Apium graveolens*)
- **Parts used:** Bruised celery seeds but occasionally the whole plant.
- **Action:** Diuretic; reduces flatulence and expels gas from the intestines; tonic; nervine; useful in promoting restfulness.
- **Indications:** Tying-up syndrome; arthritis. It is also used to combat fungal infections (externally). In Ayurvedic medicine it is used for asthma, bronchitis, and as a nerve tonic.
- **Preparation:** Celery seed can be taken internally or used externally.
- **Note:** Celery is an aromatic biennial with bulbous fleshy roots and solid, grooved stems. Do not give this to pregnant mares, although an infusion of celery seeds is helpful for mares who are lactating.

Chamomile

Chamomile (*Matricaria recutita*) or German Chamomile
- **Parts used:** Flowering tops.
- **Action:** Sedative.
- **Indications:** Gas and digestive pain; nervous colic; geriatric horses; skin health; allergies.
- **Preparation:** For skin, use as a wash prepared from the infusion. You can use just the dried flowers, but the infusion is gentler. Add 1 cupful (240 ml) of chamomile infusion or dried flowers to the horse's food once or twice a day during stressful periods. Don't use chamomile as a regular part of your horse's diet, however, because it can affect the liver over long periods. For internal use, an infusion of freshly crushed seeds is prepared.
- **Note:** German chamomile is an annual that grows tall. It contains a volatile oil as well as flavonoids. In addition, it contains high levels of calcium and magnesium and also potassium, iron, manganese, and zinc. The essential oil promotes calmness and eases worries and fears; it also helps to dull muscular pain and stimulate the liver and spleen. Chamomile flowers are available commercially in liquid form as well.

Chickweed (*Stellaria media*)
- **Parts used:** All above-ground parts, freshly harvested.
- **Action:** Demulcent; soothing to the skin.
- **Indications:** Upset stomach; skin problems; insect bites; lymphatic blockages. Internally, chickweed is used for arthritis, as well as chest infections.
- **Preparation:** For stomach upset, give a handful of fresh, bruised herb half an hour before feeding. For skin conditions, apply a chickweed compress or poultice to the affected area.
- **Note:** Chickweed is a spreading annual with brittle branches, ovate leaves, and small, white star-shaped flowers. It grows wild throughout the world and is a very safe herb.

Cleavers (*Galium aparine*)
- **Parts used:** All above-ground parts.
- **Action:** This herb is beneficial to the lymphatic system; diuretic.
- **Indications:** Swelling in the legs; ulcers and digestive cysts; skin problems, such as eczema and greasy heel. Useful for any swelling, especially from allergies.

- **Preparation:** Add a handful of the fresh herb to the feed.
- **Note:** Cleavers is the herb of choice for airborne allergies.

Coltsfoot (*Tussilago farfara*)

- **Parts used:** Leaves, stems, and flowers.
- **Action:** Antispasmodic.
- **Indications:** Coughs that spring from secondary bacterial infection; bronchitis.
- **Note:** This plant has been used for hundreds of years to treat lung ailments, including asthma. However, coltsfoot contains pyrrolizidine alkaloids, and chronic consumption may induce liver disease. Use with caution and never for more than ten days. Never feed this herb during gestation.

Comfrey (*Symphytum officinale*)

- **Parts used:** Leaf and all above-ground parts, as well as roots and rhizomes.
- **Action:** Supports the immune system; soothing to tissues.
- **Indications:** Wound and tendon healing; bone bruises; gastric ulcers and ulcerative colitis; bone repair, including fractures; sarcoids. It reduces inflammation and controls bleeding.
- **Preparation:** Use a poultice with whole herbs for wound healing and bone repair. Comfrey ointment is available; it can be used as a healing salve.
- **Note:** Comfrey is a bristly haired, perennial herb, with thick roots and tapering lance-like leaves. Comfrey contains pyrrolizidine alkaloids and is rich in vitamins A and C. Chronic consumption may induce liver disease. Use with caution.

Dandelion Leaf (*Taraxacum officinalis*)

- **Parts used:** Leaf or root, with the latter having the stronger action.
- **Action:** Diuretic that helps to remove toxins from the system.
- **Indications:** Flatulent colic; skin and coat problems; laminitis; tying-up syndrome. It basically works on any liver, kidney, or joint problem. It's also good after your horse has had a long rest.
- **Preparation:** Use leaves as a tea or extract.
- **Note:** Dandelions are an excellent source of potassium, and when used as a diuretic do not deplete the body of potassium the way most drugs do. It's what used to be called a "spring tonic," especially for the liver and digestive system, and is particularly useful during this time of year. There is a plant called flatweed or false dandelion, which looks disturbingly like a dandelion and is found in the same places. A fungus grows on this plant that is thought to contribute to stringhalt by damaging certain nerves.

Devil's Claw (*Harpagophytum procumbens*)

- **Parts used:** Dried, sliced root.
- **Action:** Anti-inflammatory; astringent; digestive aid; pain reliever.
- **Indications:** Devil's claw is used externally to treat swollen, arthritic joints as well as boils, sores, and skin ulcers. Internally, it is used for back pain.
- **Preparation:** Use as a decoction internally or a poultice externally.
- **Note:** Devil's claw is a tender trailing perennial, with tubers and many round to oval-shaped stems. It should not be combined with other painkillers, especially willow. Do not give this herb to pregnant mares or horses with gastric ulcers.

Dill (*Anethum graveolens*)

- **Parts used:** All aerial parts, seeds.
- **Action:** Soothes the stomach.
- **Indications:** Gas and digestive pain; urinary tract infection.
- **Preparation:** Use as a poultice over the gums to fight infection. Otherwise, it is not used externally. It is prepared as an infusion using mashed dill seeds and boiling water.

Many herbs that are perfectly safe for people are dangerous for horses. The same is true of medicine. Don't use your own experience with an herbal remedy to dose your horse. Seek professional advice.

- **Note:** Dill is indigenous to Southwest Asia. This is a very gentle, safe herb.

Echinacea (*Echinacea spp.*)

- **Parts used:** Root of *Echinacea purpurea* or leaves and flowers of *Echinacea angustifolia.* The former is usually considered somewhat more effective, although it is also more expensive because the entire plant has to be dug up.
- **Action:** Antimicrobial; blood cleanser; soothes stomach. It is a bitter herb with some aromatic properties.
- **Indications:** Urinary tract problems; chronic viral or bacterial infections; skin problems; immune system booster. Use at the onset of infections.
- **Preparation:** Externally, it can be used as a poultice or compress. Internally, use echinacea only for three weeks at a time because its effectiveness diminishes after that.
- **Note:** This plant is indigenous to North America. It is a tall perennial with lance-like leaves. This is an easily grown plant. However, many of the active compounds in echinacea are damaged by processing. The best way to preserve the healing properties is by freeze-drying it. It is a good "autumn tonic." Do not use in horses with heart problems.

Fennel

Eyebright (*Euphrasia officinalis*)

- **Parts used:** Flowering plant.
- **Action:** Astringent; anti-inflammatory; some antibiotic properties.
- **Indications:** Conditions of the eye and mucous membranes; conjunctivitis. Eyebright's antibiotic and astringent properties tighten membranes and mucus surrounding the eyes.
- **Preparation:** Use as a tea.
- **Note:** This plant is overharvested in the wild. Use only commercially grown herbs, or grow your own.

Fennel (*Foeniculum vulgare*)

- **Parts used:** Seed.
- **Action:** Expels gas and relieves indigestion.
- **Indications:** Dieting (also called "the dieter's herb" because fennel represses the appetite). Recovery from flatulent colic, gas, flatulence, digestive pain.
- **Preparation:** Make an infusion from the seeds and add to the feed. Safe and effective. Store in a cool, dark, dry place. Seeds will stay fresh for two years. Ground fennel will keep for six months to one year if stored properly.
- **Note:** Fennel seed is an ancient aromatic spice from Egypt, China, and India. The seed is similar that of anise but is sweeter and milder. Horses love the licorice taste of fennel, but a small pony who feeds on large amounts could show signs of fennel poisoning. One of the major constituents, anethol, has expectorant qualities and can make the animal slobber, too.

Fenugreek (*Trigonella foenum-graecum*)

- **Parts used:** Seeds and fresh leaves
- **Action:** General tonic for horses who have been ill or who have lost condition. The saponins (soapy compounds) in the herb are the secret!
- **Indications:** Stimulates appetite and helps to reduce complications caused by gastric ulcers. It also increases

milk flow in lactating mares. It is used externally for skin inflammations.

- **Preparation:** Seeds are mixed in a cup of water, mashed into a paste, and added to the feed. You also can use the dried plant.
- **Note:** Fenugreek is an erect annual with tri-foliate leaves. A long taproot sends up a round stem with a few branches. Do not use on pregnant mares.

Feverfew (*Chrysanthemum Parthenium*)

- **Parts used:** Flowers.
- **Action:** Antithrombotic; carminative; diaphoretic; diuretic; febrifuge; nervine; tonic.
- **Indications:** Arthritis (long-term support), coughs.
- **Preparation:** Infusion of the flowers. Feverfew is typically available as a tea, tincture, or capsule. As a topical ointment, fresh feverfew flowers can be rubbed on the skin as a natural insect repellant.
- **Note:** Feverfew is a common flowering aromatic plant. Do not give to pregnant mares.

Garlic (*Allium ursinum* or *Allium sativum*)

- **Parts used:** Cloves.
- **Action:** Garlic is considered nature's "natural antibiotic." It also acts as an expectorant and helps to lower blood pressure.
- **Indications:** Coughs that spring from secondary bacterial infection; laminitis and prevention of laminitis; respiratory problems; prevention of skin problems.
- **Note:** Garlic is high in sulfur, and some people believe that it helps to repel flies and stinging insects, although there's no scientific evidence to support this. You can feed a horse three cloves of fresh garlic a day. Do not give to pregnant or lactating mares.

Ginger (*Zingiber officinale*)

- **Parts used:** Root.
- **Action:** Vasodilator.
- **Indications:** This warming herb is useful for horses recovering from all sorts of illnesses; colic.
- **Preparation:** For older and arthritic horses, as a general tonic, slice some of the root very thin and put it in the bottom of the water bucket during cold weather. An old Indian proverb says "Everything good is found in ginger." Ginger contains gingerol, a combination of volatile oils and resin that accounts for its characteristic aroma.
- **Note:** Ginger from the West Indies is considered the best.

Ginkgo (**Ginkgo biloba**)

- **Parts used:** Leaves.
- **Action:** Antioxidant.
- **Indications:** Circulation, especially in the kidneys, legs, and brain; urinary tract irritations; joint problems; geriatric; immune system.
- **Preparation:** Add 1 cup (240 ml) of the cut leaf to the feed once or twice a day.
- **Note:** Do not use during pregnancy or lactation.

Goldenrod (*Solidago*)

- **Parts used:** Leaves and flowering tops.
- **Action:** Anti-inflammatory; astringent.
- **Indications:** Irritable bowel.
- **Preparation:** Use externally to treat slow healing wounds, insect bites, and ulcers. It can be used internally as an infusion.
- **Note:** Goldenrod is a bitter perennial herb.

Goldenrod

Hawthorn (*Crataegus spp.*)
- **Parts used:** The dried leaves and flowers are usually used, but the fruits also can be used.
- **Action:** Cardiac; diuretic; astringent; tonic.
- **Indications:** Circulation, especially in the legs; geriatric horses; laminitis; to improve cardiac output.
- **Preparation:** The powdered berry is given daily with the feed.
- **Note:** Hawthorn is a small deciduous tree. The herb is aromatic. Hawthorn can be used with pregnant mares who have a history of premature labor.

Hops (*Lupulus strobula*)
- **Parts used:** The cone and grains of the hops flower, dried and cut.
- **Action:** Sedative; anthelmintic (wormer); digestive aid.
- **Indications:** Helps the horse focus; calming.
- **Preparation:** Teas, infusions, tinctures, or capsules.

Hawthorn

- **Note:** The plant is a twining climber, with bristly stems and coarsely toothed leaves. The active constituents, humulone and lupulone, must be aged for a year or two before they form their sedative chemicals. Fresh hops, on the other hand, supply only bitters that stimulate digestion. (These bitters are also found in the aged herb.)

Horsetail or Scouring Rush or Shave Grass (*Equisetum arvense*)
- **Parts used:** All above-ground parts of the plant are used, both fresh and dried; berries.
- **Action:** Circulatory regulator; diuretic.
- **Indications:** The stems are high in silica, which helps to form collagen. The herb helps to boost the regrowth, strength, and elasticity of connective tissues. It has many minerals and salts to nourish blood and improve the skin, coat, and hoofs. It can act as a diuretic. It is often used for bone injury and degenerative joint disease, including bone spurs and chips; urinary tract infections; skin and coat problems; ulcers; burns; sprains; wounds (stops bleeding).
- **Preparation:** Use as a decoction. Add a little sugar to make it more palatable and to extract the silicon constituents. Horsetail preparations should be stored in well-sealed containers to ensure protection from light.
- **Note:** The use of this herb dates back to ancient Roman and Greek medicine. Another species of horsetail, *E. palustre,* is poisonous to horses. It combines well with garlic, marshmallow, and dandelion.

Kelp or Seaweed (*see Bladderwrack*)

Lemon Balm (*Melissa officinalis*)
- **Parts used:** Leaves, stems, flowers.
- **Action:** Sedative; antispasmodic; calmative; carminative; diaphoretic (when used as an infusion).
- **Indications:** Anxiety, especially in young horses; chronic mild colic.
- **Preparation:** Add as a tea to the horse's feed at night.
- **Note:** Lemon balm is a perennial plant that is common in the Mediterranean area and the Middle East, but it is also naturalized in some places in the United States. This is a very safe herb.

If you have a whole lot of fresh herbs, you can throw them into a blender and make herb juice. But you'll need a lot.

Licorice (*Glycyrrhiza glabra*)
- **Parts used:** The powdered root.
- **Action:** Blood cleanser; expectorant; anti-inflammatory (similar to steroids); protector of the mucous membranes. It is also used as a mild laxative. It may help to improve fertility.
- **Indications:** Allergic and other respiratory problems, such as COPD; skin problems; coughs; immune system; liver disease; arthritis; gastric upset, including stomach ulcers. General digestive aid.
- **Preparation:** Use externally for skin problems. Internally, don't give for more than three months because it reduces potassium levels. To prevent this from happening, add dandelion leaves.
- **Note:** Licorice is a variable perennial with downy stems and pinnate leaves, with pale blue or violet flowers. Not recommended for pregnant mares.

Marjoram (*Origanum vulgare*)
- **Parts used:** Whole plant.
- **Action:** Reduces flatulence and expels gas from the intestines; diaphoretic; mildly tonic.
- **Indications:** Marjoram has a long history of being used as a liniment by farriers, and it can be used to relieve painful swellings, colic, and arthritis.
- **Note:** This herb was highly valued by the ancient Greeks as a remedy against poison and convulsions. (If it grew on a grave, it was regarded as particularly auspicious, meaning that the departed has gone on to a happy life.) An essential oil is also extracted from it.

Marshmallow (*Althea officinalis*)
- **Parts used:** Root.
- **Action:** Antimicrobial; soothing and protecting to the tissues. It works by binding and eliminating the toxins.
- **Indications:** Respiratory; digestive (including ulcers); diarrhea and urinary irritation; coughs that spring from secondary bacterial infections (leaves); gastric distress; colic (root).
- **Preparation:** Leaves for secondary bacterial problems; root for colic and gastric trouble.
- **Note:** Marshmallow is an upright perennial with a fleshy taproot, downy stems, velvety leaves, and pale pink flowers. Some researchers have suggested a relationship between marshmallow and stringhalt, but this is not confirmed. In case you were wondering, marshmallow sweets were once made from the root extract.

Meadowsweet (*Filipendula ulmaria*)
- **Parts used:** Dried flowers and other above-ground parts.
- **Action:** A soothing herb with astringent, aromatic, and antacid properties.
- **Indications:** Allergies; chronic stomach trouble; diarrhea; joint pain; blood purifier.
- **Preparation:** Dried flowers are added to the feed.
- **Note:** This plant contains salicylic acid and is known as the "herbal aspirin." It is high in flavonoids, which may be helpful against joint disease.

Mint (*Mentha spp.*)
- **Parts used:** Leaves.
- **Action:** Flavenoids to help to relax the digestive tract.
- **Indications:** Gas and digestive pain.
- **Preparation:** Just sprinkle on the feed. You also can use a mint leaf to relive itching from a bug bite, as long as the skin is not broken.
- **Note:** Common mints include peppermint (*M. piperita*) and spearmint (*M. spicata*). Both are easy to grow and

Mint

may help to prevent colic; use daily. Use fresh mint if possible because the action of the volatile oils is largely lost in the drying process. Horses are very partial to mint.

Mullein (*Verbascum thapsus*)
- **Parts used:** Dried flower petals.
- **Action:** Demulcent; emollient; astringent.
- **Indications:** Hives. It also helps to remove mucus from the lungs.
- **Preparation:** Infusion.
- **Note:** Mullein is a hardy biennial with gray-green, woolly leaves and yellow flowers. It is a bitter, cooling herb.

Larger pieces of herbs will last longer than those that are shredded, so if you plan to use only a small bit over a long period, choose the largest pieces you can.

Nettle (*Urtica spp.*)
- **Parts used:** Leaves.
- **Action:** Astringent for eyes and skin.
- **Indications:** Sweet itch or other irritating skin conditions; geriatric horses.
- **Preparation:** Serve with the leaves a little wilted to "disarm" the nettles. Dried nettle is also safe, or you can make a tea.
- **Note:** Stinging nettle (*U. dioica*) is an excellent general tonic, especially in the spring. It is full of vitamin C and iron. A few horses develop a rash if they eat nettles; obviously, if this occurs, discontinue.

Oregon Grape (*Mahonia aquifolium*)
- **Parts used:** Root.
- **Action:** All-purpose antimicrobial, especially for bacterial infections of the teat or bladder. Stimulates liver function.
- **Indications:** Anti-inflammatory for eyes, mouth, mucous membranes. Works well with a little echinacea.
- **Preparation:** The powered root is given in a tincture, tea, or decoction.

Passionflower (*Passiflora incarnate*)
- **Parts used:** Leaves and stems.
- **Action:** Nervine; antispasmodic.
- **Indications:** Used for relaxing and reducing irritation, as well as for nerve injuries. Very good for horses with longstanding nervous habits. Works well with hops, vervain, valerian, and chamomile.
- **Preparation:** Add 2 teaspoonfuls (10 ml) of the powdered herb daily or 1/2 cup (120 ml) of the dried leaves and stems.

Plantain (*Plantago major*)
- **Parts used:** All above-ground parts of the plant.
- **Action:** Diuretic; expectorant; antimucus.
- **Indications:** Astringent for skin; respiratory, GI or urinary tract problems, same as for slippery elm; to control bleeding.
- **Preparation:** Tea. It can be used externally as a cold compress.

Raspberry Leaf (*Rubus idaeus*)
- **Parts used:** Dried leaves.
- **Action:** Astringent; uterotonic; laxative; diuretic; can

Rose Hips

also be used as a nutritive.
- **Indications:** Astringent for the eyes, skin, and uterus; toning the uterus; diarrhea.
- **Preparation:** Can be used as an infusion, poultice, or tincture.
- **Note:** Do not use after the mare is pregnant.

Rose (*Rosa canina*)
- **Parts used:** Fruits (hips), leaves, bark.
- **Action:** Astringent; nutritional (hips).
- **Indications:** Immune system; laminitis.
- **Preparation:** Give as a strong tea or use commercially available syrup.
- **Note:** Rich in vitamin C and rosehips; also contains vitamin A, thiamine, niacin, riboflavin, and vitamin K. Rosehips are touted as a wonderful spring and autumn tonic.

Sage (*Salvia officinalis*)
- **Parts used:** Foliage.
- **Action:** Antimicrobial.
- **Indications:** Wounds and infections of the skin and mouth; respiratory infections.
- **Preparation:** Add 1 quart (.95 l) to 1/2 cup (120 ml) to the feed daily.

Sage

Siberian Ginseng (*Eleutherococcus senticosus*)
- **Parts used:** Root.
- **Action:** Nervous disorder; stomachic; tonic.
- **Indications:** Immune system; recovery from viral or bacterial infections.
- **Preparation:** Powdered herb.

Skullcap (*Scutellaria spp.*)
- **Parts used:** Aerial parts, dried or fresh.
- **Action:** Nerve tone; sedative; antispasmodic.
- **Indications:** Nervousness; skittishness; pain.
- **Preparation:** Tea.

Slippery Elm (*Ulmus fulva*)
- **Parts used:** Powdered inner bark.
- **Action:** Demulcent; astringent.
- **Indications:** Soothes the lining of the digestive tract; regulates intestinal flora; good for abscesses.
- **Preparation:** Mix with a little honey to make a paste. If the horse won't eat it, use a non-needle syringe to get it into the horse. Use as a poultice for wounds, rain rot, and mud fever.
- **Note:** Do not combine with other medications unless advised to do so by your veterinarian because it can limit their effect.

Saint John's Wort (*Hypericum*)
- **Parts used:** Flowering plant.
- **Action:** Increases blood flow and lowers blood pressure; reduces nerve pain.
- **Preparation:** Tea, tincture.
- **Note:** Do not use this herb with other medicines because it may react badly with them. It causes photosensitivity in some horses. Use with care.

Common medicinal herbs to avoid using with horses include several kinds of clover, melilot, horsetail, onions, and cherry bark. Saint John's Wort may be used with care.

Tea Tree Oil (*Melaleuca alternifolia*)
- **Parts used:** Oil.
- **Action:** Emollient.
- **Indications:** Wounds; itches; flea repellent.
- **Preparation:** Tea tree oil ointment is useful as salve for various types of sores and itches.
- **Note:** Tea tree oil toxicosis has been reported in cats whose owners used the pure oil, so it is wise to dilute before use.

Valerian (*Valeriana officinalis*)
- **Parts used:** Roots and rhizomes.
- **Action:** Sedative; analgesic; antispasmodic.
- **Indications:** Anxiety; seizures; hormone imbalances in mares; nervousness during training; colic pain.
- **Preparation:** Variable—often used in loose form. This tranquilizing herb is also available as a capsule or tablet. (It is often sold as a powder.)
- **Note:** This is a banned herb for most performance events. It can be combined with skullcap or chamomile. Horses seem to like this herb and will often eat it quite freely. This is amazing to me because it really smells bad, but this is the best calming herb. Because valerian is banned, some companies offer a valerian-free mixture that may achieve the same results. It also contains vervain, lemon balm, chamomile clovers, dandelion, and passionflower.

White Willow (*Salix alba*)
- **Parts used:** Powdered bark.
- **Action:** Analgesic; anti-inflammatory; tonic; astringent; antiseptic; febrifuge.

Best Herbal Picks for Senior Horses

The following herbs are especially good for senior horses with arthritis:

- burdock
- chamomile
- devil's claw
- meadowsweet
- white willow
- yucca

- **Indications:** Laminitis; arthritis.
- **Preparation:** Given in powder form.
- **Note:** This is a bitter herb.

Yarrow (*Achillea millefolium*)
- **Parts used:** Flowers, leaves, stems.
- **Action:** Diaphoretic, astringent, tonic, stimulant, and mild aromatic
- **Indications:** Wounds (can be used undiluted to stanch wounds); digestive tract problems; circulation in the legs.
- **Preparation:** The infusion is made with dried herb and boiling water, then drunk warm.
- **Note:** If you recognize the name "Achilles" in the scientific name of this herb, you are very astute! It is said that the Greek warrior Achilles used the leaves from this plant to stop bleeding on the battlefield. Do not give to pregnant mares.

Yucca (*Yucca schidigera*)
- **Parts used:** Root.
- **Action:** Anti-inflammatory; cleansing.
- **Indications:** Arthritis and other joint inflammations.
- **Preparation:** The root can be boiled in water and several cups given daily.
- **Note:** Excessive, long-term use may slow absorption of some-fat soluble vitamins. It has a high saponin (natural antimicrobial) content, and it is an excellent herb for older horses.

Chapter 8

Chinese herbal medicine is one component of a great and comprehensive system of treatment called traditional Chinese medicine (TCM), which includes acupuncture, moxibustion, massage therapy, food therapy, and other modalities. In this chapter, though, we'll be concentrating on herbs. Chinese herbs don't really work any differently from herbs grown elsewhere, of course, but the Chinese people have evolved a whole medical theory behind their use that is rather different from Western ideas of health care. In the West, medicines (including herbal medicines) are used as

Chinese Herbal Medicine

an antidote to disease. Disease is usually considered the result of a particular pathogen. In traditional Chinese medicine, on the other hand, treatment is focused not on countering a specific disease but on restoring balance to the whole body, mind, and spirit. Used with horses in China thousands of years ago, herbal therapy has become increasingly popular with modern horse owners.

ADVANTAGES
- DESIGNED TO TREAT A WIDE RANGE OF ILLNESSES.
- AVAILABLE WITHOUT A PRESCRIPTION.
- MANY ARE EFFICACIOUS.
- MANY COME IN PREPACKAGED FORMULAS FOR EASE OF USE.

DISADVANTAGES
- MANY MAY NOT BE SAFELY PREPARED OR PACKAGED, ESPECIALLY THOSE IMPORTED FROM CHINA.
- MANY CAN BE UNSAFE IF NOT USED PROPERLY.
- THIS IS A COMPLEX MODALITY THAT TAKES MANY YEARS TO MASTER.
- BEST AND SAFEST USED WITH THE GUIDANCE OF A SKILLED VETERINARY CHINESE HERBAL PRACTITIONER.

BALANCE AND HARMONY

To understand the methodology behind Chinese herbal medicine, you must first understand its guiding doctrines. As revealed in the great text the *Tao Te Ching*, Chinese philosophy and Chinese medicine operate using the same principles of balance and harmony. So it seems that to be an effective practitioner of traditional Chinese medicine, you need to be something of a philosopher as well.

YIN AND YANG

Most fundamental to the application of this form of medicine is the cornerstone of Chinese philosophy, which is centered on the principles of yin and yang. According to this belief system, all forces in nature are thought to have yin and yang states, and the two are in constant motion. These are not opposites, however, but complementary primordial energy forces. They cannot exist without each other in the universe, and a healthy balance between them is essential to all life, as well as to the good health of all beings.

Yin and yang are present everywhere—from the farthest star to your nearest blood cell. Together they account for the push, pull, and flow of healthy life. When one element falls out of balance, disharmony (or sickness) follows. Chinese herbs are used to help to restore that balance.

You may already know that yin embodies the female energies of the earth, water, and moon, while yang embodies the male energies of the sun and heavens, but this concept is carried into the internal organs of the body as well. In traditional Chinese medicine, the understanding of the body is based on a holistic understanding of the universe, and diagnosis and treatment of illness is based on this theory of interrelationship between nature and the body.

THE EIGHT PRINCIPLES

While yin and yang are the most familiar terms used in relation to balance and harmony, there are six other terms used in Chinese medicine to divide symptoms into groups, and they are always presented as pairs. Together they compose the "eight principles," which are:

Horses as Natural Healers

The Chinese recognized horses as natural healers. A story is told that during the rule of the Han dynasty in the first century, the army was staying in an unfamiliar area and began to suffer from a disease that caused blood in their urine. The legend says that the horses who were grazing on a certain plant were spared the bloody urine—and when the soldiers ate the plants too, they were cured. The therapeutic plant they ate was Asiatic plantain (chequian), which is still used in Chinese medicine today.

- yang–yin
- eternal–internal
- hot–cold
- excess–deficiency

Like yin and yang, these other guiding principles are complementary opposites. However, they are still dominated by yin and yang: Yang energy is the first part of each pair, and yin energy is the second. Yin and yang are just further defined, or "expressed," by these additional states. Yet all eight elements must be in balance for an individual to attain a state of health.

The eight principles are used to analyze and differentiate the energetic imbalances in the body to determine the nature of a patient's condition. For example, in making a diagnosis, diseases may be classified as cold (yin) or hot (yang) diseases. Yin diseases are said to occur most often in the winter and spring, and yang diseases are said to occur in the summer and autumn. Yin diseases are said to reach inward (internal), and yang diseases pour outward (external). Yin is "empty" and stores the vital forces of life; yang is "full" and protects the body from outside pathogens. Those affected by a yin (cold) disease need a yang (hot) herb, and vice versa. Balance is the name of the game!

THE FIVE ELEMENTS

Along with the philosophy of yin and yang, Chinese medicine also employs the theory of the five elements. In this unique system of diagnosis, the relationship among the organs is much more complex than the simple saying "the knee bone's connected to the thighbone" of Western schoolyard lore. It's more like playing "rock paper scissors."

In traditional Chinese medicine, treatment is focused not on countering a specific disease but on restoring balance to the whole body, mind, and spirit.

The Whole Horse Wellness Guide

Diagnosis and the Five Elements

In traditional Chinese medicine, the five elements (wood, earth, fire, water, metal) are used as guides to interpret what's happening in the body so that the practitioner can diagnose the problem and choose the appropriate cure. Herbs will be chosen based on their ability to correct, or rebalance, disharmonies in the body. According to Chinese medical theory, temperature and taste give herbs their "healing" properties. When administered in the right combinations, they influence the yin and yang patterns of energy in the body, thus restoring balance and good health.

	Wood	Fire	Earth	Metal	Water
Flavors	sour	bitter	sweet	pungent	salty
Zang	liver	heart	spleen	lung	kidney
Fu	gall bladder	small intestine	stomach	large intestine	urinary
Senses	eye	tongue	mouth	nose	ear
Tissue	tendon	vessel	muscle	hair/skin	bone
Directions	east	south	center	west	north
Changes	germinate	grow	transform	reap	store
Color	green	red	yellow	white	black

For instance, in this model, the heart controls the lungs, the lungs control the liver, the liver controls the spleen, the spleen controls the kidneys, the kidneys control the heart, and so on. And it all has to do with the flow of energy, which is dictated by the five elements.

In the Chinese theory of life, there are five "elemental" energies that inform the universe, and in turn, the body. These are the energies of wood, fire, earth, metal, and water. They combine and recombine to form everything that exists in the world. Likewise, according to this theory, the internal organs are thought to have the same properties as the elements, and they interact with each other in the same ways. Therefore, parallels can be drawn between the phenomena occurring in the natural world and in the body. For example, the five elements represent the following:

- fire: drought, heat, flaring, ascendance, movement, etc.
- wood: germination, extension, softness, harmony, flexibility, etc.
- metal: strength, firmness, killing, cutting, cleaning up, etc.
- earth: growing, changing, nourishing, producing, etc.
- water: moisture, cold, descending, flowing, etc.

In turn, each of the five elements has a season, specific organs, and senses (taste, color, sound) associated with it:

- winter, ruled by water, is associated with the kidney and the bladder
- spring, ruled by wood, is associated with the liver and the gall bladder
- early summer, ruled by fire, is associated with the heart and small intestine
- late summer, ruled by earth, is associated with the stomach and spleen
- autumn, ruled by metal, is associated with the lungs and large intestine

In addition, each energy (wood, fire, metal, water, wood) has its particular flavor:

- bitter for fire
- sweet for earth
- salty for water
- sour for wood
- pungent for metal

The Chinese believe that every being is oriented toward one of the five elements, but because of the constant movement of energies, aspects of each element are present in living beings at different times. In other words, in this scheme, a deficiency or excess in one element can mean trouble all down the line because balance is essential for well-being.

But how does all this relate to healing horses? Well, in several ways. These five energies are used as a guide to interpret what's happening in the body so that the practitioner can diagnose the problem and choose the appropriate cure. A practitioner of Chinese medicine will size up your horse to decide if he is "water," "wood," "fire," "earth," or "metal." Horses with the constitutional type of "water" have a timid personality and are prone to kidney and bladder conditions. "Wood"-type horses can be bullies with a tendency to a bad liver (horses do not have gall bladders). "Fire"-type horses are happy but excessively needy. They may have problems with the heart or small intestine. The "metal"-type horse is wheezy and subject to lung and colon problems. And the "earth"-type horse tends to be placid but obese. Their problems tend to get worse during the season ruled by each energy. Each type should receive an herb that will counteract his basic personality. So for example, a sweet-tasting earth herb might be used to treat diseases of the spleen, pancreas, or stomach, which are ruled by the earth element.

Organ Groups

Because Chinese herbal medicine is holistic, the organs are considered part of a specific body system. Of course, Western medicine does this as well—there's the digestive system, the renal system, the circulatory system, and so forth. Each organ is also a reflection of all the others, which of course is simply common sense. When something goes seriously wrong with the heart, for instance, the lungs will suffer also. This is all very familiar. Not as familiar is the idea in Chinese medicine that some of the "organs" are not physical structures at all! An example of such an "organ" is the San Jiao, known as the "triple warmer," or the three bowls of the body, which comprise the chest, abdomen, and sacrum. Known as the "organ" that delivers and metabolizes fluid in the body, the three bowls must work in concert for good health.

Obviously, the Chinese concept of "organ" is fairly abstract and does not correspond to Western notions. While in most cases there is a relationship between the name of the organ and a physical structure, the physiological "properties" of the organ are what are considered important and relevant here. In other words, it's the "work" of the organ that the practitioner considers more than the organ itself. The heart, for example, has the function of moving blood through the body, and it's that pumping function that the practitioner takes into consideration. Moreover, in this model the individual "organ" was never studied by itself (there are no TCM heart specialists) but was part of a

Based on a holistic understanding of the universe, Chinese medicine is centered on the theory that the processes of the body are interrelated and in constant interaction with the environment.

larger concept often called the "organ system," which includes the associated channel of the body, the tissues, surfaces, functions, and other features.

Also, as we have seen, in Chinese medicine two organs are paired functionally according to the philosophy of balance and flow. For example, the heart is yin and the small intestine is yang; the kidneys are yin and the bladder is yang; and so forth. (Chinese medicine is not monolithic, however, any more than Western medicine is; different subsystems within the broad umbrella of Chinese medicine do not always agree about which organ is yin and which is yang.)

Storing Organs and Excreting Organs

Another critical aspect of the Chinese concept of anatomy is the way in which organs are grouped together: There are five "storing" organs and five "excreting" organs. The storing organs, or yin organs, also sometimes known as "solid," "internal," or "zang," are the lungs, liver, spleen, heart, and kidneys. These organs store, secrete, make, and transform special substances that nourish the body. Some of these substances are easy to picture, like blood or fluids. Others, like Qi (spirit or shen: the mental function) and essence (the body's genetic vitality), are much more abstract.

The yin organs are mainly concerned with controlling water in the system. Let's take the kidneys, for example. Kidneys store the essence of the body and so are considered the fundamental root of everything. In the Chinese system, the kidneys control water metabolism, reproduction, secretions (not just urine but also semen and vaginal secretions), and even certain brain functions. Even stranger is that in TCM, there is only one "kidney," which includes both the left and right kidney. The left kidney is the yin and the right is the yang. It may sound odd, but remember,

the Chinese are talking about a system here, and there is indeed only one renal system. The space between the two kidneys is the mystical San Jiao, the pathway by which the fluid of the body is distributed. Other yin organs (lung, spleen) are also involved with water distribution. This is all very important because the proper level of body fluids (yin) keeps the body system from overheating (yang).

The yang organs, or the excreting organs (also called "hollow" or "Fu" organs), are the large intestine, small intestine, stomach, urinary bladder, and gallbladder. Their main function is to receive and digest food, absorb nutrients, and excrete waste.

In addition, there are "heater" or "warmer" organs sometimes referred to as the "pericardium" (unrelated to the anatomical pericardium) and "triple heater." These are conceptual organs; they have protective and energetic attributes but no actual mass. (However, some authorities believe that they are part of the lymphatic system, which is otherwise ignored in Chinese medicine.)

The Six Evils of Disease

Armed with all the appropriate medical and philosophical doctrines, the Chinese herbal therapist, like a Western veterinarian, needs to consider what causes the sickness before she can apply the correct herbal remedy. She can't just guess and pull out a random herb, and people who approach Chinese herbal therapy in this way are not likely to obtain a good result.

Very often the culprit is one of the "six external evils of disease":

- **Wind**: Wind is a spring energy. When in season, it produces refreshing breezes and healthy responses. But when wind appears out of season, it becomes the hot wind of summer, the dry wind of autumn, and the bitter wind of winter. These "unseasonable" winds appear suddenly and cause sudden illness, especially of a respiratory nature. (Their effect is intensified because they carry pollutants.)
- **Cold**: Cold energy is associated with winter. If cold settles in the abdomen, it can cause colic and diarrhea, as well as poor circulation in the legs and hooves. In Chinese theory it is associated with air conditioning and other unnatural attempts to produce cold out of season, as well as with overprescribing antibiotics.
- **Heat**: Heat energy is associated with summer. In excess, it can produce irritability and profuse sweating.
- **Dampness**: Damp energy is associated with the seasonal turn from summer into fall. This is a time when mist, drizzle, and fog more regularly appear. It can produce fatigue and arthritic pains, as well as trouble in the spleen, pancreas, and adrenal glands (Cushing's disease).
- **Dryness**: Dryness is associated with fall and produces trouble in the respiratory tract when it appears out of season or in excess. It is also associated with constipation and colic.
- **Fire**: Fire is an extreme evil that comes from prolonged exposure to any of the five evils mentioned earlier; it produces the most extreme symptoms.

When these "external evils" occur in excess or out of season, illness can develop, not because of anything special in the dampness or wind, but because the evil's untoward appearance knocks the body's defenses out of kilter.

This is not far off from the modern Western understanding of illness. While rain and bitter weather don't cause colds, they can weaken our defenses to cold viruses. Because Chinese medicine is a natural, holistic system, it also explains why overheating a barn can cause problems for a horse—it is natural for winter to be cold, and a horse's

Moxibustion Warning

One commonly used Chinese herbal technique is called moxibustion or moxa. It is used to enhance healing by increasing circulation, especially for arthritic horses. It can be used in concert with acupuncture, although this is not strictly necessary. However, this technique has two major drawbacks. First, it requires the burning of an herb on or near the area of the body needing treatment, which is often near an acupuncture point (and burning anything is not a good idea around horses). In addition, the technique uses a small amount of mugwort (*Artemisia vulgaris*), a small, spongy herb that is toxic to horses in large amounts. While veterinarians skilled in Chinese medicine may use moxibustion very successfully, this is not something you should attempt yourself.

Practitioners of TCM believe that analyzing signs of disharmony outside as well as inside the body helps them to understand, treat, and prevent illness and disease. For example, excesses in your horse's immediate environment must be remedied along with the internal illness.

instincts tell him it is supposed to be cold, so he won't know how to deal with the unnatural conditions.

In general, heat injures the heart, cold injures the lungs, dryness harms the kidneys, and wind is bad for the liver. However, even here there are complexities. It is the east wind especially that injures the liver (as well as the throat and neck). The south wind can have a bad effect on the heart, chest, and ribs, while west winds attack the lungs, shoulders, and back. The north wind is a killer for the kidneys and hips. It also appears that the wind can enter the body and do damage, and many Chinese herbal remedies are designed to "expel wind," by which we do not necessarily mean "gas." Chinese herbs are designed to help the horse "right" himself and get back into balance.

Of course, in addition to these external causes of disease, there are also internal causes that can be traced not to the weather but to pathogens and bad training.

Equine conditions that may be particularly amenable to Chinese herbal medicine include:

- pain and soreness
- arthritis
- emotional or behavioral problems
- laminitis and navicular disease
- anhydrosis
- chronic respiratory disease
- Cushing's and hypothyroidism
- skin problems
- gastric ulcers
- chronic colic

CHINESE HERBS

In Chinese medicine, every herb has a host of attributes, all of which must be considered when choosing a remedy. As the body is divided into yin and yang organs and diseases are classified according to their yin and yang effects, so are the herbs used to treat diseases of those parts. Therefore, there are yin herbs and yang herbs. In general, yin herbs are intended to cool and calm the system, while yang herbs heat it up. Yin and yang herbs attempt to get the body to achieve a balance.

For instance, every herb has a flavor: sweet, sour (astringent), pungent (hot or spicy), bitter, and salty. Each flavor is said to work along a different meridian or channel in the body. Each also has a function. Sweet herbs are considered strengthening, sour herbs are drying and soothing, pungent herbs disperse energy, bitter herbs detoxify, and salty herbs help to soften masses and tumors.

In like manner, each herb is considered to be hot, warm, cool, or neutral, which can be used to correct the elemental problem affecting the horse. If, for example, a horse is affected by "fire," then a cooling herb is appropriate. Herbs even have a "direction": upward (which is said to increase circulation) and downward (which is calming and cooling).

Herbs are also classified according to the effect they produce. There are "sweating" herbs, "vomiting" herbs, "draining downward" herbs, "harmonizing" herbs, "warming" herbs, "clearing" herbs, "reducing" herbs, and "tonifying" herbs; these are mixed and prescribed in accordance with your horse's particular needs.

When a Chinese herbal medicine is ingested, the essence and healing benefits of the formula are distributed throughout the bloodstream and along the meridian complex.

The formulas chosen and the duration of treatment depend on the individual. Medicines for illnesses that occur in front of or above the chest are traditionally given after meals. Medicines for the lower regions are given before meals. For example, for an illness affecting the legs, the horse is treated early in the morning before he eats. But if it's a bone problem, the medicine is given in the evening after the last meal. Generally, a course of Chinese herbs is given for seven to ten days.

PREPARATION

Of course, there is more to Chinese herbal medicine than deciding which herbs to use. Preparation is extremely important. Some herbs are dissolved in water or alcohol; others are taken as dried extracts or pills. Some are even used externally.

Herbs are best prepared in earthenware containers, never in metal containers. (Modern herbalists are known to use Pyrex, however.) In fact, even cutting herbs with metal is a bad idea in Chinese theory. The ancient Chinese authors recommend bamboo for cutting herbs, but not everyone has a bamboo knife lying around the house. All herbs should be stored in airtight containers.

Pulse Diagnosis

Traditional Chinese medicine often uses pulse diagnosis as part of the diagnostic exam. The herbal practitioner feels the pulse to help to detect the inner condition of the animal. There are twelve pulses that correspond to the inner organs. The frequency, rhythm, and volume of these pulses reveal possible sources of disease. Every "internal organ" has its own special kind of pulse. For instance, the heart pulse should sound like "the ringing of a sickle," rich at first, then trailing off. The spleen pulse should beat in an alternating rhythm. The lung pulse should "move like a feather in the wind." The kidney pulse should beat in a solid way "like a stone hitting the earth," while the liver pulse should be "mellow as a stringed instrument." Wait, there's more. Pulses also can be divided into Piao, or "superficial pulses," and Li, or "sunken pulses." These pulses can be divided even further. But the main point is that diseases (or impending death) can be diagnosed by taking the various pulses. They also are used to determine the sex of a fetus.

DECOCTIONS

The most common way to prepare Chinese herbs is to make a decoction (*tang*, a concentrated form of tea) from them, although pills and other forms of administration are also used occasionally. A decoction is generally the best way to extract the medicinal qualities of the herbs; also, they are most easily absorbed into the body when administered in this way.

To make a decoction, herbs are measured into a ceramic or Pyrex pan along with several cups (1 cup=240 ml) of pure water. The mixture is heated and brought to a boil until about half the original liquid is left. The herbs are then strained out and the broth is reserved. Then more water is added to herbs and it is all boiled up again. This is strained and added to the first broth. The dregs are thrown away, and the new broth is served (warm if possible) to the horse, poured over his feed. I should warn you that some of the stuff tastes pretty foul, so you may have to add something tempting to the feed to encourage consumption. Honey or molasses will usually work.

POWDERED HERBS

If the time and effort involved in preparing a decoction doesn't suit you, you can grind herbs into a powder (*san*). Again, this can be shaken into your horse's hard feed, but the taste might be repellent, so add a little honey or molasses. To make a simple infusion of powdered herbs, add them to boiling water and let the mixture steep for five minutes. It is usually added to the feed three times a day or as directed.

OINTMENTS

Herbal ointments (*yio*) can be made by blending finely ground powered herbs into an oil base (such as almond oil or beeswax) for external use. The base is heated until it is warm, and then the powdered herbs are stirred in. A poultice (*fu yao*) can be applied by mixing the herbs with water to form a thick paste, then spreading the mix onto a bandage and wrapping it securely to the affected area. This is excellent for problems of the joints, muscles, and ligaments.

More Than Herbs

While most of the medications used in Chinese herbal medicine are herbs, not all are. Animals, insects, reptiles, venoms, corals, shells, soils, minerals, and even pulverized rocks also have been used. However, the Chinese herbal medicine practiced in the United States is almost totally limited to bona fide plant products such as leaves, flowers, tubers, roots, and bark. Syrups, suppositories, ointments, and even injections are also sometimes used.

Made in the USA

It may seem counterintuitive, but when purchasing Chinese herbal medicines, stick with products grown and manufactured in the United States. There have been far too many cases of contaminated herbs and other products coming from China—with the contamination in some cases being arsenic, lead, mercury, and other heavy metals. Arsenic is no better for horses than it is for people. In addition, some Chinese "herbals" include nonsteroidal anti-inflammatories, corticosteroids, caffeine, and sedatives.

PREPARED FORMULAS

In addition to specific herbs, it is common practice in Chinese herbal medicine to market certain "patent medicines" or formulas. Many have been developed specifically for horses. However, Chinese herbs are best used under the advice of a skilled and experienced practitioner.

COMMONLY USED CHINESE HERBS

Here is a brief list of some of the more common Chinese herbs used with horses. The entire *materia medica* is far too large to include here! There are more than 600 herbal formulations in common use.

Bai hao or Peony Root (*Paeoniae lactiflorae*)
- **Parts used:** Root.
- **Traditional function:** Tonifies (supplements and fortifies) blood and liver energy. Relieves pain caused by "constrained liver yang." Protects the yin.
- **Function:** Calming. Alleviates foot pain. Helps to build the blood. It is good for problems in the lower abdomen.
- **Flavor:** Bitter/sour.
- **Administration:** Decoction, 10 grams, three doses per day.
- **Note:** The white peony is supposed to be better for infections; the red variety improves circulation.

Bai zhi or Chinese Angelica (*Angelicae anomala* or *A. dahuricae*)
- **Parts used:** Root.
- **Traditional function:** Expels wind.
- **Function:** Sedative. Alleviates pain, itchy skin, and toothache.
- **Flavor:** Bitter and pungent.
- **Administration:** Decoction, whole root, three doses per day.
- **Note:** Do not use with fresh ginger.

Cang Zhu or Atractylodes *(Rhizoma atractylodes)*
- **Parts used:** Rhizome of the plant.
- **Traditional function:** Expels dampness.
- **Function:** Dries out swollen, painful joints in the foot and leg.
- **Flavor:** Bitter.
- **Administration:** Decoction, 10 grams, twice daily.
- **Note:** Do not give to dehydrated horses.

Dong Quai or Angelica (*Angelica sinensis*)
- **Parts used:** Root
- **Traditional function:** Disperses cold in chronic obstructions caused by damp, windy conditions.
- **Function:** Especially useful for mares. In the Chinese system, it is considered a "warming" herb and is therefore good for arthritis-type pains, especially in the winter. It also may help to relieve constipation and emotional stress. It is a great invigorator. It is used primarily for muscle or joint damage and diseases of the female reproductive system. It is also a blood cleanser and is said to disperse cold in COPD.
- **Flavor:** Bittersweet and slightly pungent.
- **Administration:** You can add 1 teaspoon (5 ml) of Dong Quai in the feed up to three times a day.

Traditional Chinese herbs

It also can be given as a decoction.

- **Note:** This is an herb containing many volatile oils, and in fact it is considered a perfectly balanced yin general tonic. (Ginseng is the perfectly balanced yang tonic). It should not, however, be given to a pregnant mare because it causes uterine contractions. Do not give to horses with diarrhea. It is not compatible with ginger or bladderwrack.

Fang Feng or Ledebouriella Root (*Ledebouriellae divaricatae*)

- **Parts used:** Root.
- **Traditional function:** Expels wind.
- **Function:** Alleviates pain, especially in the shoulders and neck.
- **Flavor:** Sweet and pungent.
- **Administration:** Decoction, 15 grams, twice a day.
- **Note:** Especially useful for mares with problems in the reproductive system. Do not use in cases of profuse, chronic sweating.

Fu Ling or White Poria (*Porio Cocos*)

- **Parts used:** Fungus that grows on the roots of various conifers.
- **Traditional function:** This is a drying remedy that strengthens the spleen and kidneys, removes phlegm, sedates heart energy, and calms the nerves.
- **Function:** Sedative. It relieves thirst and can help appetite.
- **Flavor:** Sweet.
- **Administration:** Decoction, 15 grams, twice a day.

Ginseng (*Panax ginseng,* or its American relative *Panax quinquefolius*)

- **Parts used:** Root.
- **Traditional function:** Deficient energy, empty lung and spleen energy.
- **Function:** Recommended for anemia, chest or stomach aches, respiratory diseases, nervous exhaustion, heart failure, eye problems, arthritis, and weakness due to old age. It helps to prevent and heal stomach ulcers. It has been shown to have anti-tumor properties, and it stimulates almost all liver functions.
- **Flavor:** Sweet or slightly bitter.
- **Administration:** 20 grams (steam decoction) once in the morning. Also can be given as a powder or paste.
- **Note:** This is a completely balanced yang herb. Do not use in cases of pneumonia.

Huang Qi or Astragalus (*Astragalus membranaceus*)

- **Parts used:** Mature (at least three years old) roots.
- **Traditional function:** Tonifies primordial energy.
- **Function:** Immune system booster (helping to improve T-cell function), helping to fight the "six evils." It helps chronic fatigue and is especially prized as helping to fight cancer and viral infections. It is used for early treatment of respiratory infection.
- **Flavor:** Sweet or slightly sour.
- **Administration:** Decoction, 15 grams, three times per day.

Not for Horses!

Many Chinese medications use monkshood, which contains a large amount of deadly aconite. This powerful herb should be used only by a certified professional herbalist because the difference between an effective dose and a deadly dose is exceedingly narrow. While the herb is used mainly against coughs and other respiratory diseases, there are other safer and equally effective herbs for this purpose. It is also used against smallpox, which horses do not get. Mugwort (wormwood, or *Ai yen*) is another common Chinese herb that should definitely not be used. Ephedra (*Ma huang*) is another potentially dangerous Chinese herb. You have to be careful when using this herb.

Licorice root

- **Note:** While you can easily grow this herb yourself, it's not safe to do so in areas where the soil has high selenium levels.

Gan Cao or Licorice (*Glycyrrhiza uralensis*)
- **Parts used:** Root.
- **Traditional function:** Tonifies spleen and stomach energy; calms heart fire.
- **Function:** Moderates spasms and alleviates pain, especially bronchial congestion. It may inhibit tumor growth. As an external wash, it can be used for skin rashes. It is best if the root is dug before the plant bears fruit.
- **Flavor:** Sweet.
- **Administration:** Decoction, 8 grams, served warm twice a day or as a wash for skin.

Long Dan Cao or Chinese Gentian Root (*Gentianae longdancao*)
- **Parts used:** Root.
- **Traditional function:** Dispels damp heat and quiets "liver fire."
- **Function:** Stimulates digestive organs. Good for chronic digestive disorders and helps the body absorb nutrients from food. It also can be used to help problems relating to liver disease, diarrhea due to excess heat, swollen eyes, and arthritic pains.
- **Flavor:** Very bitter.
- **Administration:** Decoction (5 grams), powder (6 grams), or infusion (6 grams), two times per day.
- **Note:** There are actually 57 different bitter herbs that go by the name Long Dan Cao, but all are regarded as the same in Chinese medicine.

Nui p'ang tze or Great Burdock (*Arctium lappa*)
- **Parts used:** Root, seeds, and leaves.
- **Traditional function:** Expels wind dampness and wind heat.
- **Function:** Promotes bowel and urinary movement. Helps bronchitis and can be used to remove phlegm. It also helps with skin problems when used as a compress.
- **Flavor:** Pungent /bitter.
- **Administration:** It can be given three times a day as a decoction or used as a compress for skin problems.
- **Note:** Not for long-term internal use.

Niu xi or Achyranthes Root (*Achyranthis bidentata*)
- **Parts used:** Root.
- **Traditional function:** Tonifies liver and kidney energy.
- **Function:** Invigorates the blood, circulation, and joints. This remedy is good for all traumatic injuries to the bones and joints. It relieves pain in the lower back, knees, and legs. It clears bruising and is especially recommended as a diuretic.
- **Flavor:** Bitter/sour.
- **Administration:** Decoction, 10 grams, twice a day.
- **Note:** Do not use for horses with painful swelling in the legs.

Sheng (Gan) Di Huang or Rehmannia (*Rehmannia glutinosa*)
- **Parts used:** Root.
- **Traditional function:** Tonifies blood and heart energy; cools the blood; generates fluids.
- **Function:** Good for damaged tendons and sprains.
- **Flavor:** Sweet.
- **Administration:** Decoction, 10 grams, twice a day.
- **Note:** Do not use for horses with weak digestion.

Acupuncture and Herbs

The theories of natural balance and energy flow used in Chinese acupuncture apply equally to Chinese herbal medicine; both modalities are part of the traditional Chinese system of medicine. After a diagnosis is made, the practitioner decides whether acupuncture, herbs, or a combination of both is the appropriate treatment.

Chapter 9

Ayurvedic medicine is the traditional medicine of India. Its roots go back at least 5,000 years. It is older than Chinese medicine and may have served as a partial basis for it. The word "ayurveda" means the "science of life." As is true with all sacred Hindu knowledge, the earliest masters handed down their knowledge orally. Only in the fifth and sixth centuries B.C.E. was the material committed to writing. More than 1,000 remedies are listed in these traditional holy texts.

Ayurvedic Medicine

Today, the most well-known proponent of Ayurvedic medicine is Deepak Chopra, M.D., who has written many books on physical and mental wellness. More recently, this method of healing also has been used in the West to treat animals as either a primary or adjunct treatment with many healing therapies used for diseases of the horse.

ADVANTAGES
- MOSTLY NONINVASIVE.
- HOLISTIC.

DISADVANTAGES
- NOT ALL REMEDIES ARE SCIENTIFICALLY PROVEN.
- MAY BE DANGEROUS IF INCORRECTLY APPLIED.

LIKE BODY, LIKE MIND

More than any other system of medicine, Ayurveda focuses on disease prevention and lifestyle changes that make disease less likely to occur in the first place. For both humans and horses, this means proper exercise, rest, diet, and attitude. While all medicinal systems recognize that the body and mind can influence each other, in classical Hindu philosophy, the body and mind are ultimately identical! Modern science is coming around to this point of view as well, but whereas most Western scientists believe that the entire organism (mind and body) is ultimately a physical entity, the Ayurvedic viewpoint is that the body and mind are aspects of a total all-encompassing state of being called Brahman. One goal of Ayurvedic philosophy is to get closer to that realization.

All right. Your horse will never know he is Brahman because he is not evolved enough to make the connection. However, whether or not the horse realizes his true state, the fact is that, according to this philosophy, his proper care and training may be undertaken only with this idea in mind. Not only is your horse identical with ultimate reality, but you are identical, in some fundamental way, with your horse. You may be surprised to find just how much this understanding changes and improves your relationship with him.

MAINTAINING BALANCE

The foundation of Ayurvedic medicine rests on the understanding that illness is as much a thought process as it is a physical state. So knowing the "true self" means gaining an understanding of the body as a part of the entire mental, physical, and spiritual cosmos. This involves the implicit belief that all things are joined together in the universe and that all beings are born in a state of balance within themselves *and* in relation to the universe.

However, this state of balance can be disrupted by the processes of life, which can be physical, emotional, spiritual, or a combination of these elements. Imbalances weaken the body and make it susceptible to disease. Therefore, a disease arises when a being is out of harmony with the universe, and good health only can be achieved if a wholesome interaction with the immediate environment is restored. These ideas form the basis of how Ayurvedic practitioners think about the problems that affect health.

THE THREE DOSHAS

Ayurveda has some basic principles about how the body functions. The body itself is thought to be made up of a mixture of three different types of energies called doshas, which control the activities of the body. Every being—human and animal—is born with them. "Dosha" is one of the most important concepts in Ayurvedic medicine. The idea goes all the way back to the ancient Indian sage, Charaka. He believed that each of the three doshas refers to a particular kind of energy: Vata, which is airy energy; Pitta, which is fiery energy; and Kapha, which is watery energy. Every being on earth is composed of one or more of these energy types. While it may seem logical to think that the doshas must be "in balance," this is not as simple as it sounds. It all depends on the individual—or in this case, the kind of horse you have. A fine-tuned race horse is likely to be more Vata and Pitta than Kapha, and that is just the way

you want it! A child's riding pony can do without a lot of Pitta. The doshas don't necessarily have to be equal, but the basic proportions of the original doshic makeup should be maintained in order for your horse to enjoy good physical and mental health.

The purpose of Ayurvedic medicine is to find your horse's "natural balance" and maintain it throughout his life. That means that you don't want any one dosha to overaccumulate in the body; it can cause disease as much as if the dosha were missing completely.

The way the three doshas are balanced has a lot to do with how people and animals behave, and to a large extent it determines their personalities. The combination of the doshas inherited at conception is called the prakriti, which means the body's original constitution. Factors such as diet, climate, environment, pollution, social bonds, type of work, and even the passage of time can cause imbalances. And when the doshas are out of balance, the immune system can be weakened, leaving the body susceptible to illness and emotional problems. An Ayurvedic healer can assess all these factors and make changes to the diet and environment, as well as recommend herbal remedies and other healing therapies to reestablish proper doshic balance.

Individuals with only one type of dosha (Vata, Pitta, or Kapha) are considered monotypes. Dual types, the most common, are Vata-Pitta (or Pitta-Vata), Pitta-Kapha (or Kapha-Pitta), and Kapha-Vata (or Vata-Kapha). While Pitta-Kapha and Kapha-Pitta types both combine Pitta and Kapha, the dosha listed first is predominant. The balanced or triple type is, of course, Vata-Pitta-Kapha. It should be very clear that all three doshas exist throughout the whole body in every cell; however their balance is different, depending on the individual.

The word "ayurveda" means the "science of life."

Healing Principles of Ayurveda

One of the basic principles of Ayurveda is that both people and animals are composed of a mixture of different types of energy known as "doshas." Doshas inform and describe an individual's physical and psychological makeup. For an individual to be healthy—in body, mind, and spirit—the important thing is to maintain balance of the doshas that are unique to him. When doshas are out of balance, the immune system can be weakened, leaving the body more prone to illness and emotional problems.

The Ayurvedic healer works to rebalance the body through the use of an ayurvedically balanced diet, herbs, and other healing therapies.

Many veterinarians are now looking toward nutritional and alternative ways of holistically supporting an animal's body so that it can heal itself.

THE FIVE ELEMENTS

Each of the doshas is composed of a pair of the five primeval elements (*panchmahabhuta*), which are ether (or space), air, fire, water, and earth. Combining in dynamic pairs that are always in flux, these elements powerfully affect health because the proportion of the two elements in each dosha also determines how active the dosha is in the individual. This is because the five elements also make up the body's physiology, and each dosha has a particular relationship to body functions, which can become upset for different reasons:

- Earth represents matter in its solid state, and it symbolizes strength, rigidity and structural body parts such as bones, teeth, and cell membranes. It is related to the nose and sense of smell.
- Water represents fluidity and change. Most of your horse's body is made from water, and it changes constantly. Blood and lymph fluid are the primary body parts represented by water. Water is related to the tongue and the sense of taste.
- Fire is the transforming element, and in the body it represents metabolism, the nervous system, and mental processes. In traditional thought, it is most closely related to the eye, and most of us have indeed seen the "fire" in a horse's eye!
- Air represents respiration, and it is the basis for fire, which cannot burn without it. In traditional thought, it is most closely related to the skin.
- Ether is the space or environment in which the body and mind live. In traditional thought, it is most closely related to the organ of hearing.

Because individuals, their health, and the universe are all integrated, an imbalance in the five elements can create health problems. Also, an imbalance in a dosha will produce symptoms that are unique only to that dosha and not any other. Therefore, once the individual's primary dosha is determined, the Ayurvedic healer can assess all these factors to determine in which specific areas the animal is lacking (i.e., where the imbalance lies). Then, she can offer the appropriate means of restoring proper balance for that individual and ultimately help him regain good health.

Vata

Air and ether combine to form the dosha known as Vata, which means "wind," or more scientifically, perhaps, "anabolism," which means the building of new cells. Its main element is air. This is the dosha of movement.

Vata is often considered the most dominant of all the doshas because it controls breathing, movement, the nervous system, heartbeat, eye blinks, cell movement, and emotions such as lightness, ungroundedness, fear, and

anxiety. Vata is stored in the colon and adjacent parts, and it rules the lower body.

Too little Vata results in nerve loss, congestion, constipation, and thoughtlessness. Too much can mean nerve irritation, flatulence, and confusion. Vata increases in areas with dry climates and during cold, windy autumns, so Vata horses are most in danger of getting ill during the dry, windy season. (Because Vata also tends to increase with age, older horses are more at risk during this time.)

Vata horses, or horses overbalanced in the Vata direction, are changeable, even unpredictable. They have plenty of restless energy and are often rambunctious. They tend to be on the thin side and have rough hooves. The Vata horse is subject to psychological disorders (such as anxiety and phobias), nervous problems (relating to a neurological dysfunction), bloat, and arthritis.

Is your horse a Vata? Vata-predominating horses:

- tend to belong to a Vata breed such as the Thoroughbred
- have plenty of restless energy
- are quick thinking
- thrive on a regular routine
- are generally friendly
- have a strong need for both emotional and physical warmth
- dislike winter and cold weather
- have a tendency toward thinness
- may appear physically underdeveloped

Kapha, Vata, and Pitta are designations for body types, each with their own particular type of energy. For example, Pitta horses have a strong, moderate build and plenty of restless energy—the Arabian is the ultimate example.

- may have a poor coat and dry skin
- may have brittle hooves (and dislike farriers)
- are long lived (although many seem to suffer more illnesses)
- may be unpredictable and easily agitated
- tend toward psychological disorders such as fear, nervousness, noise phobias, and anxiety
- tend toward physical problems such as arthritis (especially in the back), colic, flatulence, constipation, bone and joint problems, and other digestive trouble
- may be vocal
- may suffer bladder, colon, and heart problems

Pitta

Fire and water combine to form the dosha known as *Pitta*, or metabolism, the burning of energy. Its main element is fire. Metabolism is the process that converts matter (food) into energy like movement and thought.

Pitta controls enzymatic and hormonal activity, the digestive processes, metabolism, hunger and thirst, body temperature, skin type and pigmentation, the luster of the eyes, intelligence, and understanding. Interestingly, in Ayurvedic thought, digestion is the most important function of the body, and poor digestion is the source of most diseases. Pitta controls the central part of the body.

Emotionally, too much Pitta arouses anger, hatred, and jealousy. It is stored in the small intestine, bile, stomach, sweat glands, blood, fat, eyes, and skin. Too little Pitta results in indigestion, sluggish metabolism, and dullness of mind. Too much can mean ulcers, hormonal imbalance, irritated skin, and anger. It is most common in hot summers and in adolescent and adult horses; thus, summer is the time when Pitta horses are most in danger of becoming sick.

Is your horse a Pitta? Pitta-predominating horses:

- have a strong, moderate build; these are usually extremely handsome horses—the Arabian is the ultimate example
- are intelligent
- are hardworking, focused, and energetic
- are good with other animals, especially cats and dogs
- make excellent working and performance horses
- have a tendency toward dominance; if challenged, they may not yield
- are impatient and short tempered
- have a tendency toward jealousy, irritability, anger, impatience, and aggression
- dislike hot weather and bright light
- tend to be more nocturnal than other horses
- have a good appetite and digestion
- need smaller, more frequent meals
- tend toward the following physical problems: indigestion, diarrhea, eye disorders, stomach/digestive disorders, Cushing's disease, diabetes, hives, fever, and skin problems

Kapha

Water and earth combine to form the dosha known as Kapha. Its main element is water. It provides structure and lubrication for the body, or in some renderings of the theory, catabolism, or cellular breakdown.

Kapha controls the immune system, wound repair, joint

Body Types

The terms Vata, Pitta, and Kapha bear a resemblance to the Western scientific designation of body types ectomorph (naturally thin, like Thoroughbreds), mesomorph (average build, like Tennessee Walkers), and endomorph (chunky, like quarter horses), although the Ayurvedic understanding is more comprehensive and includes more than just body type. It also includes personality. Body and mind are equally responsible for both health and disease, and an individual might be any combination of doshas.

lubrication, mucus secretions, memory retention, and the emotions of clinginess, greed, and long-standing envy. In the correct balance, it supplies calmness and forgiveness. It is stored in the chest.

Too little Kapha can result in a dry respiratory tract, stomach problems, and an inability to concentrate. Kapha rules the upper part of the body and also regulates Pitta and Vata.

Is your horse Kapha? Kapha-predominating horses:

- have a solid, heavy build and may belong to a draft horse breed
- have large, beautiful eyes
- have strong, shiny hooves
- have a thick, heavy coat
- are gentle
- are methodical and calm
- sleep a lot
- are well behaved and trainable, even when young
- are great with big horses
- have excellent long-term memories
- are very attached to and dependent on their owner and suffer if the relationship with their owner is not healthy
- have difficulty accepting change
- tend toward ailments such as respiratory problems, allergies, and joint pain

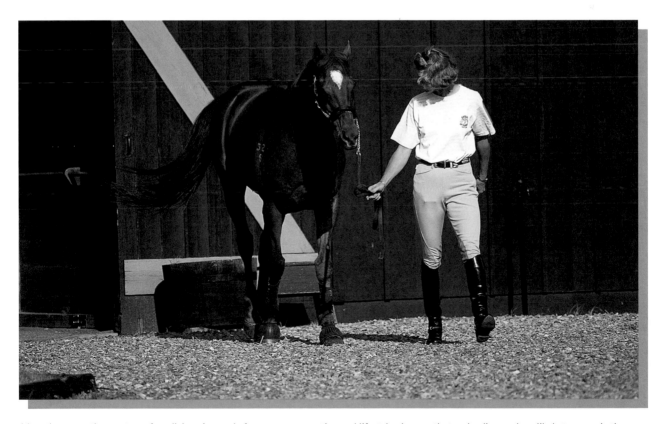

More than any other system of medicine, Ayurveda focuses on prevention and lifestyle changes that make disease less likely to occur in the first place. For both humans and horses, this means proper exercise, rest, diet, and mental attitude.

- are possessive and gluttonous
- have a strong liking for sweets
- are the healthiest of all three types but tend to get sick in winter and early spring

HOW IT WORKS: DISEASE AND DIAGNOSIS

Once the practitioner determines an individual's primary dosha and examines the state of the physical body and the emotional and environmental conditions the horse is in, she will seek to discover the underlying causes of his illness. Not all the information she relies on to make her diagnosis and design her treatment protocol will have to do with the symptoms. Ayurvedic thought maintains that disease has two ways to grab hold of the individual (whether human or animal):

- **external factors,** such as those brought on by seasonal change, infection, trauma, outside pollution, or even a supernatural cause such as a curse or planetary influence
- **internal factors**, which are generally believed to be caused by the accumulation of toxic material within us

These two elements are not always completely distinguishable, of course. They interpenetrate. One thing is well known: External forces have less power over a body that is pure and unpolluted, or as mainstream veterinary practitioners might say, "when the immune system is strong." This is why a healthy lifestyle is at the heart of Ayurveda—it makes for a strong defense against disease.

No matter what the cause, disease follows a basic progression:

Sanchaya is the first stage of disease. At this stage, toxins begin to accumulate and "clog" the system. Disease may first enter through the food route and attack different areas of the body according to the predominant dosha: Vata tends to settle in the colon, Pitta in the small intestines, and Kapha in the stomach. This is the accumulation stage. It can occur because of diet, excess dosha, weather changes, stress, or the invasion of pathogens. Signs are mild and often indefinable; however, some Ayurvedic physicians actually can detect this stage in the pulse.

Prakopa is the second stage of disease in which the doshas are overexcited and cause more blockages. The cause can be improper food, exercise (or lack of it), and seasonal effects. This is the aggravation or provocation phase.

Prasara is the third stage of disease in which the toxins "overflow" in the gastrointestinal tract and begin to move through the body. This is the distribution phase. During this phase, getting rid of the causative agent may not be enough because it frequently is in the first two phases. However, the disease is still completely reversible at this point.

Cycles of Disease

The stage at which a dosha builds up is known as the "accumulation" phase. If it reaches the point that it causes disease or imbalance, it is called the "provocation" or "aggravation" stage. When the doshic imbalance (disease) begins to subside, it is called the "pacification" stage. It is quite natural for a dosha to flow through the body in a cycle like this. Horses are not static beings!

Sthanasamsrya is the fourth stage of disease in which the toxin finds a "weak spot" (*dhatus*) in which to settle and cause illness. This is the deposition or infiltration phase. Here, degenerative disease or infection really can take hold. Malfunction or structural damage occurs, even though you may not notice it yet.

Vyakti is the first appearance of the disease itself. This is the manifestation or augmentation phase; this may be the first time that you actually notice that anything is seriously wrong with your horse. Many different symptoms may appear.

Bheda is the most serious, chronic, and widely disseminated form of the disease. It can result in permanent structural or physiological damage.

The sooner you can spot and treat a disease, the more likely it is that you will be successful in eliminating it. In many cases, you will need the advice of a skilled Ayurvedic practitioner to catch an illness in its earliest stages.

THE AYURVEDIC HEALTH CHECK

In keeping with good Ayurvedic practice, a trained horse owner

examines the horse carefully for early signs of disease.

Activity Level: A drop in normal activity level could indicate a serious problem. It is important to assess your horse's capacity for work and exercise.

Appetite: Horses, especially Kapha horses, are programmed to be hungry most of the time. A reduced appetite may be the first sign of a toxic buildup. It often may indicate the depression that accompanies many illnesses, including fever and any disease-producing nausea. A bad tooth also can cause a decrease in appetite. In the same way, a sudden, unexplained increase in appetite or a "depraved" appetite can indicate problems. Increased appetite could mean Cushing's disease, diabetes mellitus, or other Kapha-type diseases.

Breathing: The average resting respiratory rate for a healthy horse is 12 to 20 breaths per minute. (Count breaths for 15 seconds and multiply by four.) The breath should be steady and unrestricted. Labored breathing can indicate pneumonia, heart failure, anemia, or fluid in or around the lungs. Accompanied by a cough, it could mean COPD or other respiratory ailments.

Feces: Constipation, diarrhea, or feces that look or smell abnormal may be signs of a health problem. Vata-aggravated feces tend to be hard, dry, and grayish. Excess Pitta can turn feces liquid. Excess Kapha may produce mucus-coated feces.

Eyes: Eyes should be full of shine and luster. Squinting, swelling, redness, opacity, and apparent pain can mean trouble. Watery eyes indicate too much Kapha, while red eyes may suggest too much Vata or Pitta. Excessive blinking may be a sign of fear or nervousness. Yellow conjunctiva may suggest a weak liver.

Ears: Redness, infections, and debris in the ears are obvious signs of imbalance somewhere in the system.

Emotions: There are emotional waste products (*ama*) as well as physical ones. The basic question to ask is does your horse seem happy? Do you provide a stable, loving environment? Do you have a strong bond with him? Do you spend enough time with him? Knowing your horse's basic dosha will help you understand when something goes wrong. The normally placid Kapha plunges into lethargy, the energetic and focused Pitta becomes aggressive, and the energetic Vata becomes flighty when something is amiss.

Hooves: Dry and brittle hooves can be a sign of disease; they are most common in Vata-type horses. Overly soft hooves can affect Kapha types. They should feel lukewarm.

Joints and Movement: Your horse should move freely on well-lubricated joints. "Dry" horses like Vata animals are particularly low in lubrication, so they are most likely to be affected by stiffening joints.

Mouth and Gums: Breath and teeth should be clean and the gums pink. Simply lift the skin around the canine tooth and take a look. Pale, dark red, blue, or purple gums may indicate trouble. If you have difficulty examining your horse's mouth, he may have a tooth problem, as there may be swelling.

Nostrils: The nose can provide some important health clues. A discharge from the nose, either bloody, mucus, or purulent, can signal disease. Your vet can sometimes figure out the problem by flushing out the nose and examining the fluid, but often the horse will need to be sedated or anesthetized to get a clearer picture. Possible problems can include a nasal tumor, infection, a clotting problem, or a broken blood vessel.

Pulse: You can learn how to take a pulse Ayurvedically. Although you probably will not be able to use the pulse to make a diagnosis, you can learn more than you might think. A pulse occurs with every heartbeat, so the pulse rate and heart rate are the same. In traditional Ayurvedic practice, the best time to take a pulse is in the early morning,

before the horse has had breakfast but after he has defecated. Do not take the pulse after strenuous exercise or when the animal has a fever.

For male animals, take the pulse on the right leg. For females, take the pulse on the left leg. You also can take the pulse under the lower jaw or on the foreleg even with the knee joint.

The normal pulse for a horse ranges from 32 to 44 beats per minute, with Vata pulses at the higher end of that scale and Kapha pulses at the lower end. (Take the pulse for 15 seconds and multiply by four.) Don't be alarmed if the pulse rate seems to change. The pulse will be faster when the horse breathes in and slower when he breathes out. This is perfectly normal and even has a fancy name, sinus arrhythmia.

In Ayurveda, the pulse is taken with three fingers. The forefinger feels for the energy generated by ordinary circulation and respiration, the second finger detects metabolic activity, and the ring finger checks for structural health supported by the muscles, bones, and joints. When Vata is strong in the constitution, the index finger will feel a strong, irregular pulse that moves in waves like the motion of a serpent. This type of pulse is called a "snake pulse." If the pulse is felt most strongly in the middle finger, this is the Pitta pulse, which is an excited, jumping-around-like-a-frog pulse. It is indeed called a "frog pulse." The ring finger is most attuned to the Kapha pulse, or "swan pulse," which is a slow, floating sort of pulse. The kind of pulse you feel will indicate what dosha is most active. You need to feel many pulses on many horses to begin to confidently evaluate these pulse qualities.

Skin and Coat: The horse's skin and coat should be clean, supple, and free from sores, lumps, and infections. Vata-aggravated skin tends to be coarse, rough, and cool to the touch; skin overbalanced in the Pitta direction feels hot and moist; cold skin indicates too much Kapha.

Temperature: Ancient Ayurvedic physicians had no accurate way to measure temperature, but contemporary ones do not shun a thermometer. The correct temperature for a horse is 99.5° to 101.5°F (35.3° to 38.6°C). The hooves should feel lukewarm.

Thirst: Excessive water consumption is a sign of many illnesses, including diabetes, kidney failure, liver disease, high blood calcium, and so on.

Tongue: The tongue can reveal volumes to a skilled observer. A dry, rough, blackish tongue suggests an overbalance in the Vata direction; an overly red tongue can suggest too much Pitta (and is classic sign of heatstroke); and a whitish, slimy, coated tongue indicates too much Kapha.

Urine: Urine is collected via a free-catch method into a clean glass container. Normal urine should be comparatively odor free and light colored. Variations such as the following signal an imbalance among the doshas: Vata urine is pale yellow, with an "oily" consistency; Pitta urine is an intense yellow or a reddish color; Kapha urine is white, foamy, or muddy. Very dilute, watery urine may indicate a problem. Horses who have problems urinating or who suddenly seem to be urinating more than usual may have a medical condition. Certain drugs also may have this effect. In traditional Ayurvedic medicine, a drop or so of sesame oil is added to the urine to see which doshas may be at work: a snake-like form indicates Vata; an umbrella-shaped one suggests Pitta; and a pearl-shaped drop represents Kapha.

Voice: Your horse's whinny can tell you a lot about his condition, especially when there is a change in quality, volume, or frequency. Ayurvedic medicine places great emphasis on hearing the individual's voice.

MAINTAINING AND RESTORING BALANCE

The Ayurvedic practitioner develops a treatment plan specifically designed for the individual. Many plans will require a change in diet, environment, and daily routine. The goals are to eliminate impurities, reduce symptoms, eliminate physical and psychological disturbances, reduce stress, and increase harmony. A holistic form of medicine, Ayurvedic uses many tools to accomplish this.

The Three Wastes

A primary aim of Ayurveda is to cleanse the body of any substances that will cause disease, which naturally will reestablish the individual's well-being. This is why food and diet, and how things are ingested and eliminated, are important components of Ayurvedic practice.

The body can be thought of as a complex exchange system. It takes in air, food, and water and turns them into the seven tissues (plasma, blood, muscle, fat, bone, marrow, and eggs or sperm). It excretes in the feces, urine, and drool or sweat. Here are the Three Wastes (Mala)—like everything else, they comprise the five elements (earth, water, fire, air, and space):

1. Purisa, or feces, is the waste remaining after nutrients from digested food have been absorbed in the small intestine and transferred elsewhere. The large intestine takes up most of the remaining water and salt and expels the rest as fecal material.

2. Mutra, or urine, is produced by the renal system—the kidneys, bladder, and urethra. This system also regulates the fluid balance and maintains blood pressure.

3. Sweda, or sweat (perhaps you can see the etymological connection), passes through the pores of the skin; it controls body temperature and helps to regulate the electrolytic balance.

To stay in good health, the body must eliminate waste, or mala, in the proper amount and with the correct frequency. The Ayurvedic practitioner pays careful attention to these waste products to learn about her horse's internal balance.

The Balanced Ayurvedic Diet

In the Ayurvedic tradition, diet is a critical part of health maintenance. In fact, there is a saying, "Aaharah pranah," which means "Food is life." This verse alone is enough to show how important food is in Ayurvedic medicine!

In this modality, diet is more than nutrition; it is also used to balance the doshas. For instance, horses who are overbalanced in the Vata direction do best on a diet that includes some Kapha or Pitta foods. It is believed that different foods have different effects on the doshas. While these balancing diets were designed for human beings, they easily can be adjusted to fit a horse's natural diet. In Ayurveda, the distinction between food and medicine is not as rigid as it is in the Western understanding of these terms.

Ayurvedic foods are classified as sweet, salty, bitter, pungent, sour, or astringent. Each "taste" increases certain doshas and decreases others:

- to increase Vata: pungent, bitter, astringent
- to decrease Vata: sweet, sour, salty
- to increase Pitta: pungent, sour, salty
- to decrease Pitta: sweet, bitter, astringent
- to increase Kapha: sweet, sour, salty
- to decrease Kapha: pungent, bitter, astringent

Or to put it another way:

- sweet reduces Vata and Pitta but increases Kapha
- sour reduces Vata but increases Pitta and Kapha
- salty reduces Vata but increases Pitta and Kapha
- pungent reduces Kapha but increases Pitta and Vata
- bitter reduces Pitta and Kapha but increases Vata
- astringent reduces Pitta and Kapha but increases Vata

Many foods have more than one taste, which doesn't just refer to the flavor but also to the effects of the foods. Tastes are also classified as cooling or warming and are used accordingly, which relates back to an individual's original dosha, or constitution.

In the Ayurvedic view, foods cause a chain taste response or "taste cascade." The first taste is the immediate flavor on the tongue, called rasa, referring to one of the six tastes. The second phase of the taste process is virya, the heating or cooling effect during digestion as the food moves through the body. Pungent, sour, and salty foods are considered heating. Bitter, astringent, and sweet foods are considered cooling. The third phase is vipaka, during which the foods resolve into their final effect on the body.

When treating a disease, Ayurvedic practitioners try to find a combination of foods that will restore a natural balance. This is obviously a complicated process in which you'll need the aid of an Ayurvedic practitioner.

Ayurvedic Foods for Horses

Although you should prepare a complete regimen according to your own horse's dosha, the following are some examples of Ayurvedic foods that are common to most equine diets:

When treating a disease, Ayurvedic practitioners try to find a combination of foods that will restore natural balance. In this modality, different foods are used to correct imbalances in the body based on the individual's body type or dosha.

- **Grains:** Barley is a cooling grain and is best used in the summer; corn and oats are warming grains that are better fed in the winter. These grains are also all classified as "sweet" and are thus better for Vata and Pitta horses than Kapha horses. Kapha horses really do best with very little grain.
- **Treats:** Vata horses thrive on carrots, apples, and even sweet potatoes and green beans. Don't feed a Vata horse anything with white sugar or soy products. Pitta horses do well on carrots, broccoli, and potatoes. They don't do well with molasses or honey. Kapha horses do best without sweet juicy vegetables (including apples) or sugar. They do well on carrots, broccoli, and green beans.

AYURVEDIC MEDICINAL PLANTS

While Ayurvedic medicine goes down many paths, practitioners agree that herbal therapy is its most effective healing tool. The ancient Indian sage Charaka identified 350 medicinal herbs, divided into 50 groups. Part of the division depended on whether the herbs in question had healing effects or preventive effects. However, as mentioned, Ayurvedic medicine does not draw a line between nutrition, supplements, and medicine. That is a Western distinction.

There is nothing especially magical about the Indian herbs traditionally used in Ayurvedic medicine. Some of them are also used as kitchen spices, and many of these have found their way into homes throughout the world. Others are used primarily for medical purposes and seem more exotic, at least to Westerners. Many Western plants have exactly the same Ayurvedic properties as do Indian herbs. However, the medical system we call Ayurveda was based upon Indian herbs, and it is only recently that Western Ayurvedic practitioners have begun looking for Western herbal equivalents. This requires a careful study of each herb to learn whether it is Vata enhancing, Pitta reducing, Kapha balancing, and so on. Work in this area is ongoing.

That said, we should mention some plants that are often used in Ayurvedic medicine to keep horses healthy and to remedy imbalances among the doshas.

Ajwain or Ajwan (*Trachyspermum ammi*)
- **Parts used:** Crushed seeds.
- **Ayurvedic function:** Conquers Kapha and Vata.
- **Action:** Antispasmodic.
- **Indications:** For coughs and digestive problems, including colic and flatulence. This is a favorite remedy to disperse wind in the bowels. It is also used as a dewormer. A poultice of the crushed herb can be used for arthritis.
- **Note:** It is believed that thymol, a major constituent of Ajwain, is especially potent against coughs.

Aloe (*Aloe spp.*)
- **Parts used:** Leaves.
- **Ayurvedic function:** Decreases Pitta.
- **Action:** Antiseptic.
- **Indications:** For healing minor wounds and burns and for problems in the small intestine.

Amla or Amalaki (*Emblica officinalis*)
- **Parts used:** Fruit.
- **Ayurvedic function:** Balances Pitta.
- **Action:** Rejuvenator.
- **Indications:** Rejuvenates blood, bones, eyesight, liver, and heart; good for many chronic conditions. It also helps the hooves grow faster.
- **Note:** Amalaki is also called Dhatri ("the nurse" in Sanskrit) because of its healing properties.

Asafetida (*Ferula asafetida*)
- **Parts used:** Resin and gum.
- **Ayurvedic function:** It reduces Vata and Kapha and raises Pitta.
- **Action:** Antispasmodic. Also used as a digestive and nerve aid.

Choosing Ayurvedic Herbs

When using herbs, experienced Ayurvedic practitioners will take into account the mix of dosha types in an individual at the time and not just the individual's physical condition. This is because the herbs that are used to maintain or restore health also have personality or energy types of their own, and these patterns must be matched to the dosha of the animal or person eating them for maximum effect.

- **Indications:** Convulsions.
- **Note:** Contains the highest amount of vitamin C in any plant (30 percent more than in oranges).

Ashwaganda or Indian Ginseng (*Withania somnifera*)
- **Parts used:** Roots and leaves, dried.
- **Ayurvedic function:** Rejuvenation for Vata horses, it reduces Vata and Kapha. Increases Pitta.
- **Action:** Good as a tonic, astringent, diuretic, and nerve aid. Also has antitumor, antistress (adaptogen), and antioxidant properties.
- **Indications:** It addresses general debility, liver problems, and exhaustion and can be used to treat arthritis, COPD, and weak eyes. It gives energy and vitality. Good for aged horses. It also has tissue-building properties.
- **Note:** This plant is actually supposed to smell like a horse.

Bala (*Sida cordifolia*)
- **Parts used:** Seeds, roots, leaves, stems.
- **Ayurvedic function:** Strengthens Pitta and balances all three doshas.
- **Action:** For inner strength and nervous disorders.
- **Indications:** It removes toxins and builds immunity.
- **Note:** This is one of the most frequently used Ayurvedic herbs because it simultaneously balances all three doshas. Give as a decoction. (Caution: While this herb has been safely used in Indian medicine for hundreds of years, do not attempt to medicate using this herb without guidance from a qualified practitioner. It is placed here for your information only, as it is so widely used.)

Brahmi (*Bacopa monniera*)
- **Parts used:** Whole plant
- **Ayurvedic function:** Balances all the doshas.
- **Action:** Mild sedative.
- **Indications:** It is used for brain problems and age-related mental decline. Supports memory. Acts as a blood cleanser and fever reducer. Produces calmness and mental clarity. Stimulates hair and hoof growth. May prevent excessive scar formation by inhibiting the production of collagen.

Forskolin (*Coleus forskohli*)
- **Parts used:** Mostly the root, occasionally the leaves.
- **Ayurvedic function:** Decreases Vata.
- **Action:** Antispasmodic, smooth muscle relaxant, anticoagulant, anti-allergic.
- **Indications:** It is used for heart disease (strengthens cardiac contractility), abdominal colic, respiratory disorders, convulsions, and COPD.

- **Note:** Cook the roots in water and add it to the horse's feed. Add cooked leaves to increase lactation.

Frankincense or Shallaki (*Boswellia serrata*)
- **Parts used:** Bark and dried resinous gum.
- **Ayurvedic function:** Reduces Vata.
- **Action:** Anti-inflammatory, antiarthritic, diuretic, appetite stimulant, antifungal.
- **Indications:** It is used for arthritis (especially of the knee joint), chronic lung disease, diarrhea, liver disorders, ringworm, and inflammatory skin conditions.

Guggul (*Comminphora mukul*)
- **Parts used:** Gum resin from the stem.
- **Ayurvedic function:** Reduces Kapha and Vata. Increases Pitta.
- **Action:** Demulcent, appetite stimulant, nervine, analgesic, antiseptic.
- **Indications:** It is used for arthritis, skin diseases, low back pain, nervous disorders, weakness, bronchitis, and digestive disturbances. It can be an aid to fat metabolism and may enhance thyroid function.
- **Note:** This plant is closely related to myrrh. It is the most important resin in Ayurvedic medicine. It is said to have purifying and rejuvenating powers.

Gymnema (*Gymnema sylvestra*)
- **Parts used:** Root and leaves.
- **Ayurvedic function:** Reduces Kapha.
- **Action:** Astringent, stomachic (settles the stomach), tonic.
- **Indications:** It is used as a spleen and kidney tonic.

Jatamansi (*Nardostachys jatamansi*)
- **Parts used:** Bark, heartwood.
- **Ayurvedic function:** Balances all the doshas.
- **Action:** It is used as a sedative (related to the Western herb valerian).
- **Indications:** Flatulence, allergies, skin conditions.

Licorice (*Glycerrhiza glabra*)
- **Parts used:** Root.
- **Ayurvedic function:** Reduces Vata.
- **Action:** It is used as a tonic.
- **Indications:** Good for treating COPD. It also calms the mind and harmonizes the body.

Mint (*Mentha*)
- **Parts used:** Leaves.
- **Ayurvedic function:** Reduces Pitta.
- **Action:** It is used as an anti-inflammatory.
- **Indications:** This is a cooling herb for digestion; it also helps to relieve emotional strain.

Neem (*Azadirachta indica*)
- **Parts used:** Root bark, bark, gum, nuts, leaves, flowers, and young fruit.
- **Ayurvedic function:** Reduces Pitta and Kapha. Increases Vata.
- **Action:** It is used as a dewormer, antiseptic, diuretic, antifungal, and insecticidal.
- **Indications:** Good for treating eye problems, chronic low fever, skin diseases, ulcers, wounds, blood disorders, parasites, gum disease, arthritis, and chronic fatigue.

Mint

Phyllanthus (*Phyllanthus amarus*)
- **Parts used:** Whole plant.
- **Ayurvedic function:** Reduces Kapha and Pitta. Increases Vata.
- **Action:** It is used as a liver protectant, astringent, stomachic (settles the stomach), diuretic, and fever reducer.
- **Indications:** Good for treating eye problems, constipation, gastric pain, edema, and eczema.

Sandalwood (*Santalum album.* **Also known as chandana, white sandalwood, white saunders, yellow sandalwood. In India: chandan, chandanam, srigandha**)
- **Parts used:** Wood and volatile oil.
- **Ayurvedic function:** Reduces Pitta.
- **Action:** Gentle blood cleanser (alterative), antibacterial, antiseptic, astringent, carminative, disinfectant, diuretic, expectorant, haemostatic, refrigerant, sedative, stimulant.
- **Indications:** Skin disease (including allergies), eye disease, infections of the urinary tract.
- **Note:** A few horses have an irritated skin response to sandalwood. Do not use in horses with lung congestion.

Shatavari (*Asparagus racemosus, A. sarmentosus, A. gonoclados,* **or** *A. adscendens*)
- **Parts used:** Root.
- **Action:** Antidiarrhetic, antispasmodic, aphrodisiac, antidysenteric, demulcent, diuretic, nutritive, mucilaginous, stomachic (settles the stomach), tonic
- **Ayurvedic function:** Increases Kapha, decreases Pitta and Vata. It is particularly useful for balancing Pitta.
- **Indications:** Blood cleanser, nourishes mucous membranes, skin problems (including allergies), diarrhea, colon problems, stiff joint, female reproductive problems, cancer. Boosts the immune system.
- **Note:** This herb works better with female horses and is the female "equivalent" of ashwagandha.

Tulsi or Holy Basil (*Ocimum sanctum*)
- **Parts used:** Leaf, seeds, root.
- **Ayurvedic function:** Maintains the digestive fire (*agni*).
- **Action:** Antioxidant.
- **Indications:** It is used to fight stress and balance the mind. Good for treating ailments of the throat, chest, and lungs.

COMMON USES

While there are too many Ayurvedic herbs to give more than just a sample, here is a brief compendium of some of their more common uses:
- **Joint Support:** Guggul, boswellia, devil's claw root, guduchi leaf, willow tree bark, angelica root, cinnamon bark, sarsaparilla root, prickly ash bark, licorice root, gotu kola leaf, triphala, ginger root, turmeric root, haritaki fruit, celery seed, asafoetida gum, ajwan seed, pippali fruit, Fenugreek seed, shilajit, cubeb, sesame oil and its seeds, **castor oil**
- **Heart Support:** Arjuna, amalaki, cinnamon, manjishta, guggul, pippali, tamarind, hawthorn, ginger, haritaki, cardamom
- **Respiratory Support:** Elecampane, mullein, licorice, yerba anta, thyme, black pepper, shilajit, flaxseed, amalaki, ginger, clove, manna, haritaki, cardamom, turmeric, pippali, bhibitaki, myrrh, cubeb, asafoetida, tulasi, ajwan, coffee

Triphala

Triphala is a remedy made from equal parts of the fruit of three trees: Amla (*E. officinalis*), Baheda (*T. belerica*), and Harada (*T. chebula*). It is used for detoxification and cleansing. A balancing herbal combination, it works best when taken over a long period of time. It is unlike the other remedies because it is a commercially made preparation.

A true holistic therapy, Ayurveda also may include medicinal herbs and massage among other things. Massage is especially helpful when used during winter.

- **Weight Loss:** Bhibitaki, guggul, sage, Pippali, Elecampane, uva ursi, aokshura, ajwan, cinnamon, damiana, dandelion, parsley, nettle, shilajit, black pepper, ginger, turmeric, triphala, clove, cardamom

COMPLEMENTARY AYURVEDIC TREATMENTS

Ayurvedic treatment is more than herbs. It is a true holistic therapy that also may include music, massage, and aromatherapy, among other things. Here are just a few therapies.

ABHYANGA: AYURVEDIC MASSAGE

Whole body massage (Abhyanga) plays an important role in Ayurvedic medicine, both for relaxation and revitalization. It is used to manage and correct dosha imbalances and thus improves the basic functioning of the body. As with any massage, Abhyanga stimulates and tones the skin, muscles, circulatory system, and nervous system. It strengthens the lungs and regulates digestion, helping the body eliminate toxins and waste. It also promotes stamina and flexibility. This type of massage is especially useful for aged horses and animals with overabundance of Vata. It should be used in the winter.

AYURVEDIC CRYSTAL THERAPY

In Ayurvedic crystal therapy, there are nine traditional gems, each with its own special quality and use. In general, red, yellow, and orange stones lower Vata and Kapha. Green and blue stones reduce Pitta. Purple stones balance

all doshas. For excellent all-around results, many people purchase bangles composed of all nine Ayurveda gems (navaratnas). These are considered to have powerful effects in nullifying bad karma.

Here are the main crystals used in Ayurvedic healing:

- **Ruby:** This is the stone of the Sun and the king of gems. It is considered a life-protecting gem. A clear, medium-red, transparent stone is of the most efficacy. It is beneficial for diabetes, anemia, fevers, and other blood problems, as well as for digestive problems and fevers. It will decrease Vata and Kapha and increase Pitta very powerfully. If worn, it should be placed on the right side of the halter.

- **Pearl:** The pearl is associated with the Moon and should have a moon-like, shining quality. The pearl is said to provide strength, produce mental calm, and reduce aggression. A pearl with a reddish tint is said to increase intelligence. It is also good for coughs, infertility, kidney disorders, and heart failure. It pacifies Pitta, but this gem is really balancing to all doshas. Pearls should be bought on Monday when the moon is waxing and set in silver. Some people make "pearl water" by allowing the gem to stand in a glass of water overnight. If worn, it should be placed on the left side of the halter.

- **Yellow Sapphire:** This is the stone of Jupiter. It should be a clear, bright, uniform color and of symmetrical shape. It is said to confer groundedness. Yellow sapphire is beneficial for horses suffering from insect bites and other poisons, digestive ailments, and liver troubles. It is a balancing stone and can be used equally well by all doshas, although it may slightly increase Kapha.

- **Zircon:** The yellow zircon is symbolic of the shadowy planet Rahu. The best color, say the ancient texts, is the same color as cow's urine. Considering the esteem in which the cow is held in India, this may be taken as a compliment, but canary yellow or gold might be better in American culture. It improves skin quality, reproductive ability, and intelligence. It helps all doshas.

- **Emeralds:** This is the stone of Mercury. It is not possible to find a flawless natural emerald, so do the best you can, or select a flawless synthetic. (Some synthetic emeralds include flaws on purpose to make them appear more natural, but you don't want flaws in stones used for healing purposes.) Before use, the stone should be immersed overnight in cow's milk. This cooling gem is a great stone for Pitta and Vata illnesses, mental disorders, nervous diseases, abdominal pains, heart trouble, and fever.

- **Diamond:** The diamond is associated with Venus. It energizes the life force and is an excellent stone for an animal recovering from electrical shock, heart problems, paralysis, hernia surgery, or psychological issues. Colorless diamonds reduce Pitta and increase Vata and Kapha. Red diamonds, on the other hand, tend to increase Pitta.

- **Moonstone:** This mysterious stone belongs to the mystic, shadowy orb called Ketu in Indian astrology. It is strongly linked with psychic ability. This cooling stone increases Vata but is helpful to all doshas. Medicinally, it is used to increase physical strength and to help cure wounds, skin diseases, and joint pain.

- **Blue Sapphire:** The blue sapphire belongs to Saturn. It calms Vata and Kapha and increases Pitta. It is considered a very spiritual stone. It is good for skin diseases, nervous disorders, skeletal system problems, and bloat.

- **Red Coral:** Coral is identified with Mars. It gives courage, energy, and strength. It can be used in cases of dry coughs, arthritis, inflammations, eye problems, lactating mares, and fever. It increases Pitta, according

Amethyst

In Ayurveda, aromas, sounds, and even colors are thought to have healing powers. For example, a blue blanket is thought to be calming and good for the heart.

to most authorities. Others believe that it lowers Pitta and Vata and raises Kapha due to its association with water. Coral is a traditional Ayurvedic gem, but because of environmental reasons, it should be used with care.

Other stones not included in the traditional nine are also used from time to time in Ayurveda:

- **Amethyst:** This is a good stone for mental clarity. It reduces Pitta and Vata. It is a stone of love, compassion, and hope and is the perfect stone for rescue horses. It is beneficial for Vata horses.
- **Aquamarine:** Aquamarine can be used as substitute for emerald. Both are beryls. It is good for Pitta horses.
- **Jade:** Jade is a stone for longevity. It helps the kidneys and is said to be useful for the prevention of cataracts. It can be used for all doshas.
- **Lapis Lazuli:** Lapis is considered a spiritual stone that is generally tonifying. It calms Vata and Pitta and increases Kapha. It is good for eye ailments, liver, and skin diseases.
- **Opal:** Opal is the stone of Neptune. It is said to strengthen the bone marrow and nerves. It is beneficial for Vata and Kapha horses.

COLOR THERAPY

While horses do not see colors in the same way we do, they are not strictly color-blind, and colors are believed to have important healing effects on them. Some Ayurvedic practitioners use color by pouring pure water into a bottle of the appropriate color and allowing the bottle to sit out in the sun for a period of time—when cool, the water can be poured into the horse's bucket. Or you can use a blanket of the appropriate color.

- **Blue:** Blue reduces Pitta and aggravates Kapha and Vata. This antistress color is said to be good for disorders of the liver and all problems in the throat area.
- **Green:** Calming, comforting green reduces Pitta but aggravates Kapha and Vata. It is said to help heal wounds and ulcers, and it is also good for the heart.
- **Indigo:** This balancing color is good for all the senses but especially vision, hearing, and the spiritual third eye. This is a color that increases stability in all dosha types.
- **Orange:** Vibrant orange is warm and healing. It balances Kapha and Vata but can aggravate Pitta, just like red can. This is a good color for horses who are fighting infections; it is said to be antibacterial. It is also good for spleen, kidney, and lung ailments.
- **Pink:** Pink has similar but milder effects than red does. It is also more calming than red, helps to heal grief, and promotes relaxation. Pink may make Kapha horses lethargic, however.
- **Purple:** Purple, a truly transformational color, increases Vata but balances Pitta and Kapha. It creates a lightness of body that is excellent for hunters and jumpers.
- **Red:** Red is a warm color that reduces Kapha and Vata. It increases Pitta and promotes deep healing and energy. It is also good for blood formation and circulation. However, Pitta horses who are overexposed to red may be in danger of conjunctivitis and other inflammatory ailments.
- **Silver or Gray:** These colors are associated with the moon. They reduce Pitta and increase Kapha and Vata.
- **Yellow or Gold:** Yellow reduces Vata and Kapha. It is good for horses with respiratory problems. It is also good for nervous system problems.

Ayurvedic Aromas

While aromatherapy is its own modality, it is also used in Ayurvedic medicine. The pure essence is usually put in a bottle and sprayed around the barn. Here are its uses:

- air purification: camphor or frankincense
- cleansing: sandalwood or myrrh
- congestion: eucalyptus or sage
- digestion: cardamom or clove
- foot problems: peppermint oil in warm water
- immune system problems: myrrh, rose, or frankincense
- infections: eucalyptus or cedar
- pain: myrrh or cinnamon
- rejuvenation: frankincense, myrrh, rose, or guggul
- soothing and calming: sandalwood or rose
- stimulation: cardamom or fennel

Sound and Music the Ayurveda Way

Sound plays an important part in Ayurvedic healing. In fact, the original Holy Scriptures, the Vedas, were not written down but sung and chanted. In Ayurveda, sound has a powerful healing effect, and healing "mantras," or short mystical phrases, are used.

Healing and Balancing Mantras

While your horse cannot chant a mantra, you can! A mantra is recited many times (often 108 times) with a pause between each repetition. This pause is very important, and it represents the "unstruck" chord, or essential silence at the

Tablas

core of the universe. Here are some of the most well-known one-word healing mantras that you can use separately or put together creatively. The syllables, for the most part, have no individual meaning.

- **Aum:** This is the ultimate syllable. The most powerful word in any mantra is "Aum." Each letter is pronounced separately, with a slight pausing breath after the word. The "a" sound represents the creation of the universe as you open your mouth to speak the word. The "u" sound represents the maintenance and preservation of this same cosmos. And the "m" sound symbolizes the inevitable destruction of the universe. The following pause is an emblem of the hiatus before the cosmos recreates itself, forever and ever. This is a mind-altering mantra that empowers all others. Recite with your hand on the horse's head. This is a good mantra for Pitta and Kapha horses.
- **Aym:** This mantric syllable improves concentration and is excellent for performance horses. A good mantra for Pitta and Kapha horses.
- **Ham:** This syllable energizes the respiratory system. Recite with your hand on the horse's throat.
- **Hoom:** "Hoom" is said to ward off negative influences, burn Ama, and clear channels. This is a great mantra for both Vata and Kapha horses.
- **Hrim:** This is a cleansing and purifying mantra. It is a great detoxifier for animals who are recovering from poisoning. It also is good for use while cleaning stables and other areas.
- **Klim:** This Kapha-increasing mantra provides strength and emotional control for horses who are excessively angry or fearful.
- **Krim:** This mantra is empowering for action. It is great to use at the start of horse events.
- **Ksham:** This mantra gives peace and is connected with the "third eye." Recite with your fingers on the horse's forehead, above and between his eyes.

- **Lam:** Lam is the "earth" mantra and is excellent for problems of the excretory system. Recite with your hand on the horse's hindquarters.
- **Ram (with an AH):** "Ram" is probably the second most powerful mantric syllable. This mantra brings strength and peace and is ideal for calming mental disturbances and fears. Medicinally, it is said to strengthen ojas (vitality from nourishment) and build the immune system. This is an excellent mantra for Vata horses.
- **Ram (pronounced with a short "u" sound):** Ram is the fire mantra and increases will, energy, and motivation. Recite with your hand on the horse's abdomen.
- **Sham:** This is the peace mantra. It creates calm, alleviates stress, and is said to be good for chronic degenerative nervous system disorders. Excellent for Pitta horses.
- **Shrim:** This mantra is said to promote overall health. It is especially good for the plasma and reproductive fluids. It is superior for Pitta horses.
- **Shum:** This sound increases vitality and fertility.
- **Som (rhymes with home):** This sound is a general tonic for the whole system.
- **Vam:** Vam is the water mantra and helps the reproductive system.
- **Yam:** This "air" mantra helps the heart, clears the circulatory system, and provides all-around energy. Recite with your hand on the horse's chest.

Before using the mantras directly on your horse, purify the healing area by reciting Aum and Hoom several times.

Music Therapy

Music therapy is also an important part of the Ayurvedic system. There's an old story that the Indian master musician Thyagaraja brought a dead person back to life with one of his compositions, but that's a little much to expect even from Ayurveda!

In Indian music, the basic melody or form is known as the raga. About 75,000 classical ragas exist, each grouped under ten "parent scales." Each raga has its own mood and healing power, and it is ideally played at a certain time of day or season of the year. Some are very specific; one of them—the *Ahir Bhairav*—is to be played only when the very first ray of the sun is spotted at dawn. Indian classical instruments include the dhapli, dholak, duff, flute, sitar, shahnai, tablas, and mridangum.

In scientific terms, it is believed that music stimulates the pituitary gland, which in turn controls many aspects of the nervous and metabolic systems. Most people have discovered that the right kind of music can ease pain, cure headaches, and dispel anger. There is no reason to suppose it acts differently with horses. The key is to find the right music for your horse's dosha. Ayurvedic musicians have produced music to raise or lower the various doshas, so it is for you to decide what needs to be balanced. You can purchase such music almost anywhere.

HOLISTIC HORSE SENSE

Like our own doctors, many veterinarians seek complementary, nutritional, and alternative methods of supporting the body so it can heal itself. With good reason, Ayurveda is known as the "science of life." It not only offers an understanding of the processes that cause disease, but it also teaches how to live in balance with one's internal environment and the environment outside of the body in order to maintain health. More than a medical therapy, it's a philosophy, an art, and a lifestyle. It uses diet, herbs, meditation, massage, and crystal therapy. It heals the body, invigorates the spirit, focuses the brain, and awakens the mind. And, as we have just seen, it's not just for humans.

Chapter 10 Aromatherapy

$\mathcal{S}$mell is magical. Linked to the most primitive and deepest centers of the brain, it has the power to make us feel invigorated, relaxed, or nauseated. It also can cure. And unlike the tongue, which can detect only a few basic tastes, the nose is able to savor (or be repelled by) about 10,000 different odors. However, aromatherapy involves much more than walking around and sniffing roses. It uses the science of smell to promote well-being. Aromatherapy is undoubtedly one of the fastest-growing fields

and Essential Oils

in alternative medicine, but if you think that it's only for people, you're quite wrong. It is used more frequently and probably with greater success in horses than in any other animal. The father of modern aromatherapy, French chemist René Maurice Gattefossé, first experimented with horses and dogs before trying his ideas on human beings. He is also the one who coined the term "aromatherapy." And while its therapeutic application is new in the United States, French veterinarians and physicians make regular use of these fragrant plant materials in their treatment protocols.

ADVANTAGES
- NONINVASIVE.
- OFTEN EFFECTIVE.
- PLEASANT TO USE—HORSES LOVE IT.
- CAN BE USED WITH OTHER THERAPIES.

DISADVANTAGES
- NOT ALWAYS EFFECTIVE.
- IN RARE CASES, IT CAN BE DANGEROUS.
- CAN BE EXPENSIVE.

FOUNDATIONS OF AROMATHERAPY

Aromatherapy is both ancient and worldwide; its foundations date back to Egypt, India, and the Far East thousands of years ago. The modern incarnation of this healing modality began in 1912 or so, and its development was actually provoked by an accident. During a lab experiment in his perfume factory, chemist Gattefossé was badly burned. Looking for immediate relief, he plunged his hand into the nearest vat of cool liquid, which happened to be the essential oil of lavender. He was surprised to find how quickly his hand healed and that there was no residual scarring. This led him to experiment with other essences. He eventually used lavender, clove, lemon, and thyme oils medicinally for their antiseptic properties and for their ability to improve and speed healing.

Gattefossé wrote several books on his research with essential oils and would later define aromatherapy as the use of aromas, aromatics, and essential oils to promote healing and to create a feeling of well-being in the patient. Today we understand the practice of aromatherapy to refer to the use of essential oils, hydrosols, and absolutes to effect a cure.

Aromatherapy Roots

The roots of aromatherapy go even deeper than you might imagine—all the way back to the days of the ancient Egyptians. Their theories about the properties of plants were not very scientific, though, as they matched the purpose of the plant with its shape and color. For example, they believed that red plants were stimulating and blue plants were calming. The theory extended to the parts of the plant used as well. For example, plant leaves were supposed to heal respiratory disorders because they were the "lung" of the plant, and roots were used for "grounding." Nevertheless, these ideas became the foundation for the usage of many plant essences in healing today.

THE SCIENCE OF SMELL

To really understand the theory behind aromatherapy, you need to know something about the science of smell.

A smell, or scent, consists of tiny aromatic particles. Precisely how they work is still unknown, but somehow the information they contain gets delivered to the brain via olfactory nerves in the nasal cavity. These scent molecules eventually get transferred to the bloodstream, where they are carried throughout the body. Smells also go directly to the hypothalamus, which is the organ that regulates many bodily functions, including hunger, thirst, emotions, and even temperature. But it's not just a physical interaction. When inhaled, a scent also directly affects the ancient, limbic area of the brain, which is related to emotions and memories. This is why an odor or aroma can suddenly call up memories from childhood or long ago times.

AROMATHERAPY AND SMELL

Employing our "organ" of smell, aromatherapy works by using the aromatic oils extracted from plants, fruits, and flowers to enhance the body's natural self-regulating and self-healing abilities.

According to scientific studies, we respond to aromas in less than three seconds, and because oil molecules are so small, they diffuse into the bloodstream quickly to have some effect almost immediately, at least emotionally. More importantly, essential oils are thought to oxygenate the bloodstream, thereby stimulating the immune system and increasing vitality so that toxins can be eliminated from the body. They can be calming or stimulating, they can be used to relieve muscle soreness and pain, and some even have specific medicinal properties. Often combined with the healing power of touch through massage, this holistic treatment is believed to benefit body, mind, and spirit.

ESSENTIAL OILS

Nowadays, the use of essential oils to treat common physical and behavioral problems in animals has become increasingly popular, especially with pet owners who are concerned about the potential side effects of many pharmaceuticals. Because we know that animals in the wild instinctively seek out plants and herbs as natural remedies to ease their ailments, it follows that this form of therapy would be a preferred alternative for domestic animals deprived of this choice in their manmade environments. At least that's the theory.

Essential oils are generally chosen to treat a specific condition but may be changed by the herbal therapist as treatment progresses. They are used for the following conditions in horses:

- allergies
- arthritis
- behavioral problems
- colic
- COPD
- digestive problems
- headshaking
- hoof and foot conditions
- parasites
- laminitis
- mud fever
- muscular problems
- navicular problems
- pest control
- respiratory conditions
- sarcoids and warts
- skin conditions
- stress
- sweet itch
- urinary disorders
- viruses
- wounds

Aromatherapy uses the science of smell to promote well-being. It is used more frequently and probably with greater success in horses than in any other animal.

Not all animals are treated in the same way, however (i.e., you wouldn't use the same oils or the same concentrations on horses and dogs), and some oils may be toxic to your animal. Essential oils can be harmful if used incorrectly, so only use them under the supervision of a trained herbalist or aromatherapist who has worked with horses. Also, as always, it's best to consult with your vet before beginning therapy.

WHAT ARE ESSENTIAL OILS?

Contrary to what many people think, essential oils are not fragrances or perfumes. They are organic liquids that are derived from the leaves, flowers, stems, roots, bark, skin, or other parts of a plant or fruit. (However, not every plant produces an essential oil.) Although they originate from the plant oils that are located within sacs along the surface of some plant tissues, the essential oils used in aromatherapy are concentrated substances derived from these plant parts through the use of steam or water distillation, manual expression (hand-pressing), carbon dioxide extraction, or solvent extraction.

Used externally, essential oils are absorbed through the skin and into the body to produce healing. (Essential oils are among the few substances with this characteristic. If you put a drop of water on your skin, it stays there.) Highly volatile, they are also easily absorbed into the body through the blood/brain barrier via the olfactory system (the nose and its accompanying parts). On rare occasions, they are ingested. While they are not classified as medicine, they do help to balance the system and may even fight disease.

Concentrates, Hydrosols, and Absolutes

Essential oils are very strong, highly concentrated liquids, but despite the name, they are not oily at all. Interestingly, they can be processed for therapeutic use in different forms: pure concentrates, hydrosols, or absolutes.

A pure essential oil is generally derived by steam distillation of the plant materials, but a hydrosol, the water by-product of distillation that remains after the oil is skimmed off the condensate, is also produced during this process. A hydrosol contains only the water-soluble parts of the plant and a little tiny bit of the essential oil. In other words, hydrosols are like essential oils but in far less of a concentration. Also known as floral waters, they are much gentler in their action than pure essential oils but perhaps not as effective. They can be used externally on the skin, sprayed into the environment as a mist, or administered internally as a tonic. Hydrosols are used more often in small animal practice, especially with cats.

Another form of essential oil called an absolute is extracted in a more complex manner. This process uses a chemical solvent such as acetone to extract the plant material. (The solvent is later removed during the final stages of production.) Absolutes are extremely concentrated, so a little goes a long way. This method is used when regular distillation does not remove enough of the oils from the plant source or when delicate and precious plant materials may be harmed by hot steam. Because a tiny amount of solvent may remain after processing, absolutes are primarily used in the perfume industry.

Most essential oils are extracted by distillation, although citrus oils are often cold-pressed. In this process, the whole fruit is pressed to squeeze the juice from the pulp and to release the essential oil.

In equine practice, pure essential oils themselves are preferred.

CHEMICAL COMPONENTS

Essential oils are mostly liquid at room temperature, usually colorless or pale yellow, and they are highly diluted before use. They are also very complex—any single oil might have more than 200 constituents. Depending on what your horse's needs are, it may help to know what these components are and what they do.

Many oils belong to the chemical class called monoterpenes. Found in most plant matter, these naturally occurring chemical compounds have known detoxifying qualities and other

---

Natural Versus Synthetic Oils

Most substances that are passed off as aromatherapy products actually should be called "fragrance oils" because they are synthetic, not natural. Only naturally obtained substances should be considered as proper aromatherapy materials.

Synthetic substances are high in alcohol content, which you should be able to smell. To receive the maximum benefit from essential oils, use only oils made from pure, raw materials. Synthetically made oils simply don't work.

positive medical effects. Some monoterpenes, like camphor, a waxy substance that comes from an evergreen tree called *C. camphora*, occur in an almost pure form; however, most occur as complex mixtures.

Monoterpenes are among the gentlest of essential oils. One example of this class of oils is monoterpene alcohols, which include eucalyptus, peppermint, rose, rosewood, tea tree, thyme linalool, and thyme thujanol. Generally, these have tonifying and immune-enhancing effects. Another class is monoterpene hydrocarbons, which include pine and citrus oils. These are stimulating and antiviral. Because they can be irritating, however, do not use them directly on the horse's skin, although they can be good for him to smell.

Other valuable classes of oils include:

Aromatic essential oils extracted from plants, fruits, and flowers are used by aromatherapists to enhance the body's natural self-regulating and self-healing abilities.

- **Esters:** Examples of the ester class include lavender, clary sage, geranium, ylang ylang, and Roman chamomile. These gentle oils have antifungal effects and are used for balancing.
- **Oxides:** Oxides are expectorants. They are found in tea tree and eucalyptus essential oils.
- **Sesquiterpene Alcohols:** Sesquiterpene alcohols are anti-inflammatory, liver stimulating, and antiallergic. They include sandalwood, carrot seed, spikenard, vetiver, and sage.
- **Sesquiterpene Hydrocarbons:** Sesquiterpene hydrocarbons are anti inflammatory and antiallergic oils. The most important member of this group is German chamomile.
- **Aldehydes:** Aldehydes include lemongrass, melissa, and eucalyptus citriodora. They smell like lemon and have a calming effect. However, they must be highly diluted to be safe for use.

Not all essential oils are good for use with horses, such as:

- **Phenols:** Phenols include oregano, savory, and thyme. They should never be used with animals because they are too dangerous and irritating.
- **Ketones:** Ketones such as thuja, yarrow, pennyroyal, rue, hyssop, wormwood, and mugwort also should be avoided with horses. Some oils with fewer ketones, however, such as helichrysum, rosemary verbenon, Atlas cedarwood, and vetiver may be safely used with supervision. Some horses are sensitive to peppermint, which has ketones.

While most aromatherapy substances smell wonderful, remember, they are a curative therapy, not a cosmetic or a bubble bath. Essential oils do have many medicinal uses. They fight bacteria and fungi, stop itching, help tissue grow, fight inflammations, and tone and balance the body. They also can have a strong invigorating or relaxing effect on the mind. Each oil can be used for a specific purpose. However, aromatherapy is always considered an adjunct to, not a replacement for, regular veterinary care.

ADMINISTRATION OF ESSENTIAL OILS

The most common way to administer essential oils to a horse is by topical application, but they also can be inhaled (essential oils start evaporating right away), or with proper care, some can be taken internally.

Inhalation is the safest method, and many practitioners believe that it is the best and most reliable. Theoretically,

if you saturated the air with essential oils on a very hot day and there was no ventilation, you might smother your horse, but you'd really have to work at that.

At any rate, topical application is considered to be the most effective method, especially for skin problems. The diluted oils are applied to the windpipe, poll, or chest area, or specifically to the area of discomfort. They should remain on the horse for at least 12 hours, if possible. Never use essential oils around the eyes.

In chemistry, the word "volatile" simply means that the oil evaporates on contact with the air. It does not mean "explosive," although that's what people seem to think when they hear the word.

HOW IT WORKS

Whatever method you choose, pick a time when your horse is quiet and relaxed (not right before feeding!). It is standard practice to allow the animal to smell the aromatherapy oil first, and most horses show great interest in them. Do this every time you offer treatment. Hold the open bottle a few inches (1 inch=2.5 cm) from your horse's nose, but hang onto it! Some horses will try to snatch it away. Pull the bottle far enough away to see if your horse extends his neck toward it. (Most will smell the oil one nostril at a time.)

If your horse exhibits strong interest toward the oil, you can go ahead and use it a couple times a day. If he shows a little interest, try it once a day. Do not use an oil that your horse rejects. In this way, he can actually participate in his own healing. One way a horse shows interest in an oil is by curling his lip upward, which is called the Flehmen response. This allows him to pull in and examine more scent molecules. If you plan to use more than one oil, wait 20 minutes between "sniffs." Do not let your horse overinhale. Remember, essential oils are medicine, not treats. Horses will vary their response from day to day and may lose interest over time.

Preliminary Testing

With topical applications, it's a good idea to pretest all oils on yourself first. Place a smear on the inside of your elbow. If you experience redness, pain, or itching, dilute the oil until these signs are gone.

You can purchase a ready-to-use preparation, or you can buy essential oils undiluted, in which case you add them to your own base oil or other carrier.

In like manner, if your horse exhibits a strong negative reaction to a particular oil, don't use it! Such horses may pace, salivate, snort, rub the affected part against the stall wall, or indicate by similar body language that the treatment is not acceptable. If this occurs, discontinue treatment. On the other hand, some horses have liked the scent of the oils so much that they have been known to gobble up the entire bottle. That's not good either. In any case, let your horse check out the oil before every application. And don't use any essential oil for more than two weeks without your veterinarian's approval.

PREPARATION

You can purchase a ready-to-use preparation, or you can buy essential oils undiluted, in which case you add them to your own base oil or other carrier.

To begin preparation, an essential oil is usually diluted by adding two to three drops of pure concentrate to 5 ml of a base oil. (Most good commercial brands contain 2.5 percent of the essential oil.) Then the diluted mixture is added to a carrier, which is either in oil form, a cream, or a paste, depending on what condition it is being used to treat. A good-quality cold-pressed oil or aloe vera gel is often used as a base oil or carrier. Some of the more common carrier oils include:

As a rule, using an essential oil as a rub has the best physical effects; using it as an inhalant has the best psychological effects.

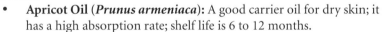

- **Apricot Oil (*Prunus armeniaca*):** A good carrier oil for dry skin; it has a high absorption rate; shelf life is 6 to 12 months.
- **Avocado Oil (*Persea americana*):** High in proteins and vitamins A, D, and E; shelf life is 12 months.
- **Grapeseed Oil (*Vitis vinifera*):** A light oil pressed from the seeds of various kinds of grapes; it feels less greasy than most others. Stored correctly, the shelf life is a year or more.
- **Coconut Oil (*Cocos nuciferas*):** A solid at "room temperature," but the stuff turns liquid at higher temperatures; this is a good massage oil, too; shelf life is indefinite.
- **Hazelnut Oil (*Corylus avellana*):** This oil is easily absorbed by the skin; shelf life is 6 to 12 months.
- **Jojoba Oil (*Simmondsia chinensis*):** A great moisturizer and good for blending more than one oil; shelf life is indefinite.
- **Olive Oil (*Olea europaea*):** Use first pressing ("extra virgin"); a good and nutrient-rich moisturizer; some practitioners recommend avoiding olive oil, which they feel is too acidic for the horse's skin (I have not had any trouble with it); shelf life is indefinite.
- **Sesame Oil (*Sesamum indicum*):** This oil is said to have anti-inflammatory properties; shelf life is 6 to 12 months.
- **Sunflower Seed Oil (*Prunus dulcis*):** This is my favorite all-purpose oil; it is inexpensive, full of vitamins A and E, and quickly absorbed; shelf life is about six months.
- **Sweet Almond Oil (*Helianthus annus*):** This oil contains vitamins A and E; it moisturizes the skin and is easily absorbed; shelf life is 6 to 12 months.
- **Walnut Oil (*Juglans regia*):** This oil has a high absorption rate; shelf life is 6 to 12 months.

There are many other suitable choices for carriers, such as rose hips oil, pecan oil, castor oil, and so on. Good oils for ointments, creams, or pastes include mango, cocoa, shea butter, kokum butter, and beeswax. Use what works best for your horse's needs.

Mixing and Matching

While it is common practice to mix and match oils, don't use more than four at any one time. It is also generally agreed that when mixing oils, it's wise to use a combination that includes the various "notes."

The "note" is the kind of aroma a substance has, and like a musical note, it tends to be high (top), medium (middle), or low (base). Oils with top notes take effect quickly and also evaporate very quickly. Their scent tends to be light, fresh, and uplifting. Base note oils take longer to detect and to evaporate. They often have a rich, heavy fragrance (and are often the most expensive). They are very relaxing and tend to slow down the evaporation rate of the other oils. Middle notes are midway between the other two. These fragrances, which take a couple minutes to establish themselves, tend to be soft and warm. These are the notes most commonly used. They balance out the blend and give it a certain "body."

You can purchase already mixed essential oils; this will save you the time and money that would otherwise be spent on buying oils individually. However, a disadvantage to doing so is that you have no control over the amount of each oil in the blend. It is best to use single oils, not mixes, for emotional conditions.

There are more than 200 essential oils available to use with your horse. Here are a few of my favorites.

BEFORE YOU BEGIN

- Do not apply undiluted essential oils or other concentrated essences directly onto the skin.

- Do not use any citrus oils, especially bergamot, if your horse will be exposed to the sun within four hours of application because most will cause photosensitivity.

- Never combine more than four oils. Responses can get too complicated after that. If your horse doesn't like a specific oil used by itself, you can "hide" a little bit of it by blending it with a larger amount of an oil of which he approves.

- Thoroughbreds, especially chestnuts, seem to be more sensitive to essential oil treatment than other breeds (they are famously "thin-skinned"), and so aromatherapy may not be appropriate for them. Gray horses seem most tolerant, although grays can be particularly sensitive to citrus oils and bergamot.

- Liniments containing eucalyptus, peppermint, or rosemary may be considered "performance enhancing" and may be prohibited in competitions adhering to Fédération Equestre Internationale (FEI, the international governing body of equestrian sport) regulations. If competing, stay away from any essential oil containing camphor, menthol, phenol, or thymol.

- For utmost safety, don't use oils on pregnant mares.

- Do not apply oils directly on sores or abscesses.

- Do not apply oils directly on the face unless absolutely necessary.

Basil (*Ocimum basilicum*)
- **Parts used:** Leaves and flower tops.
- **Fragrance:** Herby, green, sweet, licorice-like, camphorous.
- **Color:** Clear.
- **Note:** Top to middle.
- **Emotional effect:** Balancing. Basil is good for focusing and calming because it evaporates slowly.
- **Indications:** Bronchitis, colds, colic coughs, exhaustion, flatulence, flu, insect bites, laminitis, muscle soreness and spasms, arthritis, sinusitis. It also can be used as an insect repellent.
- **Remarks:** Use sparingly because some horses are sensitive to it. Don't use on pregnant mares.

Bergamot (*Citrus bergamia*)
- **Parts used:** Fruit rind.
- **Fragrance:** Light, fresh, sweet, citrusy/fruity.
- **Color:** Gold, with a green note.
- **Note:** Top.
- **Action:** Antifungal, helps to kill airborne bacteria, cleansing.
- **Emotional effect:** Balancing, cleansing, spirit lifting, toning, relaxing.
- **Indications:** Abscesses, arthritis, itching, tumors, warts, sarcoids, anxiety, cystitis, depression, ear infections, folliculitis, fungal infections, halitosis, lice, loss of appetite, stress, including anxiety and fear. Most skin complaints respond favorably to it.
- **Remarks:** Photosensitive—avoid in gray or white horses. Even horses of other colors should be kept stabled for 6 to 12 hours after its use. There is a photosensitive-free variety of this oil, but you have to look for it. This oil needs to be well diluted.

Bergamot

Birch (*Betula Lenta, B. carpinifolia*)
- **Parts used:** Wood and bark.
- **Fragrance:** Sweet, bracing.
- **Color:** Pale.
- **Note:** Top to middle.
- **Action:** Removes toxins mainly by producing increased sweating.
- **Emotional effect:** Soothing.
- **Indications:** Reduces lactic acid concentrates that cause stiffness and pain in muscles. Also good for arthritis, urinary tract disorders.
- **Remarks:** Do not use with pregnant mares. Sometimes what is sold as "birch oil" is actually wintergreen. These oils have similar effects. Combines with clary sage and cedar for use with muscle soreness. Don't use undiluted oil directly on the skin. It can be combined with chamomile, eucalyptus, lemon, lavender, or cedarwood.

Cardamom (*Elettaria cardamom*)
- **Parts used:** Seeds.
- **Fragrance:** Sweet and spicy.
- **Color:** Clear.
- **Note:** Middle.

The oils used in aromatherapy can be difficult to remove, so don't slosh them all over your horse. Besides, they are expensive.

- **Action:** Antiviral, aphrodisiac.
- **Emotional effect:** Warming, soothing.
- **Parts used:** Flower heads.
- **Fragrance:** Crisp, sweet, fruity, herby.
- **Color:** Gray-blue.
- **Note:** Middle.
- **Action:** Antispasmodic, analgesic, anti-inflammatory.
- **Emotional effect:** Calming.
- **Indications:** Colic prevention, problems with the central nervous system, wound care, sweet itch, mud fever, muscle aches, teething.
- **Remarks:** This is the chamomile that chamomile tea comes from. It is reported to be soothing for mares who become irritable when they come into estrus. In fact, this is one of the best oils for "difficult" horses. Always dilute this oil.

Clary Sage (*Salvia sclarea*)

- **Parts used:** Flowing tops and leaves.
- **Fragrance:** Earthy, warm, nutty, herby, with a slight fruity undertone.
- **Color:** Light golden yellow.
- **Note:** Middle.
- **Action:** Regulates hormone balance, antiseptic, antispasmodic.
- **Emotional effect:** Uplifting, calming, euphoric.
- **Indications:** Asthma, COPD, coughing, exhaustion, gas, muscle spasms, hair growth, nervous irritability, labor pains. Excellent massage oil.
- **Remarks:** Mix with eucalyptus, frankincense, and tea tree oil for a refreshing spray around the barn if you have horses with breathing problems. Use in small amounts. Do not use on pregnant mares.

Eucalyptus (*Eucalyptus radiata*)

- **Parts used:** Leaves and branches.
- **Fragrance:** Penetrating, camphorous, like cough drops.
- **Color:** Clear.
- **Note:** Middle.
- **Action:** Antiviral, strongly antiseptic, inhibits bacterial and fungal growth, especially airborne bacteria. Insect repellent.
- **Emotional effect:** Stimulating.
- **Indications:** Flu, inflammation, insect bites, respiratory infections, allergies, congestion, muscular pains.
- **Remarks:** The *radiata* variety of eucalyptus I am referring to here is gentler than the stuff they use to make chest rubs. It smells better too; in fact, it makes a very nice barn deodorizer. Mix with clary sage, frankincense, and tea tree oil for a refreshing spray around the barn if you have horses with breathing problems. If you are treating your horse homeopathically, do not use eucalyptus oil at the same time. The remedies can cancel each other out. This oil can be irritating to sensitive skin. Never give this oil internally. This is a good oil to use in the

Eucalyptus

summer because it is cooling.

Fennel (*Foeniculum vulgare*)

- **Parts used:** Fruit.
- **Fragrance:** Aniseed.
- **Color:** Mostly clear, slightly yellow.
- **Note:** Middle/top.
- **Action:** Eliminates toxins.
- **Emotional effect:** Strengthening.
- **Indications:** Aids in recovery from illness, increases milk flow, digestive stimulant.
- **Remarks:** Especially good for mares. Use sparingly. Do not use with pregnant mares or foals.

Frankincense, sandalwood, and cedar, among others, are considered sacred herbs in some cultures. These herbs are said to have a spiritually cleansing effect.

Frankincense (*Boswellia carterii*)

- **Parts used:** Resin.
- **Fragrance:** Fresh, camphorous, warm, balsamic, somewhat fruity.
- **Color:** Light yellow.
- **Note:** Base.
- **Action:** Antibacterial, anti-inflammatory, antidepressant. Slows breathing.
- **Emotional effect:** Toning, calming, stimulating. Addresses past and present fears.
- **Indications:** Frankincense is great for older horses who need an immune system boost. It eases coughs and shortness of breath characteristic of COPD. Good for fearful or grieving horses.
- **Remarks:** Mix with eucalyptus, clary sage, and tea tree oil for a refreshing spray around the barn if you have horses with breathing problems. Do not use with pregnant mares.

Geranium (*Pelargonium graveolens*)

- **Parts used:** Flowers, leaves, and stalks.
- **Fragrance:** Floral, green, sweet.
- **Color:** Clear.
- **Note:** Middle.
- **Action:** Antifungal, analgesic, diuretic. Insect repellent.
- **Emotional effect:** Relaxing, stabilizing, balancing.
- **Indications:** Pain, bruising, and skin problems, including lice and even ticks.
- **Remarks:** Evaporates slowly. Do not use with pregnant mares. Use caution in animals with sensitive skin. More inexpensive than most.

Grapefruit (*Citrus paradisi*)

- **Parts used:** Fruit.
- **Fragrance:** Fresh, crisp, citrus.
- **Color:** Yellow.
- **Note:** Top.
- **Action:** Antiseptic; astringent.
- **Emotional effect:** Energizing, antiseptic, uplifting. Clears negativity. Supposedly helps with jealous horses.
- **Indications:** Stimulates the lymphatic system and has a general internal cleansing effect; has a tonic effect on the skin.
- **Remarks:** Evaporates quickly. This oil is photosensitive but not as much as other citrus oils. Don't expose the horse to sunlight for four hours after application.

Helichrysum of Immortelle (*Helichrysum italicum*)

- **Parts used:** Flowers.
- **Fragrance:** Odd, deep, disgusting to some, pleasant to others.

- **Color:** Light yellow.
- **Note:** Base.
- **Action:** Antibacterial; analgesic.
- **Emotional effect:** Uplifting, antidepressant.
- **Indications:** In humans, the oil of this herb can be used for migraines, but in animals it is more often employed for chronic respiratory problems, liver ailments, and skin conditions resulting from allergies. It is also useful for bruises and bacterial infections, as well as for nervous exhaustion.
- **Remarks:** Sometimes called "everlasting oil," or Immortelle.

Hops (*Humulus lupulus*)

- **Parts used:** Female flowers.
- **Fragrance:** Bitter, aromatic.
- **Note:** Base.
- **Action:** Anodyne (painkiller), anthelmintic (dewormer), diuretic, febrifuge, hypnotic, nervine, sedative, soporific, tonic, aphrodisiac, stomachic.
- **Emotional effect:** Calming.
- **Indications:** Nervous diarrhea, restlessness, gas, ulcers, poor circulation, muscle cramps.
- **Remarks:** Do not use for prolonged periods.

Jasmine (*Jasminum officinalis*)

- **Parts used:** Flowers.
- **Fragrance:** Warm, exotic.
- **Color:** Golden brown.
- **Note:** Middle.
- **Emotional effect:** Relaxing.
- **Indications:** Colic caused by wind sucking/cribbing or weaving. It also can be used for depression and helps self-confidence. Excellent for horses who have been abused. Good for difficult foaling.
- **Remarks:** This is an especially good oil for stabled horses when massaged along the neck and head.

Juniper (*Juniperus virginiana*)

- **Parts used:** Berry, flowers.
- **Fragrance:** Like a cedar chest: clean, woodsy, and mild.
- **Color:** Clear.
- **Note:** Base.
- **Action:** Astringent, antiseptic. Helps to clear toxins when used along with massage.
- **Emotional effect:** Energizing, cleansing.
- **Indications:** Arthritis, bronchitis, coughs, dermatitis, eczema, insect and tick repellant, muscle aches, stress, anxiety. Juniper is said to remove worry.
- **Remarks:** Juniper can cause irritation and sensitization in some animals. Do not use with pregnant mares because it has a stimulant action on

Citrus essential oils are recovered from the peel, which contain the oil sacs located irregularly in the rind.

Jasmine

Don't Pick the Flowers!

As with herbal medications, do not gather wild plants for aromatherapy use. They can be endangered in the wild or sprayed with any number of noxious substances. Besides, plants grown for therapeutic use are subject to very careful quality control. Many factors, including climate, weather changes, altitude, watering and feeding, and other horticultural variants affect the quality of the oil. In addition, there is always the possibility that you'll gather the wrong one.

Buy your aromatherapy oils from a legitimate dealer, or create your own from organically grown commercial plants.

the uterine muscles and may cause abortion.

Lavender (*Lavendula augustifolia*)
- **Parts used:** Flower tops.
- **Fragrance:** Fresh, floral, slightly fruity.
- **Color:** Mostly clear, slightly yellow.
- **Note:** Top/middle.
- **Action:** Astringent, analgesic, antiseptic, antibacterial, stops itching, insect repellant.
- **Emotional effect:** Calming, soothing.
- **Indications:** Skin conditions, allergies, eczema, wound healing (bruises, scarring, sores, burns, cuts), anxiety, arthritis, asthma, flatulent colic, depression, insect bites, itching, labor pains, muscle aches, rain rot, sprains, strains, stress.
- **Remarks:** This is the most versatile (and essential) of all essential oils. It can be used undiluted on minor wounds to keep flies away. Be sure to use natural lavender, not "Lavender 40/42," a synthetic blend. This is a good oil to use in the summer because it is cooling.

Lemon (*Citrus limonum*)
- **Parts used:** Fruit peels.
- **Fragrance:** Fresh, crisp, citrusy.
- **Color:** Yellow.
- **Note:** Top.
- **Action:** Antibacterial, antiseptic, astringent, tonic.
- **Emotional effect:** Refreshing, uplifting, helps a horse focus.
- **Indications:** Cleanses, refreshes, cools. Ancient remedy for warts. Acts as a pesticide. Helpful for respiratory problems, especially in the winter, and kidney stones.
- **Remarks:** Evaporates quickly. Do not use lemon for four hours prior to sun exposure.

Lemon Balm (*Melissa officinalis*)
- **Parts used:** Leaves.
- **Fragrance:** Fresh, sweet, herbal.
- **Color:** Yellow/brown.
- **Note:** Middle.
- **Action:** Sedative, antiviral, antioxidant, antidepressant.
- **Emotional effect:** Calming.
- **Remarks:** This essential oil is often adulterated with mixtures of lemongrass, citronella, or lemon oil. If used directly on the skin, dilute well. Don't use with pregnant horses.

Lemongrass (*Cymbopogon citratus*)
- **Parts used:** Grass.
- **Fragrance:** Fresh, lemony, very sweet, earthy.

- **Color:** Yellow.
- **Note:** Middle/top.
- **Action:** Deodorant, antiseptic, insect repellent.
- **Emotional effect:** Relaxing.
- **Indications:** Muscle aches, mental stimulant.
- **Remarks:** Evaporates slowly. Do not use on damaged skin. Use sparingly because some horses are sensitive to it.

Marjoram or Sweet Marjoram (*Origanum majorana*)

- **Parts used:** Flowering top.
- **Fragrance:** Warm, herbaceous, woody, with spicy undertones.
- **Note:** Middle.
- **Action:** Sedative, anti-aphrodisiac, antibacterial.
- **Emotional effect:** Calming.
- **Indications:** Can be used to relieve muscle aches, especially in the winter. Often calms or even sedates horses who do not respond to other oils. It is rather an antiaphrodisiac.
- **Remarks:** Evaporates slowly. This oil contains camphor and should not be used with competition horses. Do not use with pregnant mares.

Lemon Balm plant

Neroli (*Citrus aurantium*)

- **Parts used:** Blossoms.
- **Fragrance:** Floral, citrusy, sweet.
- **Color:** Brown.
- **Note:** Middle.
- **Emotional effect:** Calms angry and resentful horses.
- **Indications:** Depression, scars.

Nutmeg (*Myristica aromata, M. fragrans, M. officinalis, Nux moschata*)

- **Parts used:** Fruits.
- **Fragrance:** Spicy.
- **Color:** Clear.
- **Note:** Middle.
- **Action:** Antiseptic, muscle relaxant.
- **Emotional effect:** Calming, centering, aphrodisiac, euphoric.
- **Indications:** Digestive system, muscle relaxant.
- **Remarks:** Can be toxic if used in large quantities. Use very diluted.

Orange (*Citrus sinensis*)

- **Parts used:** Fruit peels.
- **Fragrance:** Fresh, citrusy.
- **Color:** Orange.
- **Note:** Top.
- **Action:** Astringent.
- **Emotional effect:** Uplifting and calming.
- **Indications:** Shyness. This essential oil provides self-assurance and acts as a digestive aid.
- **Remarks:** Photosensitive. Do not use if the horse will be exposed to sunlight in the next 12 hours.

According to scientific studies, we respond to aromas in less than three seconds. Also, the nose is able to savor or be repelled by about 10,000 different odors!

Peppermint (*Mentha piperita*)
- **Parts used:** Aerial parts of the plant.
- **Fragrance:** Minty, sweet.
- **Color:** Clear, slightly yellow.
- **Note:** Top.
- **Action:** Anti-inflammatoy, stimulates and opens airways.
- **Emotional effect:** Refreshing; stimulating to some, calming to others.
- **Indications:** Travel anxiety, digestive aid, stimulates circulation, good for overworked muscles, clears the mind.
- **Remarks:** This is a stimulating oil and should be applied in the morning. Do not use with pregnant mares. (You also can use spearmint oil for most of these purposes, although the effect is weaker.) A few horses are sensitive to it. This is a good oil to use in the summer.

Rose (*Rosa damascena*)
- **Parts used:** Flowers.
- **Fragrance:** Sweet, floral.
- **Color:** Deep red or light yellow, depending on the method of extraction.
- **Note:** Middle.
- **Emotional effect:** Balancing and calming, especially for mares.
- **Indications:** Soothes angry and resentful horses, separation anxiety, stabilizing to the central nervous system.
- **Remarks:** This "Queen of Oils" may help to bring breeding mares into season but calms and relaxes those out of season. Rose oil is one of the most expensive oils.

Rosemary (*Rosmarinus officinalis, R. coronarium*)
- **Parts used:** Leaves and flower tops.
- **Fragrance:** Herbaceous, camphorous.
- **Color:** Clear.
- **Note:** Middle.
- **Emotional effect:** Energizing.
- **Indications:** Relieves muscle aches and both physical and mental fatigue, good tonic for the skin, boosts the immune system, improves circulation, promotes hair growth.
- **Remarks:** Do not use with pregnant mares or with animals with a seizure disorder. Dilute well.

Sandalwood (*Santalum album*)
- **Parts used:** Wood.
- **Fragrance:** Warm, sensual, buttery.
- **Color:** Clear, slightly yellow.
- **Note:** Base.
- **Action:** Antiseptic, emollient, astringent, anti-inflammatory.
- **Emotional effect:** Relaxing.
- **Indications:** Skin conditioner, insect repellent, eye infections, joint discomfort. Good for fearful horses.

GEOTA

While aromatherapy is natural and usually safe, some oils can be toxic if misused. If you decide to use this therapy, get guidance from a qualified animal aromatherapist, such as a member of the Guild of Essential Oil Therapists for Animals (GEOTA).

Rose

Tea Tree (*Melaleuca alternifolia*)
- **Parts used:** Leaves and stems.
- **Fragrance:** Medicinal, fresh, woody, and herby.
- **Color:** Clear, slightly yellow.
- **Note:** Middle.
- **Action:** Antiseptic, antibacterial, antifungal, antibiotic, antiviral.
- **Emotional effect:** Energizing, toning.
- **Indications:** Foot infections like thrush, rain rot, mud fever, cracked heels, and corns; ringworm. Relieves itching, especially when added to aloe vera gel. Effective for wound cleaning.
- **Remarks:** Mix with eucalyptus, frankincense, and clary sage for a refreshing spray around the barn if you have horses with breathing problems. This is generally a safe oil that can be used on minor wounds, although it can irritate sensitive skin. You can disinfect blankets and brushes with this oil. Tea tree oil has been shown to have a temporary paralyzing effect on dogs but not with horses. This is a good oil to use in the summer because it is energizing.

Vetiver (*Vetiveria zizanioides*)
- **Parts used:** Root.
- **Fragrance:** Woody, earthy, herby, even smoky.
- **Color:** Golden brown.
- **Note:** Base.
- **Action:** Emollient.
- **Emotional effect:** Calming, relaxing, grounding, centering.
- **Indications:** Poor circulation, cuts, muscular aches, depression, exhaustion. It can be used to prevent colic caused by wind sucking/cribbing. Wonderful for depressed or nervous horses. Evaporates slowly.

Yarrow (*Achillea millefolium*)
- **Parts used:** Dried herb.
- **Fragrance:** Sharp, woody.
- **Color:** Dark blue.
- **Note:** Middle.
- **Action:** Sedative, anti-inflammatory.
- **Emotional effect:** Releasing.
- **Indications:** Chest infections, minor wounds, fever, coat care, urinary tract infections.
- **Remarks:** This is generally a safe oil that can be used undiluted on minor wounds. Do not use with pregnant mares.

Ylang Ylang (*Cananga odorata*)
- **Parts used:** Flowers.
- **Fragrance:** Intense, floral, exotic.
- **Color:** Pale yellow.
- **Note:** Middle.
- **Action:** Antidepressant, antiseptic, sedative.
- **Emotional effect:** Calms angry and resentful horses.
- **Indications:** Anxiety, intestinal problems, stress.
- **Remarks:** Use in small amounts—this is an overpowering oil. It comes in several grades; be sure to select only the best.

Yarrow

POOR CHOICES

The following oils should not be used with horses because they can be dangerous to them:

- ajowan (*Trachyspermum copticum*)
- almond, bitter (*Prunus dulcis var. amara*)
- anise (*Pimpinella anisum*)
- arnica (*Arnica Montana*)
- boldo leaf (*Peumus boldus*)
- broom, Spanish (*Spartium junceum*)
- calamus (*Acorus calamus var. angustatus*)
- camphor (*Cinnamomum camphora*)
- clove, leaf or bud (*Eugenia caryophyllata*)
- deertongue (*Carphephorus odoratissimus*)
- horseradish (*Armoracia rusticana*)
- jaborandi (*Pilocarpus jaborandi*)
- melilotus (*Melilotus officinalis*)
- mugwort (*Artemisia vulgaris*)
- mustard (*Brassica nigra*)
- onion (*Allium cepa*)
- oregano (*Origanum vulgare*)
- pennyroyal (*Mentha pulegium*)
- rue (*Ruta graveolens*)
- sassafras (*Sassafras albidum*)
- thuja (*Thuja occidentalis*)
- wintergreen (*Gaultheria procumbens*)
- wormseed (*Chenopodium ambrosioides var. anthelminticum*)
- wormwood (*Artemisia absinthium*)

Chapter 11

$\mathcal{W}$hat's a safe combination of herbal medicine, homeopathy, and aromatherapy? Flower essences! Like homeopathy and several other therapies, Bach flower essence remedies are considered to be a vibrational therapy that is similar to homeopathy. Like homeopathic medications, they are also physically dilute. However, it is worth noting that because they are prepared in decoctions like herbs, flower essences are sometimes considered herbal medicine, and Dr. Bach himself, the founder of this modality, considered himself an herbalist.

Flower
Essences

The makeup of Bach flower remedies is very simple. Flower essences are developed from the blossoms of 38 separate flowering plants. Each plant remedy is meant to treat a specific emotional state or condition of mind. Unlike many other methods of healing, these remedies do not treat physical ailments directly. Instead, they are created to treat the negative emotional states that may give rise to disease. Bach flower essences work by "flooding out" negative feelings.

ADVANTAGES
- SAFE.
- EASY AND PLEASANT TO USE.
- READILY AVAILABLE IN HEALTH FOOD STORES.

DISADVANTAGES
- NOT USEFUL FOR PHYSICALLY BASED DISEASES.
- DESPITE A GREAT DEAL OF ANECDOTAL SUPPORT FOR FLOWER ESSENCES, ESPECIALLY THE EVER-POPULAR RESCUE REMEDY, THERE IS NO REAL SCIENTIFIC EVIDENCE THAT IT WORKS. REMARKS: PERCEPTION MEANS A LOT. IF YOU THINK IT WORKS, YOU MIGHT FEEL CALMER AND MORE READY TO TACKLE THE SITUATION.

How It Works

"Our work is steadfastly to adhere to the simplicity and purity of this method of healing," wrote Dr. Edward Bach, a London homeopathic physician who developed this alternative natural therapy in 1936. Bach devoted his life to understanding the emotional basis of illness, and he isolated 7 pathological character traits—pride, cruelty, hate, self-love, ignorance, instability, and greed—that produce the 12 emotional states of fear, uncertainty, apathy, loneliness, oversensitivity, despondency, overconcern, weakness, self-distrust, impatience, overenthusiasm, and pride (or aloofness). Bach considered disease to be "a kind of consolidation of a mental attitude," and this is the theory that grounds his work. He believed that behind every disease lie "our anxieties, our greed, our likes, and our dislikes" and that "there is no true healing unless there is a change in outlook, peace of mind, and inner happiness."

The remedies are said to contain the "energetic signature" of the flower, which can be transmitted to the user with the idea that positive energy can redirect or neutralize negative energy. Each flower is believed to impart specific qualities. When used with animals, these essences are believed to have a calming effect and to improve problem behaviors.

Remedies may be prescribed by a naturopath (a holistic practitioner who avoids drugs and surgery and emphasizes the use of natural agents and physical means to treating illness), or an individual may choose the combination they feel best suits the situation. Unlike homeopathic remedies, they are all derived from nontoxic substances. Because the remedies are extremely dilute, they do not have a characteristic scent or taste of the plant. They are usually administered orally.

THE REMEDIES

The Bach flower essences are completely safe and work in conjunction with herbs, homeopathy, and standard medications. Most are made from fresh-picked flowers soaked in spring water and placed in sunlight for a period of time before being preserved with brandy.

The most popular and well-known Bach flower essence combination for horses is the readily available Rescue Remedy. (It is used for human beings as well.) It comprises impatiens, Star of Bethlehem, cherry plum, rock rose, and clematis. Designed to work quickly on emergency stress, it is used more for emotional issues than for deep-seated chronic problems. It can be used to calm a horse in the case of cuts or trauma or to help the horse cope with the stresses of ordinary life. It also can be used for early stages of colic.

This remedy is usually given at double the standard dose, and the doses can be repeated as needed. Horse owners who use Rescue Remedy should follow

Flower remedies are designed to be used in conjunction with other therapies and were never meant to replace standard veterinary care.

crisis treatment with a thorough examination of the root causes and use some of the 38 remedies either separately or in a customized mixture to address the problem at its source.

While no scientific support exists for the effectiveness of Bach flower remedies, many holistic veterinarians and horse owners report some amazing success stories.

APPLICATION

Bach remedies come as liquids preserved in brandy. (Maybe that accounts for part of the calming effect.) To prepare the remedies for use, you usually put two drops of each essence you wish to mix in a 1-ounce (30-ml) amber glass bottle and add three parts spring water to one part alcohol (preferably brandy, but vodka also can be used). The mixture is stored in a cool place away from direct sunlight and heat. Dosage can vary, but a general rule is three drops of the prepared mixture taken orally one to four times a day. (Obviously the amount of alcohol actually ingested by the horse is miniscule.)

To administer them, the horse's lips are opened, and the remedy is slid into the side of the mouth. (Some remedies, like Rescue Remedy, also come in a spray form.) Alternatively, a few drops mixed with an eyedropper full of water can be placed onto a sugar cube. It's quite usual to give six or seven remedies together at the same time.

Bach flower essence remedies are developed from the blossoms of 38 separate flowering plants. When used with animals, these essences are believed to have a calming effect and to improve problem behaviors.

FLOWER ESSENCES FOR HORSES

The 38 flower essences and their uses with horses are as follows:

Agrimony (*Agrimonia eupatoria*): Agrimony is vital for "tough" horses who soldier on despite pain. It will allow a horse to express the pain he really feels, and the results will be a happier, healthier animal and a safer ride for you. It also can be used for animals who pace in their stall or for skin irritations. Horses who respond best to agrimony are usually those who are sensitive to their owners and will often respond badly when they see the humans around them quarrel. They also are restless in general and dislike being left alone.

Aspen (*Populus tremula*): Aspen is given to "spooky" or nervous horses who fear the unknown. These horses are likely to jump or bolt for no discernible reason. It is often given before or during a storm or fireworks display. Some veterinarians have noticed that bladder problems seem to clear up with a dose of aspen therapy.

Beech (*Fagus sylvatica*): Beech is for aloof, fussy, or distant horses. It will make them more friendly and accepting of a rider. It also works for intolerance to heat or cold. This remedy also may make horses friendlier to children or to other horses. Some vets have found it useful in the treatment of arthritis and allergies.

Centaury (*Centaurium umbellatum*): Centaury is for the kind, overly submissive horse, especially one who has been neglected or abused. It will give him more self-confidence. It is good for horses who allow themselves to get pushed around in their corrals by other horses.

Cerato (*Ceratostigma willmottiana*): Cerato is the remedy for distrustful, flighty horses who need reassurance. It helps with horses who are barn-sour, those who have developed bad habits, those who have discipline problems, and those who are easily distracted during training.

Cherry Plum (*Prunus cerasifera*): Cherry plum is for fearful, wild, out-of-control horses, especially ones who suffer from fear-related aggression. It helps horses in competition who are stressed by strange people or ones who become frantic when traveling. It is also used as a remedy for hives.

Chestnut Bud (*Aesculus hippocastanum*): Chestnut bud is made from the bud of the white chestnut. It is for horses who have difficulty during training and who continually make the same mistakes. These horses lack focus and observation.

Chicory (*Cichorium intybus*): Chicory is the remedy for manipulative, possessive, dominant horses. These animals are usually very demanding of attention.

Clematis (*Clematis vitalba*): Clematis is used to help horses who are having training problems. They are vague, absentminded, and unfocused. It increases their attention span. This remedy is especially good for horses used in hunting and similar sports.

Crab Apple (*Malus pumila*): Crab apple is the essence for vain, self-conscious horses, the ones who don't like being ridden in the rain. These horses like to be clean; even the smallest bit of grime on them reduces their performance. It also can be used to hasten recovery after surgery or trauma, and it is used as a remedy for hives.

Elm (*Ulmus procera*): Elm is a remedy for temporary loss of confidence, and it is ideal for a usually capable horse who is overwhelmed by too many things happening at once. It is recommended for use at shows.

Gentian (*Gentiana amarella*): Gentian is for withdrawn, doubtful, despondent horses. Their behavior usually can be traced back to a specific setback, such as the loss of a companion or owner.

Gorse (*Ulex europaeus*): Gorse is used in cases of illness in which a horse seems to have lost the desire to get better emotionally. The remedy is indicated when a horse has failed to respond to any sort of other encouragement.

Heather (*Calluna vulgaris*): Heather is a remedy for horses who cannot bear to be left alone and who crave attention.

Holly (*Ilex aquifolium*): Holly is the remedy for horses who seem hateful and mean. It helps with most cases of aggression.

Honeysuckle (*Lonicera caprifolium*): This is the remedy for horses who seem unable to "get with it" and who may be brooding over a former life. It may also help in cases of loss of blood.

Hornbeam (*Carpinus betulus*): Hornbeam is the remedy for horses who are slow and lethargic in the morning.

Impatiens (*Impatiens glandulifera*): As the name suggests, this remedy is used to help the impatient horse relax. It is especially useful for horses who are anxious before a race or event or for those who seem fatigued at work. It is also good for pain.

Larch (*Larix deciduas*): Larch is the remedy for timid horses who lack confidence. It is a wonderful remedy for horses who have suffered abuse.

Mimulus (*Mimulus guttatus*): Mimulus is the remedy for fearful or anxious horses. Usually, the horse is afraid of specific known things.

Mustard (*Sinapis arvensis*): Mustard is the remedy for moody horses, especially when the problem has suddenly appeared.

Heather

Like Owner, Like Horse?

Alternative therapists often note that a troubled horse takes his "cue" from his owner. High-strung owners tend to have horses who develop nervous problems and the like. It is recommended that owners work to eliminate traits in their characters that might lead to the development of problems in their horses.

Hawaiian Flower Essence Therapy

In addition to the well-known Bach flower essences, other essences from different plants found around the world are also being used. For example, in Hawaiian flower essence therapy, a common combination to clear negativity includes African tulip, ti, hila hila, naupaka, and glory bush. To help to increase focus and awareness, passion flower, hau, paka lana, lotus, and bougainvillea are combined. For emotional release, nicotiana, oleander, lantana, kukui, and water hyacinth are used. These essences are often added to crystal therapy for increased effectiveness. To release tension, try yellow ginger, false lilac, orange, comfrey, and dandelion.

Oak (*Quercus robur*): Oak remedy is used to help depressed horses, often those who are on forced stall rest. These individuals will work past the point at which they become really ill. It is also good for horses with a disability.

Olive (*Olea europaea*): Olive is the remedy for mentally or physically exhausted horses or ones who have suffered a chronic illness.

Pine *(Pinus sylvestris):* Pine is the remedy for submissive horses.

Red Chestnut (*Aesculus carnea*): Red chestnut remedy is for horses who project worry and seem to anticipate ill luck. It is good for horses who seem to fear separation.

Rock Rose (*Helianthemum nummularium*): Rock Rose is a calming remedy, especially useful in horses who fear loud noises. It is also good to use after a terrifying event.

Rock Water: Rock water, which is the only standard remedy not made from plants, is a remedy for rigid or stubborn horses. Some vets use it for degenerative arthritis.

Scleranthus (*Scleranthus annus*): Scleranthus remedy is for indecisive, negative horses. It also helps with loss of balance and lack of coordination.

Star of Bethlehem (*Ornithogalum umbellatum*): Star of Bethlehem treats emotional trauma, especially after the loss of a horse friend. It also can be used during the weaning process. Note that this plant is toxic if ingested in any amount, and so it is safe only when used as directed. Don't give your horse this herb in the whole form.

Sweet Chestnut (*Castanea sativa*): Sweet chestnut is the remedy for desolate horses.

Vervain (*Verbena officinalis*): Vervain horses are insistent, high-strung, and perhaps overenthusiastic. Horses who pace or weave in their stall also can benefit from this remedy.

Vine (*Vitis vinifera*): Vine is for horses who are overly dominant, inflexible, or aggressive. These horses tend to be difficult to train.

Walnut (*Juglans regia*): Walnut is the remedy for horses who are overinfluenced by outside developments.

Water Violet (*Hottonia palustris*): Water violet is the remedy for proud but sad horses. These individuals tend to be antisocial.

White Chestnut (*Aesculus hippocastanum*): White chestnut is the remedy for horses who are agitated and distracted by their own thoughts. They lack focus.

Wild Oat (*Bromus ramosus*): Wild oat is a remedy for older horses who are bored in retirement. They need a job, too! Horses in need of this remedy may be cribbers.

Wild Rose (*Rosa canina*): This is the remedy for the drifting, apathetic horse.

Sweet Chestnut

Willow (*Salix vitellina*): Willow is the remedy for resentful, bitter horses. It helps with destructive behavior.

Sometimes the best way to get a positive response from your horse is to be emotionally balanced yourself. If you think that flower essence therapy works on your horse, you can use it yourself! Flower essences were originally designed, after all, for people.

SAMPLE USES

Quite often, several essences can be used to treat a particular condition, either individually or in combination. The best way to ascertain which therapy will work best is to consult an herbalist who works specifically with horses. Here is a brief guide to some different situations and the essences that may help them:

- **anemia:** walnut, chestnut bud, olive, Star of Bethlehem
- **detoxification:** crab apple, walnut, chestnut bud, olive, gentian
- **diarrhea:** walnut, crab apple, olive, Star of Bethlehem, five-flower formula
- **environmental stress:** spray a mixture of walnut, mustard, wild rose, and crab apple
- **fear:** walnut, chestnut bud, mimulus, aspen, rock rose, larch
- **grieving:** Star of Bethlehem, walnut, honeysuckle, chestnut bud, gentian
- **immune disorders:** walnut, chestnut but, scleranthus, olive, Star of Bethlehem, crab apple
- **infections:** walnut, crab apple, olive, gentian, five-flower formula
- **low confidence:** walnut, chestnut bud, centaury, larch
- **new mother (to relieve stress):** red chestnut, five flower formula, walnut, larch, gentian, olive
- **quarreling horses:** walnut, chestnut bud, beech, willow, holly
- **skin problems:** crab apple, walnut, chestnut bud, five-flower formula
- **trailering:** walnut, chestnut bud, olive, clematis, impatiens, wild oat
- **trauma:** walnut, crab apple, gentian, olive, Star of Bethlehem, five-flower formula

No-Refill Guarantee

One flower essence company basically offers their customers a no-refill guarantee. It advertises that you can refill the formula without needing to add the original essences. Simply add approximately two parts of pure water and one part vodka (or another hard alcohol) or one part pure water and one part apple cider vinegar, shake the bottle vigorously, and you will have the same essence that you started with. You can do this at any time, whether the bottle is 90 percent full or 10 percent full—it makes no difference. The liquid is said to hold the vibrational or energy pattern; it does not hold any amount of physical substance from flowers.

THE INNER ESSENCE OF FRUITS AND VEGETABLES

Other plant essence protocols are constantly being developed. One, called Master Essences, is based on the work of Swami Paramhansa Yogananda, which is centered on his interpretations of the psychological and spiritual qualities of fruits and vegetables and how they can be transferred to other beings. This therapy is available commercially. It was first designed for people but is now used with pets too. Some people even use it on their houseplants!

Here are a few fruit and vegetable essences that can be used with horses:

- **almond:** self-control
- **apple:** peaceful clarity
- **avocado:** good memory
- **cherry:** cheerfulness
- **corn:** mental vitality
- **date:** tender sweetness
- **fig:** flexibility
- **grape:** love
- **lettuce:** calmness
- **orange:** enthusiasm
- **pear:** peacefulness, emergency support
- **pineapple:** self-assurance
- **raspberry:** kindness
- **tomato**: strength, endurance

Part 2 **Common Equine**

Diseases and
Treatment Options

ABSCESSES

An abscess is a collection of pus beneath the skin, often accompanied by fever and lethargy. Abscesses are warm to the touch and painful. Causes can range from a foreign body to an internal infection like strangles. Abscesses are especially common in the hoof, where they are extremely painful. If left untreated, they will follow the path of least resistance up the hoof wall. Tetanus vaccinations must be kept up to date.

Treatment options include:

- **Essential Oils:** Blue (German) chamomile, lavender, juniper, tea tree to stimulate the immune system.
- **Herbal Therapy:** Cleavers (hoof abscess). An herbal therapy compress can be made of comfrey leaf, slippery elm bark, or marshmallow.
- **Homeopathy:** Hepar sulphuricus (30C twice daily if the discharge is thick and pus filled; especially good for hoof abscesses), silicea (same as silica; if the discharge is thin or watery), sepia, belladonna (for accompanying fever).
- **Low-Level Laser Therapy:** To increase circulation in the abscessed area by dilating the blood vessels and also to increase the formation of new capillaries by replacing damaged ones. In addition, this therapy is said to increase phagocytosis, the process in which phagocyte cells scavenge for and devour dead or damaged cells.
- **Medical/Surgical:** The abscess must be drained. If the puncture site is visible, clean it carefully with an iodine-based scrub like Betadine to remove dirt. Put a hot pack on the area to draw out the infection. Clean twice a day. It also helps to soak the hoof in warm water and Epsom salts. The vet also may make a small channel in the hoof tissue leading to the infection. She may wish to prescribe antibiotics and give an antitetanus vaccine. Abscesses should be kept open until they are thoroughly drained.
- **Nutritional Therapy:** Vitamin C.

ALLERGY (HYPERSENSITIVITY)

An allergy is the result of an overactive immune system, usually manifesting as hypersensitivity to a foreign protein. It may take months or even years of exposure to develop an allergic reaction, which can affect horses of any age or breed.

Allergies can be brought on by molds, spores, vaccinations, stings, changes in food, or medications (especially those applied to the skin) such as acepromazine, bute (phenylbutazone), Banamine (flunixin meglumine), and dewormers. Many allergies can appear as skin rashes, irritations, or hives. They can be a reaction to insect bites, diet, or drugs. Hives usually appear 12 to 14 hours after exposure and may be present all over the body. Initially they tend to be small, but later they may grow together. They are usually very itchy and often will indent, or "pit," if you press them. High-protein grains or hay may cause hives. The horse may seem depressed or have a slight fever as well. Horses with hives usually recover uneventfully.

The most acute and dangerous form of allergic reaction is anaphylaxis, a condition in which your horse may not be able to breathe and will show signs of extreme anxiety. If you suspect that this is the case, get your horse to an area that is adequately ventilated, call your vet, and try to identify the source of the allergic reaction. Usually an emergency injection of steroids or other anti-inflammatory agents is necessary.

Treatment options for allergies include:

- **Acupuncture:** To stimulate the immune system.

- **Ayurvedic Therapy:** Triphala.
- **Crystal Therapy:** Celestite (to ease breathing).
- **Essential Oils:** Chamomile (either type), lavender, lemon, tea tree oil, and lavender.
- **Flower Essences:** Agrimony (hives) cherry plum (hives), crab apple (hives).
- **Homeopathy**: Apis mel (apis mellifica; 30C twice daily for five days for moderate signs with insect bite allergies); arsenicum (6C to 12C for allergic reactions); sulfur (6C twice daily for seasonal allergies).
- **NAET:** NAET therapy utilizes Muscle Response Testing, which is said to indicate the kinetic imbalance in the body caused by allergens. The therapist stimulates pressure points along the spine from the neck to the sacrum while the patient is in contact with an allergen. The patient must completely avoid the allergen for 25 hours following the treatment. Allergens are treated one at a time in a specific sequence.
- **Nutritional Therapy:** Check the diet for allergies. Many horses are allergic to corn. Give the digestive enzyme protease twice a day at ten times the human dose.
- **Shiatsu:** Lung meridian (for hives).
- **Tissue Salts:** Natu mur (natrum muriaticum; two tablets three times a day for ten days).
- **Western Herbal Therapy:** Calendula (20 grams of dried herb daily), cleavers (15 to 20 grams of dried herb), kelp (20 to 25 grams of dried herb daily), meadowsweet (25 grams of dried herb daily), nettle (20 grams of dried herb), powdered root of licorice. Antihive Combination 1: Anise, fenugreek, garlic, slippery elm, marshmallow, and mullein. Antihive Combination 2: Burdock, yellow dock, St. Mary's thistle, cleavers, and dandelion. Compress/Rinse: Comfrey, chamomile, and witch hazel in equal parts in boiling water. Let cool, strain away herbs, and apply them as a rinse or in a cold compress.

ANEMIA

Anemia is a condition in which the blood fails to carry enough oxygen. Because this is the job of hemoglobin in red blood cells, anemia usually means that there is problem with or a reduced number of red blood cells. Anemia can result from:

- general blood loss (trauma)
- increased red blood cell destruction (maple leaf toxins, drug toxicity, parasites, tumors)
- insufficient red blood cell production (the most common form is seen in horses with cancer, equine infectious anemia, or vitamin or mineral deficiency)
- iron, copper, or cobalt deficiency in the diet
- stress due to overwork

Signs include:

- depression
- discolored urine
- elevated heart rate (more than 50 beats per minute)
- exercise intolerance
- lack of appetite
- nosebleeds
- pale mucous membranes

Treatment depends on the cause. In terms of general care, keep the stable warm and dry because the horse's circulatory system (which helps to keep mammals warm) is not working at full efficiency. Halt all fast work (the need for oxygen increases with fast exercise). Make sure that your horse gets plenty of greens because they are a good source of iron. And of

course, see your veterinarian for a diagnosis before considering various other care options. Here are some suggested treatments:

- **Acupressure:** Bladder meridian 13 (located a couple of inches [about 5 cm] behind the shoulder blade, between ribs eight and nine).
- **Chinese Herbs:** Ginseng.
- **Crystal Therapy:** Yellow stones.
- **Nutritional Therapy:** Injections of iron, B12, or folic acid.

ANHYDROSIS (DRY COAT)

Horses sweat to keep cool; during exercise, a horse's temperature can rise to 104°F (40°C). Anhydrosis is the inability to sweat. (Horses and humans are among the few animals capable of perspiring freely.) The condition occurs because of a permanently high blood adrenalin level. Nobody knows exactly why it happens, although there are a lot of theories. It can occur when a horse is moved from a cool climate to a tropical one and the regulatory system fails to adjust.

Signs include:

- flaky, dry skin
- high temperature after exercise
- sweating confined to just a few areas, such as the crest of the neck

Care and treatment options include:

- **Crystal Therapy:** Green or white. (Rock crystal therapy is best.)
- **Nutritional Therapy:** Because the digestion of proteins and forages generates a fair amount of heat, put the horse on a diet as high in fat as he will tolerate, which will generate less heat.
- **Physical Management:** Keep your horse as cool as possible. Only exercise during the coolest part of the day, and hose him down afterward. In some cases, frequent shampooing may help the coat stay healthier. Many horses fail to recover and must be moved to a cooler climate.
- **Supplements:** Vitamin E or thyroid supplementation also may help.

ARTHRITIS (DEGENERATIVE JOINT DISEASE, OSTEOARTHRITIS)

Arthritis, the inflammation of the joints, is a major cause of horse lameness. It usually affects the fetlocks, hocks, coffin joints, and navicular bone. A particular form of arthritis affecting the knee joint is called carpitis. This is common in horses who do a lot of jumping or turning. Arthritis is most common in older horses, but any animal can be affected, especially those heavily involved in athletic events. If only one joint is affected, the likely cause is trauma.

In healthy horses, a thick layer of cartilage cushions meeting bones and prevents them from rubbing against each other. It also acts like a shock absorber, taking up the various jolts that come from normal activity. The problem with cartilage, though, is that it doesn't have its own blood supply. When it's damaged, it just doesn't heal as fast or as well as tissue with a vascular supply. In arthritis, stress to the joint damages not only the tissues that surround it but also the joint capsule itself and the synovial fluid that fills the capsule and lubricates the joint.

White blood cells enter the area and begin to chomp away at the joint cartilage. Eventually the horse will become lame and the joint will be swollen and warm to the touch.

The signature sign of arthritis is a warm, firm swelling that is painful to the touch. Long before swelling sets in, there will be heat at the joint and perhaps mild swelling. Pay attention to these signs. As time goes on, the swelling becomes harder, cooler, and less painful, but by then joint movement may be severely restricted. Performance horses may show a reluctance to execute moves that put strain on their joints. The presence of arthritis can be confirmed with X-rays.

Care and treatment options include:

- **Prevention:** Because this disease is more likely to affect horses with poor conformation, take note of any horse with legs that are less than perfect and of specific problems like toeing out. These horses are at a higher risk of developing arthritis and should not participate in events that put a lot of stress on those imperfect joints. Aged horses are of course at increased risk, partly because of a lifetime of stress and partly because after the age of 15, horses use up more new cartilage than they can produce. Don't feed your young horse a high-protein diet (more than 12 percent). A diet too rich in protein may contribute to the development of OCD (osteochondritis dissecans) and other problems.
- **Acupuncture:** Acupuncture helps the body attain homeostasis (a "steady state") so that it can better heal itself. It may help to normalize the flow of oxygen and nutrients to the damaged area.
- **Ayurvedic Therapy:** Mixture of the herbs triphala and boswellia. Warm baths are also recommended.
- **Chinese Herbal Therapy:** Ginseng, various patent combinations.
- **Crystal Therapy:** Sapphire.
- **Herbal Therapy:** Alfalfa and aloe vera (be careful when using aloe internally), which may counter the adverse side effects of nonsteroidal anti-inflammatory drugs (NSAIDs); apple cider vinegar (1/3 pint [0.15 liters] in the food or water); bladderwrack (long-term support); celery seed (long-term support); comfrey; dandelion; feverfew (long-term support); ginger (long-term support); yucca root (liquid); combination of devil's claw, meadowsweet, and white willow (for acute pain, blended equally to make 2 tablespoons [30 ml]).
- **Homeopathy:** Apis mel (6C if accompanied by swollen joints); arnica (6C-30X three times a day or arnica lotion); belladonna (if accompanied by heat and swelling); bryonia (12C-30X 3 times a day for hot, swollen joints and if the lameness grows worse with movement); hekla lava (6C-30X twice a day for problems in the coffin joint or navicular; ledum (especially if the arthritis is in the hock); rhus tox (rhus toxicodendron; 30C three times a day for hot, painful swellings).
- **Magnetic Therapy:** To help with pain by amplifying certain beneficial electrical currents in the body.
- **Massage and Physical Therapy:** Cold hydrotherapy (that's just ice) if there is no sign of infection; you also can hose the area with cold water. Heat therapy (sweats) and corrective shoeing also may be useful.
- **Medical:** NSAIDS work to reduce inflammation, fever, and pain. They include phenylbutazone, Banamine, and aspirin. While useful, these medications do nothing to destroy the destructive enzymes that may be present in the joint. If NSAIDs are used by themselves, they can be harmful because they reduce pain so well that the horse may further damage the joint when self-exercising. NSAIDs should be used along with sodium hyaluronate (HA) or polysulfated glycosaminoglycans (PSGAGs). These compounds are designed to protect the cartilage. PSGAGS are particularly useful when there is inflammation and mild

cartilage damage. Corticosteroids also can be injected directly into the joint. These work fast to eliminate pain and to destroy harmful free radicals. They too are often used in combination with HA or PSGAGs. HA is naturally present in the joint and can be given as an injection directly to the joint or intravenously (which will treat several joints). PSGAGs have similar properties to the components of normal cartilage; they reduce inflammation, relieve pain, stimulate the production of HA, and help cartilage heal. They also can be injected into the joint or muscle. Glucosamine and chondroitin supplements (related to other cartilage components) also may be effective.

- **Nutritional Therapy:** Chondroitin and glucosamine in powder or liquid form; Vitamin C (work up to 8 grams per day); MSM (methylsulfonylmethane); flaxseed; fish oils.
- **Rest and Moderate Exercise:** In the early stages of arthritis, before damage to the cartilage occurs, the first and best option is rest for at least several days and perhaps several months. It also may help to put a pressure bandage on the affected area while waiting for a diagnosis. Later, moderate exercise with plenty of warm-up time is helpful.
- **Rubs:** Arnica lotion; chili oil, available from health food stores, rubbed into the joint; DMSO (dimethyl sulfoxide); essential oil rubs (use a 2.5 percent solution in olive oil) such as blue (German) chamomile, bergamot, rosemary, juniper, or lavender.
- **Shiatsu:** Lung meridian.
- **Shoeing (Therapeutic):** Absorption pad, neoprene shoes.
- **Stem Cell Therapy:** Fat-derived stem cell treatments from the animal's own body are injected at the arthritic site to repair tendons and ligaments.

AZOTURIA (*see Tying Up*)

BACK PAIN

Just about every movement a horse makes gets translated through the back, which includes the vertebrae and related muscles, tendons, ligaments, and nerves. Horses were not originally designed to carry people around, so it shouldn't be surprising that sore backs are an extremely common problem.

Signs include:

- bucking
- difference in strength of diagonals at the posting trot
- difficulty in backing up or turning short
- difficulty in making movements such as touching the muzzle into the shoulder
- head tossing and tail swishing
- muscular spasms
- oversensitivity to grooming or even tenderness on fingertip pressure
- resistance to being saddled or mounted
- saddle sores
- short stepping on affected side
- stiffness and limited movement
- tendency to drop the back when being mounted
- tripping
- uneven shoe wear and trouble on lateral work

Back problems can be "low grade" and so subtle that the rider isn't aware of them. She may not realize how the pain is

diminishing the horse's performance.

There can be many causes of back pain, including something as simple as an ill-fitting blanket or saddle. Saddles and blankets come in different sizes and styles, and what works for one horse may not work for others. The saddle should have sufficient clearance in the gullet and through the channel between the panels. Saddle makers suggest checking saddle panels every 6 to 12 months. If your horse has a sore back, get some expert help in assessing whether the saddle fits properly.

Other nonmedical causes of a sore back include poor riders who may be unbalancing the horse or forcing the neck into a position that leads to back pain. An unbalanced seat can cause pressure points and keep the saddle tree from distributing weight evenly. Uneven muscular development in the horse is another possibility.

In other cases, back pain could be related to lameness, or a bone may be putting pressure on spinal nerves or touching other bones. Chiropractors may detect a subluxation of the vertebrae. There also may be lesions in the spinal canal.

It is important to establish the cause of the pain before attempting to treat it. If the problem is in the muscle, the condition may respond to manipulation or laser therapy. If the back problem is in the muscle, spinal manipulation will be of limited usefulness. Spinal problems are particularly prevalent in jumpers.

Treatment options include:

- **Acupuncture/Acupressure:** Bladder meridian 37: located about 5 inches (12.7 cm) below the point of hip (in the crease on the side and toward the tail, kidney meridian).
- **Ayurvedic Therapy:** Mixture of herbs: kaishore, guggul, and dashamoola basti.
- **Chinese Herbs:** Dong quai.
- **Chiropractic Care:** To treat any misalignments that have been diagnosed by a veterinarian.
- **Crystal Therapy:** Indigo stones, gold.
- **Homeopathy:** Rhus tox and bryonia alba combined; arnica.
- **Massage:** Effleurage on the back muscles.
- **Medical:** Sarapin, a vegetable-based pain reliever, injected along the back to relieve spasms.
- **Shiatsu:** To maintain the back in good condition, a practitioner of shiatsu may use pressure techniques on the bladder meridian.

BEHAVIORAL AND PERFORMANCE PROBLEMS

Most behavior problems respond best to kind, consistent training. But because this is a book on health and wellness, and not training, I am including only therapies designed to be used as adjuncts to good training in this section.

AGGRESSION/QUARRELSOMENESS

- **Flower Essences:** Vine.
- **Homeopathy:** Belladonna, sepia.

ANGER, RESENTMENT

- **Essential Oils:** Bergamot, jasmine, neroli, orange, Roman chamomile, rose, valerian, vetiver, yarrow, ylang ylang.
- **Flower Essences:** Cherry plum.

ANXIETY, APPREHENSION

- **Essential Oils:** Bergamot, geranium, dashamoola basti, patchouli, mandarin, rose.
- **Homeopathy:** Aconite, calcarea carbonica (30C twice daily), scutellaria.

- **Tissue Salts:** Mag phos (magnesia phosphorica or phosphate, which can be combined with valerian and thiamine).
- **Vitamin/Mineral Therapy:** Thiamine, calcium (for mild cases).

CRIBBING/WIND SUCKING

- **Essential Oils:** Carrot seed, jasmine, bladderwrack, vetiver, violet leaf, frankincense, nutmeg, Roman chamomile, ylang ylang.
- **Homeopathy:** Sulfur.
- **Massage:** Craniosacral massage.
- **Physical Management:** This condition is caused by boredom. Get a companion for your horse, give him more turnout time, or exercise him more. Or all three.

DEPRESSION

- **Crystal Therapy:** Lapis lazuli.
- **Essential Oils:** Jasmine, lavender, vetiver, clary sage, geranium, helichrysum, mandarin, orange, rose, ylang ylang, frankincense, neroli, sandalwood.
- **Flower Essences:** Mt. Shasta Essences, oak, gorse, cranesbill.
- **Herbal Therapy:** Celery seed, especially when the depression is caused by arthritis.
- **Shiatsu:** Bladder or kidney meridian.

DISOBEDIENT, HEADSTRONG, STUBBORN

- **Crystal Therapy:** Thernadite.
- **Essential Oils:** Jasmine, nutmeg, vetiver.
- **Flower Essences:** Vine, clematis.
- **Homeopathy:** Belladonna, calcarea carbonica.

FEARFULNESS, SKITTISHNESS, INSECURITY, SPOOKINESS

- **Crystal Therapy:** Azurite, citrine, thernadite.
- **Essential Oils:** Bergamot, clary sage, frankincense, grapefruit, jasmine, juniper, lavender, lemon, lemon balm, orange, Roman chamomile, rose, vetiver, violet leaf, sandalwood.
- **Flower Essences:** Aspen, rock rose, Rescue Remedy.
- **Herbal Therapy:** Chamomile flowers (dried), chasteberry, hops (1/2 to 1 tablespoon [7.5 to 15 ml] mixed with grain), lemon balm, meadowsweet, passion flower, skullcap, Saint-John's-wort (use for horses with a gloomy disposition), valerian.
- **Homeopathy:** Aconite, gelsemium, silicea, nux vomica, arsenicum, kali phos.
- **Nutritional Therapy:** Magnesium supplement.

IRRITABILITY

- **Essential Oils:** Mandarin, frankincense, sandalwood.
- **Flower Essences:** Cherry plum.
- **Herbal Therapy:** Chamomile (especially when caused by gastrointestinal upset), valerian (when the irritability is caused by tension), passion flower,

bladderwrack.
- **Homeopathy:** Apis mel, bryonia.

LACK OF FOCUS
- **Crystal Therapy:** Lead.
- **Essential Oils:** Basil, lemon, cypress, black pepper, hyssop, peppermint.

LONELINESS
- **Essential Oils:** Bergamot, frankincense, Roman chamomile.

LOW CONFIDENCE
- **Bach Flowers:** Walnut.
- **Essential Oils:** Bay laurel, cypress, jasmine, rose.

RESTLESSNESS
- **Essential Oils:** Chamomile (both Roman and German).
- **Homeopathy:** Arsenic, belladonna.

SEPARATION ANXIETY
- **Essential Oils:** Neroli, rose, violet leaf.
- **Flower Essences:** Mimulus.

SHYNESS
- **Essential Oils:** Jasmine, juniper, sweet orange.
- **Flower Essences:** Bach's aspen, Mt. Shasta columbine.
- **Homeopathy:** Pulsatilla, especially with gentle mares.
- **Shiatsu:** Kidney meridian.

STALL-WEAVING
This condition is caused by isolation and anxiety and is a difficult vice to cure once begun.
- **Flower Essences:** Verbatim.
- **Homeopathy:** Arsenicum album.
- **Physical Management:** Stimulus. Use deep straw bedding.

STRESS
- **Essential Oils:** Clary sage, geranium, jasmine, Roman chamomile, sandalwood.

WEAKNESS, FATIGUE, EXHAUSTION
- **Crystal Therapy:** Gold.
- **Essential Oils:** Helichrysum, basil, cypress, peppermint, lemon, sandalwood.
- **Nutritional Therapy:** DMG (dimethylglycine), magnesium supplement.

BIGHEAD (BRAN DISEASE OR MILLER'S DISEASE)
Bighead is caused by an imbalance of calcium and phosphorus. It's often seen in horses who graze on mostly tropical grasses such as buffelgrass and setaria; these contain oxalates that bind calcium in the intestine. Signs include shifting lameness and reluctance to move. In severe cases, there is a swelling around the jaw, which gives the disease

its name. Horses who feed primarily on high-phosphorus grains also may be susceptible.

Care and treatment options include:

- **Crystal Therapy:** Seashells.
- **Environmental/Nutritional Therapy:** Remove the horse from the pasture or add a high-calcium feed supplement designed for bighead. If the horse is on a high-grain diet, add 40 grams of calcium carbonate daily.

BOG SPAVIN

Bog spavin is associated with inflammation of the joint capsule. Usually it is cosmetic only and doesn't affect the usefulness of the horse. The typical sign is a soft, fluid-filled area on the upper and inner side of the hock. It is not usually accompanied by heat or pain. Causes include poor conformation and turning suddenly.

Care and treatment options include:

- **Acupuncture:** To reduce inflammation.
- **Crystal Therapy:** Indigo stones.
- **Homeopathy:** Aesculus hippocastanum, apis mel, ledum, bryonia, rhus tox.
- **Medical:** Drain the fluid or inject an anti-inflammatory into the joint capsule.
- **Rest and Physical Treatment:** Rest, cold water hosing, pressure bandage.

BONE SPAVIN

Bone spavin is basically arthritis of the hock joint. The joint capsule is usually swollen and filled with fluid. You usually can feel a bony enlargement that doesn't often cause lameness. However, in some causes there can be lameness without any swelling at all. Causes include poor conformation or stressful activity.

Care and treatment options include:

- **Acupuncture:** To reduce pain and inflammation.
- **Corrective Shoeing:** The hoof should be rasped square and fitted with a shoe with a raised heel and rolled square toe. This should alleviate the strain on the inside of the hock.
- **Crystal Therapy:** Indigo stones.
- **Herbal Therapy:** Dandelion to relieve excess fluid.
- **Homeopathy:** Ledum, bryonia, rhus tox.
- **Physical Treatment:** Rest for at least six weeks. Anti-inflammatory agents, radiation, or surgery may be prescribed.

BRUISES

A bruise is a traumatic injury of the soft tissues that results from breakage of the capillaries and leakage of red blood cells into the area. Most bruises go away within a few days. (*See also* Wounds.)

Treatment options include:

- **Essential Oils:** Combination of geranium, lavender, and marjoram in a 2.5 percent solution (in aloe gel; may be combined with flower essences).
- **Flower Essences:** agrimony, star-of-Bethlehem; use 6 drops in aloe gel for both.
- **Herbal:** Tincture of yarrow, calendula cream, or ointment.

- **Homeopathy:** Arnica (30C twice a day following injury or excessive exercise), phosphorus, hamamelis.

BURSITIS

Bursitis is an inflammation of the bursa, the sac that surrounds and lubricates the joints and other areas where friction can occur.

Treatment options include:

- **Acupuncture:** May be of benefit, but the horse must rest.
- **Homeopathy:** Ruta graveolens.
- **Medical:** Anti-inflammatory pain medication, along with rest, is often effective, especially for bursitis of the hock.
- **Surgical/Medical:** Subacromial bursitis (often caused by the bacteria *Streptococcus spp.*) can sometimes be treated by debridement surgery.

CALCIUM/PHOSPHORUS IMBALANCE

Calcium is absorbed mostly in the small intestine; phosphorus is mainly absorbed in the large intestine. Both are dependent on receiving sufficient vitamin D (the sunshine vitamin, which actually works more like a hormone) to be properly absorbed. The ideal levels are about 1.2 to 2 parts calcium to 1 part phosphorus, although growing horses need a somewhat higher percentage of calcium. Calcium is critical for many bodily functions other than bone building, such as muscle contraction and blood clotting. If horses can't get sufficient calcium from their diet, the body will obtain it from the bones, and that's bad news. On the other hand, too much calcium can interfere with the absorption of copper, zinc, and magnesium—three vital minerals.

It is important to understand that the ratios between calcium and phosphorus are more critical than the absolute amount. If calcium and phosphorus are not properly balanced, numerous bone disorders and other problems can develop. Calcium deficiency can occur when horses are fed a high-phosphorus grain like bran (especially rice bran). In fact, most cereal grains are deficient in calcium and high in phosphorus. Here are the approximate calcium/phosphorus ratios in some common feeds:

Feed	Calcium (percent)	Phosphorus (percent)
alfalfa hay, mid-bloom	1.24	0.22
Bermuda hay, 29 to 42 days	0.30	0.19
oat hay	0.29	0.23
orchard grass hay, early bloom	0.24	0.30
Timothy hay, mid-bloom	0.43	0.20
barley grain	0.05	0.34
beet pulp, dehydrated	0.62	0.09
corn grain	0.05	0.27
oat grain	0.05	0.34
rice bran	0.09	1.57
wheat bran	0.13	1.13

You usually can get a balance by feeding a good grass hay (other than orchard grass) plus beet pulp. For more energy, add a little vegetable oil, which will not upset the proper calcium/phosphorus balance.

However, diet is only part of the picture. Calcium deficiency also can occur if the pasture contains oxalates that hinder calcium absorption. Horses also can have disease conditions that affect calcium absorption in the body.

As for phosphorus, some horses lack the enzyme phytase, which enables them to digest phytates, the primary dietary source of phosphorus in many plants.

Other treatment options include:

- **Chinese Herbs:** Dong quai.
- **Crystal Therapy:** Indigo stones.
- **Homeopathy:** Calcarea carbonica.

CANNON KERATOSIS (CANNON SCALD)

Cannon keratosis is characterized by a patch of crusted or scaly skin in the region of the cannon bones, which are the long bones that extend from the knee to the pastern. These lesions generally require lifelong management. Despite its strange appearance, the condition is not caused by a fungus, bacterial infection, rain rot, scratches, or urine scald. It is actually produced by overactive sebaceous glands.

Care and treatment options include:

- **Crystal Therapy:** White stones.
- **Physical Management:** Soak the affected leg with medicated shampoo to remove the excess keratin, and then clean the legs with cool water. Dry the legs and apply a human acne cream containing 10 percent benzoyl peroxide. Wrap with vet wrap, and keep the horse confined for a couple of hours. Then unwrap the legs, wet them, and lather the area with povidone iodine shampoo or Betadine. Rinse. Soothe the area with cotton soaked in witch hazel. To prevent recurrence, move the horse to a better pasture. You may have to continue the treatment because a cure is not known. (You also can buy a benzoyl peroxide shampoo for pets that does the same thing.)

CAPPED ELBOW (SHOE BOIL)

A shoe boil is a soft, fluid-filled swelling on the point of the elbow. It is really a very common form of bursitis. However, unlike most kinds of bursitis, it is not usually painful. In most cases, the cause is a horse lying down in such a way that the shoe rubs against the sore spot or a high-stepping horse who actually can hit his elbows with his hooves. The best treatment is to remove the cause of the trauma.

Care and treatment options include:

- **Acupuncture:** To reduce inflammation.
- **Homeopathy:** Arnica (30C twice a day for ten days), apis mel (6C three times a day for three days for swelling).
- **Medical/Surgical:** If the cap is recent, the vet may be able to drain it off. Old shoe boils can be removed surgically.
- **Physical Management:** Cold compresses, exercise reduction (walk only), corrective shoeing (using a shoe boil or "doughnut roll," a soft padded roll that fits around the fetlock like a bracelet).

CHOKE

Choke occurs when food gets stuck in the esophagus. This is considered a medical emergency. However, your horse can still breathe, so do not panic. Call your vet immediately. Signs include:

- distress
- extended neck
- frothy nostrils
- nasal discharge that has bits of feed in it
- pawing
- refusal to eat

Choke usually happens because, for one reason or another, the horse has insufficient saliva to moisten food properly or because dry food can swell up quickly on contact with saliva. Do not give water or any food. You actually may be able to see a bit of a lump on the lower side of the horse's neck. Gently try to move it, but don't use force. You still should call your vet.

Horses who tend to bolt their food are most in danger. Wild horses, who munch slowly on grass all day, do not have this difficulty. It's just another "blessing" of domestication. Horses who eat in groups also tend to choke more than horses who are fed singly because there's no competition for horses who feed alone.

Treatment options include:

- **Acupuncture:** To relax the area around the choke.
- **Crystal Therapy:** Barite, yellow-orange stones.
- **Flower Essences:** Bach Rescue Remedy.
- **Homeopathy:** Arnica (30C).
- **Medical:** Usually, a slow flush via a stomach tube clears the blockage. Standard muscle relaxers, intravenous fluid therapy, analgesics, and/or surgery are also options, depending on the situation. Researchers at the University of Mississippi have recently experimented with the administration of oxytocin to relax the muscle. This seems to work well in uncomplicated cases but should not be used with pregnant mares.
- **Tissue Salts:** Mag phos (12C four times, 15 minutes apart).

CHRONIC OBSTRUCTIVE PULMONARY DISEASE (HEAVES, BROKEN WIND, BRONCHIAL ASTHMA)

Chronic obstructive pulmonary disease (COPD) is a constriction of the small airways, called bronchioles, in the lungs and is the equine equivalent of asthma. In most cases, the condition is caused by an allergic reaction to dust or fungal spores. Signs usually appear gradually, and most affected horses who develop the condition are over the age of four. The disease, unfortunately, seems to be on the increase—probably as a result of the way in which we keep our horses.

Signs include:

- breathing in without much difficulty, but breathing out requires an abnormal muscular force
- chronic cough, perhaps with a clear nasal discharge
- exercise intolerance

Care and treatment options are as follows:

- **Acupuncture:** Many horse owners have had success using acupuncture against the allergy causing this condition. Seek a qualified practitioner.
- **Chinese Herbal Therapy:** Ginseng, dong quai.
- **Crystal Therapy:** Orange stones.
- **Essential Oil:** Cedarwood, peppermint, spearmint, fennel, clary sage, eucalyptus, violet leaf, frankincense, sandalwood, lavender. Combination: You can make a refreshing barn spray by adding a few drops each of clary sage, eucalyptus, and frankincense to a pint (470 ml) of water. This may help your horse breathe easier. Chest rub: Aloe vera and 2.5 percent dilution of a selected oil.
- **Homeopathy:** Arsenicum, nux vomica, bryonia, carbo vegetabilis (carbo veg).
- **Medical:** Antihistamines or allergy medication. In some cases, your vet may prescribe the bronchodilator clenbuterol to help the airways clear more quickly.
- **Physical Management:** When the source of the allergy is removed, the horse usually can breathe normally again. The major allergens are fungal spores found on hay, so the best plan often is to turn the horse out to pasture. When you feed hay, it may help to dampen it beforehand to keep the dust down. The stable should be well ventilated. The horse should sleep on dustless bedding such as wood shavings or even shredded paper. (At last, a use for that shredder you bought.) Keep the stable washed down regularly. Don't expect immediate results; it may take twice as long for the condition to clear as it did to develop, so it may be weeks or months before the horse returns to normal.
- **Tissue Salts:** Nat sulph.
- **Western Herbal Therapy:** Licorice. Combination tea: chamomile, mullein, and comfrey added to the feed.

COLIC

The term "colic" simply means pain in the abdomen, but it strikes fear into the hearts of horse owners, and with reason. Colic is the number-one killer of horses. About 10 percent of horses suffer colic every year. It is probably the most common disease affecting them, although technically speaking, the word refers to a number of different conditions. The horse's intestine bends at more than 180 places. These flexures are often sites where colic can develop.

Not all cases of colic are life threatening. However, it is often difficult to tell in the early stages whether a particular colic episode is merely a passing discomfort or a medical emergency requiring immediate surgery. Some really violent-looking cases turn out to be quite mild, and vice versa. *All* cases of colic should be treated as life threatening as a matter of prudence, and all cases should receive veterinary attention. Time is critical.

Signs include:

- capillary refill time of more than four seconds (This means that if you press down on the inside of the horse's lip, the white spot will not return to a normal pink color for four seconds. In a healthy horse, it should only be second or two. Capillary refill time is an indicator of blood circulation. This is true for all animals, humans too!)
- increased pulse rate (above 60 bpm)
- looking at or kicking at the belly with the front hoof
- lying down or lying down and getting up repeatedly
- passing of hard, dry manure
- pawing at the ground
- repeatedly curling the upper lip
- standing stretched out
- violent rolling may occur in later stages, or the horse may lie on his back almost completely still

The vet may make a rectal exam to check for colic, but don't attempt this yourself because it is easy to tear the bowel wall. Horses with repeated episodes of colic may be more likely to founder also.

There are several different kinds of colic, each with a different cause. In many cases, the cause is simply not known:

Spasmodic Colic: Spasmodic colic, the most common form, is really a disorder of the nervous system that affects the bowels, which have abnormal and increased contractions. It is caused by fear and stress. The pain is severe but intermittent.

Flatulent Colic: Flatulent (gas or tympanitic) colic is formed by large amounts of gas in the large intestine. It stretches the intestine and results in intense pain. It can cause very violent signs and can be serious, although it usually will respond to medical treatment.

Impaction Colic: Impaction colic occurs when the intestine becomes blocked by a firm mass of food in the large or small intestine, usually at the site of one of the flexures. Signs usually develop slowly. The blood flow is cut off from the affected part of the intestine, and the tissue dies. Impaction colic may resolve relatively easily with proper care, which includes administering mineral oil via a tube into the horse's stomach. Be alert, though—an impaction may be just the first obvious sign in a more complicated case. Never give a laxative to horse with an impaction because the bowel could rupture.

Twisted Gut (Displacement or Volvulus/Torsion): These kinds of colic almost always require emergency surgery. Although displacement colic and colic resulting from volvulus or twisted gut are slightly different, both conditions need to be immediately treated surgically if the horse has any chance of surviving. In torsion, parts of the horse's gastrointestinal tract (usually in the small intestine) may twist upon themselves. The blood supply is cut off, causing rapid deterioration and requiring emergency surgery. Intussusception, a related form, occurs when part of the intestine "telescopes" within a portion of itself. This most often occurs in young horses and requires emergency surgery.

Gastric Distension/Rupture: Gastric distension/rupture can occur when a horse gorges himself on grain or a feed that expands when wet, like beet pulp. Horses have small stomachs considering their large size, and when the contents of the stomach swell up, the horse is in trouble. Horses are not able to vomit, and this combination of events may cause the stomach to burst. The result is death. Obviously, it's important to get veterinary help before this happens.

Enteritis/Colitis: This is an inflammation of the small (enteritis) or large (colitis) intestines. In either case, it requires immediate veterinary attention.

We still don't know enough about colitis. Most of the knowledge we have comes from careful surveys of horses who have had colic and those who have not. Once a horse has had colic, he has increased chances of getting it again. Horses between the ages of two and ten seem most at risk.

Here are some preventive measures and care suggestions that may help:

- Avoid sudden changes in your horse's diet. For example, if your horse has been on pasture and you want to stable him and begin training, don't suddenly switch to a high-grain diet. Start feeding just hay for a few days, then gradually add the grain. Keep turning your horse out to pasture for a week or so, but gradually decrease the time he spends there. The more gradual the changes, the more likely you are to avoid an episode of colic.
- Feed hay before grain.
- Maintain a regular feeding schedule.
- Do not keep your horse in a stall for more than 12 hours a day. Horses need regular exercise.
- Feed a consistent diet of high-quality hay or pasture, with plenty of fiber. This is very difficult, as hay quality

varies widely from crop to crop. Hay that contains too much roughage can lead to gas, and that leads to colic. It is possible that mixing a consistent fermentable "hay chop" with grain rations may reduce the risk of colic.

- Make sure that your horse always has access to fresh water (5 to 10 gallons [20 to 40 l] per day). Depriving your horse of water, even for a couple of hours, increases the risk of colic because it slows down the movement of food through the digestive system.
- If you can avoid feeding grain, do so. Feeding 5.5 pounds (2.49 kg) of grain or more per day seems to increase the risk.
- If you do feed a balanced grain meal to your horse, do not add extra corn (beyond what is already mixed into it).
- If your horse bolts his feed, add some chaff to slow down the eating pace. You also can add a coarser grain mix to make him spend more time chewing.
- If you can, divide meals, especially grain meals, into as many small meals during the day as possible. Remember that horses are natural grazers and prefer to eat low-value meals constantly throughout the day rather than a high-value meal once a day.
- If your horse spends all day in a stall, he should have a fairly constant supply of hay. The fiber in it will help to prevent colic.
- Keep your horse on pasture as much as possible. Access to several different pastures also may be helpful.
- Be careful about suddenly reducing exercise and increasing stabling time. This has been shown to increase the risk of colic.
- Keep down the stress factor. Solitary horses would do better with a companion.
- Cool your horse down gradually after a workout.
- Keep your horse properly dewormed (although many studies do not show a correlation between parasite burden and colic—but it doesn't hurt).
- Herbal therapy prevention includes chamomile, valerian, mint, and marshmallow. A chamomile infusion is especially good for horses who are prone to nervous colic.
- Take the fleshy part of the fennel stems and add liberally to the feed every day.
- Essential oil prevention includes inhalation of bergamot, jasmine, fennel, juniper, frankincense, vetiver, basil, or marjoram.

If you notice signs of colic, take your horse's pulse and respiration rates and call your vet for further advice. Take away all food.

Here are suggested treatment options:

- **Acupuncture/Acupressure:** To stimulate the bowel (may be somewhat useful for impaction colic) and soothe the intestine. The master point for the abdomen is stomach meridian 36, located about 3 inches (7.6 cm) below the stifle joint and 1 inch (2.5 cm) to the outside of the tibial crest (the ridge of bone below the knee). Bladder meridian 18: located about 3 inches (7.6 cm) from the midline in the middle of the back between ribs 13 and 14. Bladder meridian 25: located about 3 inches (7.6 cm) from the midline above the flank and in front of the hip (especially good for colic resulting from

problems in the large intestine).

- **Crystal Therapy:** To be used while waiting for the vet, not in place of medical or surgical care: citrine or any yellow-orange stone (for gaseous-type colic), sapphire (nervous type colic).
- **Essential Oils:** To be used while waiting for the vet, not in place of medical or surgical care: lavender (waft under horse's nose to help horse cope with stressful pain), lemon, hops and lavender mix, bergamot (waft under horse's nose to help horse cope with stressful pain), frankincense (waft under horse's nose to help horse cope with stressful pain), melissa, comfrey to reduce stomach lining inflammation (present in certain kinds of colic). Massage oil: Blend up to any four of the following: chamomile (German or Roman), juniper, basil, orange, geranium, or fennel in 2.5 percent solution in oil or aloe vera gel, and gently rub the abdomen area.

- **Flower Essences:** To be used while waiting for the vet, not in place of medical or surgical care: Rescue Remedy in the early stages (four drops every half hour), water violet (for colic pain), sweet chestnut, impatiens, rock rose.
- **Homeopathy:** To be used while waiting for the vet, not in place of medical or surgical care. In all cases, give a 30C dose for milder signs, 200C for more severe signs. Possibilities include belladonna (6C to 12C), colocynthis (for colic of unknown causes; for spasmodic colic, give one dose and wait for a response), aconite (6C to 30X every hour; may be useful in the early stages of any sort of colic), nux vomica (6C to 30X for grass colic, mild cases), colchicum (for tympanitic or gaseous colic, if the liver or kidney is not involved), euonymus europaeae (for tympanitic or gaseous colic if the liver is involved), magnesia phosphorica (gaseous colic), carbo vegetabilis (30C for gaseous colic every three hours), zingiber (gaseous colic), china, arsenicum, zincum metallicum (gaseous colic, especially recurrent cases), veratrum album (gaseous colic), euphorbium, dulcamara (colic caused by stress), lycopodium (chronic cases of colic).
- **Massage (Reflexology):** Massage the ears for stomach pain.
- **Medical/Surgical:** Antispasmodics to return bowel movements to normal, nasogastric intubation (tube through the nose), Xylazine hydrochloride (Rompun), a powerful painkiller and stomach muscle relaxer. Many kinds of colic can be helped by administering dioctyl sulfosuccinate (DSS), which reduces surface tension in the fecal mass, letting water penetrate more easily. It also helps the intestines secrete more water. Give no more than once in a 48-hour period. *Note:* DSS should not be given at the same time as mineral oil. It causes the mineral oil to break up into tiny particles that can be absorbed into the bloodstream. Surgery to release the gas pressure (tympanitic colic) or to untwist the intestine may be needed. Psyllium, found in many constipation products (for impaction colic).
- **Physical Management:** Take away all food. Take your horse for a little ride in the trailer. The jiggling may get things back on track, so to speak. At the least, it will keep your horse standing. Rolling can compound the problem. It does no real good to keep walking a colicked horse. This only serves to tire the horse out but does not treat the disease. Even if the horse stops rolling, he does so only because he has become distracted.
- **Shiatsu:** To be used while waiting for the vet, not in place of medical or surgical care: Stomach meridian.
- **Tissue Salts:** To be used while waiting for the vet, not in place of medical or surgical care: Mag Phos (every 30 minutes).
- **Western Herbal Therapy:** To be used while waiting for the vet, not in place of medical or surgical care:

Chamomile, peppermint, or valerian tea if your horse is still eating or drinking (for nervous colic; these herbs also will help a horse recovering from colic), comfrey (to reduce stomach lining inflammation that is present in certain kinds of colic), dandelion (leaf or root) and fennel are helpful for flatulent colic, ginger is helpful for recovering horses (add 1 tablespoon [15 ml] of the grated root or a cup of a strong infusion), marshmallow (to coat the digestive tract, 20 grams per day). Recovery Blend: For aftercare, one part each of marshmallow, St. Mary's thistle, meadowsweet, slippery elm, and comfrey root, combined with half a part of licorice root. Offer 1 tablespoon (15 ml) or so up to one month after the colic episode.

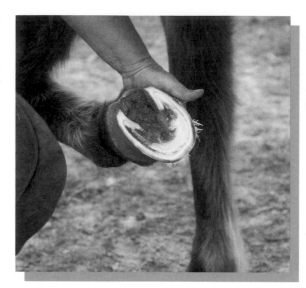

CORNS AND BRUISED SOLES

Corns are reddish bruises on the sole of the foot, usually toward the rear. Causes include bad, uneven, or infrequent shoeing (with the heel of the shoe turning inward and putting pressure on the sole), or work over rough surfaces. The horse is usually lame.

Treatment options include:

- **Acupuncture:** For pain and inflammation.
- **Essential Oils:** Tea tree (to help to prevent infections), bergamot (to help to prevent infections), lavender (add to Epsom salt soak), geranium (add to Epsom salt soak). Use all as aromatherapy once a day every other day
- **Herbal Therapy:** Bladderwrack (to strengthen feet; use for several months), Hawthorn (to strengthen feet; use for several months), rose hips (to strengthen feet; use for several months), comfrey poultice.
- **Homeopathy:** Arnica (30C to 200C, depending on the severity of the bruise, twice a day for five days). Or soak in arnica lotion mixed with warm water 20 minutes twice a day. Calcarea fluorica (30C).
- **Medical:** Make sure that there is drainage from the area. Apply povidone iodine to the opening. Soak in a drawing agent like Epsom salts. Tetanus injection. Iodine spray to toughen the feet. Be careful not to get too much iodine around the coronary band because it can cause inflammation.
- **Physical Management:** E-Z boots, rest, proper shoeing.

COUGHING

A cough is not a disease in and of itself but rather a mechanical reaction to an irritant such as dust or other allergens, or it is a sign of a major viral or bacterial infection. It is important to determine the cause of the cough, especially if it persists for any length of time. However, the following may help to lessen your horse's discomfort:

- **Ayurvedic Therapy:** Shatavari.
- **Essential Oils:** Cardamom, cedarwood, eucalyptus, peppermint, sandalwood.
- **Flower Essences**: Chicory, crab apple, gorse.
- **Herbal Therapy:** Garlic; combination: echinacea, mullein, and fenugreek. (Add 1 cup [240 ml] of blended herbs to feed morning and evening.)
- **Homeopathy:** Belladonna (6C to 200C, depending on severity of cough), bryonia (6C to 200C, depending on severity of cough), phosphorus (6C to 200C, depending on severity of the cough), carbo veg. Combination: Rhus tox and bryonia.

- **Tissue Salts:** Give two tablets two or three times a day for at least ten days: ferr phos (for mild cough), mag phos (for loud, spasmodic coughs with no phlegm), kali sulph (for yellow phlegm, rattling coughs), nat mur (for clear, watery phlegm), calc sulph (for bloody phlegm), silica (for chronic cough).

CURB

A curb is a ligament tear or sprain just below the point of the hock. Most of the time there is no lameness. This is a common condition of cow-hocked or sickle-hocked horses. It can be treated in much the same way that other tendon and ligament damage can.

Treatment options include:

- **Electro-Acupuncture:** Use of a multi-microcurrent has been successful in treating some cases. It is said to increase oxygen and blood supply to the area.
- **Medical:** Anti-inflammatory.
- **Physical Management:** Cold hosing, compress, or wash.

CUSHING'S DISEASE (PITUITARY ADENOMA)

Dogs, horses, and people all can be victims of Cushing's disease. Equine Cushing's disease is caused by hyperactivity of the pituitary gland. The original cause is usually a nonmalignant but destructive tumor on the gland. However, there may be other unknown factors as well.

The condition occurs because the affected gland overproduces hormones like MSH (melanocyte-stimulating hormones), beta-endorphin, and ACTH (adrenocorticotrophic hormones) but underproduces dopamine, an important neurotransmitter. This, in turn, damages the immune system. The disease is most common in older horses and ponies. In fact, ponies seem particularly vulnerable.

You often can spot a Cushing's horse from a distance. He has developed a potbelly (typical of dogs with Cushing's as well) and an accompanying swayback. This is due to the muscle loss typical of the disease. However, the classic sign of Cushing's in horses is the appearance of the coat, which is heavy, curly, and often matted and in poor condition. It loses its sheen and quality. The Cushing's horse does not shed his winter coat, probably because the hypothalamus has been pressured by the pituitary gland.

Other signs include:

- abscesses on the sole of the foot and in the mouth
- bouts of colic
- depression
- excessive thirst and hunger, often without weight gain and sometimes with weight loss (affected horses may drink 20 gallons [75.7 l] a day)
- fat deposits redistributed on the body, including over the eyes
- frequent infections of the skin
- hair on Cushing's horses often seems to stand on end while they are being worked
- infertility
- laminitis, a particularly nasty and chronic type, often occurring in the fall or winter (there may be a relationship between the breakdown of the intestinal wall characteristic of Cushing's disease and the development of laminitis)
- lower resistance to intestinal parasites
- pneumonia

- sweating less than normal, even on hot days

While a vet often can diagnose Cushing's from the horse's history and symptoms, blood and urine tests are available for suspected cases. These tests include the DST (dexamethasone suppression test) and ACTH stimulation. Recently, a test combining the DST with a TRH (thyroid-stimulating hormones) test was developed by a team at the University of Tennessee. This is an especially accurate test, but repeat testing may be necessary for this disease. A complete blood count also should be done to assess the horse's immune status.

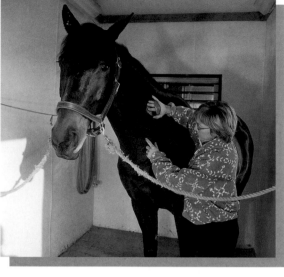

While no one knows exactly why horses get Cushing's, some holistic veterinarians are drawing a connection between the overfeeding of sugar with the development of the disease. Apples and carrots are high in sugar, by the way.

Proper stable management and grooming can help to keep your affected horse more comfortable:

- Keep your horse as stress free as possible; Cushing's horses have little resistance to stress. He should have a safe, comfortable stall of his own, with fresh water and hay available at all times. A regular feeding and turnout schedule also will help to reduce stress.
- Groom (and clip) your horse. Because he probably has a heavy shaggy coat that won't shed, it's up to you to keep him comfortable in the summer by removing as much of the excess hair as you can. In the winter, provide him with a blanket. Good grooming also will keep his skin in the best possible condition.
- Keep the hooves closely trimmed. Cushing's horses *always* develop laminitis if they live long enough.
- Keep the teeth in good shape with regular examinations. Cushing's horses may develop abscesses and other infections due to a weakened immune system.
- Keep your horse up to date on vaccinations and away from new horses who may be carrying other diseases. Your horse's weakened immune system needs all the help it can get.
- Deworm your horse every month or so. Cushing's horses are in more danger from worms than healthy horses.

No treatment will cure Cushing's, although it can be managed. Mild cases respond best. Horses who have already developed chronic laminitis and chronic infections may be too far gone to be saved. Currently, there is no method of removing the tumor from the pituitary gland. However, many owners have found the following treatments helpful:

- **Acupuncture:** Acupuncture is a traditional treatment for Cushing's; many people have had great success with it.
- **Chinese Herbal Therapy:** According to this theory, affected horses, especially those with laminitis, have a classic kidney yang deficiency that produces sore back muscles, weakness, infertility, excess urination, vacuum heat due to yin deficiency, and qi-yin deficiency. The formulas used to treat the disease include rhemannia 14 (for kidney yang deficiency), mai men dong san (for vacuum heat due to yin deficiency), and rhemannia 11 (for qi-yin deficiency). A practitioner skilled in this art also may use other formulas.
- **Crystal Therapy:** Barite, feldspar, tin (for the pituitary), and topaz and tourmaline for the immune system.
- **Essential Oils:** Frankincense helps to boost the immune system.
- **Herbal Therapy:** Some anecdotal evidence shows that chasteberry is effective for the early stages of Cushing's. It is said that horses on this treatment begin shedding within three weeks, and high blood glucose and insulin levels drop within four to six weeks. Herbs used are: apple cider vinegar, burdock, cleavers, bladderwrack, nettle, clover, rose hips, milk thistle, aloe vera, slippery elm, and garlic. Give the herbs in tincture, and monitor carefully. Combination: chasteberry, cleavers, dandelion, nettle, ginkgo, and

peppermint. (Some recipes call for wormwood, but this is dangerous.)

- **Homeopathy:** Homeopathy pituitary is a remedy made from the posterior lobe of the pituitary gland. It purports to help to balance the actions of the gland. Give it in low potencies (30C) over a long period of time, and monitor closely. In the early stages of the disease, try homeopathy formic acid.
- **Medical:** One drug commonly used is cyproheptadine, a serotonin blocker. It comes in tablet form, and it is easily absorbed. (The normal beginning dose is about 0.13 mg/kg, about 58 mg for an average 440-kg horse.) The dose is increased until the horse shows improvement. This is usually done by measuring the amount of water drunk, the first symptom of improvement, although even this takes six to eight weeks. After the horse has shown improvement for a month, the dosage is cut back to a maintenance level. This drug is effective in about three-quarters of Cushing's horses but may retain its benefits only for a year or two.

  Another drug used successfully is Permax (pergolide mesylate), which was once used to treat Parkinson's disease in people. It appears to replace the function of the neurotransmitter dopamine in the horse's system. At first, pergolide was considered a failure because it constricted the blood vessels and led to even worse laminitis. However, it was later discovered that it was effective in smaller doses against the symptoms of Cushing's disease without worsening the laminitis. Horses improve on a daily regimen of this drug quite rapidly, usually within 3 weeks, with the horse stabilizing at about 21 weeks. Horses on this drug need to be checked regularly.

  All these drugs can add productive years to your horse's life.
- **Nutritional Therapy:** Eliminate simple carbohydrates like sugar from your horse's diet, especially if the horse has diabetic-like signs. A high-fiber, lower-carbohydrate diet is recommended. Alfalfa hay should not be used alone or fed to a fat horse. Consider supplementing with coenzyme Q10, which has been shown to be useful in reversing free radical damage. This can be especially valuable if your horse has some of the common side effects of Cushing's, such as wounds, laminitis, or skin infections. Omega-3 essential fatty acids are also important. Fish oil is your best source, but if your horse refuses it (most do), use flax or hemp oil. If the Cushing's is accompanied by laminitis, add wheat bran as a source of fiber, taking care to keep the calcium/phosphorus ratio in balance in the overall diet. You can add blue-green algae to the bran to provide important amino acids and trace minerals. Grass or other lower-protein hays can be given free choice.
- **Orthomolecular Treatment:** Vitamin C (for Cushing's disease due to pituitary adenoma, 3 to 6 grams per day), beta-carotene, vitamin E, magnesium, chromium, vanadium, and MSM (methylsulfonylmethane).

DENTAL PROBLEMS

Unlike people teeth, equine teeth continue to grow throughout the life of the horse. (The expression "long in the tooth" therefore refers to one who has lived a very long time.) One sure sign of dental problems in your horse is "quidding," in which he drops half-chewed food from his mouth. Such horses also may chomp at their bits.

What happens in most cases is simple: The cheek or molar teeth wear unevenly and develop sharp points, usually on the outside edge of the upper teeth and the inside edge of the lower teeth. This can be alleviated by filing the affected teeth. Some horses need to be sedated for this procedure. Another common problem occurs when a horse loses a tooth—the corresponding tooth in the opposite jaw may get very long and cause trouble.

Even more serious are tooth abscesses, which usually occur in the upper molars. These molars are seated in large spaces in the jaw, which can accumulate an amazing amount of pus. Most people don't normally go poking around in their horse's head, so the first sign that anything is wrong may be a purulent discharge from the nostrils, leading one to think that the problems is in the lungs. The suspect tooth will have to be removed; this usually requires general anesthesia.

Care and treatment options include:

- **Prevention:** Horses should get their teeth checked every six months or so. This gives the vet an opportunity to locate any decayed, loose, abscessed, or chipped teeth, as well as to file down (float) teeth that have developed sharp points. Horses who have "wolf teeth" (small, peg-like, vestigial premolars) should have them removed. Even though these extra teeth may not cause trouble in and of themselves, they can interfere with the bit in riding horses, resulting in a lack of control for the rider. There is no easy treatment for horses who have severe congenital problems such as parrot mouth, where the upper and lower incisors do not meet. These animals have a hard time grazing but often can manage hay and grain.
- **Crystal Therapy:** Fluorite.
- **Essential Oils:** Roman chamomile.
- **Medical/Surgical**: For abscesses of the tooth, the offending tooth must be removed. For fractured teeth, the sharp edges of the fractured tooth can sometimes be removed without resorting to extraction of the entire tooth.

DIARRHEA

Diarrhea is a sign of a problem rather than a disease. It can be caused by many different factors. Specific treatment depends on the cause, which can include an improper feeding regimen, antibiotics, viruses, loss of important gut bacteria, bad teeth and consequent failure to chew food properly, contamination of food, toxic plants, and worms.

Diarrhea in foals and adults is usually quite different. Foal heat diarrhea is common in animals 7 to 14 days old. It is called foal heat diarrhea because the foal's dam usually is having her first estrus cycle since foaling during this time. Foals often will continue to nurse and remain in good spirits, however, and there is no fever. The cause of the diarrhea is unknown but may be the result of changes in intestinal cell bacterial populations. Usually it gets better on its own.

Some parasites such as strongyloides, viruses such as rotaviruses, and bacteria such as salmonella also can cause diarrhea in foals. Overcrowding and poor hygiene have been associated with these outbreaks. These foals become very sick very fast and can die if not treated aggressively. Some can even get diarrhea from nursing and become lactose intolerant. A formula can replace the mother's milk. Foals who are between several weeks and several months of age can develop gastric ulcers, which cause chronic diarrhea. Such animals may show colic-like signs and grind their teeth. These ulcers can be treated medically. To prevent diarrhea in foals:

- Disinfect the foaling stall between uses.
- Do not use prophylactic antibiotics in foals.
- Use wood shaving bedding rather than sawdust or straw.
- Wash the mare's udder before the foal nurses.
- Work the mare in her last trimester.

People who tend a sick foal should wash their hands with a povidone iodine scrub. A phenolic solution should be used as a foot bath for anyone entering the stall with the foal, and all equipment also should be disinfected.

Adult horses with chronic diarrhea may be more likely to founder. Always consult your vet if your horse shows signs of illness along with the diarrhea.

Care and treatment options for diarrhea are as follows:

- **Prevention:** Avoid sudden or extreme dietary changes, especially from poor to rich pasture. Avoid sudden reduction in fiber. Do not overfeed protein. Deworm your horse properly. Check food for contamination. Supplement the diet with a lactobacillus or acidophilus product.
- **Acupuncture:** Can improve gastrointestinal function and boost the immune system.
- **Crystal Therapy:** Green stones
- **Essential Oils:** Bergamot, patchouli, sandalwood.
- **Flower Essences:** Add to drinking water or use your hand to wipe across the abdomen: agrimony (10 to 20 drops), impatiens (10 to 20 drops), mimulus (10 to 20 drops).
- **Herbal Therapy:** Meadowsweet (dried flowers or infusion), raspberry leaf tea (1 to 2 cups [240 to 480 ml] poured over feed), slippery elm bark powder (combined with cooked pumpkin once or twice a day).
- **Homeopathy:** China (30C twice a day or 200C once for violent diarrhea), colocynthis (30C twice a day or 200C once if diarrhea is accompanied by colicky pain), nux vomica (30C three times daily for diarrhea caused by overfeeding), podophyllum (6C three times a day).
- **Medical:** Rheaform (the antiprotozoal drug clioquinol), kaolin (a porcelain clay used especially to treat foal diarrhea).
- **Nutritional Therapy:** Stop feeding concentrates. Give only hay and water.
- **Tissue Salts:** Give two tablets every half hour: calc phos (a general remedy), ferr phos (sudden diarrhea containing undigested food), kali sulph (watery, yellow droppings), nat sulph (for older horses with dark-colored diarrhea), nat phos (green foul-smelling droppings)

EAR PROBLEMS

Horses are prone to two different kinds of ear problems: ear infections and ear mites. In both cases, the horse may rub and shake his head. Because it is not always easy to discern the trouble with the naked eye, you may need your vet's assistance. Antipesticide or antibiotic drops will take care of the problem.

Ear ticks are common in horses and extremely hard to remove. Your veterinarian can provide you with a medication to kill them. Ear warts are also common but don't usually require removal. In fact, they are best left alone.

Treatment options for ear ailments include:

- **Acupressure:** On the acupoints around the ear.
- **Crystal Therapy:** Blue stones.
- **Essential Oils:** Bergamot, especially for fungal infections. (Don't use in gray or white horses.)
- **Homeopathy:** Graphites (for ear infections and ear warts), belladonna (if accompanied by pain), sulphur (for ear mites).

ENCEPHALOMYELITIS (SLEEPING SICKNESS, ENCEPHALITIS)

This serious neurological viral disease comes in three varieties: Eastern (EEE), Western (WEE), and Venezuelan (VEE). All are transmitted by swamp-loving mosquitoes (*Culiseta melanura*) and can be transmitted from horse to horse via mosquitoes hanging around the paddock. The horse isn't a natural host for the virus, though. Birds are the normal natural reservoir of the virus, but it is passed on to horses through the bite of a mosquito. An infected horse can't pass the disease on to people or other horses directly, but your horse doesn't ever have to leave the barn or see another horse to get it.

EEE and VEE are lethal in up to 90 percent of recognized equine cases. WEE is less lethal, with a mortality rate of about 40 percent. In the US, EEE occurs mainly in the eastern region of the country, from New England to Florida and along the Gulf Coast.

Encephalomyelitis is a terrible and potentially fatal disease that affects the brain. Signs include:

- abnormal gait and circling
- convulsions
- drooping ears
- drowsiness (hence the common name)
- head pressing
- high fever
- nervousness
- wandering

The best course of action is prevention.

- **Prevention:** You can administer a vaccine against all three forms of the disease that also includes a tetanus toxoid. Commonly given in one shot, this vaccine is called the VEW-T or 4-way vaccine. Initial vaccination is followed by a second dose in two to three weeks or four to six weeks, depending on the specific vaccine used. An annual or six-month revaccination is given thereafter. The vaccine is a combination of killed viruses. Protection of horses from mosquitoes is also important.

    Encephalitis vaccine is best given in the spring and fall, but in northern regions (with shorter mosquito seasons), a spring vaccination may suffice. There have not been sufficient studies to determine the length of immunity. Manufacturers recommend that the vaccine be given annually. However, some vets believe that an initial vaccination at five months and again at six months, followed by a booster every three years, is quite sufficient. Discuss your options with your vet. It is probably not necessary to vaccinate any horse over the age of 15 unless an outbreak has occurred.

- **Treatment:** There is no treatment of any kind.

EQUINE GASTRIC ULCER SYNDROME

Equine gastric ulcer syndrome (EGUS) may be caused by stress and can develop within five days. It is estimated that about 80 percent of horses suffer gastric ulcers at one time or another.

Signs include:
- change in eating habits
- diarrhea
- dull coat
- recurrent colic
- weight loss

Care and treatment options include:
- **Prevention:** An FDA-approved product called ULCERGARD may be helpful. The active ingredient in ULCERGARD is omeprazole, which suppresses acid production in a horse's stomach. (In general, 1 mg/kg of omeprazole per day for 28 days effectively prevents the onset of ulcers in horses exposed to stressful conditions.) The products come in a cinnamon-flavored oral paste that is readily accepted by horses. Gastrogard is a similar product.
- **Acupuncture/Acupressure:** To help to reduce stress.
- **Ayurvedic Therapy:** Ashwagandha.
- **Crystal Therapy:** Blue-violet.
- **Homeopathy:** Aconite, arsenicum, phosphorus (12C to 30C), kali bichromicum (30C three times a day for two weeks), nux vomica (6C to 30C three times a day for three weeks).
- **Medical:** Cimetidine (Tagamet), ranitidine (Zantac). Coat stomach with 4 teaspoons (20 ml) of milk of magnesia twice a day.
- **Physical/Environmental Management:** Soak hay, avoid feeding pellets. Feed the same time every day.
- **Western Herbal Therapy:** Aloe vera, comfrey leaf, fenugreek, marshmallow root (15 grams mixed with water twice a day), meadowsweet, powdered licorice root (15 grams per feeding).

EQUINE INFECTIOUS ANEMIA (SWAMP FEVER)

Equine infectious anemia (EIA), a disease that attacks the immune system, affects horses all over the world. The disease is caused by a virus related to the AIDS virus, although it doesn't infect humans.

EIA is usually transmitted by bloodsucking insects, particularly the large horsefly. It thrives in damp humid areas characteristic of the Gulf Coast—hence its nickname, "swamp fever." But it can show up anywhere its main disease-transmitting organism, the large horsefly, lives. Deerflies and mosquitoes also have been implicated. The virus doesn't live long in the horsefly—maybe as little as 15 to 30 minutes—so horses must be in close proximity for the disease to be passed along. The incubation period is 8 to 14 days.

EIA has three stages. In stage one, which lasts for several days, the horse is lethargic, sweaty, feverish, and uncoordinated. His eyes may be bloodshot. Approximately one third of infected horses will die of this acute form within a month. In the second stage, the horse is anemic and weak, suffering weight loss and recurrent fever. Mares can abort.

Horses who survive will enter a chronic stage in which they may appear normal. Some may be slightly anemic, others poor keepers. Few or none die from the disease at this stage. However, they are carriers, and they can develop

recurring bouts of EIA if subjected to stress. Infected mares can pass the disease to their foals.

Despite testing and measures to eradicate EIA, about 2,000 new cases are identified every year in the United States. An annual blood test, called the Coggins test, detects antibodies in the bloodstream. Annually, more than 1 million horses are screened for EIA this way. Blood samples must be sent to a state-approved laboratory. Horses who test positive must be confined or isolated from other horses. (While horses don't pass the disease directly to each other, if a horsefly bites an infected horse, it can transmit it to others.) A new EIA test called ELISA (enzyme-linked immunosorbent assay) is sometimes used to detect the disease. It offers faster results; however, ELISA may not be as accurate as the Coggins test. A positive ELISA reading is verified by a Coggins test anyway.

There is neither a known cure nor an effective vaccine as of yet. Some authorities recommend that horses who test positive be euthanized to keep the disease from spreading.

Care and treatment options include:

- **Prevention:** Testing for EIA should be done at least annually for all horses and more often for competitive horses. Disposable needles and syringe—one per horse—should be used when giving vaccines and medications. Instruments need to be sterilized after each use and before use on another animal. Current negative Coggins certificates should be required before introducing any new horses to the barn. New horses must be quarantined for 45 days. Barns should be kept clean and dry at all times.
- **Crystal Therapy:** Topaz.
- **Homeopathy:** Belladonna or aconite (for the fever).
- **Nutritional Therapy:** Feed mostly high-protein feed.

EQUINE PROTOZOAL MYELITIS (EQUINE PROTOZOAL MYELOENCEPHALITIS [EPM])

Equine protozoal myelitis (EPM) is a protozoal neurological disease that is somewhat similar to Wobbler disease, although it can be detected in more than one area of the spine. It is one of the most common neurological diseases in horses. Most horses will respond to aggressive early treatment and can achieve complete recovery.

The incubation period for EPM is variable—from two weeks to two years from the time of exposure to the development of clinical signs. The causative agent of this disease is the pathogen *Sarcocystis falcatula*, formerly *Sarcocystis neurona*. There is an antibody test and DNA test to detect it. Researchers are not sure of the entire life cycle of this pathogen, although it is thought that the definitive host for *Sarcocystis* is believed to be opossums. These animals don't get sick themselves, but they shed the parasite for months. Horses may eat the opossum sporocysts along with their hay, water, or pasture grass; however, they are not "normal" hosts for this disease. After ingestion, the pathogen travels to the brain and spinal cord, causing a wide variety of neurological problems, including lameness, muscle wasting, lack of coordination, and paralysis.

Horses cannot transmit the organism to other horses. Also, not all infected horses get sick. Many ingest the sporocysts, but their immune system destroys the organisms before they reach the central nervous system. This is a serious long-term illness. Even after horses have seemingly recovered, stress can make the symptoms return.

Because the protozoa might infect any part of the central nervous system, many different signs are possible. The disease usually starts out slowly, but many cases can have a rapid onset as well. Definitive diagnosis is difficult and requires analysis of spinal fluid.

Signs include:
- behavioral changes
- bucking (perhaps due to back soreness)
- dragging or spastic movement, perhaps on one side only
- fever
- holding the head to one side
- locking up of the stifle
- muscle atrophy in the jaw, resulting in eating difficulties and facial twisting
- snoring due to airway abnormalities or blood from a nostril
- toe dragging and stumbling

Care and treatment options are as follows:
- **Prevention:** Cover tightly anything that an opossum can get into in the barn or stable area, including cat and dog food. Do not leave feed out. Feed attracts opossums at night and birds during the day. Steam crimping and pelleting grain kills off the sporocysts, so using processed grains also may decrease the exposure to EPM as long as you keep the opossums out of the feed bin! Opossums are nocturnal, so you need to be especially vigilant when leaving the barn for the night.

    Most horses improve with treatment, but fewer than 25 percent recover completely. Relapses are possible in some horses. The vaccination for this disease has only recently become available. It is given as an intramuscular injection initially and then again two to three weeks later. Do not use chiropractic or massage in horses with this condition.
- **Acupuncture:** To stimulate the immune system.
- **Chinese Herbs:** Dong quai.
- **Crystal Therapy:** Barite, sapphire, tourmaline. Any blue or yellow stone.
- **Essential Oils:** Lemon aromatherapy.
- **Herbal Therapy:** Herbs to boost the immune system, improve the nervous system, and purify the blood. One commercial company uses a mix of burdock, cascara, dandelion, echinacea, garlic, gingko, golden seal,

gota kola, kelp, myrrh, Oregon grape, pau d'arco, rose hips, skullcap, and yarrow.

- **Homeopathy:** Belladonna or aconite (for the fever), causticum, rhus tox (3C to 30C three times a day for one week), gelsemium.
- **Medical:** Some horses are able to clear the disease without treatment; others require long-term sulfa drugs and antimalaria medication. The only FDA-approved treatments for EPM are ponazuril and nitazoxanide, both available as paste formulations. Another choice is pyrimethamine in combination with sulfadiazins. Horses should remain on both drugs for the duration of treatment because the protozoa can become resistant to pyrimethamine in the absence of sulfas. Pyrimethamine decreases the availability of folic acid in the body, so horses on this treatment may need folic acid supplements. Trimethoprim *is not recommended*. I add this because some drug combinations include it automatically in the compounding formula, but it can be harmful here. It is best to use the patented formula specifically designed for this disease. Anti-inflammatories are helpful for acute cases, including phenylbutazone or Banamine. DMSO (dimethyl sulfoxide) can be added either intravenously or by nasogastric tube.
- **Nutritional Therapy:** Folic acid may be added to the diet to prevent drug-induced anemia. Vitamin E supplements (8000 to 9000 IU) may be helpful for nerve healing. The use of both of these supplements is currently controversial, but they are probably harmless at worst. Don't use either of the adjunct therapies in pregnant mares, however. Colloidal silver can be given (1 teaspoon [5 ml] per day).

EQUINE RECURRENT UVEITIS (MOON BLINDNESS, PERIODIC OPHTHALMIA)

Equine recurrent uveitis is one of the most common eye diseases in horses. This painful, immune-mediated condition is the most common cause of equine blindness, which can occur in one or both eyes.

Interestingly, there are three different stories about how this disease received its folk name, "moon blindness." One version claims that the name comes from the fact that affected horses could not stand bright light and were sometimes said to be blinded by the moon. Another idea is that the cloudy, pale blue color of the affected eye resembled a full moon. A third story claims that because the disease seemed to come and go, it must be dependent on moon phases. It was once believed that white horses were especially vulnerable to moon blindness, but there is no truth to that theory. However, it does seem that Appaloosas have a greater predilection to this disease than other breeds.

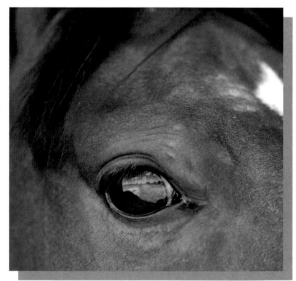

Uveitis is actually an inflammation of the uvea, which is the inner lining of the eye. Well-supplied by blood vessels, it is prone to infection and inflammation. Uveitis is serious, and inappropriate or tardy treatment can lead to blindness. Unfortunately, uveitis is often diagnosed as something far less serious, and so critical time is lost. As with most things, fast diagnosis and treatment produce the best chance for recovery.

This is a condition for which there are many possible causes: bacterial (leptospirosis), viral (herpes virus and influenza virus), parasitical (onchocerca, transmission by a biting midge, and *Toxoplasma gondii*), allergies, or trauma.

The bacterial infection called leptospirosis is by the far the most suspect cause. Horses can acquire the disease through drinking water infected with the urine of deer, fox, skunks, or cattle. *Leptospiria* can survive in water for up to 20 days and in manure up to 61 days. However, the exact relationship between leptospirosis and equine recurrent uveitis is unclear.

Even though it is often responsible for uveitis, the eye condition may not show up for months or even years after a bout with lepto. Other bacterial infections implicated include *Streptococcus equi*, *Escherichia coli*, *Rhodococcus equi*, and *Brucella*.

The major viral infections linked to equine uveitis are respiratory equine herpes virus and influenza virus.

The most common parasite connected with uveitis is the parasitic worm onchocerca. Culicoides, a biting midge of the *Ceiatopogonidae* family, is believed to be the primary transmitter. The adult onchocerca lives in the connective tissue of the horse's neck and the microfilariae (larval offspring of the onchocerca) travel throughout the body. The most common signs of it are sores breaking out on the midline of the horse's stomach and base of the mane and withers, as well as uveitis in the horse's eye. In this case, the condition occurs when there are large quantities of dead microfilariae in the eye. Normally, the eye can handle the live ones, but the dead ones give off large amounts of antigens that cause inflammation. This is one case where deworming can be dangerous. When the horse is dewormed, the microfilariac die and the disease starts. However, horses who are routinely dewormed are in very little danger of this happening, as not enough of the parasites have built up to cause trouble.

Regardless of the specific course or cause of the disease, the inflammation eventually leads to secondary changes in the eye. Signs in the eye include:

- constriction of the pupil in the dark and avoidance of light
- redness, puffiness, or cloudiness
- swelling, squinting, or discharge
- white spots or bleeding in the eye

Other signs may include:

- head shaking
- loss of appetite
- loss of balance
- runny nose

A more specific diagnosis is obtainable via blood count; serum biochemical profile; urinalysis; leptospirosis, toxoplasmosis, and brucellosis titers; and a fecal exam for parasites. Because an acute attack of uveitis may be just the first sign of systemic disease, your vet will perform a complete physical examination, not just an exam of the eye.

The word "recurrent" in the disease name is important. After the original episode has been successfully treated, the eye may look normal. However, the signs usually will reappear at some time in the future. Wind, pollen, stress, and many other factors can set it off again. Every time the problem resurfaces, more eyesight is lost. Progression of the disease can be halted only by aggressive and long-term treatment. Options include:

- **Prevention:** There is a vaccine against leptospirosis, but it's not officially approved for horses and is therefore not routinely given.
- **Acupuncture:** Some alternative vets have found acupuncture helpful in treating moon blindness.
- **Chiropractic:** Chiropractic may be helpful for some cases.
- **Crystal Therapy:** Pearl and topaz for the immune system, tourmaline for both the eyes and immune system.
- **Essential Oils:** Frankincense (to boost the immune system).
- **Homeopathy:** Euphrasia or a homeopathic preparation of MSM
- **Medical/Surgical:** For the short term, the eye is dilated by atropine, and then a topical steroid in drop or ointment form and/or an antibiotic is prescribed. It is very important that a steroid not be given without

a vet's okay; a steroid given to an ulcerated eye can cause blindness, and you cannot always tell without a special instrument. Also, extended use of 1 percent or 4 percent atropine can lead to colic because of its effect on gut motility, so it is important to limit use. Flunixin meglumine (a painkiller and NSAID), given intravenously, is sometimes used in acute cases. This is the most effective treatment of acute uveitis. Both steroidal and nonsteroidal topical medications are commonly used. Large doses of antibiotics can sometimes stop the progression of the disease. An antihistamine may be prescribed to stop the itching. Two new surgical techniques are also promising: core vitrectomy, which removes the vitreous (thick, transparent substance that fills the center of the eye) through an incision. The vitreous is then replaced with either saline or a balanced salt solution. The theorized benefit of this procedure is that T lymphocytes or organisms in the vitreous contribute to the chronic inflammation of equine uveitis. Another procedure is the implantation of a cyclosporine disk. Although this procedure is still regarded as experimental, early results have been encouraging. In cases where nothing can be done, the eye can be removed, which will stop the pain. Horses adjust quite well to having only one eye.

- **Nutritional Therapy:** Vitamin E, bee pollen, MSM (methylsulfonylmethane) supplements to help the immune system. At one time it was believed that a riboflavin deficiency might have something to do with moonblindness, but that idea has now been discredited.
- **Physical Management:** In the short term, a fly mask can be used to cut down on light. Make sure that the long hairs around the eye are not curling into it, causing further irritation. Hot and cold compresses.

EQUINE VIRAL ARTERITIS

Equine viral arteritis (EVA) is an acute, contagious, viral disease that arrived in the United States from Poland. The disease is self-limiting; the vast majority of horses recover fully.

Signs include:

- abortion (also can result in death of young foals)
- colic
- conjunctivitis (brick-red eyes)
- depression
- edema of the limbs (especially hind limbs) and scrotum
- fever lasting two to nine days
- nasal discharge

This disease is transmitted through both respiratory and venereal routes, and stallions can be carriers. The virus is shed constantly in the semen. After aerosol exposure, the virus multiplies in bronchial and lung tissue, and within 48 hours, inhabits the lymph nodes. It also can attack the blood vessels. Constipation and colic are also common, as are subclinical infections. Standardbreds and warmbloods seem most affected.

- **Medical:** Eye ointment to ease the pain of conjunctivitis.
- **Physical Management:** This is a disease that can be controlled by sound stable management. Rest is necessary for one month after signs disappear. The stable area should be carefully disinfected after incidence of infection.

EYE PROBLEMS, COMMON

One of the most common eye problems in horses, fly irritation, is comparatively easy to address. Simply attach a fly fringe to the halter, and your poor horse should get some relief. The root cause should always be investigated, however. Don't settle for treating the symptoms only. (*See also* Equine Recurrent Uveitis.)

Treatment options for eye problems include:

- **Acupuncture:** Some owners have had success in using acupuncture for certain eye problems in horses.
- **Ayurvedic Therapy:** Amla, triphala, licorice.
- **Essential Oils:** Lemon aromatherapy.
- **First Aid:** If an infection is present, bathe the eye with 1 teaspoon (5 ml) of bicarbonate of soda mixed with warm water.
- **Flower Essences:** Bach crab apple.
- **Homeopathy:** Euphrasia can be used for conjunctivitis or injuries (two or three times a day), pulsatilla (for conjunctivitis), rhus tox (for conjunctivitis), silicea (for conjunctivitis or eye infection).
- **Medical:** Aspirin relieves the signs of eye inflammation. Atropine causes the eye muscle to relax and dilate, which relieves pain and spasm.
- **Western Herbal Therapy:** Bathe the eye in a solution of eyebright (euphrasia) and water for watery red eyes due to allergy, as well as for infections. It can be used as an eye wash, using one part herb to four parts water. Boil the herb in the water for half an hour, strain, and add one part vegetable glycerin. Refrigerate. To use, mix a spoonful or so of the stock with a cup of distilled or sterilized water. Wash the eye carefully. You can use this herbal therapy treatment every hour if you'd like. (Taken internally, eyebright is good for respiratory problems or allergies.) A diluted celandine wash also may prove helpful.

FEVERS

For complete treatment, it's important to get at the underlying cause of a fever; however, reducing the fever itself may be in your horse's best interest. The following treatments are helpful:

- **Homeopathy:** Aconite, belladonna.
- **Topical Treatment:** Some vets recommend an alcohol bath to reduce fever. Because it evaporates very quickly and has a cooling effect, this is probably not a bad idea. However, high concentrations of alcohol can be irritating to the skin, so proceed with caution.

FISTULOUS WITHERS

A fistula is a long, narrow ulceration that may be infected. It can have a systemic cause such as the *Brucella* pathogen or a physical cause such as a poorly fitting saddle. It may develop slowly or quickly and occur on one or both sides. The earlier the problem is addressed, the better. It is a good precaution to keep horses separate from *Brucella*-infected cattle and cattle separate from horses with discharging fistulous withers.

Treatment options include:

- **Homeopathy:** Silicea or sulpharis calcareum.
- **Medical:** Antibiotics or surgery may be necessary if the fistula is extensive. The most successful treatment is complete removal of the infected bursa.
- **Physical Management:** Bathe the swelling several times a day for ten minutes with very warm water. Apply a suitable drawing agent.

FRACTURES

A fracture is a broken bone. It can be an injury as tiny as a bone chip or as large as a completely shattered limb. Fractures occur more frequently in the front legs than in the rear ones because the front legs bear more weight and are locked into a more rigid position.

In earlier times, a fracture often meant euthanasia. It still can, but modern veterinary medicine often can save the life of the horse and in some cases can return him to useful work. Younger, smaller, and calmer horses have the best chance of recovery. Lower limb fractures have a better chance of healing than those above the knee and hock; bones that bear weight have a worse prognosis.

Signs of a fracture include:

- lameness
- pain
- sweating
- swelling
- trembling

Obviously, fractures require veterinary treatment as soon as possible. Other adjunct treatments include:

- **Acupuncture:** To stimulate healing after standard veterinary care.
- **Crystal Therapy:** Indigo stones.
- **First Aid**: While waiting for your vet to arrive, keep the horse as quiet as possible. Use a tranquilizer if your vet so recommends; however, do not use one for horses in shock. Apply a splint to prevent further damage to the leg. (A broom handle works well to stiffen the splint.)
- **Flower Essences**: Administer Rescue Remedy until help arrives.
- **Homeopathy:** Not to be used in place of standard veterinary care: phosphorus (30C every 15 minutes), plus arnica (30C three or four times a day for several days).
- **Magnetic Therapy:** To stimulate healing after regular veterinary care. Do not use if the horse has a metal pin or other appliance.
- **Medical:** Your vet has a wealth of new treatment options available, including new materials and methods for applying casts, immersion tanks, and so on.
- **Stem Cell Therapy:** To help heal the fracture; it is hoped that it will help the horse generate new bone to stabilize the fracture.

GRASS SICKNESS (EQUINE DYSAUTONOMIA)

This odd and horrible disease first appeared in Scotland back in 1907. Equine dysautonomia, or grass sickness, later spread to England and eventually to other northern European countries. It is now reported in North America in the same geographic area (Midwest) that has a high prevalence of canine dysautonomia, a similar condition that also results in loss of autonomic nervous system function.

Grass sickness is a very unpleasant disease in which there is damage to the parts of the nervous system that control the function of the horse's digestive tract, producing the main symptom of gut paralysis. This seems to occur most often after horses have been grazing in cold, damp spring pastures.

This disease affects horses, ponies, and donkeys. (It even killed a zebra in a zoo.) It kills about 200 animals a year in Scotland, which is still at the center of the disease. The illness occurs in horses of all ages from 4 months to over 20

years, but most affected animals are between ages 2 and 7. Cases occur during every month of the year, but most are seen between April and July.

No one knows the exact cause, although it's strongly associated with grazing. However, a few cases have been seen in animals with no access to pasture; hay is presumed to be the culprit in those cases. The assumption is that there is a fungal toxin at work, but it has not yet been identified. The *Fusarium* fungus is a suspect, though, as is *Clostridium botulinum*. More research needs to be done. The type of pasture doesn't seem to matter. Stress seems to be a factor in the appearance of the disease.

Signs include:
- depression
- in chronic cases, profound loss of appetite and weight loss occurs
- in the more acute condition, the stomach fills with a greenish liquid, intestinal movement ceases, and the contents of the intestine get hard and dry; acute cases are always fatal
- rapid heartbeat and patchy sweat
- the horse is unable to swallow, and muscle twitching sets in
- tucked-up stance

Options for treatment are currently few:
- **Prevention:** Stabling at-risk stock for part of the day.
- **Acupuncture:** Can increase intestinal motility and may be helpful in mild cases.
- **Crystal Therapy:** Green stones.
- **Homeopathy:** Lathyrus, plumbum metallicum.
- **Medical:** In less acute cases, cisipride can help to get the intestines moving again, but the more acute cases are almost always fatal. Horses must be euthanized to prevent their suffering. Administration of fluids may give temporary relief.

GREASY HEEL (SCRATCHES, MUD FEVER)

Greasy heel is a dermatological infection that occurs around the fetlock, pastern, or heel, usually on nonpigmented skin. It is most commonly seen in horses kept in small, muddy pens, especially in clay-based soils. It occurs most frequently in the rear legs.

The condition arises from continual wetting of the skin, so it usually occurs in the autumn or winter. When the natural protective oils of the skin are removed, the bacterium *Dermatophilus congolensis* takes over, producing all sorts of different skin problems, including rain rot in addition to greasy heel or cracked heel. Make no mistake, this is a painful condition.

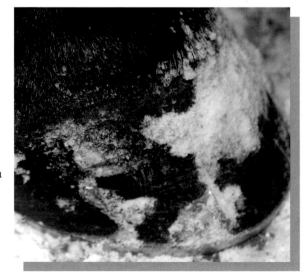

Signs include:
- lameness on the affected leg
- raw areas and bleeding
- swelling and hair loss

Care and treatment options include:
- **Acupuncture:** To reduce stress and pain.
- **Essential Oils:** Roman chamomile, or a solution of tea tree oil (ten drops to 1 pint [0.5 l] of water) applied topically. You also can make a gel by adding a bit of tea tree oil and lavender to aloe vera gel or petroleum jelly and apply topically. Combination One: 10 drops lavender, 20 drops tea tree oil, 5 drops Roman

chamomile, 5 drops yarrow or German chamomile, and 4 drops of garlic in aloe vera gel. Combination Two: ten drops frankincense, ten drops myrrh, ten drops patchouli, and ten drops yarrow in aloe vera gel.

- **Herbal Therapy:** Cleavers, comfrey, marshmallow, or slippery elm poultice. As a separate treatment or after using the poultice, apply aloe vera gel, let it soak in completely, and then let the area dry.
- **Homeopathy:** Arnica, arsenicum album, graphites, kali, bichromicum, sulfur, thuja.
- **Physical Management:** Brush away dirt and dead hair. Cleanse and soften the area with zinc ointment cream, and apply an emollient dressing, like baby oil, overnight. If the skin is already soft, apply gentian violet to dry it out. Then wash the area again with a made-for-people acne cleanser containing 10 percent benzoyl peroxide. Leave on for ten minutes, then rinse and towel dry. Then clip the hair away from the affected site and dress the area with povidone iodine ointment. For best results, leave the area open. Alternatively, use sulfur tablets ground into a paste and apply to the cleaned, dried area. Then wash with a shampoo, leave on for about ten minutes, and clean and dry again.

Keep the horse in a clean and dry area for about three days, and repeat the cleansing regimen each day. The cleaner and dryer the area, the better. Even straw and hay can aggravate the condition, which will take up to two weeks to heal. A little exercise will help to reduce the swelling.

HEMATOMAS (BLOOD BLISTERS)

A hematoma is a blood blister that is usually the result of a damaged blood vessel. It is cool to the touch and painless, unlike an abscess. If the blood can be drained away from the site, the blood vessel will heal itself. If it is not drained, the hematoma may become infected. (*See also* Wounds.)

Treatment options include:

- **Chinese Herbal Therapy:** Yunnan Paiyao (very sparingly, and give no more than once a month).
- **Essential Oils:** Geranium.
- **Flower Essences:** Bach Rescue Remedy, either orally or topically.
- **Homeopathy:** Arnica gel (two or three times a day), arnica 30C (three or four times a day for five days), plus phosphorus 30C (every 15 minutes for an hour or so).
- **Western Herbal Therapy:** Comfrey (cold compress of slightly crushed fresh leaves).

HOOF PROBLEMS

No hoof, no horse, as they say. Because it takes much of the brunt of day-to-day living, the hoof is subject to a plethora of conditions, including thrush, puncture wounds, and other ailments.

The misuse of horse shoes is one factor contributing to the decline of a horse's hoof. Shoes decrease the hoof's ability to absorb shock; they vibrate at a rate that may cause tissue damage, decrease blood circulation, and reduce traction and contraction—not to mention the damage caused by nails. Early shoeing is particularly damaging to the development of the hoof. While riders cannot always avoid shoeing their horses, many animals can get along quite well if their hooves are properly trimmed (not a simple "pasture trim") and well cared for. Even horses ridden on trough terrain may go unshod if

they wear special boots for this purpose.

Also, it is not necessary to wash your horse's feet in soap and water. In fact, this practice can lead to excessive drying. On the

other hand, normal hooves don't need to be dressed or oiled either.

Care and treatments for hoof problems include:

- **Crystal Therapy:** White stones.
- **Hoof Dressings:** Many effective products are used alone or in combination as hoof dressings. Herbal therapy dressings include allantoin (an extract of comfrey, noted for its healing and soothing properties), almond oil, aloe vera, coconut oil, and castor oil.
- **Nutritional Therapy:** Many cases of weak or poor-quality hooves result from a deficiency in biotin (B7, a B-complex vitamin) or DL methionine (an amino acid), substances that are needed to form the sulfur bonds that make hooves strong and healthy. Without sufficient biotin and DL methionine, the hoof can crack and become more vulnerable to infection. Supplement these substances in your horse's feeds. Remember that hooves grow slowly, and you shouldn't expect to see any results for at least six months at the earliest. Flaxseed oil also may be helpful.

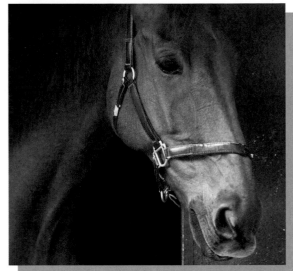

- **Physical Management:** Regular exercise will actually make hooves grow faster. As the horse trots around, the cycle of pressure and release stimulates circulation to the hoof, which brings increased nourishment. Corrective shoeing, usually involving cutting a groove at right angles to the crack, can help a cracked hoof.
- **Western Herbal Therapy:** Horsetail.

HYPERKALEMIC PERIODIC PARALYSIS

Hyperkalemic periodic paralysis (HYPP) is an inherited muscular disorder primarily affecting quarter horses, paints, and Appaloosas who can trace their lineage back to the sire Impressive. More than 2 percent of all quarter horses (about 55,000 animals) carry this dangerous gene. There is a genetic marker to detect its presence, and the American Quarter Horse Association is addressing this issue with admirable straightforwardness.

However, it is almost certain to creep into other breeds in time. The trouble occurs when, for some unknown reason, potassium leaks out of the muscle cells and sodium moves into the cells. This in turn creates an electrical charge that overstimulates the muscles and creates an elevated blood-potassium level, which results in uncontrolled muscle twitching or profound muscle weakness. Other signs include:

- difficulty breathing
- muscle cramping
- paralysis
- tremors

Death can occur from heart or respiratory failure, although many horses with the condition lead healthy lives. Care and treatment options include:

- **Prevention:** Check the breeding of your horse, and buy only horses who do not carry the genetic marker for HYPP. If your horse already has the marker, take the prophylactic step. Reduce the amount of potassium-high alfalfa, and replace it with oat or Bermuda grass hay. Also, add beet pulp for fiber. (Beet pulp is low in potassium.) There are also commercial diets that are made for horses who need to restrict their potassium intake.
- **Crystal Therapy:** Barite.
- **Medical:** Diuretics such as acetazolimide will increase potassium secretion by the kidneys, which may help.

INFLUENZA (FLU, EQUINE INFLUENZA)

Equine influenza is a common viral disease affecting horses in North America, Europe, and Asia. Two types have been recognized. Type 1 was first isolated in Prague in 1956, and the Type 2 strain was isolated in Miami in 1963. It is especially prevalent in animals who meet in showing or racing competitions.

This acute, highly contagious upper respiratory disease is caused by myxoviruses, which are transmitted by contact and contaminated droplets. The incubation period is one to five days. Horses remain infective for six to ten days after the onset of the clinical signs. The clinical signs of the disease can vary from mild (or even unapparent) to severe. However, it's rarely fatal in horses (although donkeys, and believe it or not, zebras, can die from it). A "carrier state" is not recognized for equine influenza, which is one good thing.

It takes the respiratory tract tissue about three weeks to regenerate, and during this period, the horse is at increased risk of secondary bacterial complications such as pneumonia, pleuropneumonia, and chronic bronchitis. Clinical signs, which begin abruptly, include:

- depression
- dry, harsh, nonproductive cough (may persist for three weeks)
- nasal discharge, which is clear at first and then becomes mucopurulent (containing mucus and pus) and foul smelling
- shivering
- sudden fever in the first few days

Although they are quite ill, most horses recover completely in a week or two, while others may take two or three months. A few animals can develop pneumonia, pleurisy, or damage to the heart muscle. The disease also can lower resistance to infection. Foals are especially vulnerable.

The signs of this disease are just about identical to those of equine herpes virus (EHV) infection. There is a rhino/flu combination vaccine containing influenza strains and rhinopneumonitis EHV-4, which may be advisable for show horses, race horses, or horses kept in close quarters with unknown horses.

Care and treatment options are as follows:

- **Prevention:** The early equine flu vaccines (beginning in the 1960s) were not particularly effective, and they gave a bad name to all vaccines. But times have changed, and as with human flu vaccines, manufacturers constantly update their vaccines to keep up with the latest strains of flu virus.

  The vaccine usually includes the two most common strains of the flu virus. Some animals are revaccinated every three or four months and others only once a year. However, it is mandatory for all race horses and for many other event horses participating in events in which there is a governing body. Many other kinds of competitions also require proof of flu vaccination. During a flu outbreak, it may be wise to take an unvaccinated horse out of hard training to let the immune system rev up to fight an incipient infection. Remember that even if your horse stays home, you can bring it home if you are in contact with other horses. Isolate new horses for at least two weeks.
- **Acupuncture:** Can stimulate the immune system and improve respiratory symptoms.
- **Crystal Therapy:** Topaz (to boost the immune system).

- **Essential Oils:** Frankincense (to boost the immune system).
- **Homeopathy:** Belladonna or aconite (for the fever), baptisia tinctoria (especially if the horse is weak or lethargic), eupatorium perfoliatum, gelsemium sempirvirens, curare, lobelia, or lathyrus (for post-influenza weakness).
- **Medical:** Bronchodilators, antibiotics (to clear secondary infections or when fever persists beyond three or four days), NSAIDs (nonsteroidal anti-inflammatory drugs recommended for horses with a fever over 104°F [40°C]).
- **Physical Management:** Rest and supportive care for four weeks is necessary. The more rest the horse gets, the faster he will recover. Keep the horse hydrated and comfortably warm. Keep the stable area as well ventilated and dust free as possible to prevent secondary infection.

INSECT BITES AND STINGS

Even when there is no allergic reaction (*see* Allergies), insect bites can be painful. Signs include sudden painful swelling or hives.

Care and treatment options are as follows:
- **Prevention:** Use fly repellents, veils, sprays, and strips. Remove manure promptly.
- **Ayurvedic Therapy:** Apply sandalwood paste to the site of the bite or sting.
- **Essential Oils:** Blue (German) chamomile (one to two drops undiluted), yarrow (one to two drops undiluted), tea tree oil (one to two drops undiluted), lemongrass and juniper (as a repellent).
- **Flower Essence:** Bach Rescue Remedy for a frightened animal.
- **Homeopathy:** Apis (30C every 15 minutes for 2 hours for serious bites), arnica (30C every hour along with apis 30C), arsenum (6C), sulphur.
- **Medical:** Antihistamines are frequently used to counteract the itching and swelling of insect stings.
- **Physical Treatment**: Cold hosing of the area is soothing. It is also helpful to apply a cold clay poultice.

LAMINITIS (FOUNDER)

Laminitis is an extremely painful condition that results from inflammation of the laminae, the soft tissues between the hoof wall and pedal bone. This is the disease that nearly killed the Kentucky Derby winner Barbaro after he broke his leg. If left untreated, permanent damage to the internal structure of the hoof will occur. In a few cases, the damage left by laminitis is minimal. In other cases, it can be devastating. And while the apparent pain the animal is suffering may be a rough indication as to the severity of the episode, it's not a sure thing.

In horses with laminitis, not enough oxygen is reaching the tissues because of a restricted blood supply. If too many of the laminae are destroyed, the coffin or pedal bone is no longer secured and can twist or rotate downward toward the sole. As it does so, it tears through more tissue. Unfortunately, by the time you notice anything is wrong, most of the damage already may have occurred.

Signs include:
- characteristic stance in which the horse "leans back" trying to take the weight off the front feet, which are most commonly affected (however, laminitis can affect all four feet)
- refusal to eat

- reluctance to move or turn
- stiffness traveling on hard surfaces
- tendency to lie down

A number of factors can be responsible, including a diet too rich in sugar or carbohydrates, such as one consisting of too much grain. The rich, overfertilized grass commonly fed today takes its victims. Too many carbohydrates disrupt the normal bacterial activity in the gut. The stomach responds by releasing endotoxins that cause blood vessel constriction. (Endotoxins are potentially toxic natural compounds found inside pathogens such as bacteria.) Other causes can involve gastrointestinal disease, severe concussion of the hoof due to overwork on hard ground, respiratory problems, reproductive ailments, kidney problems, endocrine system conditions, skin problems, and musculoskeletal and immune system disorders. Toxins such as those in black walnut shavings or those produced by salmonella are also possible causes. Laminitis may follow a serious illness such as diarrhea, colic, or strangles.

A University of Queensland study suggests that glucose starvation of the laminar tissue contributes to the development of laminitis because glucose is a critical energy source for most body cells. The inability to absorb adequate amounts of glucose can lead to changes in the laminae.

Laminitis is on the increase, which appears to be a result of overweight, overheated, underexercised horses. The tiny feet of fat ponies and chubby quarter horses seem most at risk, while thinner horses who are well exercised have reduced incidences. Laminitis can be permanently disabling to its victims. Call a vet immediately if you suspect that your horse is suffering from this condition.

Care and treatment options are as follows:

- **Prevention:** Some say that adding fresh garlic to the feed (one or two cloves) will help to prevent laminitis.
- **Acupressure/Acupuncture:** Some practitioners use the small intestine and large intestine (colon and cecum) acupuncture energy meridians at their "end points," the coronary band around the hoof.
- **Chinese Herbal Therapy:** Custom formulations may be needed. Consult a practitioner.
- **Crystal Therapy:** Petrified wood, wulfenite.
- **Essential Oils:** Lemon (diluted for massage to the coronary band), juniper.
- **Flower Essences:** Bach Rescue Remedy (ten drops in drinking water while condition persists).
- **Herbal Therapy:** Dandelion, garlic, and nettle to cleanse the blood; milk thistle to help the liver clear toxins from the body; devil's claw and cleavers. Combination: infusion of garlic, nettle, dandelion, and fenugreek. After the initial episode, add 1 cup (240 ml) of this powdered combination: burdock, hawthorn, and celery seed. Chamomile tea poured over the feed (1 cup [240 ml]).
- **Homeopathy:** In the early stages, give aconite (30C repeated every 30 minutes for six doses). If the horse has a rapid pulse, combine with belladonna (1M or 200C once a day for three days). Nux vomica (30C to 1M every half hour) will help the circulation. Calcarea fluorica (30C) will help the hoof structure heal if the damage is not too severe before being treated. Bryonia (30C once a day for three or four days) is helpful after the initial episode has passed.
- **Magnetic Therapy:** Apply to the cannon bone.
- **Medical:** Acepromazine (Ace) is sometimes prescribed because it increases circulation to the feet. Aspirin helps to prevent the formation of blood clots in the hoof. You can get aspirin in the form of tablets, powder, or boluses. Anti-inflammatory agents such as DMSO (dimethyl sulfoxide). Isoxsuprine hydrochloride (dilates peripheral blood vessels)

- **Nutritional Therapy:** MSM (methylsulfonylmethane) is a source of organic sulfur, an important component of disulfide bonds in the laminae. Sulfur may be an important nutrient for affected horses and can be fed free choice or by controlled supplementation. Flax and hemp oil provide palatable omega-3 fatty acids, although cold water fish oils are even better.
- **Physical Management:** The horse needs extensive rest, preferably in a deep sandy bed, with as much of the weight off the foot as possible. Do not remove the shoes unless instructed to do so. Cold hosing (20 minutes on and off) or ice may relieve some of the pain. The most common treatment is corrective trimming and shoeing of the hoof, but unless the underlying cause of the disease is treated (such as Cushing's disease), it can recur. Reduce food intake. Old folklore says that foundered horses should be walked—don't do this.
- **Tissue Salts:** Silica (two tablets) for two months.

LEPTOSPIROSIS

Seven types of leptospirosis can attack horses, and all of them love warm, damp areas. Because leptospirosis is a bacterial disease, horses can acquire it from infected water or grain, or grain or hay contaminated by the urine of infected animals such as cattle, pigs, deer, rats, raccoons, skunks, and foxes. It is even possible for one horse to catch it from another. Humans also can pass the disease from one animal to another via hand contact. Lepto is extremely common and can survive in water for 20 days and in manure for 2 months. It can cause abortion, stillbirth, or illnesses in foals, including renal or eye problems (very common). It also can affect humans.

Signs include:
- abnormal milk production
- conjunctivitis
- fever

Care and treatment options include:
- **Prevention:** Vaccines approved for cattle and swine have been developed, although there is no vaccine specifically formulated for horses. These five-way vaccines cover all of the lepto varieties except L. autumnalis and L. bratislava, both of which are found in horses. While some horses react poorly to the vaccine, there are places in the United States where lepto is so prevalent that horses are routinely vaccinated against it. Keep horses from drinking stagnant water. Manage manure carefully, and practice good barn hygiene.
- **Homeopathy:** Belladonna or aconite (for the fever).
- **Medical:** Antibiotics such are streptomycin, chlortetracycline, oxytetracycline, and penicillin are given.

MANGE

Mange is a disease caused by the infestation of microscopic parasites, generally mites that breed just beneath the skin. It is due to an allergic reaction and is characterized by an unsightly skin rash and inflammation. Mange in horses is caused by any one of three mites: sarcoptic mange mites (scabies), which usually occur around the neck; psoroptic mange mites, which live around the ears, mane, or tail; or chorioptic mange mites, which live around the fetlocks and usually show up in cold weather. These mites are almost impossible to see with the naked eye. A contagious disease transmitted through close contact, mange can be a stubborn condition. However, mange

mites do not cause visible signs in every animal.

Sarcoptic mange is the most serious in horses, but fortunately, it is rare in the United States. However, chorioptic (leg) mange is common in heavy breeds of horses in the US.

Care and treatment options include:

- **Prevention:** Proper bathing and good nutrition will help to prevent mange mites from infesting your horse.
- **Essential Oils:** Bergamot, lavender, chamomile, and tea tree oil (2.5 percent, mix together to help healing).
- **Flower Essences:** Crab apple (ten drops in food or water for emotional support), aspen (ten drops in food or water for emotional support), gorse (ten drops in food or water for emotional support).
- **Herbal Therapy:** Powdered burdock (1 tablespoon [15 ml] to promote hair growth after mites are killed), echinacea and nettle (two parts each) combined with burdock root and bladderwrack (one part each).
- **Homeopathy:** Sulphur (start with 6C twice a day; if ineffective, try 200C once a week).
- **Physical Management:** Thick scabs and crusts should be removed or at least loosened. You also can try a rubdown. For this to be successful, you have to rub down nearly the whole horse. Mange mites have areas of retreat under the tail and similar hard-to-get-at places, including the feathering around the fetlocks. You can make an oil of garlic rub. Crush six cloves of garlic into a jar with cold-pressed vegetable oil and leave overnight. Rub over the infected area. Repeat every ten days to kill the eggs. Or use a cedar extract and neem (an Asian and African tree) rub. Repeat every ten days to kill the eggs.

Affected animals should be isolated and all tack, equipment, and grooming implements disinfected.

MELANOMA

This is a word that strikes fear in the heart because it is a deadly disease in humans. Luckily, it is usually treatable in horses. Gray horses are especially vulnerable, as are older horses.

Melanoma is a cancer that develops in the melanin cells of the skin. The tumors appear as hard, smooth, round black growths on the skin. They usually appear around the base of the ears, eyes, neck, jugular groove, and under the tail. They don't seem to be painful and are only slightly invasive, growing slowly throughout the life of the horse. In rare cases, they can occur internally. In many cases, owners elect to skip treatment.

Care options include:

- **Acupuncture:** To stimulate the immune system.
- **Cryotherapy:** (Freezing to a very low temperature with liquid nitrogen). Usually the tumor is "debulked" first (surgical removal of a large bit of it) and then frozen to -20°F (-28.9°C) two or three times. Often this procedure is repeated in the future to keep the tumors at a manageable size.
- **Crystal Therapy:** White or blue-violet stones.
- **Essential Oils:** Lemon to stimulate the immune system.
- **Homeopathy:** Thuja (30C three times a day during medical treatment), nux vomica (6C three times a day).
- **Medical:** The ulcer drug Tagamet (cimetidine), a histamine-blocking agent, may dramatically reduce the size of some melanomas, although it does not cure the cancer. It must be given for up to three months or even more. There is also a sort of anticancer vaccine made from the horse's own tumor cells. This vaccine has been successful in reducing the size of tumors on the face, body, and legs. However, tumors under the tail and along the jugular groove are more recalcitrant.
- **Nutritional Therapy:** Vitamin C supplements (up to 8 grams daily).
- **Surgical:** Some vets feel that surgical removal somehow activates the tumor to produce others. However, if the tumor interferes with function, it needs to be removed, often with laser surgery, which cuts and seals the blood vessels in one neat action.
- **Western Herbal Therapy:** Echinacea (20 grams).

MUSCLE SORENESS

Muscle pain is a double whammy. Not only can it cause local pain, but the effort the horse puts forth to avoid the pain can result in lameness to one or more of his limbs. This is sometimes called "compensatory lameness."

Sore muscles can occur because of an unbalanced load due to slipping, falling, jumping, overly strenuous work, or poor shoeing. It also can be progressive. Signs of an injured muscle include:

- heat
- pain
- reluctance to move the muscle
- swelling

Treatment options include:

- **Acupuncture:** Can be effective in reducing pain in many cases.
- **Chiropractic:** Can very effective in reducing pain in some cases.
- **Essential Oils:** Basil, chamomile (German and Roman), eucalyptus, fennel, geranium, juniper (to decrease toxins; use a few drops as a rinse), lavender (to relieve pain), lemongrass, mandarin, marjoram, rosemary. Combination: 15 drops white birch, 15 drops peppermint, and 15 drops wintergreen in aloe vera gel applied to the area.
- **Flower Essences:** Impatiens, rock water (for tight muscles), water violet (for stiffness).
- **Herbal Therapy:** Chamomile (German and Roman), devil's claw.
- **Homeopathy:** Arnica (6C to 30C).
- **Laser Therapy:** Use of this therapy is said to trigger a biological response that results in stimulation of the immune, lymphatic, vascular, and neural systems.
- **Massage:** Use especially for new injuries.
- **Medical:** Ketoprofen (a NSAID [nonsteroidal anti-inflammatory drug] similar to ibuprofen that can be given intravenously), DSMO (dimethyl sulfoxide), hyaluronate sodium (Legend, used for chronic cases).

- **Physical Management:** Rest the injured muscle.
- **Tissue Salts:** Magnesium phosphate (6C to 30C three times a day for spasms).
- **Ultrasound:** To relieve muscle tension and stimulate repair of soft-tissue injuries.

NAVICULAR DISEASE

The boat-shaped navicular bone in the foot works as a kind of pulley for the deep flexor tendon. Navicular disease is the degeneration of this bone, resulting in lameness. In fact, navicular is not really one disease but a common name given to an assortment of different problems with this bone, most often a degenerative joint disease. The cause is unknown, but it is thought to be related to overwork, especially quick turning and stopping. Warmbloods are particularly affected.

Almost always presenting as front leg lameness, navicular disease is notoriously hard to diagnose. Often, a nerve block and X-rays are needed to correctly diagnose and treat the condition. It may be hereditary.

Signs include:
- difficulty moving, especially when trotting
- lameness, especially in both front feet
- short stepping in the later stages
- slight shifting of the front leg lameness in the early stages

Care and treatment options include:
- **Acupuncture:** Very successful in some cases.
- **Crystal Therapy:** Indigo.
- **Homeopathy:** Bryonia alba, calcarea fluorica, arnica (30C three times a day).
- **Medical:** Surgery, anti-inflammatory drugs like phenylbutazone, steroids, anticoagulant agents, isoxsuprine hydrochloride (to dilate peripheral blood vessels).
- **Physical Management:** Corrective shoeing (raised heel/rolled-toe shoes). Refrain from exercising the horse on hard surfaces.

PEMPHIGUS FOLIACEUS

This autoimmune disease produces multiple sores and hairless areas, especially around the head and face. Some animals have sores in the mouth, stiff muscles, pale gums, and a swollen belly.

Treatment options include:
- **Crystal Therapy:** White stones, tourmaline.
- **Medical:** Immunosuppressive drugs such as cyclophosphamide or azathioprine, sometimes in combination with glucorticoids.

PLEURITIS (PLEUROPNEUMONIA, SHIPPING FEVER)

This is a very painful condition that can be caused by stress, such as shipping (hence the name.) Signs include fever and a resistance to flexing or bending. Some horses are so sensitive that they react even to being touched on the rib cage.

Treatment options include:
- **Crystal Therapy:** Chalcedony, for safety in travel.

- **Homeopathy:** Aconite (to prevent and treat shipping fever), belladonna, bryonia.
- **Medical:** Metronidazole (Flagyl), an antimicrobial drug often used to treat chest infections.

PNEUMONIA

Pneumonia is an inflammation of the lungs, and it may have many causes. One sort commonly appears in nursing foals. In this case, the culprit is the bacterium *Rhodococcus equi*, which can cause abscesses in the lungs. Another type can result from the inhalation of liquids, which get sucked down in the alveoli (tiny air pockets) of the lungs, and this is also common in foals who suckle from a bottle, although it can occur with naturally nursing foals as well. This type of pneumonia, caused by *Corynebacterium equi* is also called "rattles." If it has appeared before on your property, give antibiotics at birth.

Pneumonia is quite hard to treat, especially because horses spend most of their time standing. Gravity keeps pulling the bacteria deep into the lungs, and it's harder for the horse to cough them out. Lung tissue is also very well supplied with blood, which makes a good environment in which bacteria can grow.

Pneumonia both in foals and adult horses is often a complication of stress or other primary disease processes such as viral upper respiratory conditions, strangles, colitis, and aspiration due to esophageal obstructions. Transporting horses over long distances is associated with increased incidences of infectious pneumonia. Moderate to severely excessive exercise or training also can contribute to susceptibility.

Signs include:
- breathing difficulty that may be accompanied by coughing, especially when moving
- cough, especially if productive—horses often look as though they are chewing or swallowing after a productive cough
- decreased exercise tolerance
- dullness
- enlarged submandibular lymph nodes (they lie under your horse's jaw)
- fever
- foul-smelling nasal discharge
- increased respiratory rate
- poor appetite
- weight loss

Care and treatment options include:
- **Acupuncture:** Can stimulate the immune system and improve lung function.
- **Ayurvedic Therapy:** Herbal mixture of sitopaladi, punarnava, pippali, abhrak bhasma, and chyavanprash.
- **Crystal Therapy:** Orange or yellow-orange stones.
- **Essential Oils:** Eucalyptus.
- **Homeopathy:** Aesculus hippocastanum (if accompanied by coughing).
- **Medical:** High doses of broad-spectrum antibiotics, especially rifampin given in combination with erythromycin.
- **Physical Management:** Give your horse plenty of time to recover if he has just undergone strenuous exercise because his immune system will be down. Whenever possible, don't tie your horse's head up when in transit, and avoid hay bags. If your horse is already sick, keep him in a temperate, well-ventilated but draft-free environment; and avoid damp, poorly ventilated barns. Try to avoid dusty bedding or moldy, dusty hay.

POTOMAC HORSE FEVER (EQUINE EHRLICHIAL COLITIS, EQUINE MONOCYTIC EHRLICHIOSIS)

Potomac Horse Fever (PHF) is a seasonal disease. It was first identified right down the road from where I live, so I have a particular aversion to it. Many horses died in the initial outbreak. It is caused by the rickettsial parasite *Ehrlichia risticii*, and the disease can be lethal. It is believed that the horse ingests the pathogen during grazing in marshy areas, but transmission is usually through a tick bite. Fresh water snails have been identified as carriers.

Signs (which are similar to salmonellosis) include:

- decreased appetite
- depression
- high fever
- laminitis on all four feet several days after diarrhea starts
- low white blood cell count
- watery diarrhea within 24 to 48 hours

The mortality rate for this disease is high no matter what treatment is given.

- **Prevention:** Vaccinations can reduce the severity of the clinical signs but may not prevent the disease in an outbreak.
- **Medical:** Intravenous fluids, antibiotics, and supportive care.
- **Homeopathic:** Aconite, belladonna.

RADIAL PARALYSIS

The radial nerve, which serves several joints and muscles in the front leg, can be easily damaged by trauma. The condition may cause the horse to have a partially paralyzed foreleg, or he may have great difficulty bringing the affected leg forward. It can occur as a result of many types of injury or even from a horse lying too long on his side.

Treatment options include:

- **Acupuncture:** Can help stimulate nerve regeneration.
- **Crystal Therapy:** Petrified wood.
- **Homeopathy:** Hypericum 30C, gelsemium, plumbum metallicum.
- **Medical/Surgical:** Anti-inflammatory drugs.
- **Physical Therapy:** Massage to improve circulation and to stimulate healing. Rest is necessary.

RESPIRATORY PROBLEMS

Respiratory infections, next to colic, are a major concern of horse owners. The most common problems are the viral infections equine influenza and rhinopneumonitis (equine herpes), as well as chronic obstructive pulmonary disease (COPD), discussed earlier.

An observant owner can tell a lot about the condition of her horse by the color and consistency of his nasal discharges. A horse with no respiratory problems usually has no discharge at all, although some horses have a thin, watery discharge in very

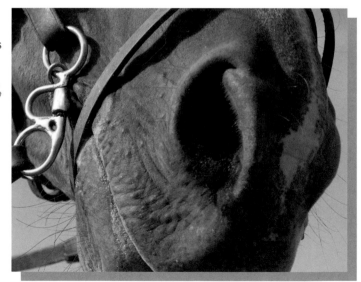

cold weather (as do some people!) A great deal of water discharge coupled with a purplish color in the membranes of the eye suggests rhinopneumonitis. A discharge with pus may indicate a sinus infection, strangles, or a secondary infection stemming from influenza. If the discharge is in one nostril only, suspect something localized. (*See also* Influenza, COPD, and Rhinopneumonitis.)

Care and treatment options are as follows:

- **Prevention:** While viruses and bacteria can cause many different types of respiratory illnesses, you can help to reduce their seriousness by careful environmental management. Anything that lowers a horse's resistance to infection can contribute to all kinds of respiratory difficulties, including overwork, inadequate food, and parasites. One reason that so many horses come down with respiratory problems is that they spend hour after hour in a dusty barn sucking in dirty air. Horses were meant to move freely on a grassy plain. The more time your horses spends in a barn, especially in the company of other horses who might be harboring infection, the more likely it is that he will become prey to one of many communicable diseases. Even if he is by himself and the barn is bacteria-free, the dust alone can cause serious problems. To give your horse the highest-quality environment, provide him with an airy but draft-free home. Remove as much dust from the environment as possible, including bedding. A seriously affected horse will do better on paper over rubber matting. If this is not possible, the horse may do well outdoors, with access to a three-sided shelter. Also, dry your horse thoroughly after exercise. Each horse should have his own grooming kit, which is not shared by other horses.

  Food is also a factor. The hay your horse eats is more loaded with dust, mold, and spores than the fresh grass he was meant to have. Feed high-quality haylage instead of hay. Feed garlic, especially in the winter, for is antiviral effects.

- **Acupuncture/Acupressure:** Bladder meridian 10: located about 2 inches (about 5 cm) from the center of the mane in a groove just behind the atlas (the big bone below and behind the ear); bladder meridian 13: located about 2 inches (about 5 cm) behind the shoulder blade, between ribs eight and nine.
- **Chinese Herbal Therapy:** Astragulus (huang qi).
- **Crystal Therapy:** Orange, tin.
- **Essential Oils:** Helichrysum, eucalyptus, frankincense, and lemon (for a refreshing spray to ease signs); bergamot; carrot seed; frankincense; garlic; hops; peppermint; tea tree oil.
- **Homeopathy:** Aconite (especially for viral disease accompanied by high fever), hepar sulphuris calcareum (if there is pus), phosphorus (30C three times a day), sulfur (12 to 30C three times a day).
- **Medical:** Antihistamines can sometimes relieve coughing and other signs of respiratory problems.
- **NAET:** May be useful if the problem is caused by an allergy.
- **Nutritional Therapy:** Feed extruded grains rather than whole grains. Wet down hay before feeding to reduce dust.
- **Shiatsu:** Lung meridian.
- **Western Herbal Therapy:** Licorice, echinacea (quick boost to the immune system), garlic, ginger (a good warming herb, also can be used to increase effectiveness of others), eyebright (as a tea or sprinkled directly on the feed). Combination 1: garlic, anise boneset, alfalfa, licorice, and marshmallow (1 cup [240 ml] in the feed once or twice a day). Combination 2: eyebright, hawthorn, mullein, peppermint, and sage (1 cup [240 ml] in the feed once or twice a day).

RHINOPNEUMONITIS (EQUINE HERPES VIRUS)

This upper respiratory viral infection is spread by direct or indirect contact with the nasal secretions of infected animals. It can move quickly through an entire barn.

There are two types of equine herpes virus (EHV): EHV-1 and EHV-4. Both occur in horse populations worldwide, with EHV-4 being more common. Latent infections and carrier states occur with both virus types. The incubation period is thought to be from two days to two weeks.

Signs may include:

- appetite loss
- clear nasal discharge
- cough
- depression
- high fever ranging between 102° to 107°F (38.9° to 41.7°C) that can last five days

EHV cannot be differentiated from equine influenza, equine viral arteritis, or other respiratory infections based only on clinical signs. They all look pretty much alike: fever, discharge, depression, and coughing. Your vet can make a definitive diagnosis by virus isolation from samples obtained from a nasopharyngeal swab and a blood sample.

Some horses show no signs of the disease at all, even though they are infected and can infect others. Once infected, a horse carries the virus for the rest of his life in a dormant state and can continue to spread the disease. In fact, a recent study showed that 60 percent of adult horses were latently infected with EHV-1 or EHV-4, and 30 percent carry both viruses.

EHV-1 can cause epidemic and sporadic abortions (usually in the last trimester), respiratory disease, and myeloencephalitis. In pregnant mares, it can cause abortions up to four months after exposure. Usually mares who suffer abortion from this disease do not exhibit the typical respiratory signs that other horses do. Even worse, some mares exposed late in gestation may not abort but give birth to live foals with fulminating viral pneumonitis. These little ones are vulnerable to secondary bacterial infections and often die within days or even hours. The transmission of EHV-1 from the mare to the foal is a key element in the cycle of infection. Vaccinated mares can transmit EHV-1 and EHV-4 to their unweaned, unvaccinated foals. However, the vaccine may reduce the period during which the virus is shed.

The closely related EHV-4 can cause respiratory illness that can harm performance, but does not usually cause abortions. Outbreaks with some strains of EHV-1 infection also may result in neurological disease, such as weakness in the hind legs or facial paralysis. Clinical signs vary from mild uncoordination to rear-end partial paralysis to severe posterior paralysis, loss of bladder and tail function, and loss of sensation to the skin in affected areas. In a few cases, the paralysis may progress to quadriplegia and death. Prognosis depends on the severity of the signs, but in many cases, recovery can be quite slow. In the past several years, more reports have surfaced of the severe neurological disorder associated with equine herpes, although it is still uncommon.

There are eight known equine herpes viruses, but only EHV-1 and EHV-4 are associated with truly awful effects. EHV-4 alone accounts for more than 46 percent of respiratory diseases in horses. These viruses were first known as equine rhinopneumonitis viruses, but it was later found that they were members of the notorious herpes family and so were renamed. EHV-2 is found in the respiratory mucosa, conjunctiva, and white blood cells of normal horses of all ages. No one knows

exactly what it does, although some have suggested that it causes herpetic kerato-conjunctivitis. EHV-3 causes genital horsepox. All herpes viruses can have carrier animals.

There is no specific treatment for EHV infection. The following care options may help:

- **Prevention:** Many horses are vaccinated against equine influenza but not against rhinopneumonitis. And equally unfortunate, the immunity derived from vaccination for rhinopneumonitis is short lived—less than a year. However, you can give a combination vaccination for "flu/rhino" that will extend immunity.

    Also, there is recent evidence that modified live virus vaccines (MLV) are more effective at preventing herpes than other more widely used killed vaccines. Traditionally, the equine community has been wary of MLVs. There have been incidents in the past in which an MLV that was incompletely weakened caused neurological disease symptoms after it was administered. The more widely used vaccine employs a killed virus. However, well-known immunologist Klaus Osterrieder, Associate Professor of Virology with the College of Veterinary Medicine at Cornell, believes that MLV vaccines are reasonably safe and more effective than killed vaccines. Therefore, he believes that MLV should be the vaccine of choice for this condition.

    Vaccination against EHV-1 should be given to all horses on the premises. New horses and those returning from other barns should be isolated for three or four weeks before joining the rest of the group, especially pregnant mares. Rhino can be lethal to developing fetuses. However, there is a special killed vaccine for pregnant mares called Pneumabort K-1B, the only rhinopneumonitis vaccine that is currently federally approved for this purpose. It is given during the fifth, seventh, and ninth months of pregnancy.
- **Acupuncture:** Can reduce stress and improve the immune system.
- **Crystal Therapy:** Orange.
- **Essential Oils:** A mixture of several drops of clary sage, eucalyptus, frankincense, and tea tree oil dissolved in water and sprayed around the barn. Some people also use tea tree oil (ten drops in a pint of water) to disinfect grooming equipment.
- **Homeopathy:** Belladonna or aconite, especially for accompanying fever. Use belladonna after the aconite. Use bryonia if the cough is harsh or dry
- **Medical:** Antibiotics are given for secondary bacterial infections. Bronchodilators such as clenbuterol are helpful. Antipyretics are recommended for horses with a fever above 104°F (40°C).
- **Physical Management:** Rest to minimize secondary bacterial infections. Disinfect barn regularly.
- **Western Herbal Therapy:** Anise seed, coltsfoot, garlic, or marshmallow can sometimes help coughs that spring from secondary bacterial infection.

RAIN ROT (DERMATOPHILOSIS, RAIN SCALD, DEW POISONING)

Rain rot is a skin ulceration caused by anaerobic, rod-shaped bacteria (*Dermatophilus congolensis*) or fungi that attack moist skin. It also can be spread by biting insects. Unlike other kinds of infections, it does not progress further than the skin or cause abscesses.

Signs include hair loss mostly along the topline, neck, and rump. (That's where the horse gets wettest, after all!) The horse will look out of condition. Small tufts of hair will pull out easily, with crusty material at the root. Although the condition is painless and doesn't usually cause itching, affected horses often seem depressed. Rain rot is contagious and can be transmitted by shared tack or blankets or even by mutual rubbing against fence posts.

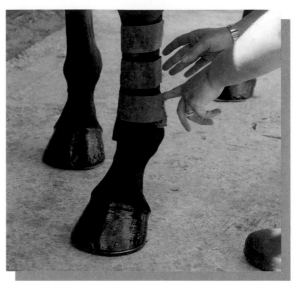

Treatment options include:

- **Crystal Therapy:** White.
- **Essential Oils:** Tea tree oil (about ten drops per pint of water). Combination paste: tea tree oil and lavender oil in aloe vera gel or petroleum jelly.
- **Herbal Therapy:** Slippery elm poultice.
- **Homeopathy:** Arnica 30C plus aconitum (6C if infection occurs), thuja, graphites (if there is a clear, sticky discharge).
- **Medical:** Keep the affected areas as dry as possible, and clip the area around the sores. First you may need to soften the scabs by applying a mixture of baby or mineral oil, 3 percent hydrogen peroxide, and tincture of iodine. Combine the ingredients in a large container, but don't seal it. Apply it to the horse and leave it there for a couple of hours. You also can use petroleum jelly. Then wet your horse down and lather him up with a povidine iodine shampoo or Nolvasan scrub. Let stand for ten minutes, then rinse. Dry thoroughly. Make sure that your horse gets plenty of fresh air and sun, and keep him as dry as you can. Keep the blankets off. You may have to repeat this treatment every day for a week or so.
- **Shiatsu:** Lung meridian.

RINGBONE AND COFFIN JOINT PROBLEMS

Ringbone is an abnormal bone growth around the pastern or coffin joint (the lowest joint in the leg), usually on the front legs. It is really a type of arthritis. Articular ringbone, which means a growth around the joint, is most often found in quick-turning performance horses or in horses with bad conformation. Nonarticular ringbone may be the result of trauma or inflammation of the periosteum (connective tissue membrane) that covers the bone.

The prognosis for ringbone usually depends on where it occurs; low ringbone has a much poorer prognosis than ringbone that occurs higher up.

Signs include:

- bony deformation in the area as the disease progresses
- firm swelling in the pastern area
- lameness
- pain if area is pressed deeply

Care and treatment options include:

- **Acupuncture:** To relieve pain. The needles are often inserted around the shoulder area.
- **Chiropractic:** Useful before ringbone sets in. May properly adjust the coffin joint.
- **Crystal Therapy:** Indigo.
- **Essential Oils:** Juniper.
- **Homeopathy:** (Choose one only.) Calcarea fluorica, calcarea carbonica, aconitum (6C to 30X three times daily), arnica (30C three times a day), ruta graveolens.
- **Magnetic Therapy:** Use small hoof magnets or a larger magnet held under the hoof with tape.
- **Medical/Surgical:** Anti-inflammatory drugs, steroids, PSGAGs (polysulfated glycosaminoglycans),

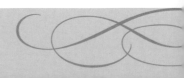

hyaluronic acid injected into the joint. Surgical intervention also may help some more advanced cases. It involves immobilizing the joint with orthopedic implants. (Because the pastern doesn't move very much, this therapy will not render a horse useless for riding.)

- **Physical Management:** Rest. Good hoof care, perhaps including a bar shoe.

RINGWORM (DERMATOPHYTOSIS OR GIRTH ITCH)

Despite its name, ringworm is a fungal infection, not a worm. The two most common species of fungi causing the problem are *Trichophyton* and *Microsporum*, which live in dirt, wooden fences, and the like. Horses pick them up through direct contact with the original source or from other animals. Infected tack or grooming utensils also can spread it.

Ringworm is common in horses. Young horses are at greater risk than older horses because immunity to the fungi develops with age. It feeds on dead skin but does not invade the tissues. Ringworm generally clusters into itchy, irritating crusty patches about the size of a quarter. Signs include circular hair loss, often around the head and neck. If the area of hair loss is larger than your hand, it could be a sign that the horse's immune system is weak.

This condition can be contagious to humans as well as to other horses, so use caution.

Treatment options include:

- **Crystal Therapy:** Tourmaline (to support the immune system).
- **Essential Oils:** A cream or ointment containing tea tree oil (2.5 percent solution).
- **Flower Essences:** Crab apple, mimulus, aspen, holly.
- **Herbal Therapy:** Echinacea, cleavers, yellow dock, and burdock (mixed equally) for hair growth.
- **Homeopathy:** Thuja (6C twice a day).
- **Medical:** Griseofulvin (given orally for a minimum of seven days). Do not give it to horses with liver disease or to pregnant mares. An antifungal wash is often prescribed.
- **Physical Management:** Disinfect brushes, towels, and blankets. Disinfect stables. Isolate affected horses.
- **Tissue Salts:** Kali sulph.

SADDLE SORES

Saddle sores are usually caused by a poorly fitting saddle, so you need to address that issue immediately. To treat the resulting sores, coat them with petroleum jelly.

Other treatments include:

- **Essential Oils:** Lavender oil in aloe vera gel (2.5 percent solution).
- **Herbal Therapy:** Fresh comfrey (added to the diet) or a comfrey poultice with aloe vera.
- **Homeopathy:** Arnica (30C once a day for three days if bruising is present), calendula (30C once daily for five days for pain).
- **Tissue Salts:** Nat mur (two tablets until healing occurs), calc sulph (two tablets until healing occurs).

SARCOIDS

Sarcoids are a common type of skin tumor in horses. They may appear singly or in groups, often around the girth area or genitals. They will not go away by themselves, and even if surgically removed, about half of them will come back. They are possibly transmitted from horse to horse.

Treatment options include:
- **Crystal Therapy:** White stones, especially white opal.
- **Medical:** In some cases, the injection of BCG (Bacille Calmette-Gu rin) vaccine will stimulate sufficient local response to destroy the tumor. A heavy-metal ointment also may work. Surgical removal is an option.

SKIN AND COAT PROBLEMS

Skin is the largest organ of the body, and because it is the nexus between the inside of the horse and the outside world, it is vulnerable to attack both internally and externally. Not only can it be torn or bitten, but nutritional inadequacies and other systemic problems often make their first appearance here. For example, if the liver, lungs, kidneys, and bowels are not working well, the effects on the skin will be soon become apparent.

The tough but flexible outside layer of the skin, or epidermis, protects the body from the environment, including the sun. It also protects it from infection and prevents excessive water loss from the body. In addition, the epidermis provides emotional cues. Stroking the skin gently, for example, promotes a feeling of well-being, while striking it sharply produces the opposite effect.

Itchy skin is a sign of an underlying problem. Aside from insect bites or stings, the cause could include liver problems like hepatitis or cholangitis, chronic granulomatous disease, parasites, leg mange, contact dermatitis, or a host of other things. In other species, insufficient fatty acids in the diet have been shown to lead to a poor coat, but the same has not been documented in horses. A good diet and regular brushing are the ways to keep a healthy horse in good coat. Contagious skin conditions require the attention of a veterinarian. (*See also* skin conditions listed separately.)

- **Bach Flowers:** Crab apple.
- **Crystal Therapy:** White stones, especially white opal, jade, copper, lead.
- **Essential Oils:** Aloe vera gel with tea tree or lavender oil. "Fly Away Combination" spray or wipe: 20 drops each of lavender, tea tree, eucalyptus, plus 7 drops of garlic and water.
- **Herbal Therapy:** Cleavers (especially to promote regrowth in tail and mane), powdered burdock (for dry, scurfy skin or sores), yellow dock, St. Mary's thistle, nettle. These powdered herbs can be mixed together and 2 tablespoons (30 ml) given morning and night. Add some licorice if the horse has previously been on steroids for the skin condition. You also can use 1 or 2 cups (1 cup = 240 ml) of fresh or dried herb in with the feed. Chickweed compress or poultice. Echinacea (if infection is present). Chamomile tea (as a wash).
- **Homeopathy:** Sulphur (for dry, itchy skin), rhus tox, apis mel, calendula, ledum, hypericum.
- **Nutritional Therapy:** Flaxseed oil.
- **Shiatsu:** Lung meridian.
- **Tissue Salts:** Nat mur, kali sulph, calcarea fluorica.

SPLINT

This is a word with two meanings. On one hand, "splint" refers to a bone in a horse's leg. Horses have two splint bones in each leg, one on each side of the cannon bone. However, when most owners complain that their horse has a "splint" they are not talking about the normal bone itself but an area of new bone that develops on the ligament that

is holding the splint bone to the cannon bone.

Splints are much easier to prevent than to repair. They form because of stress on the leg in which a ligament is torn, usually in young, overworked horses. Splints usually develop on the inside splint bone. Most of the time they cause no pain at all; sometimes they hurt for a couple of weeks. Some develop apparently overnight, while others appear only gradually. In some cases, splints even disappear over time.

Treatment options include:

- **Acupuncture:** To improve blood circulation and aide healing.
- **Chiropractic:** For the shoulder; some splints can be caused by a slight shoulder subluxation.
- **Herbal Therapy:** Powdered devil's claw (2 tablespoons [30 ml]) and powdered white willow bark (2 tablespoons [30 ml]) in the earliest stages. Comfrey ointment or poultice. Arnica lotion three times a day
- **Homeopathy:** Calcarea fluorica, calcarea carbonica, arnica (30C when heat or swelling is noticed three times daily; or use any of these as a liniment). Ruta graveolens (6C as a follow-up treatment three or four times a day for inflammation for ten days) or rhus tox.
- **Magnetic Therapy:** Magnetic boots are commonly used to increase blood flow to the damaged area.
- **Medical:** DMSO (dimethyl sulfoxide).
- **Physical Management:** Rest the horse, and apply cold compresses (or ice packs) or hose the area down with cold water 15 minutes a day. Use support bandages. If the lameness persists, have the vet check out the bone.
- **Tissue Salts:** Silica (two tablets twice a day).

STRANGLES (DISTEMPER, BARN FEVER)

Strangles is an ancient and highly contagious bacterial respiratory disease that is transmitted by direct contact or via contaminated objects such as troughs and buckets. It occurs most often when young horses are brought together for the first time. The name is due to the fact that the lymph nodes between the jaw bones are most commonly affected, and the horse does indeed sound as if he is being strangled. While it is not usually fatal, about 10 percent of untreated horses will die from it, usually from secondary pneumonia.

The responsible bacterium (*Streptococcus equi*) can survive in the environment for a time and continue to serve as a source of infection. (The bacteria are carried on the surface of the pharynx at the back of the mouth.) The incubation period is two to six days. Most affected horses are between one and five years old.

Signs include:

- clear, then purulent yellow nasal discharge from both nostrils
- depression
- fever (103° to 105°F [39.4° to 40.6°C])
- lack of appetite
- slight cough
- Usually painful, hot enlargements and abscesses of the lymph nodes under the jaw develop (hence the name). After a week or so, the abscesses may rupture through the skin. Cases where this does not occur are called "catarrhal" cases; this is more common in older horses. Rarely, these abscesses can spread to other parts of the body such as the lungs, liver, or brain. These cases are called "bastard strangles" and are often fatal.

Strangles usually shows up when a new horse is being introduced into the herd. The disease often responds well to antibiotics (like penicillin and sulfa drugs) after the lymph nodes are drained, but horses also can become carriers and transmit it to others. It helps to isolate new animals for at least four weeks because affected animals can shed the bacteria for a month after all clinical signs are gone. A veterinarian can take a series of

nasal swabs to see if a horse is shedding the bacteria.

Care and treatment options include:

- **Prevention:** Vaccination does not provide complete protection but does increase resistance. However, the immunity derived from the vaccine is very short lived. High-risk horses should probably be vaccinated every six months. Vaccinated horses who get strangles anyway almost always have a milder case. (It is a myth that horses can get strangles from the vaccine itself. The vaccine uses only a part of the culprit bacterium. There are other diseases, however, sometimes confused with strangles, that are caused by different organisms.) If an infected horse arrives at the barn and the other horses are healthy and have been vaccinated in the past, a booster might be reasonable. Foals are particularly susceptible. Recovered horses can continue to shed the bacteria for eight months. Most animals need a rest of three months before returning to work.

- **Acupuncture:** Can stimulate the immune system.
- **Crystal Therapy:** Orange or red-orange stones.
- **Homeopathy:** Belladonna or aconite for fever.
- **Medical:** Penicillin, given intramuscularly, works as a prophylactic. Some vets prefer to wait until the abscesses have burst to prevent the bacteria from being walled off in the glands. The lymph nodes may be drained surgically.

SWEET ITCH

This charmingly named condition is caused by the bite of midges (*Cullcoides*) in summer and early fall. Affected horses will rub the bases of their tail until the hair comes off and may have bald spots in other places as well. However, this family of midges is more than an annoyance. They have been linked to equine recurrent uveitis and so are very dangerous. Once a horse contracts sweet itch, it can worsen every year. Sweet itch can be resistant to treatment, so be patient.

Care and treatment options include:

- **Prevention:** Use a fly blanket and sprays to keep midges away from your horse. Ten drops of citronella to 1 pint (470 ml) of water makes a very good natural midge repellent.
- **Acupuncture:** To reduce pain.
- **Essential Oils:** Roman chamomile. Combination: lavender (ten drops), tea tee oil (ten drops), and Roman chamomile (five drops) into 1/2 cup (118 ml) of aloe vera gel, and smear it on the horse. This will also help to repel the midges. Be careful not to apply to irritated skin.
- **Homeopathy:** Graphites, arsenicum album, psorinum, thuja.
- **Medical:** Steroids. (Use with caution because they can cause laminitis.) Antihistamines (especially hydroxyzine) to control itching and antibiotics to manage any secondary infection.
- **Nutritional Therapy:** Add sulfur to the diet in the form of MSM (methylsulfonylmethane). Some owners claim success with fatty acid supplements and linseed oil, although this has not been proven scientifically.
- **Physical Management:** Shampoo based on wild geraniums to reduce itching.
- **Shiatsu:** Lung meridian.
- **Western Herbal Therapy:** A good herbal infusion combines three handfuls of nettle, rosemary, and

calendula. Pour the cooled liquid with some ice over the affected spot. You also can add some apple cider vinegar to the grain or water.

SWELLING

Swelling is not a disease but a sign of a problem. Depending on specifics, a swelling might mean a snakebite, abscess, sarcoid, hematoma, arthritis, bighead, cyst, hernia, tumor, cellulitis, infection, tooth problem, and so on. Identify the cause of the swelling before beginning any treatment.

Swelling of the lymph glands under the lower jaw usually indicates a bacterial or viral infection, usually the former. You should not be able to feel the lymph glands in a normal, healthy horse. While strangles is the most famous disease that produces lymph gland swelling, there are others. In most of these other cases, the swelling is not so dramatic, but even a tiny swelling is not normal and suggests that the horse is fighting an infection, even if he seems to be acting normally. Such horses should be rested and seen by a vet.

Helpful treatments include:
- **Herbal Therapy:** Cleavers (for leg swelling).
- **Homeopathy:** Apis mel for swellings that pit on pressure and are worse with touch. This remedy is especially indicated for horses who are irritable, suspicious, and dislike being left alone.
- **Medical:** DMSO (dimethyl sulfoxide).

TENDON TROUBLE

Tendons are strong bands of sinewy tissue that connect bone to muscle. Injuries usually occur from overwork, but some damage also can occur from poor shoeing or a stressed spine. If the horse does not show pain on pressure, the trouble may be in the foot. Try hoof testers. If the hoof testers yield a positive result, the horse may have an abscess or some other problem in the foot that has caused it to fill with pus.

The most common sort of tendon problem is "bowed tendon," which results from overwork, especially in racehorses. Horses with long, sloping pasterns are predisposed. Believe it or not, a bowed tendon can develop from an improperly fitting shipping bandage.

Signs include:
- pain on pressure
- swelling, usually in the back of the cannon area, which pits when you put pressure on it
- swollen areas that are hot to the touch

Care and treatment options include:
- **Acupuncture:** To reduce pain and aide healing
- **Crystal Therapy:** Petrified wood, iron.
- **Energetic Therapy:** Laser or ultrasound physiotherapy.
- **Flower Essences:** Impatiens, vervain.
- **Herbal Therapy:** Hawthorn (to stimulate circulation). Comfrey leaf compress.
- **Homeopathy:** Ruta graveolens (30C), apis mel (6C twice a day), silicea (silica), arncia (30C administered as soon as possible after the injury), bryonia (6C twice a day), rhus tox (internally 6C twice a day and as a liniment).
- **Magnetic Therapy:** You can buy special horse boots that incorporate magnets.

- **Medical/Surgical:** anti-inflammatory drugs, tendon splitting, tendon transplant, stem cell therapy (experimental).
- **Nutritional Therapy:** Omit concentrates, and feed only hay and water. Supplement PSGAGs (polysulfated glycosaminoglycans) in the first couple of weeks.
- **Physical Management:** Stable rest is the most important component of any treatment plan. A deep bed of straw is best. Keep off work for six months. Recovery is slow. Cold compresses may help immediately after an injury, but in serious cases, the vet may want to immobilize the tendon in a cast. Hose down the horse with cold water. Physical therapy aftercare is recommended. Shoe with a raised heel.

TETANUS (LOCKJAW)

Tetanus is a truly terrible disease. It can affect both people and domestic animals. It is caused by a toxin produced by a nasty little bacterium called *Clostridium tetani*. It is commonly found in horse manure and is more common in cultivated than uncultivated soils.

Transmission generally occurs through injury. The bacterium enters the body through a puncture. (It doesn't have to be large.) The toxin makes it impossible for the horse to control muscle contraction, and early signs may include a stiff-legged gait, with the tail held out straight and the ears pricked. Then the horse will go rigid, unable to move or eat. The third eyelid will become prolapsed. The final stage is death by asphyxiation.

This disease must be treated early and aggressively if you want to save your horse. About 80 percent of all horses who get tetanus will die of it, despite treatment. If an unvaccinated horse is injured, tetanus antitoxin should be administered to provide immediate but short-term (three weeks) protection. *At the same time,* a vaccination program should be commenced to develop long-lasting immunity. Only the tetanus vaccine provides long-lasting protection. Immunity, however, takes seven to ten days to develop, so an injured horse may develop tetanus before protection is fully achieved. The vaccine should be given along with tetanus toxoid if an injured horse has an unknown vaccination history. Even horses who have recovered from the disease are not immune to a new infection. The tetanus vaccine is administered intramuscularly on one side of the neck, while the tetanus antitoxin is injected subcutaneously on the other side of the neck.

Obviously, prevention is your best bet, but here are some care options:

- **Prevention:** The tetanus vaccine should be given at least once a year but can be given more often. It's inexpensive and an easy way to prevent your horse from contracting the disease. You should get yourself inoculated, too!
- **Crystal Therapy:** Barite, iron.
- **Homeopathy:** Cicuta virosa, hypericum perforata. However, the chances of a horse living through tetanus without antitoxin are almost zero.

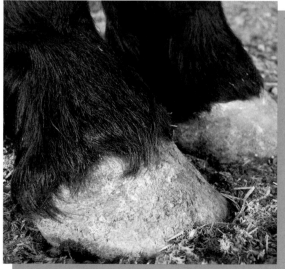

THRUSH

Thrush is an infection of the frog and horn of the hoof that produces a black, smelly discharge. The problem starts when a horse stands around in damp bedding (often soaked with ammonia-laden urine). However, a healthy hoof is much more resistant to thrush, even when the horse has to stand in foul conditions. In cases where thrush develops, there is almost always a previous condition in the frog of the hoof.

The disease occurs because when the frog softens, it can be invaded by fungi and bacteria, which do further damage and produce that characteristic nasty smell. It also may turn

black. Depending on how deep the infection goes, the horse can become chronically lame.

Care and treatment options include:

- **Prevention:** Provide the horse with a dry, clean stall, and don't let him stand in a small muddy corral day after day. Make sure that the frog is healthy.
- **Acupuncture:** To reduce pain and improve the immune system.
- **Crystal Therapy:** White.
- **Essential Oils:** Tea tree oil, lemon, lavender. Combination: tea tree and lavender oil diluted (five drops oil to 1/3 cup (79 ml) carrier oil three times a day).
- **Herbal Therapy:** Scrub the hoof with a stiff brush. Add ten drops of tea tree oil to the water. Poultice with slippery elm bark powder, comfrey leaves, or marshmallow root. You may add a few drops of tea tree, bergamot, or lavender.
- **Combination:** equal parts echinacea, cleavers, bladderwrack, meadowsweet, and burdock. (Drink 1 cup [240 ml] every day.)
- **Homeopathy:** Hepar sulph (30C for five days), followed by silicea (200C).
- **Medical/Surgical:** Have the farrier cut away all badly infected tissue. Apply an antibiotic/antiseptic treatment to the horn. One well-known effective treatment is copper naphthenate (Kopertox). This is a caustic chemical that dries the foot and kills the infective agents. It's recommended for five days. Thrush Buster is another commercial product. Some holistic veterinarians suggest a mixture of one part colloidal silver and three parts calendula ointment twice a day for seven to ten days. Simple bleach works well, as does a solution of 7 percent iodine; however, both are very drying to the hooves.
- **Tissue Salts:** Silica tissue salts (two tablets per day).

THYROID PROBLEMS

The common thyroid disease in horses is hypothyroidism, which simply means insufficient levels of thyroid hormones. Thyroid hormones regulate a horse's metabolism and affect his energy level.

The disease is difficult to diagnose. There is a simple laboratory test called the T4 test, but it is not definitive, and it needs to be repeated over a period of time to get accurate results. Another method is to stimulate the thyroid to release thyroid hormones by giving thyroid-stimulating hormone (TSH), but this test is complex and difficult to administer.

Signs of hypothyroidism include:

- depression
- hair loss around the top of the head
- moth-eaten look
- swollen legs
- lethargy
- shivering
- sweating

Horses with thyroid disorders may suffer exercise intolerance, sore muscles, lethargy, tying up syndrome, goiter, and laminitis. Many thyroid-deficient horses are obese, with a crusty neck and poor hair coat. Mares may be infertile.

Care and treatment options include:

- **Crystal Therapy:** Sodalite to balance the metabolism.
- **Herbal Therapy:** Bladderwrack to balance the metabolism. If your feed contains iodine supplement,

however, do not use bladderwrack because it is full of iodine. Use between 1 and 2 teaspoonfuls (5 to 10 ml) powdered herb in the feed daily.

- **Homeopathy:** In cases where the thyroid is depressed, you may use Homeopathy Thyroid 30C at one drop per day for three weeks, which can return thyroid levels to normal. Then recheck the levels.
- **Medical:** The horse can be treated with a synthetic thyroid hormone, but it has to be done carefully. Oversupplementation can lead to decreased production of natural thyroid hormones and can suppress the normal activity of the thyroid gland. However, in most cases, the treatment is successful.
- **Physical Management:** One cause of thyroid problems may be too much protein in the diet. Reduce alfalfa, corn, etc.

TYING UP (MONDAY MORNING DISEASE, EXERTIONAL RHABDOMYOLYSIS, AZOTURIA, MYOSITIS, SET-FAST)

First noted in draft horses in the 19th century, this disease was characterized by well-conditioned working horses becoming stiff (and sometimes unable to move) on Monday morning following a day's rest and normal grain rations. In milder cases, the horse may just "step short" on the hind legs, but the condition may progress to the point where the horse actually cannot move. The muscles are hard to the touch.

Tying up is not really one disease but a syndrome that can result from several different conditions, most of which are exercise related. Other causes can include excessive consumption of grain, dehydration, glucose depletion, electrolyte imbalances, and mineral and vitamin deficiencies (especially sodium deficiency). Hormonal factors also may play a part; it has been shown that horses with low thyroid hormone levels are also more prone to tying up.

In general, tying up occurs because the body is not dealing properly with glycogen, a starch that should convert into energy. During the process, excessive levels of lactic acid can form in the blood and muscles. This reduces cellular enzymes and blood pH. If too much forms or if the bloodstream doesn't remove it fast enough, there can be damage to the muscle fibers—they end up being in a permanent state of contraction.

Sporadic exertional rhabdomyolysis, another form of tying up, occurs suddenly in previously sound horses following exercise. It is usually due to muscle strain caused by an inadequate warm-up, preexisting lameness, and overwork. It also can occur when young horses are overloaded on grain. Horses should not be fed more than 15 pounds (6.8 kg) of grain a day and never more than 5 pounds (2.3 kg) of grain at any one time. Grain is not a natural food for horses. However, some horses not on grain diets can still tie up if they are hypersensitive to lactic acid.

Chronic exertional rhabdomyolysis occurs in horses who have had repeated episodes of tying up from a young age. Two forms of chronic tying up have been identified using muscle biopsies. One form, polysaccharide storage myopathy (PSSM), affects mostly quarter horse-related breeds, warmbloods, and draft breeds. The other form affects quarter horses, paints, Appaloosas, Thoroughbreds, Arabians, standardbreds, and Morgans.

Recurrent exertional rhabdomyolysis (RER) is a disorder of Thoroughbreds, most often young fillies, but it also can appear in standardbreds and Arabians. No one knows why fillies seem more affected than colts, but it may have something to do with estrogen levels.

Signs of tying up include:
- abnormally short strides
- dark urine or trouble passing urine
- hard, stiff muscles
- muscle contractions and pain
- obvious discomfort
- rapid breathing and pulse
- stiffness
- sweating more than expected during exercise

A blood sample can confirm the diagnosis by detecting abnormally high levels of certain enzymes.

Care and treatment options include:

- **Acupressure/ Acupuncture:** To relieve muscle tension and improve blood circulation.
- **Crystal Therapy:** Ruby, barite, petrified wood, iron.
- **Essential Oils:** Blue chamomile, lemongrass, basil, clary sage, eucalyptus, juniper, lavender, lemongrass, marjoram, Roman chamomile.
- **Flower Essences:** Vervain.

- **Herbal Therapy:** Celery seed may help in the prevention of tying up. Cleavers are recommended when the reason for tying up is unknown. Dandelion also helps.
- **Homeopathy:** Arnica (in early stages, 12X to 30C three times daily), berberis vulgaris, bryonia (helps to restore movement), elaps corallinus.
- **Medical:** Possibly IV fluids or tranquilizers. A blood test will help to determine what is needed. Muscle relaxant drugs like methocarbamol (injected or oral) or NSAIDs like naproxen may help with the muscle spasms and pain. Diuretics may be prescribed to help the kidneys eliminate the breakdown products. Injection of selenium and vitamin E also may be given.
- **Nutritional Therapy:** Make sure that all horses get adequate hydration. For horses with sporadic tying up, feed high-quality hay with little or light grain supplementation. Provide a mineral/vitamin supplement, such as EquiMin Horse Mineral. Vitamin E supplements may be helpful to rebuild the damaged muscle. An ounce (0.4 kg) of salt added to the food daily also may help. You also can add 2 to 4 pounds (about 5 to 9 kg) of shredded beet pulp to the horse's ration. Beet pulp contains more calories per pound (0.5 kg) than alfalfa and also provides added nutrition. Too much protein can depress the thyroid function, so you want to feed a ration that does not contain excessive protein but that does provide sufficient magnesium. A grain mix containing 10 percent protein with a magnesium level of at least 0.3 percent is a good choice. Horses with a history of tying up should not be given iron supplements, as too much iron can stimulate free radical production. Vitamin C supplementation is also helpful. Calcium may be helpful before a workout.

There is another theory that a low-carbohydrate, high-fat diet may be helpful because there is a suggestion that susceptible horses have a defect in the glycogen metabolic pathway and cannot manage carbohydrates efficiently. For horses with chronic tying up, change the diet to foods with higher fat and lower sugar and starch levels. Feeding 1 to 2 pounds (about 2.2 to 4.5 kg) of rice bran (20 percent fat) or vegetable oil provides a large number of calories and can greatly reduce the need for a large amount of grain. Quarter horses with PSSM benefit from daily feeding of 2 pounds (4.5 kg) of rice bran with grass hay. Other breeds affected with PSSM may need more calories and would benefit from high-fat feeds; they may require additional rice bran or vegetable oil. Add as much good-quality hay and roughage as the horse wants.

When tying up is caused by excessive grain intake, it is usually called azoturia. This is the easiest kind of tying up to manage. In race horses, it helps to replace most of the grain with a fat supplement such as Triple

Crown Rice Bran or Triple Crown Rice Bran Oil Plus. In addition to providing the necessary calories, this is a calming diet. Another option is to feed a high-fiber, high-fat, low-starch feed. DMG (dimethylglycine, an intermediate metabolite) also may be helpful.

- **Physical Management:** Immediately stop all exercise and move the horse to a well-padded stall with plenty of water. In very mild cases, you can try hand walking the horse to see if he improves. Walking helps circulation and may hasten the removal of lactic acid. In serious cases, don't move the horse. Cover him and keep him warm. Try to get him to drink fluid containing electrolytes. Your vet can order a panel of diagnostic tests to determine the precise cause of the condition. Resume training gradually and only after the horse is completely recovered. Keep the excitement level as low as possible, and maintain the horse on a moderate working schedule.
- **Tissue Salts:** Mag phos (6C or 12C three times a day for one day).

VESICULAR STOMATITIS (MOUTH BLISTERS)

This is a new viral disease so far confined to the Western Hemisphere. It affects horses, cattle, and swine. Humans also can be affected and usually develop flu-like symptoms. The mode of transmission is not entirely known, although both insect and mechanical transmission may be responsible.

The incubation period for vesicular stomatitis is five to eight days, during which time the horse may have a fever and be slightly depressed. Signs include excessive salvation, slow eating, and mouth blisters. If there are no complications, affected animals recover in about two weeks, but horses may refuse to drink and become dangerously dehydrated. A small percentage of horses also will develop foot lesions, and so some people mistake the condition for hoof and mouth disease. Many conditions can cause blisters in the mouth including phenylbutazone ("bute") toxicity, blister beetles, periodontal disease, and foreign bodies. It's wise to have your vet diagnose the problem before treatment.

Care and treatment options include:
- **Homeopathy:** Antimonium crudum.
- **Medical:** There is no specific Western medical treatment, cure, or vaccination for vesicular stomatitis. It may be helpful to use a mild antiseptic mouthwash.

WARTS

Warts are comparatively common, especially in young horses. They are caused by a virus, just like the one that causes human warts. This virus is passed from mares to foals during suckling (and so are sometimes termed "milk warts"). They usually form on the muzzle and eyelids but also can be found on the forelimbs. Transmission between young horses is common. Once a horse is older than 18 months, warts are rarely seen.

It is best to isolate an affected animal. The warts usually go away by themselves, but occasionally some extra help is needed, especially if they become infected.

Treatment options include:

- **Essential Oils:** Lemon.
- **Homeopathy:** Select one of the following: thuja occidentalis (30C to 200C once a day for ten days), causticum, calcarea carbonica (for facial warts or for a number of small, nonbleeding warts (200C once a week for three to four weeks), kali-carb (30C every other day for ten days).
- **Medical:** Antibiotics are given for infected warts.

WEST NILE VIRUS

West Nile virus is a serious and sometimes fatal disease in horses. It was originally identified in Uganda in 1937 and was later detected in New York in 1999. Since then, it has spread to 48 states and Canada and Mexico.

Transmission is through insect bites. Mosquitoes become infected when they feed on infected birds. Most birds who carry the disease do not become ill themselves, thus making them excellent carriers. In horses, the peak infection period is August and September. The disease can affect both the central and peripheral nervous systems.

Signs include:

- ataxia of the hind legs
- coma
- dementia or disorientation
- fever (sometimes)
- weakness and lying down

These signs are very nonspecific and are similar to signs of other diseases that affect the brain, such as rabies, equine herpes virus, and equine encephalomyelitis. Have your horse properly diagnosed. Any horse who exhibits neurological signs must be handled with extreme care. Even if you think it is West Nile, it *could* be rabies. Don't guess—call your vet.

Care and treatment options include:

- **Prevention:** Mosquitoes lay their eggs in standing water, so rinse and clean water buckets and any other sources of stagnant water constantly. Use equine insect repellents. Remove dead birds from the area. There is no indication that West Nile virus is spread directly from birds to people, but avian flu can be, so use rubber gloves and a rake when handling dead birds. Vaccination is available.
- **Crystal Therapy:** Blue stones.

WHITE LINE DISEASE (ONYCHOMYCOSIS, STALL ROT, HOLLOW FOOT, WALL THRUSH, YEAST INFECTION, SEEDY TOE)

In this disease, the white line (zona lamellatum) is the junction of the sole and the hoof wall. It runs all the way up the inside of the hoof but is only visible on the sole. White line disease is caused by fungi and/or bacteria that infiltrate and destroy the keratin tissue. A hoof-wall separation may not always be visible on an X-ray. It can occur in one or more feet.

Signs include:

- crumbly, soft horn tissue in the middle wall
- hollow sound if you tap on the hoof wall
- hooves become shell-like and won't hold a shoe
- laminitis-like signs
- one side of the hoof is dished, while the other bulges

Horses who have trauma to the hoof, who have foundered, or who live in filthy conditions are more prone to the disease.

Treatment options include:

- **Acupuncture:** To simulate the immune system and increase blood supply to the hoof.
- **Essential Oils:** Lavender and thyme either topically (as a hoof cleanser) or as aromatherapy (once a day for three days).
- **Surgical:** The earlier the treatment is started, the more successful it is likely to be. The affected hoof area must be removed, resected (the bad part cut away and the good parts joined together), and exposed to air and light. The underlying tissue must be treated with a broad-spectrum antibacterial/antifungal agent.

WINDGALLS

Windgalls are soft swellings around the fetlock, usually on the hind legs. The causes can include overwork on hard ground, poor nutrition, and immune system reactions. They are most common in older horses.

Care and treatment options include:

- **Herbal Therapy:** Garlic, dandelion, echinacea, yucca.
- **Homeopathy:** Apis 30C, kali bichromium, eupatorium perfoliatum.
- **Magnetic Therapy:** To increase blood flow and help the horse heal.
- **Physical Management:** Some people have success applying cooling gels containing menthol or camphor.
- **Various Applications:** Kaolin-based paste, arnica liniment, lotion.

WOBBLER SYNDROME

Wobbler syndrome is actually a group of diseases characterized by gait instability. One of the most common causes is cervical vertebral stenotic myelopathy (a compression of the spinal cord), which results in an abnormal gait. It generally affects growing horses between 4 and 12 months of age. The other common type is cervical static stenosis, which strikes slightly older horses (12 to 36 months). This condition causes a closing of the cervical vertebrae (neck) and compression of the spinal cord. Diagnosis includes a neurological examination to identify the location of the malformation. In the past, most horses with Wobbler syndrome were euthanized.

In general, there are four factors that can lead to the various forms of Wobbler syndrome: genetic predisposition, nutritional imbalance, rapid growth, physical trauma, or any combination of these. There is also a theory that the longer the neck of the horse, the more likely he is to develop Wobbler syndrome. Thoroughbreds, Morgans, and quarter horses are the most commonly affected breeds; it has not yet been reported in miniature horses. Wobbler syndrome also affects males far more often than females.

The first main sign is unsteadiness in the hindquarters, followed by noticeable incoordination, weight loss, and severe weakness in the hindquarters. Many horses also develop "Wobbler's heel," a condition in which they reach forward with the back foot and lacerate the bulb of the front hoof. These signs may be of sudden or gradual onset.

Treatment options include:

- **Acupuncture:** Can aid in nerve regeneration.
- **Medical:** Drug therapy includes medication to reduce nerve tissue swellings and intracranial pressure. Osmotic agents like mannitol, DMSO (dimethyl sulfoxide), and diuretics like furosemide are typical.
- **Nutritional Therapy:** A special restricted diet, developed by researchers at the University of Pennsylvania, can sometimes

reverse the disease in young foals if they have not become paralyzed. This diet limits both food intake and exercise. (Sometimes total confinement is required.) Eventually, the horse may completely recover. This takes time and patience, but it is the best option.

- **Surgery:** The type of procedure indicated is actually adopted from human surgery and is called the "cloward method" for fusing the vertebrae.

WORMS

Horses are prey to numerous worms, including roundworms, redworms of various types, threadworms, hairworms, tapeworms, pinworms, lungworms, liver flukes, abdominal worms, eyeworms, stomach worms, and gullet worms. Worms are more than just an ugly face (at least for those of them that actually have faces). Worms and their fellow parasites lower resistance of the immune system, steal nutrients, and cause numerous gastrointestinal problems. Those are the nice ones. The nasty ones can kill.

Most horses become infested with worms when they eat grass contaminated with worm eggs or larvae, although there are some exceptions. Once inside the horse, they may lay eggs that are voided with the feces. Some worms, such as the liver fluke, require an intermediate host.

While signs of various worm infestations vary, they can include:

- coughing
- depression
- diarrhea
- pneumonia
- poor hair coat
- recurrent colic
- sores
- tail rubbing
- weight loss

In some cases, parasitic larvae in the horse's brain can actually be activated by deworming, which can cause bizarre changes in gait and behavior.

Care and treatment options include:

- **Prevention:** Heavily infested pastures can be ploughed or harrowed. (The sun kills many larvae.)
- **Crystal Therapy:** Green, blue-violet, blue-green.
- **Herbal Therapy Deworming:** Many herbal therapists use black walnut or wormwood in place of conventional dewormers. However, these powerful herbs can be dangerous to horses, and I don't advise either of them. Bladderwrack may be used after deworming to restore balance to the intestinal system.
- **Standard Deworming:** Your horse should be on a good deworming program. Many vets prefer using one wormer twice and then rotating to a different type, using about three dewormers altogether. For horses who have suffered a great deal of parasitical damage, daily dewormers may be required.

  There are three main methods of deworming a horse: oral paste syringe, nasogastric tube, and feed additive. All are safe and effective as long as the horse gets the required amount of dewormer for his weight and as long as he ingests the whole dose. Obviously, the easiest way is to put the stuff in the horse's food, but you have to be sure the horse actually eats the stuff. Some won't. A paste might work for horses who won't simply eat the dewormer. If you have no luck there, tube deworming will work. It goes straight into the stomach and so is very effective. The problem is that horses really don't like that either. The other problem is that it takes skill to do this right; to be safe, you should have your equine vet do it.

WOUNDS

The first thing to know is that most wounds in horses are contaminated. Make sure that tetanus protection is up to date. The wound healing process consists of four stages: inflammation, debridement (scraping away the bad, infected material), repair, and maturation. Serious wounds may take two years to heal; most seriously wounded areas remain weaker than the surrounding skin. Wounds that are deep or more than 3 inches (7.6 cm) long (unless they are very superficial) require veterinary assistance.

EMERGENCY CARE

- Stop the bleeding.
- Alum, a double sulfate of aluminum and potassium, which is a major component of styptic powder, can be used to stop blood flow from a superficial wound.
- For gaping wounds, try to bandage the edges of the wound together. A pressure bandage works well on the legs.
- Use gauze to pack large open wounds.
- Clean the wound. Clip away any hair that invades the margins of the wound. The basic care for minor wounds is to wash them with clean, cool water. (Cool water reduces the chances of swelling.) Remove any leftover dirt with a clean cloth, and follow with a dilute antiseptic. One good cleanser is chlorhexidine, available in various products like Nolvasan and Chlorhexiderm. These work like povidone-iodine but act quicker and last longer. However, it is important to rinse the medicine thoroughly from the wound after applying it. Do not use hydrogen peroxide on a fresh wound. Change bandages every day.
- A combination (three-way) antibiotic will also be helpful. They work synergistically to kill most bacteria.
- A homeopathic tincture of arnica or herbal therapy preparation with calendula also may be used.

WOUND CARE

Abrasions: For abrasions, some pressure is desirable, but not enough to force the dirt back into the wound. When the wound is clean, dry it and use a powdered or spray antibiotic. You may cover it with a light gauze bandage if desired, but make sure that the wound is draining. Don't exercise the horse until you see signs of good healing.

Contusions: Contusions can be reduced by alternating hot and cold treatments. For the hot treatment, put hot water into a bucket, along with a couple of tablespoons (1 tbsp=15 ml) of salt, and soak some gauze in it. Apply the soaked gauze to the contusion. This will increase the blood circulation to the area and encourage healing, as the blood helps to carry away debris. Keep it on the area until it cools off, and then repeat. Do this for about ten minutes. Follow with a cold pack, which will constrict the blood vessels and reduce the accumulation of fluid in the site. Don't use this treatment if the contusion is accompanied by an open wound.

Lacerations: Lacerations, perhaps the most common type of wound, *sometimes* consist of whole sections of skin torn away, but are not always as painful as they look. (Many of them are caused by barbed wire.) This type of wound should be cleaned thoroughly and all foreign matter flushed out. Don't use strong antiseptics because they can damage the tissue and still may not kill all the bacteria. Clip hair away from the site. Cover the wound with gauze. Don't use a tight bandage, as that can inhibit healing. Call your vet for advice about suturing. Don't exercise the horse until the wound is healed.

Puncture Wounds: Puncture wounds should be scrubbed with iodine or a similarly based solution. If possible, open the puncture wound as much as you can to promote drainage, and remove any embedded foreign object. As long as the wound continues to drain, it should be left open. Antibiotics and antitetanus medications should be given. Because puncture wounds can escape notice until they abscess, it is really important to keep your horse up to date on the tetanus vaccine.

Incised Wounds: Incised wounds tend to be cleaner than other types, but they can be quite deep and often require suturing, preferably within eight hours of the incident.

Other treatment options include:

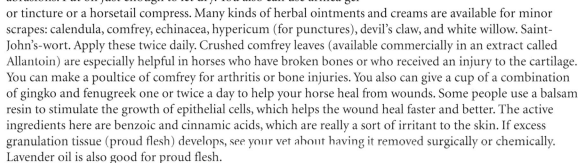

- **Crystal Therapy:** Petrified wood.
- **Essential Oils:** (Do not apply the following as a base oil; use with water or undiluted. You want the wound to dry.) Tea tree oil: Use first, especially if there is pus in the wound. Apply undiluted or use as a compress. Redress the wound twice daily. Lavender: Accelerates healing after the pus has cleared. Lavender also will keep away flies. Use eucalyptus and lavender together for aromatherapy. German chamomile, roman (blue) chamomile: Put undiluted on the wound. Thyme: Use as an infusion. Yarrow: Put undiluted on the wound.
- **Flower Essences:** Bach Rescue Remedy.
- **Herbal Therapy:** Fresh aloe gel can be applied directly to burns or abrasions. Put on just enough to let dry. You also can use arnica gel or tincture or a horsetail compress. Many kinds of herbal ointments and creams are available for minor scrapes: calendula, comfrey, echinacea, hypericum (for punctures), devil's claw, and white willow. Saint-John's-wort. Apply these twice daily. Crushed comfrey leaves (available commercially in an extract called Allantoin) are especially helpful in horses who have broken bones or who received an injury to the cartilage. You can make a poultice of comfrey for arthritis or bone injuries. You also can give a cup of a combination of gingko and fenugreek one or twice a day to help your horse heal from wounds. Some people use a balsam resin to stimulate the growth of epithelial cells, which helps the wound heal faster and better. The active ingredients here are benzoic and cinnamic acids, which are really a sort of irritant to the skin. If excess granulation tissue (proud flesh) develops, see your vet about having it removed surgically or chemically. Lavender oil is also good for proud flesh.
- **Homeopathy:** Arnica gel (for bruises and hematomas; or orally, give two doses of arnica 30C two hours apart). Calendula (30C) promotes rapid healing and granulation of the skin. The pure tincture can be applied locally or added to other healing salves. Hypericum (30C to help healing; give four times over 24 hours), alternations of hypericum (1M) and ledum palustre (30C for puncture wounds), ledum (12X-30C; three times a day for five days after the injury), hepar sulph, phosphorus (30C every 15 minutes in acute cases), silica (6C for deep wounds three times a day for six days), sulpharis calcareum (39C for fistulas).
- **Medical:** DMSO (dimethyl sulfoxide) for closed wounds. Do not use with open wounds because there is a danger of the DMSO carrying the bacteria to the interior of the body.

Acupressure: Chinese healing method that involves applying pressure to meridian points on the body to relieve pain and relax tension.

Acupuncture: The practice of inserting needles into the body to reduce pain or to induce healing.

Adaptogens: Substances that support the endocrine system, and the whole person, helping the individual adapt to stress. Herbal examples include: ginseng root, nettle leaf, licorice root, and ashwagandha.

Adjuvants: Substances, commonly mineral oil or alum, added to vaccines to enhance antigenicity.

Akasha: Free open space, ether, sky, or atmosphere in Ayurvedic medicine.

Allergy: A misguided reaction by the immune system to foreign substances.

Alterative: A substance that alters a chronic condition by aiding the elimination of metabolic toxins. A "blood-cleanser." These substances improve lymphatic circulation and boost immunity. Herbal examples include: ginseng, aloe, sandalwood, burdock, bayberry, black pepper, cinnamon, myrrh, and safflower.

Alternative medicine: Practices used instead of standard medical treatments.

Ama: In Ayurvedic medicine, the disease process that circulates in the whole body.

Analgesic: A substance that helps reduce or eliminate pain. Herbal examples include: chamomile, cinnamon, cloves, echinacea, lavender flower, cabbage leaves, wintergreen leaf, and passionflower.

Anodyne: Herbs that relieve pain and reduce the sensitivity of the nerves.

Anthelmintic: Substances that destroy and worms, fungus, yeast. Herbal examples include: goldenseal, wormseed, wormwood, ajwain, cayenne, peppers, and pumpkin seeds.

Antibiotic: A substance that inhibits the growth of germs, bacteria, and harmful microbes.

Antibody: An immunoglobulin, a specialized immune protein, produced because of the introduction of an antigen into the body.

Antigen: A foreign substance that when introduced into the body stimulates the production of an antibody.

Anti-inflammatory: A substance that prevents or reduces inflammation.

Antioxidant: An enzyme or other organic molecule or chemical compound that can oxidate damage in tissues.

Antiphlogistic: Substances that counteract inflammation; same effect as an anti-inflammatory.

Antiseptic: A substance that inhibits the growth and development of microorganisms. Herbal examples include: aloe, gudmar, sandalwood, and turmeric.

Antispasmodic: A substance that relieves or prevents involuntary muscle spasms or cramps by strengthening nerves and the nervous system. Herbal examples include: chamomile, ashwagandha, basil, guggul, licorice, myrrh, sage, jatamanshi, peppermint, sandalwood, and spearmint.

Antithrombotic: Anticlotting.

Antitussive: A substance that prevents or improves a cough.

Aperient: A mild or gentle laxative.

Aromatherapy: The use of volatile plant oils, including essential oils, for psychological and physical well being.

Aromatic: An herb with a pleasant, fragrant scent and a pungent taste.

Arthritis: Inflammation of a joint.

The Whole Horse Wellness Guide

Astringent: A substance that causes a local contraction of the skin, blood vessels, and other tissues, thereby arresting the discharge of blood or mucus. Usually used locally as a topical application. Herbal examples include: amalaki, arjuna, cinnamon, jasmine, sandalwood, and yarrow.

Ayurveda: Constituted of two words: Ayur meaning life and Veda meaning knowledge, it means the knowledge of life. An Indian modality.

Bach Flower Remedy: Water that has been patterned with the energetic vibrations of one of 38 different flowers.

Bodywork: Any of a number of therapeutic or relaxing practices that involve the manipulation, massage, or regimented movement of body parts.

Bronchodilator: Expands the spastic bronchial tube.

Carminative: A substance that helps prevent gas from forming in the intestines, and also assists in expelling it. Herbal examples include: chamomile, chrysanthemum, coriander, fennel, lime, peppermint, spearmint, ajwain, basil, calamus, cardamom, cinnamon, ginger, and turmeric.

Chiropractic: Adjustments of the spine and joints.

Chondroitin: A naturally occurring cartilage-building substance, used as a supplement, derived from bovine or porcine tracheas.

Compress: A folded cloth or pad applied so as to press upon a body part.

Connective tissue: A material made up of fibers forming a framework and support structure for body tissues and organs.

Craniosacral Therapy: Type of bodywork that manipulates the bones of the skull to treat a range of conditions.

Decoction: The extraction of water-soluble drug substances by boiling.

Demulcent: A substance that soothes and relieves the irritation of inflamed mucous membranes. Herbal examples include: barley, licorice; linseed, olive, and almond oils.

Diaphoretic: Sweat-inducing.

Diluent: Diluting agent.

Discutient: Causing dispersal or disappearance of a pathological accumulation or morbid matter (like pus).

Emollient: A substance used to soften and soothe the skin.

Expectorant: Promoting the expulsion of phlegm, mucus, or other matter from the respiratory tract.

Extruded feeds: Feeds that have been dried and blended into "kibble."

Febrifuge: A substance used to reduce body temperature and fever; also called antipyretic.

Flavanoids: Any of a large group of plant-based nutrients considered to have antioxidant and anti-inflammatory properties.

Fracture: A break in bone or cartilage.

Glucosamine: A naturally occurring synthesized substance used to repair cartilage.

Heart rate: The number of heart beats per unit time, usually per minute.

Homeopathy: System of medicine developed by Samuel Hahnemann. Based on the Law of Similars, it relies on extremely diluted and "energized" substances.

Humoral: Pertaining to elements in the blood or other body fluids.

Infection: The growth of a parasitic organism within the body.

Inflammation: A basic way in which the body reacts to infection, irritation, or other injury, the key features being redness, warmth, swelling, and pain.

Infusion: A solution obtained by steeping or soaking a substance (usually in water). A tea.

Liniment: A medicinal liquid rubbed into the skin to soothe pain or relieve stiffness.

Lymph: An almost colorless fluid that travels through vessels in the lymphatic system and carries cells that help fight infection and disease.

Lymphocyte: Any of the nearly colorless cells found in the blood, lymph, and lymphoid tissues, constituting approximately 25 percent of white blood cells.

Massage: The manipulation of muscle and connective tissue to enhance the function of those tissues and promote relaxation and well-being.

Menstruum: A solvent used to extract compounds from plant and animal tissues for drug preparation.

MSM: Methylsulonfylmethone, a naturally occurring sulfur compound used as a nutraceutical.

Nervine: A substance that calms and soothes the nerves and reduces tension and anxiety. Herbal examples include: ashwagandha, bala, and gudmar.

Nosode: A homeopathic remedy prepared from diseased tissue or the product of disease.

Nutraceuticals: Supplements that function both as nutrients and medications; most are naturally occurring substances found in the body.

Nutritive: Nutritious or nourishing.

Potentized: A substance that has gone through serial dilution and succession in homeopathy. (*Also, potentiated.*)

Poultice: Plant material that is prepared in a special way and applied to the surface of the body as a remedy for certain disorders.

Remedy: A healing medicine, as in homeopathy.

Salve: Medicinal ointment.

Saponins: Plant glucosides that form soapy lathers when mixed and agitated with water.

Sopoforic: Sleep inducing.

Stomachic: Substances that tone the stomach, stimulate digestion, and improve the appetite. Herbal examples include: amalaki, black pepper, cardamom, cedar, chitrak, cumin, ginger, licorice, and turmeric.

Strangles: An infectious disease caused by the bacterium *Streptococcus equi* and characterized by inflammation of the nasal mucous membrane and abscesses of the jaw.

Succussion: In homeopathy, the process of serial dilution by which the remedy is "potentized."

Tincture: An alcoholic extract or solution of an herb.

Tissue salts: A collection of 12 different "cell salts" used for treatment of disease in cell salt therapy.

Tonic: Herbs that restore and strengthen the entire system. Herbal examples include: aloe, bala, barberry, chirayata, katuka, gentian, and goldenseal.

Toxin: Poisonous substance.

Triturations: Reduction to a powder.

Tumor: An abnormal mass of tissue.

Vaccine: A preparation of a weakened or killed pathogen, such as a bacterium or virus, or of a portion of the pathogen's structure that upon administration stimulates antibody production or cellular immunity against the pathogen but is incapable of causing severe infection.

Vasodilator: Causing dilation of the blood vessels.

REGISTRY ORGANIZATIONS

The American Horse Council
1616 H Street, NW
Washington, DC 20006-3805
202-296-4031
www.horsecouncil.org

American Riding Instructors Association
28801 Trenton Ct.
Bonita Springs, FL 34134-3337
239-948-3232
www.riding-instructor.com

Canadian 4-H Council
930 Carling Avenue
Ottawa, Ontario
K1A 0C6 Canada
www.4-h-canada.ca

Canadian Pony Club
CPC National Office
Box 127
Baldur, MB R0K 0B0
Canada
www.canadianponyclub.org

Equine Canada
2460 Lancaster Rd.
Ottawa, Ontario K1B 4S5
Canada
613-248-3433
www.equinecanada.ca

National 4-H Council
7100 Connecticut Ave.
Chevy Chase, MD 20815-4999
301-961-2959
www.fourhcouncil.edu

The British Horse Society
Stoneleigh Deer Park
Stareton Lane
Kenilworth, Warwickshire
CV8 2XZ England
www.bhs.org.uk

The Pony Club (UK)
Stoneleigh Park
Kenilworth, Warwickshire
CV8 2RW England
www.pcuk.org

United States Equestrian Federation
The National Governing
Body for Equestrian Sports
4047 Iron Works Parkway
Lexington, KY 40511
859-258-2472
www.usef.com

United States Pony Clubs, Inc.
4041 Iron Works Parkway
Lexington, KY 40511
859-254-7669
www.ponyclub.org

EQUINE SPORTS ORGANIZATIONS

American Driving Society
P.O. Box 160
Metamora, MI 48455-0160
810-664-8666
www.americandrivingsociety.org

American Endurance Riding Conference
P.O. Box 6027
Auburn, CA 95604
530-823-2260
www.aerc.org

American Hunter and Jumper Foundation
335 Lancaster Street
P.O. Box 369
West Boylston, MA 01583

American Vaulting Association
642 Alford Place
Bainbridge Island, WA 98110-3657
206-780-9353
www.americanvaulting.org

Canadian Sport Horse Association
P.O. Box 1625
Holland Landing, Ontario
L9N 1P2 Canada
905-830-9288
www.canadian-sport-horse-org

Federation Equestre International
Avenue Mon-Repos 24
P.O. Box 157
CH-1000 Lausanne 5 Switzerland
www.horsesport.org
294 295

National Barrel Horse Association
725 Broad Street
P.O. Box 1988
Augusta, GA 30903-1988
706-722-7223
www.nbha.com

National Cutting Horse Association
4704 Highway 377 S.
Fort Worth, TX 76116-8805
817-244-6188
www.nchacutting.com

National Steeplechase Association
400 Fair Hill Drive
Elkton, MD 21921
410-392-0700
www.nationalsteeplechase.com

North American Riding for the
Handicapped Association
P.O. Box 33150
Denver, CO 80233
303-452-1212
www.narha.org

United States Combined Training Association
525 Old Waterford Rd, NW
Leesburg, VA 20176-2050
703-779-0440
www.eventingusa.com

United States Dressage Federation
220 Lexington Green Circle
Lexington, KY 40503
859-971-2277www.usdf.org

United States Equestrian Team
1040 Pottersville Road
P.O. Box 355
Gladstone, NJ 07934-9955
908-234-1251
www.uset.org

VETERINARY ORGANIZATIONS

American Animal Hospital Association (AAHA)
P.O. Box 150899
Denver, CO 80215
Phone: (303) 986-2800
Website: http://www.aahanet.org

American Association of Equine Practitioners (AAEP)
4075 Iron Works Parkway
Lexington, KY 40511
www.myhorsematters.com

American Holistic Veterinary Medical Association (AHVMA)
2214 Old Emmorton Road
Bel Air, MD 21015
Phone: (410) 569-0795
Website: http://www.ahvma.org

American Veterinary Medical Association (AVMA)
1931 North Meacham Road, Suite 100
Schaumburg, IL 60173
Phone: (847) 925-8070
Fax: (847) 925-1329
Website: http://www.avma.org

ASPCA Animal Poison Control Center
1717 South Philo Road, Suite 36
Urbana, IL 61802
Telephone: (888) 426-4435
www.aspca.org

International Veterinary Acupuncture Society (IVAS)
P.O. Box 271395
Ft. Collins, CO 80527
Phone: (970) 266-0666
Website: http://www.ivas.org

British Equine Veterinary Association
Wakefield House
46 High Street
Sawston, Cambridgeshire
CB2 4BG England
www.beva.org.uk

Canadian Veterinary Medical Association
339 Booth Street
Ottawa, ONK1R 7K1
Canada
613-236-1162
www.canadianveterinarians.net

The Academy of Veterinary Homeopathy (AVH)
P.O. Box 9280
Wilmington, DE 19809
Phone: (866) 652-1590
Website: http://www.theavh.org

The American Association for Veterinary Acupuncture (AAVA)
P.O. Box 419
Hygicnc, CO 80533
Phone: (303) 772-6726
Website: http://www.aava.org

ANIMAL WELFARE GROUPS AND ORGANIZATIONS

American Humane Association (AHA)
63 Inverness Drive East
Englewood, CO 80112
Phone: (800) 227-4645
Website: http://www.americanhumane.org

American Society for the Prevention of Cruelty to Animals (ASPCA)
424 East 92 Street
New York, NY 10128
Phone: (212) 876-7700
Website: http://www.aspca.org

Best Friends Animal Sanctuary
Kanab, UT 84741-5001
Phone: (435) 644-2001
Website: http://www.bestfriends.org

International League for the Protection of Horses
Anne Colvin House
Snetterton, Norfolk
NR16 2LR England
www.ilph.org

National Horse Protection Coalition
P.O. Box 1252
Alexandria, VA 22313
www.horse-protection.org

The Fund for Horses
914 Dallas, #403
Houston, TX 77002
713-650-1973
www.fund4horses.org

The Humane Society of the United States (HSUS)
2100 L Street, NW
Washington, DC 20037
Phone: (212) 452-1100
Website: http://www.hsus.org

Thoroughbred Retirement Foundation
PMB 351, 450 Shrewsbury Plaza
Shrewsbury, NJ 07702-4332
732-957-0182
www.trfinc.org

WEBSITES

ASPCA Animal Poison Control Center
1717 South Philo Road, Suite 36
Urbana, IL 61802
Telephone: (888) 426-4435
www.aspca.org

Healthypet
(http://www.healthypet.com)
Healthypet.com is part of the American Animal Hospital Association (AAHA) an organization of more than 25,000 veterinary care providers committed to providing excellence in small animal care.

Petfinder
(http://www.petfinder.org)
On Petfinder.org, you can search over 88,000 adoptable animals and locate shelters and rescue groups in your area who are currently caring for adoptable pets. You can also post classified ads for lost or found pets, pets wanted, and pets needing homes.

Pets 911
(http://www.1888pets911.org)
Pets 911 is not only a website; it also runs a toll-free phone hotline (1-888-PETS-911) that allows pet owners access to important, life-saving information.

VetQuest
(http://www.vin.com/vetquest/index0.html)
VetQuest is an online veterinary search and referral service. You can search their database for over 25,000 veterinary hospitals and clinics in the United States, Canada, and Europe. The service places special emphasis on veterinarians with advanced online access to the latest health care information and highly qualified veterinary specialists and consultants.

PUBLICATIONS

Books

Budd, Jackie. *Seasons of the Horse*. Neptune City, NJ: TFH Publications, Inc., 2007.

Morgan, Diane. *Feeding Your Horse for Life*. Half Halt Press, 2006.

Morgan, Diane. *Understanding Your Horse's Lameness*. Half Halt Press, 1992.

Magazines

Animal Wellness Magazine
PMB 168
8174 South Holly Street
Centennial, CO 80122

ASPCA Animal Watch
424 East 92nd Street
New York, NY 10128

Arabian Horse World
656 Quince Orchard Rd., #600
Gaithersburg, MD 20878-1472
301-977-3900
www.equisearch.com

Chronicle of the Horse
P.O. Box 46
Middleburg, VA 20018
540-687-6341
www.chronofhorse.com

Dressage Today
656 Quince Orchard Rd., #600
Gaithersburg, MD 20878-1472
301-977-3900
www.equisearch.com

Endurance News
American Endurance Riding Conference
P.O. Box 6027
Auburn, CA 95604
www.aerc.org

Equus
656 Quince Orchard Rd., #600
Gaithersburg, MD 20878-1472
301-977-3900
www.equisearch.com

Horse & Rider
656 Quince Orchard Rd., #600
Gaithersburg, MD 20878-1472
301-977-3900
www.equisearch.com

Horse Connection
380 Perry Street, #210
Castle Rock, CO 80104
303-663-1300
www.horseconnection.com

Horse Illustrated
P.O. Box 6050
Mission Viejo, CA 92690
949-855-8822
www.horseillustratedmagazine.com

Practical Horseman
656 Quince Orchard Rd., #600
Gaithersburg, MD 20878-1472
301-977-3900
www.equisearch.com

Thoroughbred Times
P.O. Box 8237496 Southland Dr.
Lexington, KY 40533-8237
www.thoroughbredtimes.com

USDF Connections
United States Dressage Federation
220 Lexington Green Circle
Lexington, KY 40503
859-971-2277
www.usdf.org

Western Horseman
P.O. Box 7980
Colorado Springs, CO 80933-7980
719-633-5524
www.westernhorseman.com

The Whole Horse Wellness Guide

INDEX

Note: **Boldfaced** numbers indicate illustrations.

A

Abhyanga, 165
abrasions, 260
abscesses, 200
absolutes, 176
Achillea millefolium, 133, 188
Achyranthis bidentata, 147
acid rain contamination, 47
aconite, 104
Aconitrum napellus, 104
acupoints
    laser therapy and, 90
    meridians and, 71, 74, 76
acupressure
    advantages, 73
    conditions treated, 74
    credentials necessary, 79
    defined, 263
    disadvantages, 73
    nutritional therapy and, 48
acupuncture
    advantages, 70
    conditions treated, 72–73
    credentials necessary, 79
    defined, 71, 263
    on diagnosis and treatment, 71–72
    disadvantages, 70
    nutritional therapy and, 46, 48
    overview, 70–71
adaptogens, 263
adjuvants, 15, 21, 263
Aesculus carnea, 195
Aesculus hippocastanum, 104, 194, 195
agate (crystal healing), 86
aged horses
    coenzyme Q10 and, 44
    digestive enzymes in, 45
    DMG and, 45
    Perna Mussel and, 45
    shiatsu and, **75**
    vitamins and, 41
Agency for Healthcare Research and
    Quality (AHRQ), 89
aggression, 205
Agrimonia eupatoria, 193
agrimony, 193
Ahir Bhairav, 171

Ai yen, 146
ajwain (ajwan), 161
akasha, 263
alcohol-extracted herbs, 119
aldehydes, 177
alfalfa, 38, 42–43, 47
allergies
    to antibiotics, 24
    anti-inflammatory drugs and, 25
    broncodilators for, 26
    defined, 263
    heavy metal contamination and, 47
    treatment options, 200–201
    to vaccines, 16, 18
Allium sativum, 127
Allium ursinum, 127
almonds, 197
aloe, 161
aloe vera, 121
alterative, 263
alternative medicine, 7, 46, 263
Alternative Therapy Health Medicine,
    102
Althea officinalis, 129
aluminum (heavy metal), 46
ama, 263
amazonite (crystal healing), 86
amber (crystal healing), 86
American Association of Equine
    Practitioners (AAEP), 13, 20, 53
American College of Veterinary
    Anesthesiologists (ACVA), 29
American Veterinary Chiropractic
    Association (AVCA), 64, 66
American Veterinary Medical
    Association, 7
amethyst (crystal healing), 86, 167
ametrine (crystal healing), 86
amla (amalaki), 161, 164
anabolism, 152
analgesic, 263
anemia, 201–202, 223–224
anesthesia, 27–29
Anethum graveolens, 125–126
angelica, 121–122, 145–146
Angelica archangelica, 121
Angelicae anomala, 145
Angelicae dahuricae, 145
Angelica sinensis, 121, 145–146
anger, 205
anhydrite (crystal healing), 86
anhydrosis, 202

animal communicators, 96–97
aniseed, 122
anodyne, 263
anthelmintic, 263
antibiotics
    advantages, 24
    colloidal silver and, 45
    defined, 24, 263
    disadvantages, 24
    DMSO as carrier, 26
    side effects from, 24–25
antibody, 14, 263
antigens, 14–15, 17, 263
anti-inflammatory
    defined, 25, **26,** 263
    MSM as, 45
    orthomecular medicine on, 48
    Perna Mussel as, 45
Antimonium crudum, 104
antimony (crystal healing), 86
antioxidants
    defined, 42, 263
    orthomecular medicine on, 48
    vitamins as, 41, 44
antiphlogistic, 263
antiseptic, 263
antispasmodic, 263
antithrombotic, 263
antitussive, 263
anxiety, 205–206, 207
anyolite (crystal healing), 86
apatite (crystal healing), 86
aperient, 263
aphthitalite (crystal healing), 86
Apis mellifica, 104
Apium graveolens, 124
apophyllite (crystal healing), 86
apples, 197
apprehension, 205–206
apricot oil, 179
aquamarine (crystal healing), 86, 167
arborvitae, 45, 111–113
Arctium lappa, 123, 147
arnica, 122
Arnica montana, 104–105
aromatherapy. *See also* essential oils
    advantages, 174
    Ayurvedic medicine on, 168
    dangerous plants, 189
    defined, 263
    disadvantages, 174
    foundations of, 172–174

smell and, 174–175
aromatic, 263
arrow poison, 107
arsenic, 46, 105
Arsenicum album, 105
Artemisia vulgaris, 141
arthritis, 202–204, 263
asafoetida, 161–162
ashwaganda, 162
Asiatic plantain, 136
Asparagus adscendens, 164
Asparagus gonoclados, 164
Asparagus racemosus, 164
Asparagus sarmentosus, 164
aspen, 193
asthma, 211–212
Astragalus membranaceus, 122,
    146–147
astringent, 264
ATP (adenosine triphosphate), 90
atractylodes, 145
atragalus, 122
attentuated vaccines, 15, 16
Aum (mantra), 169, 170
autoimmune response, 14–15, 20–21
aventurine (crystal healing), 86
avocado, 197
avocado oil, 179
Aym (mantra), 169
Ayurvedic medicine
    Abhyanga, 165
    advantages, 150
    aromatherapy, 168
    on balanced diet, 160–161
    color therapy, 167–168
    common remedies, 124
    conditions treated, 161–170
    crystal therapy, 165–167
    defined, 264
    disadvantages, 150
    diseases and diagnosis, 156–159
    five elements, 152–156
    healing principles, 152
    medicinal plants, 161–165
    overview, 148–149
    restoring balance, 159–165
    sound and music, 168–171
    three doshas, 150–151
    three wastes, 159
Azadirachta indica, 163
azoturia, 254–256
azurite (crystal healing), 86

B
Bach, Edward, 192
Bach flower remedies
    advantages, 192
    applying, 193
    conditions treated, 193–196
    defined, 191, 192, 264
    disadvantages, 192
    Rescue Remdey, 192–193
back pain, 204–205
Bacopa monniera, 162
bacterial supplements, 46
Baheda, 164
Bai hao, 145
Bai zhi, 145
bala, 162
balance
    in Ayurvedic medicine, 150–156,
        168–171
    in Chinese herbal medicine,
        136–142
banned drugs, 27
Baptisia tinctoria, 105
barberry, 106
barite (crystal healing), 86
barn fever, 249–250
basil, 181
beech, 193
behavioral problems, 205–207
Belladonna, 105
Bellis perennis, 105
Berberis vulgaris, 106
bergamot, 181
bcryl (crystal healing), 87
Betula carpinifolia, 181
Betula Lenta, 181
Bheda, 156
bighead, 207–208
Biochemic Tissue Salt Therapy, 112
bioenergetics, 92
biosonic repatterning, 46
biostimulation, 89
biotin (vitamin), 41
birch, 181
bitter apple, 107
bitter cucumber, 107
black antimony sulfide, 104
black lead, 108
black stones (crystal healing), 84
bladder meridian, 76–77
bladderwrack, 122

blood blisters, 232
bloodstone (crystal healing), 87
blue in color therapy, 168
blue sapphire, 166
blue stones (crystal healing), 83, 84
B lymphocytes, 13–14, 15
bodywork
    chiropractic, 46, 48, 64–67, 264
    defined, 52, 264
    massage therapy, 52–61, 265
    touch therapy, 61–64
bog spavin, 208
boneset, 108
bone spavin, 208
booster shots, 19, 23
Boswellia carterii, 183
Boswellia serrata, 163
Bowen Technique, 57, 61–62
Bowen Therapy Academy of Australia
    (BTAA), 57
Bowen, Tom, 61
brahmi, 162
bran disease, 207–208
British Holistic Veterinary Medicine
    Association (BHVMA), 57
British Journal of Rheumatology, 89
broken wind, 211–212
Bromus ramosus, 195
bronchial asthma, 211–212
bronchodilators, 26, 264
bruised soles, 216
bruises, 208–209
Bryonia alba, 106
burdock, 123, 133
bursitis, 209

C
cabochons, 85
cadmium (heavy metal), 46
Calcarea carbonica, 106
Calcarea fluorica, 106
calcite (crystal healing), 87
calcium, 42–43, 209–210
calcium carbonate, 109
calcium fluoride, 112
calcium phosphate, 112
calcium sulfate, 112
calendula, 123
Calendula officinalis, 106, 123
Calluna vulgaris, 194
camphor, 168, 177
Canadian Deep Muscle massage, 55–56

Cananga odorata, 188
canarypox virus, 17
cancer, 238–239
Cang zhu, 145
cannon keratosis (cannon scald), 210
capped elbow, 210
Capsicum spp., 123–124
capsules (herbal medicine), 119
Carbo vegetabilis, 106
cardamom, 168, 181–182
carminative, 264
carnelian (crystal healing), 87
Carpinus betulus, 194
Castanea sativa, 195
catnip, 117, 118
Causticum, 106–107
CAVM (complementary and alternative veterinary medicine), 7
cayenne, 123–124
celery seed, 124
celestite (crystal healing), 87
cell-mediated immunity (CMI), 14, 15
centaury, 193
cerato, 193
Ceratostigma willmottiana, 193
chakras, 85
chalcedony (crystal healing), 87
chamomile, 120, 124, 133
changes, Chinese herbal medicine on, 138
Charaka (sage), 150
chelated minerals, 43
cherries, 197
cherry plum, 193
chestnut bud, 194
chickpea, 109
chickweed, 124
chicory, 194
China, 107
Chinese angelica, 145
Chinese gentian root, 147
Chinese herbal medicine
    advantages, 136
    balance and harmony, 136–142
    classifying herbs, 143
    commonly used herbs, 145–147
    conditions treated, 145–147
    disadvantages, 136
    eight principles of, 136–137
    equine conditions amenable to, 142
    on excreting organs, 140–141
    five elements, 137–139

    on horses as natural healers, 136
    organ groups, 139–140
    overview, 134–135
    preparation, 143
    six evils of disease, 141–142
    on storing organs, 140–141
    yin and yang in, 136
chiropractic
    advantages, 65
    benefits, 66
    conditions treated, 67
    defined, 65, 264
    disadvantages, 65
    exam components, 66
    follow-up treatments, 67
    nutritional therapy and, 46, 48
    overview, 64–65
    when to seek care, 67
choke, 211
chondroitin, 44, 264
Chopra, Deepak, 149
chronic obstructive pulmonary disease, 211–212
Chrysanthemum Parthenium, 127
Cichorium intybus, 194
Cicuta virosa, 107
cinchona, 107
citrine (crystal healing), 87
Citrus aurantium, 186
Citrus bergamia, 181
Citrus limonum, 185
Citrus paradisi, 183
Citrus sinensis, 186
clary sage, 182
cleavers, 120, 124–125
Clematis vitalba, 194
clove, 168
clover, 107
club moss, 109–110
coat problems. *See* skin/coat problems
cobalt, 43
coconut oil, 179
Cocos nuciferas, 179
coenzyme Q10 (ubiquinone), 44
coffin joint problems, 246–247
Colchicum, 107
cold as evil of disease, 141
cold laser therapy, 89
Coleus forskohli, 162–163
colic, 212–216
colloidal silver, 45
Colocynthus, 107

color
    Chinese herbal medicine on, 138
    senses and, 88
color therapy, 167–168
coltsfoot, 125
comfrey, 125
Comminphora mukul, 163
Compendium of Veterinary Products, 22–23
complementary medicine, 7, 64
compresses, 120, 147, 264
Compression technique, 59
concentrates, 176
confidence problems, 207
connective tissue, 44, 264
contusions, 260
conventional medicine. *See* Western medicine
copper
    in crystal healing, 84, 87
    as homeopathic remedy, 107
    as supplement, 43, 49
coral snake, 108
corn in diet, 36, 197
corns, 216
corticosteroids, 25
Corylus avellana, 179
coughing, 216–217
Council on Biologic and Therapeutic Agents (COBTA), 23
crab apple, 194
Craniosacral Therapy, 62, 264
Crataegus spp., 128
cribbing, 206
Cross-Fiber Friction technique, 60
crystal healing
    advantages, 82
    Ayurvedic crystal therapy, 165–167
    chakra rebalancing, 85
    conditions treated, 86–89
    crystal clearing, 85
    crystal shapes, 85
    defined, 82
    disadvantages, 82
    master metals, 84
    master stones, 82–83, 84
    synthetic stones, 83
    traditional properties of stones, 86–89
Cuprum metallicum, 107
Curare, 107
curb, 217

Cushing's disease, 217–219
cuttlefish ink, 111
Cymbopogon citratus, 185–186
cytotoxic (killer) cells, 14

D

daisy, 105
dampness as evil of disease, 141
dandelion leaf, 125
dates, 197
deadly nightshade, 105
decoctions, 120, 144, 264
Deep Digital Pressure technique, 59
degenerative joint disease, 202–204
demulcent, 264
dental problems, 219–220
depression, 206
dermatophilosis, 245–246
dermatophytosis, 247
devil's claw, 125, 133
dew poisoning, 245–246
diagnostic tools
        acupressure as, 74
        acupuncture as, 71–72
        in Ayurvedic medicine, 156–159
        in Chinese herbal medicine,
                138–139
        massage therapy as, 55, 59
        shiatsu as, 76
diamond (crystal healing), 87, 166
diaphoretic, 264
diarrhea, 220–221
dicumarol, 42
diet. *See also* nutrition
        balanced Ayurvedic, 160–161
        equine digestive system, 32, 33
        extruded feeds, 37, 264
        grains in, 34–36
        grass in, 32–33
        hay in, 33–34
        mineral supplements in, 42–46
        nutritional therapy and, 46
        pelleted feeds, 36
        poisonous pasture, 37–40
        principles of nutrition, 32–33
        protein in, 38
        vitamins in, 40–42, 44
        water in, 36
digestive enzymes, 45
digestive system
        bacterial supplements and, 46
        MSM and, 45

        nutrition and, 32, 33
dill, 125–126
diluents, 18, 264
dilution, 100
dimethylglycine (DMG), 45
dimethyl sulfoxide (DMSO), 25–26
directions, Chinese herbal medicine on,
                138
discutient, 264
diseases. *See also specific diseases*
        acupuncture on, 70
        Ayurvedic medicine on, 156–159
        Chinese herbal medicines on,
                141–142
        from heavy metal contamination, 47
        homeopathy on, 100–101
        nutritional therapy on, 46
        orthomolecular medicine on, 48–49
disobedient behavior, 206
distemper, 249–250
DMG (dimethylglycine), 45
DMSO (dimethyl sulfoxide), 25–26, 45
Dodds, W. Jean, 20
dolomite (crystal healing), 87
Dong quai, 145–146
doshas, 150–151. *See also* Kapha; Pitta;
                Vata
drugs in equine practice
        anti-inflammatory, 25–26
        banned, 26
        bronchodilators, 26
        DMSO, 25–26
        hyaluronic acid, 26
        natural herbs as, 116
        sedatives, 26
dry coat, 202
dryness as evil of disease, 141
Dulcamara, 107

E

ear problems, 221
earth
        as elemental energy, 138, 139
        Kapha energy, 154
echinacea, 107, 126
EEE (Eastern encephalomyelitis), 222
Effleurage technique, 60
Einstein, Albert, 92
Elaps corallinus, 108
elbaite (crystal healing), 87
elderly horses. *See* aged horses

Electro-Acuscope Myopulse Therapy,
                90–91
electrolytes, 43, 44
electromedicine, 46, 48
Elettaria cardamom, 181–182
Eleutherococcus senticosus, 131
elm, 194
Emblica officinalis, 161
emerald (crystal healing), 87, 166
emollient, 264
encephalitis, 222
encephalomyelitis, 222
energetic medicine
        acupressure, 48, 73–74, 263
        acupuncture, 46, 48, 70–73, 263
        animal communicators, 96–97
        on bioenergetics, 92
        credentials necessary, 79
        crystal healing, 82–89
        defined, 69, 81
        Electro-Acuscope Myopulse
                Therapy, 90–91
        light therapy, 89–90
        magnetic therapy, 91–95
        on meridians, 69, 76–79
        Reiki, 95
        shiatsu, 74–76
enteritis, 213–214
ephedra, 146
Equine Craniosacral Therapy (ESCT),
                62, 264
equine dysautonomia, 230–231
equine ehrlichial colitis, 242
equine gastric ulcer syndrome (EGUS),
                223
equine herpes virus, 244–245
equine infectious anemia (EIA),
                223–224
equine influenza, 234–235
equine monocytic ehrlichiosis, 242
Equine Muscle Release Therapy
                (EMRT), 56–57
equine protozoal myelitis (EPM),
                225–226
equine protozoal myeloencephalitis
                (EPM), 225–226
equine recurrent uveitis, 226–228
Equine Sports Massage (ESM), 52, 57
equine viral arteritis (EVA), 228
Equisetum arvense, 128
Equus College of Learning and
                Research, 57

essential oils. *See also* aromatherapy
administering, 177–178
conditions treated, 181–188
listed, 179–188
overview, 175–177
preliminary testing, 178
preparing, 178–179
usage recommendations, 180
ester oils, 177
eucalyptus, 168, 182–183
Eucalyptus radiata, 168, 182–183
Eupatorium perfoliatum, 108
Euphorbium, 108
Euphrasia officinalis, 108, 126
excreting organs, 140–141
exhaustion, 207
expectorants, 264
extertional rhabdomyolysis, 254–256
extruded feeds, 37, 264
eyebright, 108, 126
eye problems, 229

F

Fagus sylvatica, 193
Fang feng, 146
Faraday's law, 93
fatigue, 207
fat-soluble vitamins, 40–42
fatty acids, 45, 48
fearfulness, 206
febrifuge, 264
Feeding Your Horse for Life (Morgan), 38
Feldenkrais Method of Functional Integrational massage, 63
feldspar (crystal healing), 87
fennel, 126, 168, 183
Fenugreek, 126–127
Ferrum phosphorus, 108
Ferula asafetida, 161–162
feverfew, 127
fevers, 229
figs, 197
Filipendula ulmaria, 129
finger pressure. *See* shiatsu
fire
as elemental energy, 138, 139
as evil of disease, 141
Pitta energy, 154
fistulous withers, 229
flavanoids, 264
flavors, Chinese herbal medicine on, 138

flaxseed oil, 45
flint, 111
flower essences, 190–197
flu, 234–235
fluoride of lime, 106
fluorite (crystal healing), 87
focus, lack of, 207
Foeniculum vulgare, 126, 183
Food and Drug Administration (FDA), 118
forskolin, 162
founder, 235–237
fractures, 230, 264
frankincense, 163, 168, 183
Fucus vesiculosus, 122–123
Fu ling, 146
Fu organs, 138, 141

G

Galium aparine, 124–125
Gan cao, 147
Gan di huang, 147
garlic, 127
garnet (crystal healing), 87
gastric distention/rupture, 213
Gattefossé, René Maurice, 173, 174
Gelsemium sempervirens, 108
gene-deleted vaccines, 16, 17
generality (homeopathy), 103
genetic engineering, 17
gentian, 194
Gentiana amarella, 194
Gentianae longdancao, 147
geranium, 183
German chamomile, 124
ginger, 113, 127
Ginkgo biloba, 127
ginseng, 146
girth itch, 247
glandular therapy, 49
glucosamine, 44, 264
glycerin-extracted herbs, 119
Glycerrhiza glabra, 163
glycoprotein, 15
Glycyrrhiza glabra, 129
Glycyrrhiza uralensis, 147
gold (crystal healing), 84, 87
goldenrod, 127–128
gold in color therapy, 168
gorse, 194
grains
in balanced Ayurvedic diet, 161

in diet, 34–36
heavy metals in, 47
manganese in, 43
pelletized, 36
selenium in, 40
grapefruit, 183
grapes, 197
grapeseed oil, 179
grasses in diet, 32–33, 40
grass sickness, 230–231
gray in color therapy, 168
greasy heel, 231–232
great burdock, 147
green in color therapy, 168
green stones (crystal healing), 83, 84
guggul, 163, 168
Gymnema sylvestra, 163

H

Hahnemann, Samuel, 100
hair/coat problems, 248
Hall's effect, 93
Ham (mantra), 169
Hamamelis, 108
Hannay, Pamela, 74, 75
Harada, 164
harmony in Chinese herbal medicine, 136–142
Harpagophytum procumbens, 125
Hawaiian flower essence therapy, 195
hawthorn, 128
hay, 33–34, 41
hazelnut oil, 179
headstrong behavior, 206
heart rate, 38, 264
heat as evil of disease, 141
heather, 194
heaves, 211–212
heavy metal contaminants, 47
Hecla lava, 108
Heisenberg, Werner, 92
Helianthemum nummularium, 195
Helianthus annus, 179
Helichrysum italicum, 183–184
helper cells, 14
hematite (crystal healing), 87
hematomas, 232
Hepar sulphuris calcareum, 109
herbal medicine. *See also* Chinese herbal medicine; Western herbal medicine
gathering herbs, 118

homeopathy vs., 102, 104, 116
judging herbal quality, 118
herd immunity, **21**
herpes virus, 244–245
Hippocrates, 64, 100
Holistic Animal Therapy Association of
Australia (HATAA), 57
holistic medicine
Ayurvedic medicine as, 171
Chinese herbal medicine as, 139,
140
defined, 7
vaccine debate, 20–22
hollow foot, 257–258
holly, 194
holy basil, 164
homeopathy
administering remedies, 103–113
advantages, 100
basic principles, 100–101
Biochemic Tissue Salt Therapy, 112
conditions treated, 103–113
defined, 7, 99, 264
on dilution, 100
disadvantages, 100
herbal medicine vs., 102, 104, 116
legal issues, 102
prescribing remedies, 102–103
remedy potency, 101
special licensing, 111
as vaccine alternative, 101–102
vaccine debate, 21–22
honeybee venom, 104
honeysuckle, 194
hoof problems, 232–233
Hoom (mantra), 169, 170
hops, 128, 184
hornbeam, 194
horse chestnut, 104
horsetail, 128
Hottonia palustris, 195
Hrim (mantra), 169
Huang qi, 146–147
humoral, 264
humoral immune response (HIR), 13–15
Humulus lupulus, 184
hyaluric acid (sodium hyaluronate), 26
hydrosols, 176
Hypericum perforatum, **108,** 109, 131
hyperkalemic periodic paralysis
(HYPP), 233
hypersensitivity. *See* allergies

I
Ilex aquifolium, 194
Illicium verum, 122
immune response, 13–15, 22–23, 45
immune system
Ayurvedic medicine for, 162, 164,
168
Ayurvedic medicine on, 154
B lymphocytes, 13–14
defenders in, 15
flaxseed and, 45
hair analysis for, 47
interferon and, 15
retained virulence and, 16
T lymphocytes, 14–15
vaccines and, 17, 22
vital force and, 103
Impatiens glandulifera, 194
incised wounds, 261
Indian ginseng, 162
Indian tobacco, 109
indigo in color therapy, 168
indigo stones (crystal healing), 84
infections, 264
inflammation, 265
influenza, 234–235
infusions, 120, 265
insect bites/stings, 235
insecurity, 206
integrative medicine, 7
interferon, 15
International Association of Animal
Massage Therapists (IAAMT),
52
iodine (I), 43
iron
in crystal healing, 84, 87
as mineral supplement, 43, 49
phosphate of, 108
iron phosphate, 112
irritability, 206–207
isopathic nosode, 101

J
jade (crystal healing), 87, 167
jasmine, 184
Jasminum officinalis, 184
jasper (crystal healing), 87
jatamansi, 163
jet (crystal healing), 87
jojoba oil, 179

Jones, W. B., 102
Jostling technique, 60
Journal of Athletic Training, 89
Juglans regia, 179, 195
juniper, 184–185
Juniperus virginiana, 184–185

K
Kali bichromicum, 109
Kali phosphoricum, 109
Kapha
balanced diet, 160–161
color therapy, 168
crystal therapy, 165–167
defined, 150
overview, 154–156
kelp
in poultices, 120
as supplement, 43, 45
in Western herbal medicine,
122–123, 128
ketones, 177
ki (life force), 95
kidney meridian, 76–77
killed vaccines, 15–16
killer (cytotoxic) cells, 14
Klim (mantra), 169
Ksham (mantra), 169
kunzite (crystal healing), 87

L
lacerations, 260
lack of focus, 207
Lactobacillus acidophilus, 46
Lactobacillus bulgaris, 46
Lam (mantra), 170
laminitis, 235–237
lapis lazuli (crystal healing), 87–88, 167
larch, 194
Larix deciduas, 194
Larson, L., 102
laser therapy, 89–90
Lathyrus, 109
lavender, 185
Lavendula augustifolia, 185
Law of Similars, 100
lead
in crystal healing, 84, 88
as heavy metal, 46
in homeopathic remedies, 110
Ledebouriellae divaricatae, 146

LEDs (light-emitting diodes), 91
Ledum palustre, 109
lemon, 185
lemon balm, 128–129, 185, **186**
lemongrass, 185–186
Leopard's bane, 104–105
leptospirosis, 237
lettuce, 197
licorice, 129, 147, 163
life force. *See also* energetic medicine
    acupoints and, 70, 71, 76
      Chinese herbal medicine on, 140
light therapy, 89–90
lignans, 45
liniment, 265
Lobelia inflata, 109
lockjaw, 252
loneliness, 207
Long dan cao, 147
Lonicera caprifolium, 194
Low-Level Laser Therapy, 89–90
lung meridian, 76, 78
Lupulus strobula, 128
Lycopodium, 109–110
lymph, 265
Lymph Drainage Massage, 57–58
lymphocytes, 13–15, 265
lyophilized vaccines, 18

M

Magnesia phosphorica, 110
magnesium, 43
magnesium phosphate, 110, 112
magnetic therapy, 91–95
Mahonia aquifolium, 130
Ma huang, 146
mainstream medicine. *See* Western
    medicine
Mala, 159
malachite (crystal healing), 88
Malus pumila, 194
manganese, 43
mange, 237–238
mantras in Ayurvedic medicine, 168–171
marigold, 106
marjoram, 129, 186
marshmallow, 120, 129
marsh tea, 109
massage therapy
    Abhyanga, 165
    advantages, 52
    basic strokes, 59–61

benefits, 52–54
    Canadian Deep Muscle massage,
      55–56
    conditions treated, 52–53, 56–58
    defined, 52, 265
    as diagnostic tool, 55, 59
    disadvantages, 52
    Equine Muscle Release Therapy,
      56–57
    Equine Sports Massage, 52, 57
    Lymph Drainage Massage, 57–58
    preparing for, 54–55
    Swedish Massage, 58
    Trigger Point Therapy, 58–59
    when to avoid, 60
    when to use, 60
master metals (crystal therapy), 84, 85
master stones (crystal healing), 82–84,
    85–89
Matricaria recutita, 124
meadow saffron, 107
meadowsweet, 129, 133
Melaleuca alternifolia, 132, 188
melanoma, 238–239
Melissa officinalis, 128–129, 185
menstruum, 119, 265
Mentha piperita, 187
Mentha spp., 129–130, 163
mercury (heavy metal), 46
meridians
    acupoints and, 71, 74, 76
    acupressure and, 73
    acupuncture and, 71, 72
    defined, 69
    important, 76–79
    shiatsu and, 76
meta-ankoleite (crystal healing), 88
metal as elemental energy, 138, 139
methylsulfonylmethone (MSM), 26, 45,
    265
milk thistle, 118
Millefolium, 110
Miller's disease, 207–208
Mimulus guttatus, 194
minerals in crystal healing, 85
mineral supplements
    chelated minerals, 43
    listed, 42–46
    NRC requirements, 47, 48
    nutritional therapy and, 46, 47
    orthomolecular medicine on, 48–49
mint, 129–130, 163, 168, 187

modified live vaccines (MLVs), 15, 16,
    23
Monday morning disease, 254–256
monkshood, 104, 146
monoterpenes, 176–177
monovalent vaccines, 16, 23
moon blindness, 226–228
moonstone (crystal healing), 88, 166
Morgan, Diane, 38
mouth blisters, 256
moxibustion, 141
MSM. *See* methylsulfonylmethone
mud fever, 231–232
mugwort, 141, 146
mullein, 130
multivalent vaccine, 16
muscle soreness, 239–240
music therapy in Ayurvedic medicine,
    168–171
mustard, 194
mutation, wild-type, 16, 19
Mutra, 159
myositis, 254–256
Myristica aromata, 186
Myristica fragrans, 186
Myristica officinalis, 186
myrrh, 168

N

NAET (Nambudripad's Allergy
    Elimination Technique), 72
Nardostachys jatamansi, 163
National Research Council (NRC), 47
natrum muriaticum, 112
naturopaths, 192
navicular disease, 240
neem, 163
Nei Jing, 70
Nepeta cataria, 117, 118
neroli, 186
nervine, 265
nettle, 130
nickel (heavy metal), 46
nosodes, 101, 102, 265
NSAIDs, 25, 121
Nui p'ang tze, 147
Nui xi, 147
nutmeg, 186
nutraceuticals, 40, 265
nutrition. *See also* diet
    analyzing grains for, 35
    from bacterial supplements, 46

hay and, 33–34
NRC requirements, 47–48
orthomolecular medicine and, 48–49
principles of, 32–33
supplements and, 42–46
vitamins and, 40–42, 44
nutritional therapy, 46–48
nutritive, 265
Nux moschata, 186
Nux vomica, 110

oak, 195
oats in diet, 35–36
obsidian (crystal healing), 88
Ocimum basilicum, 181
Ocimum sanctum, 164
Ohashi Institute (New York), 74
ointments, 144
older horses. *See* aged horses
Olea europaea, 179, 195
olive oil, 120, 179
olives, 195
omeaga-3 fatty acids, 45
1C potency, 101
onychomycosis, 257–258
onyx (crystal healing), 88
opal (crystal healing), 88, 167
orange (fruit), 186, 197
orange in color therapy, 168
orange stones (crystal healing), 83, 84, 165
Oregon grape, 130
organ system, Chinese herbal medicine on, 139–140
Origanum majorana, 186
Origanum vulgare, 129
Ornithogalum umbellatum, 195
orthomolecular medicine, 48–49
osteoarthritis, 202–204
oxides, 177
oyster shell, 106

Paeoniae lactiflorae, 145
Palmer, B. J., 64
Panax ginseng, 146
Panax quinquefolius, 146
pasque flower, 110
Passiflora incarnate, 130
passionflower, 130

pearl (crystal healing), 88, 166
pears, 197
Pelargonium graveolens, 183
pelleted feeds, 36
pemphigus foliaceus, 240
peony root, 145
peppermint, 187
Percussive Strokes technique, 60
performance problems, 205–207
peridot (crystal healing), 88
periodic ophthalmia, 226–228
Perna Mussel *(Perna caniculus),* 45
Persea americana, 179
petrified wood (crystal healing), 88
Petrissage technique, 61
Pfrimmer, Therese, 55
phenols, 177
phosphate of iron, 108
phosphorus, 42–43, 110, 209–210
photon therapy, 46, 89–90
phototherapy, 89–90
Phyllanthus amarus, 164
pine, 195
pineapples, 197
pink in color therapy, 168
Pinus sylvestris, 195
Pitta
    balanced diet, 160–161
    color therapy, 168
    crystal therapy, 165–167
    defined, 150
    overview, 154
pituitary adenoma, 217–219
Plantago major, 130
plantain, 130
pleuritis, 240–241
pleuropneumonia, 240–241
Plumbum metallicum, 110
pneumonia, 241
poison ivy, 110–111
poison nut, 110
poison oak, 110–111
poisonous plants
    for aromatherapy, 189
    listed, 37–39
    selenium and, 40
    vitamin D and, 41
polyvalent vaccines, 23
Populus tremula, 193
Porio Cocos, 146
potassium (K), 43
potassium bichromate, 109

potassium chloride, 112
potassium hydrate, 106–107
potassium sulfate, 112
potency, 101, 118
potentized, 100, 102, 265
pot marigold, 123
Potomac Horse Fever (PHF), 242
poultices, 120, 161, 266
Prakopa, 156
Prasara, 156
probiotics, 46
protein in diet, 38, 47
proteoglycan, 44
Prunus armeniaca, 179
Prunus cerasifera, 193
Prunus dulcis, 179
Pulsatilla, 110
Pulsating Electromagnetic Field Therapy (PEFT), 93
puncture wounds, 260
Purisa, 159
purple cone flower, 107
purple in color therapy, 168

Qi (life force), 70, 71, 76, 140
quantum physics, 92
quarrelsomeness, 205
quartz (crystal healing), 88
Quercus robur, 195

radial paralysis, 242
rain rot, 245–246
rain scald, 245–246
Ram (mantra), 170
raspberries, 197
raspberry leaf, 130–131
recombinant DNA technology, 16
recombinant gene vaccines, 16–17
red chestnut, 195
red coral, 166–167
red in color therapy, 168
red stones (crystal healing), 83, 84, 165
regulating body fluids. *See* electrolytes
Rehmannia glutinosa, 147
Reiki, 95
remedy, 101, 266
repertory (homeopathy), 103
repetitive stress injuries, 93
Rescue Remedy, 192–193

resentment, 205
residual virulence, 16
respiratory problems, 242–243
restlessness, 207
retained virulence, 16
retrovirus, 22
rhinopneumonitis, 244–245
Rhizoma atractylodes, 145
rhodonite (crystal healing), 88
Rhus toxicodendron, 110–111
ringbone, 246–247
ringworm, 247
Rocking technique, 61
rock rose, 195
rock water, 195
rolling, **59**
Rosa canina, 131, 195
Rosa damascena, 187
rose, 131, 168, 187
rosemary, 187
Rosmarinus coronarium, 187
Rosmarinus officinalis, 187
roughage, 33, 34
Rubus idaeus, 130–131
ruby (crystal healing), 88, 166
ruby zoisite (crystal healing), 86
rue, 111
Ruta Graveolens, 111

S
saddle sores, 247
sage, 131, 168
Saint John's Wort, **108,** 109, 131
Salix alba, 132–133
Salix vitellina, 196
salves, 120, 266
Salvia officinalis, 131
Salvia sclarea, 182
Sanchaya, 156
sandalwood, 164, 168, 187
San Jiao, 141
Santalum album, 164, 187
saponins, 266
sapphire (crystal healing), 88, 166
sarcoids, 247–248
Schuessler, Wilhelm, 112
Scleranthus annus, 195
scouring rush, 128
scratches, 231–232
Scutellaria, 111
sea shells (crystal healing), 88
seaweed, 122, 128

seedy toe, 257–258
selenium, 40, 44
senses
    Chinese herbal medicine on, 138
    color and, 88
separation anxiety, 207
serial dilution, 100
serpentine (crystal healing), 88
sesame oil, 179
Sesamum indicum, 179
sesquiterpene alcohols, 177
sesquiterpene hydrocarbons, 177
set-fast, 254–256
Shaking technique, 61
shallaki, 163
Sham (mantra), 170
shark cartilage, 46
shatavari, 164
shave grass, 128
Sheng di huang, 147
Sherrington, Charles, 97
shiatsu, 74–76, 79
shipping fever, 240–241
shoe boil, 210
Shultz, R. D., 102
Shum (mantra), 170
Shu Xue, 71
shyness, 207
Siberian ginseng, 131
Sida cordifolia, 162
silica, 111, 112
silicon dioxide, 111
silver
    colloidal, 45
    in color therapy, 168
    in crystal healing, 84, 88
Silybum marianum, 118
Simmondsia chinensis, 179
Sinapis arvensis, 194
skin/coat problems, 248
skittishness, 206
skullcap, 111, 131
sleeping sickness, 222
slippery elm, 120, 131
smell, science of, 174–175
Smith, Fritz, 64
smithsonite (crystal healing), 88
smoky quartz (crystal healing), 88
sodalite (crystal healing), 88
sodium chloride, 44
sodium hyaluronate, 26
sodium sulfate, 112

Solidago, 127–128
Som (mantra), 170
Sonchus oleraceus, 118
sopoforic, 266
sow thistle, 118
splint, 248–249
spookiness, 206
spurge gum, 108
squirting cucumber, 107
stall rot, 257–258
stall-weaving, 207
star of Bethlehem, 195
Static Magnetic Therapy, 93
Stellaria media, 124
stem cell therapy, 28
steroids, 25, 45
Sthanasamsrya, 156
St. Mary's thistle, 118
stomachic, 266
stomach meridian, 78–79
storing organs, 140–141
strangles, 249–250, 266
stress, 207
stubbornness, 206
subluxation, 65, 66
subunit vaccines, 16
succussion, 100, 266
sulfur (S)
    defined, 44
    DMSO and, 25
    in homeopathic remedies, 109, 111
    MSM and, 26, 45
    in Western herbal medicine, 127
sunflower seed oil, 179
supplements
    mineral, 42–44, 46–47
    NRC requirements, 47–48
    orthomolecular medicine on, 48–49
    other, 44–46
suppressor cells, 14
surgical procedures, 26–29
swamp fever, 223–224
Sweda, 159
Swedish Massage, 58
sweet almond oil, 179
sweet chestnut, 195
sweet itch, 250–251
sweet marjoram, 186
swelling, 251
Symphytum officinale, 125
synthetic oils, 176

T

Taittiriya Upanishad, 31
Takata, Hawayo, 95
Tao Te Ching, 136
Taraxacum officinalis, 125
Task Force for Veterinary Science, 93
T-cell receptors, 14, 146
tea tree, 132, 188
telepathic communications, 96–97
Tellington-Jones, Linda, 63, 97
Tellington TTouch Therapy, 63–64, 97
tendon trouble, 251–252
tetanus, 252
thermonatrite (crystal healing), 88
thoroughwart, 108
3C potency, 101
thrush, 252–253
Thuja occidentalis, 45, 111–113
thumpers, 56
thyroid problems, 253–254
tin (crystal healing), 84, 88
tinctures, 101, 119, 266
ting points, 76
tissue salts, 266
T lymphocytes, 14–15, 17
tomatoes, 197
tonics, 266
topaz (crystal healing), 88
touch therapy
    advantages, 61
    Bowen Technique, 57, 61–62
    conditions treated, 61–64
    defined, 61
    disadvantages, 61
    Equine Craniosacral Therapy, 62, 264
    goal, **61**
    relaxation and, 64
    Tellington TTouch Therapy, 63–64, 97
    Zero Balancing, 64
tourmaline (crystal healing), 88–89
toxins
    antibiotics and, 25
    Ayurvedic medicine for, 162
    in Chinese herbal medicine, 141
    defined, 266
    nutritional therapy for, 47, 48
    from poisonous plants, 37–39, 40
    vitamin D and, 41
Trachyspermum ammi, 161
traditional Chinese medicine (TCM),

134–135. *See also* acupuncture; massage therapy
Trigger Point Therapy, 58–59
Trigonella foenum-graecum, 126–127
triturations, 266
TTEAM, 63–64, 97
TTouch Therapy, 63–64, 97
tumors, 266
turquoise (crystal healing), 89
Tussilago farfara, 125
twisted gut, 213
2C potency, 101
tying-up syndrome, 254–256

U

ubiquinone (coenzyme Q10), 44
ulcers, 223
Ulex europaeus, 194
Ulmus fulva, 131
Ulmus procera, 194
United States Equestrian Federation (USEF), 27
univalent vaccine, 16
Urtica spp., 130
USDA (United States Department of Agriculture), 16, 24
Usui, Mikao, 95

V

vaccines
    AAEP recommendations, 20
    adjuvants and, 15
    advantages, 12
    allergic reactions to, 16, 18
    anti-vaccine myth, 20
    attenuated, 15, 16
    autoimmune disease and, 15
    basic guidelines, 24
    booster shots, 19, 23
    conventional vs. holistic debate, 20–22
    defined, 266
    diluents and, 18
    disadvantages, 12
    duration of immunity, 18
    frequency protocol debate, 22–23
    gene-deleted, 16, 17
    homeopathic alternative, 101–102
    immune system and, 13, 14
    infection and, 16
    killed, 15–16

    lymphocytes and, 13–15
    lyophilized, 18
    modified live, 15, 16, 23
    monovalent, 16, 23
    multivalent, 16
    overview, 12
    owner responsibility, 20
    polyvalent, 23
    reasons for failure, 18–20
    recombinant gene, 16–17
    route of administration, 19
    safety and effectiveness, 17–18
    side effects, 15, 21, 23
    stressed horses and, **17**
    subunit, 16
    types of, 15–17
    univalent, 16
    vectored, 16, 17
valerian, 132
Valeriana officinalis, 132
Vam (mantra), 170
vasodilator, 266
Vata
    balanced diet, 160–161
    color therapy, 168
    crystal therapy, 165–167
    defined, 150
    overview, 152–154
vectored vaccines, 16, 17
VEE (Venezuelan encephalomyelitis), 222
vegetable charcoal, 106
Veratrum album, 113
Verbascum thapsus, 130
Verbena officinalis, 195
vervain, 195
vesicular stomatitis, 256
veterinary immunologists, 23
vetiver, 188
Vetiveria zizanioides, 188
vine, 195
violet stones (crystal healing), 84
vital force (homeopathy), 100–101, 103
vitamin A, 41, 48–49
vitamin B complex, 41, 43
vitamin C, 41, 48–49
vitamin D, 41, 49
vitamin E, 41, 44, 48–49
vitamin K, 42
vitamins
    as antioxidants, 41, 44
    listed, 40–42

NRC requirements, 47, 48
nutritional therapy and, 46, 47
orthomolecular medicine on, 48–49
Vitis vinifera, 179, 195
Vodder, Hans, 57
voice, Ayurvedic medicine on, 159
volcanic ash, 108
volulus/torsion, 213
vomit, inability to, 37
Vyakti, 156

W

wall thrush, 257–258
walnut, 195
walnut oil, 179
warts, 256–257
water
        acid rain contamination, 47
        in diet, 36, 38
        as elemental energy, 138, 139
        Pitta energy, 154
        sulfur in, 44
water hemlock, 107, 122
water-soluble vitamins, 40–41
water violet, 195
weakness, 207
WEE (Western encephalomyelitis), 222
weight loss, 47, 165
Western herbal medicine
        administration of herbs, 119–121
        advantages, 116
        common herbs and uses, 121–133
        conditions treated, 121–133
        disadvantages, 116
        dried vs. fresh herbs, 118
        efficacy, 117
        naming convention, 117–118
        natural herbs, 116

roles of herbs, 118–119
Western medicine
        anesthesia, 27–29
        antibiotics, 24–25
        background, 10–11
        bioenergetics on, 92
        commonly used drugs, 25–27
        defined, 7
        reliability of, 29
        stem cell therapy, 28
        vaccinations, 12–24
West Nile virus, 257
white bryony, 106
white chestnut, 195
white hellebore, 113
white line disease, 257–258
white poria, 146
white sandalwood, 164
white saunders, 164
white stones (crystal healing), 84
white willow, 132–133
wild hops, 106
wild indigo, 105
wild oat, 195
wild rose, 131, 195
wild-type mutation, 16, 19
willow, 196
wind
        as evil of disease, 141
        Vata energy, 152–154
windflower, 110
windgalls, 258
wind sucking, 206
witch hazel, 108
Withania somnifera, 162
wobbler syndrome, 258–259
wolfbane, 104
wood as elemental energy, 138, 139
woody nightshade, 107

worms, 259
wormwood, 146
wounds, 260–261
wulfenite (crystal healing), 89
Wynn, S., 102

Y

Yam (mantra), 170
yarrow, 110, 133, 188
yeast infection, 257–258
yellow in color therapy, 168
yellow jasmine, 108
yellow sandalwood, 164
yellow sapphire, 166
yellow stones (crystal healing), 83, 84,
        165
yin and yang. *See also* energetic
        medicine
        in Chinese herbal medicine,
                136–137, 139–140
        defined, 71–72
ylang ylang, 188
Yogananda, Paramhansa, 197
yucca, 133
Yucca schidigera, 133

Z

zang, Chinese herbal medicine on, 138
Zero Balancing, 64
zinc, 44, 113
Zincum metallicum, 113
Zingiber officinale, 113, 127
zircon, 166

PHOTO CREDITS

Front cover: John Waine (Shutterstock)
Back cover: Condor 36, Alexia Khruscheva

Jacqueline Abromeit (Shutterstock): 115
Aceshot1 (Shutterstock): 127
agafon (Shutterstock): 70, 94
Terry Alexander (Shutterstock): 32
Kivrins Anatolijs (Shutterstock): 30
Galyna Andrushko (Shutterstock): 166
Tom Antos (Shutterstock): 63
Awe Inspiring Images (Shutterstock): 122
Kitch Bain (Shutterstock): 182
Jeff Banke (Shutterstock): 87
Stacey Bates (Shutterstock): 207
Mircea Bezergheanu (Shutterstock): 98
Casey K. Bishop (Shutterstock): 184
Adam Borkowski (Shutterstock): 82
Natalia Bratslavsky (Shutterstock): 273
Joy Brown (Shutterstock): 54
Magdalena Bujak (Shutterstock): 57
Ed Camelli: 8, 10, 11, 13, 17, 21, 26, 35, 42, 45,
    47, 53, 58, 64, 92, 93, 113, 148, 155, 157,
    160, 167, 201, 218, 224, 228, 229, 236,
    249, 251, 267, 268, 275
catnap (Shutterstock): 114, 172, 207
Richard Chaff (Shutterstock): 80
Yanik Chauvin (Shutterstock): 119
Lars Christensen (Shutterstock): 235
LaNae Christenson (Shutterstock): 134
Sergey Chuskin (Shutterstock): 109, 188
Cathleen Clapper (Shutterstock): 257
Stephanie Coffman(Shutterstock): 262
Condor36 (Shutterstock): 50, 223
HD Connelly (Shutterstock): 99
Alistair Cotton (Shutterstock): 210
Chris Curtis (Shutterstock): 133
Sharon D (Shutterstock): 181
Zacarias Pereire da Mata (Shutterstock): 117
R. de Man (Shutterstock): 128
Jody Dingle (Shutterstock): 217
Pichugin Dmitry (Shutterstock): 151
Melissa Dockstader (Shutterstock): 252
Jim Dubois (Shutterstock): 108
Pontus Edenburg (Shutterstock): 206
electerra (Shutterstock): 248
Elena Elisseeva (Shutterstock): 34, 40, 105, 203
Kondrashov Mikhail Evegenevich
    (Shutterstock):14, 265
Foxygrl (Shutterstock): 22
Ava Frick (Shutterstock): 61, 67, 73
Justyna Furmanczyk (Shutterstock): 224
Miodrag Gajic (Shutterstock): 100
Karen Givens (Shutterstock): 208
Rui Mauel Teles Gomes (Shutterstock): 202
GSK (Shutterstock): 169

Anthony Hall (Shutterstock): 168
Hannamariah (Shutterstock): 247
Susan Harris (Shutterstock): 234
Jean Hatch (Shutterstock): 84
Damian Herde (Shutterstock): 129
Cheryl Hill (Shutterstock): 140
Ron Hilton (Shutterstock): 205
Shawn Hine (Shutterstock): 48, 227
Daniel Hughes (Shutterstock): 178
Anita Huszti (Shutterstock): 189
David Hyde (Shutterstock): 241
Jakez (Shutterstock): 240
Verity Johnson (Shutterstock): 232
Judy Ben Joud (Shutterstock): 237
Holly Kuchera (Shutterstock): 75, 103
Cheryl Kunde (Shutterstock): 216
Simon Krzic (Shutterstock): 238
Jill Lang (Shutterstock): 132, 214
langdu (Shutterstock): 111
JD Lawrence (Shutterstock): 219
letty (Shutterstock): 131, 163
Maga (Shutterstock): 180
David Marchal (Shutterstock): 28
Peter Marlin (Shutterstock): 258
Melissa Anne Galleries
    (©istockphotos.com): 51
Sharon Morris (Shutterstock): 7, 137, 215, 222
Al Mueller (Shutterstock): 250
mypokcik (Shutterstock): 191
N. Joy Neish (Shutterstock): 255
Tropinina Olga (Shutterstock): 243
Danny Ortega (Shutterstock): 190
Carolyne Pehora (Shutterstock): 245
Wendy Perry (Shutterstock): 65, 204
Photomediacom (Shutterstock): 196
Svetlana Privezentseva (Shutterstock): 124
Puchan (Shutterstock): 4, 230
Kathryn Rapier (Shutterstock): 19
Anette Linnea Rasmussen (Shutterstock): 81
Elena Ray (Shutterstock): 9, 70, 72, 135, 146,
    162
Rebvt (Shutterstock): 173, 187
Al Redpath (Shutterstock): 107
Tina Rencelj (Shutterstock): 106, 211
Brian Rome (Shutterstock): 165
Randall Schwanke (Shutterstock): 25
Jean Schweitzer (Shutterstock): 244, 256
Josef Sedmak (Shutterstock): 38, 213
Chen Wei Seng (Shutterstock): 233
Vaide Seskauskiene (Shutterstock): 130
Vishal Shah (Shutterstock): 171
Richard Sheppard (Shutterstock): 186
Shutterstock: 197, 246
silksatsunset (Shutterstock): 170
Bruno Sinnah (Shutterstock): 3
Slobodan (Shutterstock): 86
Otmar Smit (Shutterstock): 59
B. Speckart (Shutterstock): 177
Eline Spek (Shutterstock): 79, 90, 175, 221

Claudia Steininger (Shutterstock): 180, 200
Michaela Steininger (Shutterstock): 121
Brian Stewart-Coxan (Shutterstock): 142
stocksnapp (Shutterstock): 104
Dale A. Stork (Shutterstock): 231, 261
Nick Stubbs (Shutterstock): 193
Suravid (Shutterstock): 31
Annamaria Szilagyi (Shutterstock): 68
Tatiana53 (Shutterstock): 126
Charles Taylor (Shutterstock): 144
TFH Archives: 153
Lee Torrens (Shutterstock): 242
Trutta55 (Shutterstock): 253
Vincente Barcelo Varona (Shutterstock): 210
Emily Veinglory (Shutterstock): 29
Virtuelle (Shutterstock): 195
Jenna Layne Voigt (Shutterstock): 158
Zaur Vorokov (Shutterstock): 220
Monika Wisniewska (Shutterstock): 69
Joanna Wnuk (Shutterstock): 194
Lim Yong (Shutterstock): 145
Serg Zastavkin (Shutterstock): 110
Andrejs Zavadskis (Shutterstock): 6

Illustrations: Stephanie Krautheim: 77, 78

ABOUT THE AUTHOR

Diane Morgan is an award-winning writer who is the author of many books on pet care, including Feeding Your Horse for Life, Understanding Your Horse's Lameness, and Good Dogkeeping. Over the years she has owned Thoroughbreds, Quarter Horses, Arabians, and Morgans. She teaches philosophy and comparative religion at Wilson College and resides in Williamsport, Maryland.

DEDICATION

For Lisa Wallace, for so many things.

ACKNOWLEDGMENTS

To my super editor, Mary Grangeia, for her extraordinary patience with me, go my deepest thanks. Her wise corrections made this a much better book. And also to Stephanie Fornino, who copyedited the text with eagle eyes, and Stephanie Krautheim for her expert and elegant design.

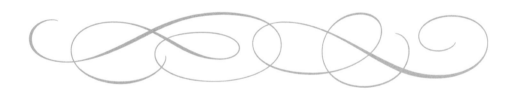

EDITOR'S SPECIAL THANKS:

To Dr. Doug Knueven, DVM, Consulting Veterinary Editor, for his expert review of this text. Dr. Doug received his veterinary degree from Ohio State University in 1987 and has been practicing veterinary medicine in Beaver County, PA ever since. He owns and operates Beaver Animal Clinic, a full-service animal hospital, and shares clinical duties with two associates. Dr. Knueven is a popular speaker at veterinary conferences, and he has lectured on holistic topics at numerous conventional and holistic veterinary conferences across the US. A pioneer in holistic pet care in the Pittsburgh, PA region, he has earned certification in veterinary acupuncture, veterinary Chinese herbal medicine, and animal chiropractic. He also has advanced training in veterinary clinical nutrition, massage therapy, and homeopathy.

To Dr. Ava Frick, DVM, who provided the photos on pp. 61, 67, and 73. Dr. Ava is the Veterinary Medical Director for Animal Fitness Center, Union, MO, a unique animal health care center that specializes in the diagnosis and management of animal injuries, disease, nutritional problems, chiropractic, acupuncture, rehab, and pain management. In 2006, she was the Hartz 2006 Veterinarian of the Year Runner Up. Learn more about the center at: www.petbodybuilders.com.